# THE GREAT URBANIZATION OF CHINA

# Series on Contemporary China (ISSN: 1793-0847)

**Series Editors:** Joseph Fewsmith *(Boston University)*
Zheng Yongnian *(East Asian Institute, National University of Singapore)*

*Published\**

Vol. 18   Oil in China: From Self-Reliance to Internationalization
*by Lim Tai Wei*

Vol. 19   China's Elite Politics: Governance and Democratization
*by Bo Zhiyue*

Vol. 20   China's New Social Policy: Initiatives for a Harmonious Society
*edited by Zhao Litao & Lim Tin Seng*

Vol. 21   Oil and Gas in China: The New Energy Superpower's Relations with Its Region
*by Lim Tai Wei*

Vol. 22   China and The Global Economic Crisis
*edited by Zheng Yongnian & Sarah Y. Tong*

Vol. 23   Social Cohesion in Greater China: Challenges for Social Policy and Governance
*edited by Ka Ho Mok & Yeun-Wen Ku*

Vol. 24   China's Reform in Global Perspective
*edited by John Wong & Zhiyue Bo*

Vol. 25   The Transition Study of Postsocialist China: An Ethnographic Study of a
Model Community
*by Wing-Chung Ho*

Vol. 26   Looking North, Looking South: China, Taiwan, and the South Pacific
*edited by Anne-Marie Brady*

Vol. 27   China's Industrial Development in the 21st Century
*edited by Mu Yang & Hong Yu*

Vol. 28   Cross-Taiwan Straits Relations Since 1979: Policy Adjustment and
Institutional Change Across the Straits
*edited by Kevin G. Cai*

Vol. 29   The Transformation of Political Communication in China: From Propaganda
to Hegemony
*by Xiaoling Zhang*

Vol. 30   The Great Urbanization of China
*by Ding Lu*

*\*To view the complete list of the published volumes in the series, please visit:
http://www.worldscibooks.com/series/scc_series.shtml

Series on Contemporary China – Vol. 30

# THE GREAT URBANIZATION OF CHINA

*editor*

Ding LU

*University of the Fraser Valley, Canada*

**World Scientific**

NEW JERSEY · LONDON · SINGAPORE · BEIJING · SHANGHAI · HONG KONG · TAIPEI · CHENNAI

*Published by*

World Scientific Publishing Co. Pte. Ltd.

5 Toh Tuck Link, Singapore 596224

*USA office:* 27 Warren Street, Suite 401-402, Hackensack, NJ 07601

*UK office:* 57 Shelton Street, Covent Garden, London WC2H 9HE

**British Library Cataloguing-in-Publication Data**
A catalogue record for this book is available from the British Library.

First published 2012 (Hardcover)
Reprinted 2017 (in paperback edition)
ISBN 978-981-3224-80-3

**Series on Contemporary China — Vol. 30**
**THE GREAT URBANIZATION OF CHINA**

ISBN-13 978-981-4287-80-7
ISBN-10 981-4287-80-6

Typeset by Stallion Press
Email: enquiries@stallionpress.com

Printed in Singapore.

# Preface

For three decades after the founding of the People's Republic of China, the government pursued policies designed to restrict urban growth. As a result, most of the population remained as farmers living in rural villages. When economic reforms initiated in late 1978 kickstarted rapid economic growth, however, this policy of restricting rural to urban migration gradually gave way to a large scale movement of rural workers to the cities and China's urbanization boom was underway. Today, more than three decades later, China has become more of an urban than rural society and that will be even more true one or two decades in the future.

In many respects, this process of Chinese urbanization has followed a more or less "typical pattern" common to countries that have achieved major increases in per capita income. But as several of the chapters in this volume indicate, government policies, for better or for worse, have led to some diversion from the more "typical pattern". China's rate of urbanization, for example, is still somewhat below what one would expect for a country with her per capita income.

The challenge China has faced during rapid urbanization has several dimensions. For many highly urbanized countries, rural to urban migration and the growth of cities took place at a slower pace, largely because the economic growth driving urbanization was also slower. In addition, urbanization took place within well established market systems. In China, by contrast, rapid economic growth and rapid urbanization began when China was still a centrally planned command economy based on the Soviet model. The gradual move toward greater reliance on market forces unleashed growth and growth made large scale rural to urban migration a necessity. Many features of a market economy as a result did not yet exist when this process got underway and some still do not exist to this day. In the beginning of this development, for example, there was no market for urban land and elaborate substitutes had to be created to free up the land needed for development and for improving the housing conditions of the urban population. Today there is an urban land market but urban governments own most of the land and use land sales as a major source of urban revenue, a practice that is not sustainable in the long term.

One feature of China's urbanization process that has all too much in common with market driven urbanization elsewhere is the increasing environmental problems facing China's cities. The air is polluted and water, particularly in the north, is in short supply. Unlike North America and Western Europe, however, these environmental problems have become serious at a much lower level of per capita income. In effect, China has been forced to deal with these major external diseconomies earlier than was the case elsewhere.

Arguably, the biggest distortion created by the old command system was the household registration system that before 1978 was used to tightly restrict rural to urban migration and since 1978, used to lower the cost of this migration by limiting the urban services available to migrants. This registration system is gradually being eliminated but the services available to migrants remain extremely limited. Migrants have little access to public housing, to urban health care, and only limited access to urban schools for their children. Urban governments, partly because of limited revenue sources, have preferred to use these limited resources to support infrastructure for economic growth and services for the existing registered urban population.

The essays in this book provide in depth analysis of these and many other issues related to China's urbanization. They describe and analyze past urbanization patterns and performance and attempt to understand whether government policies have made that performance more or less efficient. They also suggest issues that need to be dealt with going forward and offer possible solutions. The book is thus designed for both outsiders interested in understanding China's urbanization challenges and Chinese planners searching for solutions to those challenges.

**Dwight H. Perkins**
Belmont, Massachusetts
February 2011

# Acknowledgments

Thanks are due to a number of people and institutions for their assistance in the publication of this book: to Professor Zheng Yongnian, Director of the East Asian Institute at National University of Singapore (NUS), for his encouragement and suggestion to have this volume included in the Series on Contemporary China; to Research and Graduate Studies office at the University of the Fraser Valley (UFV) for the teaching load release to facilitate research related to this project; to the publishers of SAGE, Elsevier, Routledge, and Taylor & Francis for reprint permission granted through the authors of five chapters in this volume; to the librarians at NUS and UFV for their valuable services; and to Dong Lixi, Ares Tan Hui Kheng, and Zheng Danjun at the World Scientific for their patience and professionalism in administrating the publication process, editing the manuscripts, and reading the final proof.

# Contents

*Preface*                                                                                         v
*Acknowledgments*                                                                                 vii
*Contributing Authors*                                                                            xi

Chapter 1   Introduction: China's Great Urbanization                                              1
            *Ding Lu*

Chapter 2   Urbanization and City-Size Distribution                                               11
            in China
            *Shunfeng Song and Kevin Honglin Zhang*

Chapter 3   Evolution of China's Urban Development                                                29
            Strategy and Institutions
            *Ding Lu*

Chapter 4   Urban Planning for Local Development                                                  63
            *Jieming Zhu*

Chapter 5   Industrialization, Urbanization, and Land Use                                         99
            in China
            *Xiaobo Zhang, Timothy D. Mount and*
            *Richard N. Boisvert*

Chapter 6   Assessing Urban Spatial Growth Patterns                                               125
            in China during Rapid Urbanization
            *Chengri Ding and Xingshuo Zhao*

Chapter 7   Land Use Reform, Land Markets, and Urban                                              161
            Land Use in Beijing
            *Chengri Ding*

Chapter 8      From Land Use Rights to Land Development        191
               Rights: Institutional Change in China's Urban
               Development
               *Jieming Zhu*

Chapter 9      A Transitional Institution for the Emerging       221
               Land Market in Urban China
               *Jieming Zhu*

Chapter 10     Urban Land Expansion and Economic Growth         259
               *Ding Lu*

Chapter 11     Rural-Urban Migration and Urbanization           279
               in China
               *Kevin Honglin Zhang and Shunfeng Song*

Chapter 12     Demography, Migration, and Regional              301
               Income Disparity
               *Ding Lu*

Chapter 13     Epilogue                                         317
               *Ding Lu*

Appendix       Major Events of China's Urban Development        331
               (1949–2010)
               *Ding Lu*

*Index*                                                         345

# Contributing Authors

**Richard N. Boisvert**  Department of Agricultural, Resource, and Managerial Economics, Cornell University, Ithaca, NY, USA

**Chengri Ding**  Urban Studies and Planning Program and National Center for Smart Growth, University of Maryland, College Park, MD, USA

**Ding Lu**  Department of Economics, University of the Fraser Valley, Abbotsford, BC, Canada

**Timothy D. Mount**  Department of Agricultural, Resource, and Managerial Economics, Cornell University, Ithaca, NY, USA

**Shunfeng Song**  Department of Economics, University of Nevada, Reno, NV, USA

**Kevin H. Zhang**  Department of Economics, Illinois State University, Normal, IL, USA

**Xiaobo Zhang**  International Food Policy Research Institute, Washington, DC, USA

**Xingshuo Zhao**  Urban Studies and Planning Program, University of Maryland, College Park, MD, USA

**Jieming Zhu**  Department of Real Estate, National University of Singapore, Singapore

# CHAPTER 1

# Introduction: China's Great Urbanization

*Ding Lu*

The spectacular rise of China as a world economic power is one of the most important events at the turn of the 21st century. In the three decades after China launched its market-oriented reform in 1978, the world's most populated country has seen its wealth continuously grow by almost one tenth per annum. With that rate of growth, the size of the economy doubles every seven years. Thanks to hyper economic growth, hundreds of millions of people have been lifted from poverty even though income distribution has become more polarized. With a 12-fold rise in just 30 years, China's per capita income has risen from merely one tenth of the world average to about one third in the past 30 years (NBSC, 2009a). Meanwhile China has also become a global hub of manufacturing, the second-largest exporter in the world market (2009), and the second-largest economy in the world (2010). By 2008, China had lifted itself from the rank of low-income countries to be one of the middle-income countries (Fig. 1.1).

Spatial concentration of production and population through urbanization is a salient feature of modern economic development in all countries. Industrialization and urbanization are the twin processes of modernization. China is no exception. In this giant country of 1.3 billion people, as the economy puffs ahead, urbanization is taking place at a scale and pace never before seen in human history. Figure 1.2 shows that every year since the mid-1980s, 13–15 million people have been added to China's urban population. That is equivalent to expanding the urban population every year by the size of the population in New York City. With this pace, China has added an urban population of 111 million in the 1980s, 141 million in the 1990s, and about 200 million in the first decade of this century. In other words, more

1

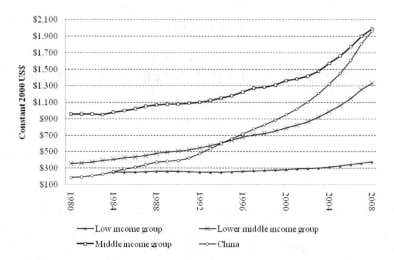

Figure 1.1.   Per capita GDP: China compared to various income groups.
*Source*: World Bank, *World Development Indicators* online database.

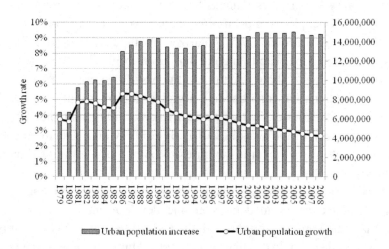

Figure 1.2.   China's urban population increase and growth rate (1979–2008).
*Source*: World Bank, *World Development Indicators* online database.

than 400 million people, nearly the combined population of the US and Mexico, have been added to China's urban population over the past 30 years.

Across China, new cities are sprouting up and the existing ones are being restructured and expanded. Hundreds of skyscrapers shadowed by numerous cranes and scaffolds are changing the city skylines day and night. The phenomenon of Shenzhen, a modern city of over eight million residents that was launched three decades ago as a special economic zone in a village-town near the border of Hong Kong, has been emulated and repeated in many places around the country. Between 1978 and 2008, the number of cities of all sizes tripled while the number of cities with one million residents or more quadrupled (Fig. 1.3). Urban city built-up areas have been expanding at an amazing pace of over six percent per annum since the mid-1980s.

Thirty years ago, China was not only one of the low-income countries but also a laggard in urbanization. From the 1960s to the 1970s, due to a series of peculiar events and policy options in a centrally planned regime, China's urbanization process stagnated and even reversed. Its share of global urban population actually declined. By 1978, its urbanization rate (percentage of population living in urban areas) was less than 19 percent. Thanks to the persistent and massive urban building drive since the early 1980s, China has nevertheless quickly caught up with the rest of the world in its level of urbanization. By 2004, China managed to raise its urbanization rate to 39 percent, surpassing that of the lower-middle-income group for the first time (Fig. 1.4). It is notable that it was not until 2008 that China's per capita income qualified it as one of the lower-middle-income

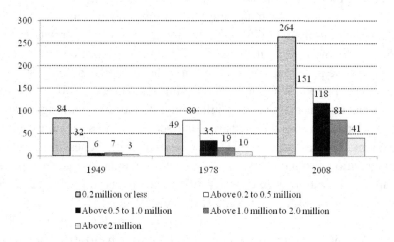

Figure 1.3. Number of Chinese cities of different population sizes (1949, 1978, 2008). *Source*: NBSC (2009b).

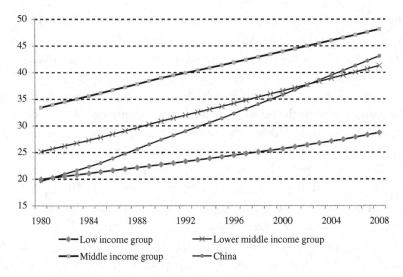

Figure 1.4.   Urban population: Percentage of total (1980–2008).

*Source*: World Bank, *World Development Indicators* online database.

countries. China's urban agglomeration level, measured by the percentage of population in urban agglomerations of more than one million residents, had even surpassed the middle-income group's by 2007: China with 18.4 percent vs. the middle-income group with 17.8 percent.[1]

The momentum of China's great urbanization seems unstoppable. As discussed by Northam (1975), urbanization has followed a growth path of an S-curve in most places in the world. When the urbanization rate is below 30 percent the pace tends to be slow since the industrialization is still at a preliminary period. When the urbanization rate surpasses 30 percent, its pace accelerates as massive rural-urban migration occurs while agricultural productivity rises and the industrial and service sectors create more and more jobs. The urbanization will slow down after it reaches 70 percent of the population. From this historical perspective, China has entered a period of rapid urbanization since the early 1990s and now is still in the middle of the second phase of the S-curve, a steep upward slope.

While China's per capita income has reached the average middle-income countries' level (as seen in Fig. 1.1), its urbanization rate is still

---

[1] World Bank, *World Development Indicators* online database.

about five percentage points lower than the latter's (as shown in Fig. 1.4). This remarkable contrast between the two indicators points to a huge potential for rapid urbanization in the coming years. According to a report by the McKinsey Global Institute (2010), if managed well, China will have 335 million more urban residents by 2025; one billion Chinese will live in cities by 2030; and the number of Chinese cities with a population of one million or more may reach 221 by 2030. In this process, approximately 40 billion sq meters of floor space will be built in five million buildings.

Moving ahead with further urbanization is indispensable to China's ambitious plan to sustain fast economic growth and raise its per capita income to the level of the high-income countries in the 21st century. The challenges and difficulties are abundant. To transform half a billion people from rural villagers to urban residents in the next three decades will not only require a colossal amount of investment in urban infrastructure and real estate but will also call for the development of many socioeconomic institutions and policies to facilitate and accommodate the massive transformation. Resource constraints, environmental pressures, social tensions, and institutional barriers all must be seriously addressed.

To understand the challenges and difficulties China faces today in this great urbanization, one must review what has happened in the unfolding events over the past decades. In particular, we must examine how various public policies have been adjusted and how institutions have been reformed to address critical issues in urbanization. To what extent have these policies and reforms been successful in meeting their challenges? In which ways are the past policies and institutions related to the issues in the coming years? Given the past experience, how likely will China's governing system meet the future challenges and solve knotty problems in urbanization?

This book aims to guide readers in comprehending some key developments in China's urbanization process. The volume collects insightful research papers by scholars on some key urbanization issues in China. These papers not only present a historical review of the evolution of public policies and institutions regarding urban development, but also a useful survey and in-depth analysis of various socioeconomic forces that define and contribute to the process of urbanization.

A good starting point is to take an overview of the whole city system in this populous country of vast territories. In Chapter 2, Song and Zhang examine the size distribution of Chinese cities and towns and compare it with the empirical observation of the so-called Pareto law of city-size distributions in other countries. Their study suggests that China's city-size distribution is better described by a modified Pareto distribution function with a quadratic term: city-size distribution appeared to be more even for large cities but less even for small urban and town areas. They also discovered that Chinese cities became more evenly distributed in the 1990s. The duo tried to interpret the phenomenon through the government intervention in urbanization: the policy that favors the development of small cities till the mid-1990s and the restriction of rural-urban migration especially for large cities.

Government policies have played a pivotal role in China's urbanization process. Chapter 3 (Lu) reviews the evolution of the country's urban development strategy at the national level. The chapter delineates major events in China's urban development since the founding of the People's Republic and describes how the central government's urban planning policies have drastically changed over time. It is interesting to observe that a new policy agenda to promote the growth of metropolitan hubs and urban clusters has emerged in recent years. The chapter also describes a series of institutional reforms since 1978 that have overhauled the resource allocation mechanisms in urban development and redefined the roles of the central government and local governments.

Local governments have crucial roles to play in China's urbanization. In Chapter 4, Zhu describes how, with the birth and growth of the urban land market, decentralization of urban land use planning to local governments has created an urban planning system conducive to economic development and rapid urbanization. He observes that this urban planning regime has been very pro-business and pro-growth by releasing land resources previously locked and underutilized in a centrally controlled system to be utilized productively in a market-based economy. However, he cautions that this transitional regime is not sustainable over a long term due to its lack of well-defined property rights and market order that provide certainty and internalization of externalities.

Rapid industrialization and urbanization have transferred more and more land away from agricultural use. The authors of Chapter 5, Zhang, Mount, and Boisvert, give a historical review of agricultural land use in China and its tension with the rising demand for urban land driven by industrialization. They then develop an analytical framework to describe what drives local governments to convert farmland for non-agricultural use and how the farmers determine the land use intensity (i.e. intensive cropping) for agricultural production. The empirical study confirms that with the deepening urbanization and rising incomes, it is inevitable that many farmers will eventually lose interest in intensive farming and move to non-farm jobs.

With more land being converted from farming uses to urban uses, the issue of assessing the efficiency of urban land uses arises. In Chapter 6, Ding and Zhao examine three typical urban spatial development forms in China — special economic zones, university towns, and central business districts — and evaluate the potential negative consequences and associated efficiency losses that may affect the long-term sustainable growth of cities. They argue that urban development in China should be focused on the creation and development of employment (sub)centers and urban spatial development in conjunction with these (sub)centers through the integration of land use and transportation.

To allocate land resources more efficiently, urban development needs not only foresight planning but also effective market mechanisms. Under the socialist legal framework, all urban land is owned by the state. In most Chinese cities before the late 1980s, urban land use rights were allocated free of charge to state-owned or state-controlled socioeconomic units (*danwei*) and there was no land market. An amendment to China's Constitution in 1988 legalized the transfer of land use rights through leasing and subleasing transactions between users, developers, and local governments. Since then, the real estate market has been burgeoning thanks to the transaction of land use rights. In Chapter 7, Ding outlines how the public (land) leasing system (i.e. land use rights system) was introduced as the foundation of today's urban land market. He uses the land transaction data of Beijing in 1997–1999 to examine the effects of the urban land market on land use patterns. His results provide evidence that market forces and prices have significant influences on the determination of urban land use and land development.

Zhu, the author of Chapter 8, describes how the land use right has evolved into the land development right (LDR) as he observed in a field study in Shanghai. By this account, the LDR was created to unlock the redevelopment process by eliminating supply-side constraints upheld by the old institution of the socialist land use right. It therefore was a major institutional innovation at the local level to facilitate urban development. However, it is also observed that this transitional institution has induced hasty capitalization of land rent and led to a suboptimal utilization of scarce land resources.

In Chapter 9, Zhu discusses the emergence of two major players in the post-reform urban development, namely the local developmental state and the *danwei*-enterprises (state-owned economic units inherited from the pre-reform regime). The spectacular urbanization and urban redevelopment in many Chinese cities have been driven by the incentives for these players to grab the rent in land use. Due to the ambiguity of entitlement to land rent, the transitional institution of the land use rights market has been associated with massive rent dissipation and wasteful investment. The author observes that the cost incurred by the institution is gradually overtaking its benefit.

A remarkable feature of China's fast economic growth and massive urbanization is the rapid expansion of urban land use. Chapter 10 by Lu applies the neoclassical growth accounting model to assess the distinctive role of urbanized land in economic growth. Using China's data of 31 provincial economies during 1996–2007, the study finds rather low contribution rates of urban land expansion to economic growth. The author interprets this finding as empirical evidence of low efficiency in urban land uses, which might be rooted in a series of institutional weaknesses of the land market, especially the monopoly power amassed by the local bureaucracy in determining the terms and conditions of land requisition and land use rights lease and sales.

Urbanization essentially converts rural residents into urban ones. Rural-urban migration is the core issue. As shown in Chapter 11 by Zhang and Song, in the two decades up to 1999, more than 75 percent of the urban population increase came from rural-urban migration and most of the migration took place across provinces, from inland rural areas to coastal urban areas. The authors of the chapter apply the rural-urban migration theories in development economics to analyze the demographic data. They conclude that both inter- and intra-province rural-to-urban migrants are motivated by the income gap between the rural home and urban destinations. They also find that the urban population size in a province has positive effects on intra-province migration while geographic distance discourages inter-province migration. The most intriguing part of this paper is its time-series analyses, which show that the nation-wide migration boom in these two decades was a consequence of China's rapid economic growth, not vice versa. This is consistent with our observation of Figs. 1.1 and 1.4: China's urbanization rate has lagged behind its economic growth. A possible interpretation of this result is that some structural bottleneck (such as urban social services for migrants) or institutional barriers have constrained the urban economy's capacity to create enough jobs for migrants.

A unique feature of China's urbanization process is the existence of various institutional barriers to rural-urban migration, such as the *hukou* (household registration) system, which defines residency status in urban areas. Due to the system, about one tenth of the country's population has become the so-called floating population, living and working in places where they do not have permanent residency status. Most of the population consists of rural migrant workers (*nongmin gong*) and their dependents. In Chapter 12, Lu discusses how this pattern of rural-urban migration may affect the welfare of migrants and the people of their homeland in the big picture of heterogeneous demographic transition across regions. The main challenge to the poor and rural regions is that the outflow of their working-age population has demographic consequences that favor the rich and urban areas. The biased impact is exacerbated by the *hukou* system since it returns rural migrant workers to their homeland when they get old and become unemployable. Several policy options are suggested for poor regions to deal with this challenge.

Finally, the epilogue highlights the major challenges to China's great urbanization in the coming years, which concern the ecological environment, urban governance, and mass migration. How China responds to these challenges will define the pace and features of the great urbanization in the coming years.

# References

McKinsey Global Institute (2010). *Preparing for China's Urban Billion.* McKinsey & Company.

National Bureau of Statistics of China (NBSC) (2009a). *Sixty Years of Social Economic Achievements of People's Republic of China — Series Report No. 1.* http://www.stats.gov.cn/.

National Bureau of Statistics of China (NBSC) (2009b). *Sixty Years of Social Economic Achievements of People's Republic of China — Series Report No. 10.* http://www.stats.gov.cn/.

Northam, R. M. (1975). *Urban Geography.* New York, John Wiley & Sons.

## CHAPTER 2

# Urbanization and City-Size Distribution in China*

*Shunfeng Song and Kevin Honglin Zhang*

China has been experiencing rapid urbanization since the economic reform starting in 1978. The number of cities increased from 191 in 1978 to 667 in 1999, while the urban share of national population increased from 18 percent to 31 percent. This paper examines China's urbanization and the evolution of its city system. It uses city-level data from 1991 and 1998 to investigate China's city-size distribution and its changes. It also discusses how economic and institutional factors affect the urban system and the patterns of city growth.

## 1. Introduction

Over the past two decades, China has experienced rapid urban growth. The non-agricultural population in urban areas increased from 172 million in 1978 to 389 million in 1999 (NBS, 1994, 2000), a 126 percent growth. This growth rate is much greater than the national population growth rate of 31 percent between 1980 and 1999. As a result, China has become more urbanized, with an urban population share that increased from 18 percent in 1978 to 31 percent in 1999. Rapid urbanization can be also observed in the increase in the number of cities. Chinese cities are administrative

* Reprinted with the authors' permission from *Urban Studies*, 39(12), pp. 2317–2327. The paper was first presented at the International Conference on China's Urbanization, Xiamen, Fujian, China, June 2001. The authors are grateful to participants for their comments and thank Guest Editor Kenneth Small and two anonymous referees of *Urban Studies* for their helpful comments and suggestions.

entities and officially designated according to political status, economic development level, and total population. In 1980, China had 223 cities, with 15 having a population size of over 1 million. In 1999, China had 667 cities, with 37 having a population size of over 1 million (NBS, 2000). Naturally, urbanization in China and China's city system have formed an important area for research.

Previous studies of the size, growth, and distribution of cities have been mostly based on Western economies. Generally, these studies have concluded that cities grow to take advantage of scale and agglomeration economies in production, consumption, and distribution. In the market economy, a free flow of labor, capital, and goods in trade is assumed to allow processes to operate and to permit choice among various locations. These choices lead to regional specialization, competition, and variable growth rates of cities in a system. Governments also intervene directly in the evolution of urban systems. Such intervention may take the form of state investments in transportation and urban infrastructure in order to correct market failure in economically viable locations or in influencing an industrial or commercial location through favoritism.

Among the many theories advanced to explain city sizes, growth dynamics of cities, and distribution of population across cities, the Pareto law, as discussed in Section 2, has been most popular. Empirically, the Pareto law has been proved a very accurate description of city-size distributions in many different countries and at different times within a country (Rosen and Resnick, 1980; Mills and Hamilton, 1994; Fujita *et al.*, 1999). Theoretically, however, this law has received much criticism due to the lack of consistent and well-defined explanations of the processes that govern city-size distribution. Several studies have argued a hierarchy of city systems (Henderson, 1988; Fujita *et al.*, 1999). But none of them has proved that the hierarchy should follow the Pareto law.

China has been a socialist economy since 1949. Its city system is unique, large, and complex. However, few studies have investigated the size, growth, and distribution of Chinese cities (Fan, 1999). This paper has three purposes. First, it examines China's urbanization and the evolution of city system. The paper shows that urbanization in China has experienced three phases since the People's Republic of China was founded in 1949 and the number of cities has increased greatly, especially during the past two decades. Second, the paper uses 1991 and 1998 city-level data and applies the Pareto law to investigate the size distribution of Chinese cities and changes in China's city system. It finds that the size distribution of Chinese cities became flatter, i.e. cities became more even in size, during the 1990s. Third, the paper discusses how economic and institutional factors affect the patterns of city growth and urban system. It argues that both economic and institutional factors are important in explaining China's city system.

This paper is organized as follows: Section 2 presents the Pareto law of city-size distributions and reviews the literature on this topic. Section 3 summarizes facts of urbanization in China and the evolution of China's city system. Section 4 estimates the parameters of the Pareto law and a generalization of it using 1991 and 1998 city-level data, in order to examine the Pareto or non-Pareto behavior of the Chinese city systems and changes in the system. In Section 5, this paper argues that in China both the market and the government play active roles in shaping China's city system. Section 6 concludes.

## 2. Size Distribution of Cities: An Overview

The Pareto law for city-size distribution can be written as

$$G_i = AP_i^{-\alpha} \tag{1}$$

where $G_i$ is the number of cities with population $P_i$ or more, $P_i$ is the population of the $i$th largest city, $A$ is a constant, and $\alpha$ is the Pareto exponent. When $\alpha = 1$, the Pareto law becomes the so-called rank-size rule. In this case, the product of a city's rank and population is a constant equal to the population of the largest city, also indicating that the third-largest city is one-third the size of the largest, and so on. When $\alpha > 1$ ($\alpha < 1$), populations of cities far down in the size distribution are greater (less) than is predicted by the rank-size rule, indicating a more (less) even distribution of city sizes. For example, the rank-size rule ($\alpha = 1$) predicts that the population of the second-largest city would be half that of the largest city, while when $\alpha = 1.2$ the Pareto law predicts that the population of the second-largest city would be 56 percent that of the largest city. Thus, the Pareto exponent measures how evenly city sizes are distributed.

There is an extensive literature on the application of the Pareto law to city-size distribution (e.g. Rosen and Resnick, 1980; Parr, 1985; Fan, 1988). Reviewing the literature, several important observations can be made. First, the Pareto law provides a very accurate description of city-size distributions in many different countries and at many different times in history. For instance, Rosen and Resnick (1980) used data from 44 countries and found that the $R^2$ value was above 0.95 for 36 countries while only Thailand had an $R^2$ value lower than 0.9 (0.83).

Second, the Pareto law gives a simple way to examine changes in city-size distribution over time for a given country and to compare size distributions across countries. Previous studies (e.g. Parr, 1985; Guerin-Pace, 1995) have shown that the Pareto exponent exhibits a U-shaped pattern over time. Rosen and Resnick (1980) found that the Pareto exponent tends to be higher for populous countries, suggesting that populous countries tend to have more evenly distributed populations.

Third, there is no general agreement as to whether the Pareto exponent is elastic, unitary, or inelastic across nations or even in a given country. In fact, estimates of the Pareto exponent vary for different studies, due to different sample sizes, different cutoffs in the low end of distributions, and using city proper or SMSA or urbanized area data. For instance, the mean Pareto exponent for 44 countries in Rosen and Resnick (1980) was 1.136 and the standard deviation was 0.196. For the United States in particular, Rosen and Resnick (1980) gave an estimate of 1.000 for 1970 metropolitan population data, 1.184 for city proper data, and 1.310 for data on the 50 largest cities in the United States. Parr (1985) used US city proper data and reported an estimated exponent ranging from 1.066 to 1.147 during 1895–1981.

Fourth, there is no theoretical reason to expect the Pareto law to hold with precision for city-size distribution, although a number of studies have theoretically derived a hierarchy in the urban system (e.g. Henderson, 1988; Fujita et al., 1999).[1] As these studies have emphasized, there is

---

[1] Gabaix (1999) theoretically proves that city-size distribution converges to a power law if all cities follow some proportional growth process (i.e. cities' growths have the same mean and same variance). He calls this power law Zipf's law and argues against using the Pareto law for city-size distribution.

a tension between external economies associated with the geographic concentration of industry within a city, on one hand, and diseconomies such as congestion costs associated with large cities, on the other. The net effect of this tension determines the optimal size of a given city. A hierarchy of city systems emerges because external economies tend to be specific to particular industries and hence vary greatly across industries, but diseconomies tend to depend on the overall size of a city. However, none of previous studies has proved that the hierarchy should follow the Pareto law or the rank-size rule. Fujita *et al.* (1999, p. 219) state that "the regularity of the urban size distribution poses a real puzzle, one that neither our approach nor the most plausible alternative approach to city sizes seems to answer". They further say that "we hope that future research will resolve this puzzle" (p. 225).

## 3. Urbanization and the City System in China

Urbanization in China has experienced three phases since the PRC was founded in 1949. In the first phase (1952–1965), China emphasized the growth of heavy industries. With this development strategy, many rural workers were recruited by state-owned enterprises and industrial cities were developed, especially in the inland areas. During this period, the urban population increased faster than the national population and China experienced a steady rate of urbanization. Table 2.1 shows that the urban population increased from 71.6 million in 1952 to 130.5 million in 1965, an 82 percent growth. During the same period, the pace of national population growth was slower, from 574.8 million to 725.4 million, a 26 percent growth. As a result, the urban population share increased from 12.5 percent in 1952 to 18 percent in 1965 (NBS, 1994).

The second phase was during the Cultural Revolution (1966–1977). During this period, urban growth was either negative or static. A major reason was the policy that required millions of urban youth to go to rural areas in order to "undergo peasants' education", which Mao thought important to prevent the younger generation from accepting capitalist influences and to channel and cultivate new revolutionary successors. In 1966–1977, 17 million urban people were resettled in the countryside

Table 2.1.   China's Population and Urbanization

| Year | Total Population (million) | Growth Rate[a] (percent) | Urban Population (million) | Growth Rate[a] (percent) | Urbanization (percent) |
|---|---|---|---|---|---|
| 1952 | 574.82 | — | 71.63 | — | 12.46 |
| 1957 | 646.53 | 2.50 | 99.49 | 7.78 | 15.39 |
| 1962 | 672.95 | 0.82 | 116.59 | 3.44 | 17.33 |
| 1965 | 725.38 | 2.60 | 130.45 | 3.96 | 17.98 |
| 1970 | 829.92 | 2.88 | 144.24 | 2.11 | 17.38 |
| 1975 | 924.20 | 2.27 | 160.30 | 2.23 | 17.35 |
| 1978 | 962.59 | 1.39 | 172.45 | 2.53 | 17.92 |
| 1980 | 987.05 | 1.27 | 191.40 | 5.49 | 19.39 |
| 1983 | 1030.08 | 1.45 | 222.74 | 5.46 | 21.62 |
| 1984 | 1043.57 | 1.31 | 240.17 | 7.83 | 23.01 |
| 1985 | 1058.51 | 1.43 | 250.94 | 4.48 | 23.71 |
| 1986 | 1075.07 | 1.56 | 263.66 | 5.07 | 24.53 |
| 1987 | 1093.00 | 1.67 | 276.74 | 4.96 | 25.32 |
| 1988 | 1110.26 | 1.58 | 286.61 | 3.57 | 25.82 |
| 1989 | 1127.04 | 1.51 | 295.40 | 3.07 | 26.21 |
| 1990 | 1143.33 | 1.45 | 301.91 | 2.20 | 26.41 |
| 1991 | 1158.23 | 1.30 | 305.43 | 1.17 | 26.37 |
| 1992 | 1171.71 | 1.16 | 323.72 | 5.99 | 27.63 |
| 1993 | 1185.17 | 1.15 | 333.51 | 3.02 | 28.14 |
| 1994 | 1198.50 | 1.13 | 343.01 | 2.85 | 28.62 |
| 1995 | 1211.21 | 1.06 | 351.74 | 2.55 | 29.04 |
| 1996 | 1223.89 | 1.05 | 359.50 | 2.21 | 29.37 |
| 1997 | 1236.26 | 1.01 | 369.89 | 2.89 | 29.92 |
| 1998 | 1248.10 | 0.96 | 379.42 | 2.58 | 30.40 |
| 1999 | 1259.09 | 0.88 | 388.92 | 2.50 | 30.89 |

*Source*: NBS (1994, 2000) and authors' calculation.

*Note*: [a] Growth rates before 1984 are average annual growth rates.

because of political reasons and the worsening situations regarding housing shortages, job opportunities, and the infrastructure in the cities (Song and Timberlake, 1996). As shown in Table 2.1, the growth rate of the national population was higher than that of the urban population between 1965 and 1975. Consequently, the urban population share stagnated, being 18 percent for both 1965 and 1978 (NBS, 1994).

The third phase is the rapid urbanization in the reform era (1978 till present). Since 1978, China has not only promoted an open-door policy and a "socialist market economy" but also encouraged urbanization. Many county towns (*xian zhen*) have been upgraded and classified as cities. The number of cities increased dramatically from 191 in 1978 to 667 in 1999, and the urban population share increased from 18 percent to 31 percent (NBS, 2000, pp. 95 and 347). As shown in Table 2.1, it took China 26 years (1952–1978) to have a 5.5 percent increase in urbanization, while it took China 21 years (1978–1999) to have a 13 percent increase in urbanization. No doubt, China experienced a faster urbanization in the past two decades.

In China, cities are classified into three levels according to their administrative status: county-level cities, prefecture-level cities, and central municipalities. In 1993, for example, China had 371 county-level cities, 196 prefecture-level cities, and 3 central municipalities. These numbers changed to 437, 227, and 4, respectively, in 1998.[2] Chongqing became the fourth central municipality in July 1997. Cities with different statuses are given different levels of authority with regard to investment decision-making and foreign-funded project approvals. The higher the level, the more directly the city reports to Beijing and the greater its autonomy and influence. Usually, larger cities have higher administrative statuses. But there are some exceptions. For example, Xiamen in Fujian Province is a quasi-province-level city but has a non-agricultural population (0.6 million in 1998) of only approximately half of Fuzhou's population (1.1 million in 1998). The latter is only a prefecture-level city even though it is the capital of the province and has a much larger population (NBS, 1999a).

The definition of a city in China is not straightforward. Chinese cities are administrative entities and must be officially designated, with the designation criteria being a function of the political-administrative status, economic development, openness, and total population of an urban place. Since a higher status in the administrative hierarchy is usually accompanied

---

[2] The 227 prefecture-level cities in 1998 include 15 quasi-province-level cities (NBS, 1999). The quasi-province level, newly designated, has an administrative status higher than the prefecture level but lower than the central level.

Table 2.2.  Number of Cities by Size of Non-agricultural Population

| Size | 1949 | 1965 | 1980 | 1991 | 1994 | 1999 |
|---|---|---|---|---|---|---|
| Total | 132 | 168 | 223 | 479 | 622 | 667 |
| Super-large (over 2 million) | 1 | 5 | 7 | 9 | 10 | 13 |
| Very large (1–2 million) | 4 | 8 | 8 | 22 | 22 | 24 |
| Large (0.5–1 million) | 7 | 18 | 30 | 30 | 41 | 49 |
| Medium (0.2–0.5 million) | 18 | 42 | 72 | 121 | 175 | 216 |
| Small (less than 0.2 million) | 102 | 95 | 106 | 297 | 374 | 365 |

*Sources*: NBS (various issues).

by greater autonomy, political power, and access to resources, local authorities are eager to pursue the upgrading of their settlements to higher statuses (Fan, 1999). Such efforts, together with relaxation of the designation criteria, have brought a significant growth in China's urban sector in the past two decades. Many county seats (*xian cheng*) were reclassified as cities (*shi*), resulting in a sharp increase in the total number of cities, from 223 in 1980 to 667 in 1999. Some county seats earned the city status even though they had a relatively small population. During the past two decades, many existing cities were upgraded by expanding their territories or merging two adjacent cities or combining a city with its surrounding county.

China also classifies its cities into five categories according to their sizes. Table 2.2 shows the definitions and the number of cities in each category in 1980 and 1999. In 1980, China had 7 super-large cities, 8 very large cities, 30 large cities, 72 medium cities, and 106 small cities. These numbers increased to 13, 24, 49, 216, and 365 in 1999, respectively. These changes indicate a rapid urban growth in the past two decades. Table 2.2 also shows that most are small cities. In fact, the primacy and intercity concentration is relatively low in China. For example, the primacy, measured by the share of the largest city's population in the total urban population, was only 4 percent in 1998, compared to a primacy of 10 percent for the US in 1990 based on urbanized area data. The urban population share of the top ten largest cities for China was 19 percent in 1998, compared to 37 percent for the US in 1990 based on urbanized area data (Bureau of the Census, 1993).

## 4. Size Distribution of Cities: The Case of China

Does the Pareto law also provide an accurate description of Chinese city-size distribution? To answer this question, we apply Eq. (1) to Chinese city systems in 1991 and 1998. The data come from *Urban Statistical Yearbook of China* compiled by the National Bureau of Statistics of the PRC (NBS, 1992, 1999a). This paper uses data on the non-agricultural population in urban areas (*shi qu*). Although the time gap between 1991 and 1998 might be small, it is interesting to examine if there is any change in the Pareto exponent and thus a change in the pattern of Chinese city-size distribution. Because city-level data are available only from 1991 and 1998, this paper is limited to these two years.

Table 2.3 presents the results that are obtained by estimating a double-log model of Eq. (1) with the OLS method. Several interesting findings are observed. First, judging from the $R^2$ values, it appears that the Pareto law explains Chinese city-size distributions well. The adjusted $R^2$ values are higher than 0.88 for both 1991 and 1998.

Second, for 1991 data, the estimated Pareto exponent is 0.92 with a standard deviation of 0.015, suggesting that the rank-size rule ($\alpha = 1$) is

Table 2.3. Regression Results on Pareto Distributions: Chinese Cities (Dependent Variable: log $G$)

| Year | Variable | Coefficient | S.D. | Sample Size | Adj. $R^2$ Value |
|------|----------|-------------|------|-------------|------------------|
| 1991 | Constant | 16.3322 | 0.1826 | 479 | 0.8870 |
|      | log $P$  | 0.9231  | 0.0151 |     |        |
| 1998 | Constant | 18.1953 | 0.1535 | 665 | 0.9119 |
|      | log $P$  | 1.0414  | 0.0126 |     |        |
| 1991[a] | Constant | 16.2754 | 0.1853 | 468 | 0.8858 |
|         | log $P$  | 0.9192  | 0.0153 |     |        |
| 1998[a] | Constant | 17.2174 | 0.1974 | 468 | 0.8894 |
|         | log $P$  | 0.9743  | 0.0159 |     |        |

*Note*: [a] Regressions are on common cities of 1991 and 1998.

statistically rejected. The estimated Pareto coefficient indicates that the size distribution of Chinese cities in 1991 is less even than that implied by the rank-size rule. For 1998 data, however, the estimated coefficient (1.04, with a standard deviation of 0.013) is statistically greater than 1, indicating that the city-size distribution became more even than that predicted by the rank-size rule.

Third, the results show a significant increase in the Pareto exponent, from 0.92 in 1991 to 1.04 in 1998. This finding implies that the city-size distribution in China became more even during 1991–1998. The question here is what caused this change. Was it caused by the inclusion of many new cities in 1998 or by the dynamic changes among 1991 cities? To answer this question, we ran regressions by using data on common cities in both 1991 and 1998. As Table 2.3 shows, the estimated exponents based on the common sample become 0.92 for 1991 and 0.97 for 1998. Considering their standard deviations, we conclude that the latter is statistically greater than the former, suggesting that cities in the common sample became more evenly distributed between 1991 and 1998. We further notice that the estimated coefficient with the full 1998 sample (1.04) is statistically greater than that obtained by using the common sample (0.97). This finding suggests that the inclusion of new cities made cities in the full sample appear more evenly distributed.

Some previous studies have shown that estimates of the Pareto exponent are sensitive to sample thresholds and size (Rosen and Resnick, 1980; Guerin-Pace, 1995). To examine whether it is also the case for China's cities, we use various thresholds of low-end cutoffs in the 1998 city-size distribution. Table 2.4 presents the results. It shows that the estimated Pareto exponent is sensitive to sample thresholds. In China's case, the Pareto exponent increases with higher cutoff thresholds, at least within the range reported in Table 2.4.

This finding suggests that the city-size distribution is more even for large Chinese cities than for smaller cities. The rise in the Pareto exponent is also illustrated by the increase in the slope of fitted curves in Fig. 2.1. Another interesting finding revealed in Table 2.4 is related to the fit of the Pareto law for different sample thresholds. As the last column shows, the $R^2$ value increases until it reaches a maximum of 0.9968 at the threshold of 190,000. This result indicates that the explanatory power of the Pareto law is also sensitive to sample thresholds. For the

Table 2.4.  Sensitivity of the Pareto Exponent to the Size of City Sample, 1998

| Threshold | Sample Size | Pareto Exponent | Adj. $R^2$ Value |
|---|---|---|---|
| Full sample | 665 | 1.0414 | 0.9119 |
| 50,000 | 640 | 1.1619 | 0.9689 |
| 80,000 | 588 | 1.2287 | 0.9842 |
| 100,000 | 535 | 1.2682 | 0.9895 |
| 120,000 | 462 | 1.3092 | 0.9929 |
| 150,000 | 383 | 1.3527 | 0.9960 |
| 170,000 | 349 | 1.3668 | 0.9966 |
| 190,000 | 309 | 1.3800 | 0.9968 |
| 200,000 | 292 | 1.3838 | 0.9967 |
| 210,000 | 272 | 1.3900 | 0.9967 |

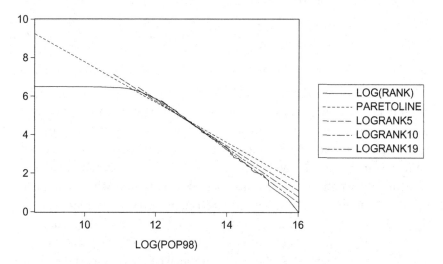

Figure 2.1.   Pareto law with different sample thresholds, 1998.

*Notes*: The solid line shows the data points; PARETOLINE is the fitted curve from the full sample; LOGRANK5, LOGRANK10, and LOGRANK19 are fitted curves from subsamples with cutoff thresholds of 50,000, 100,000, and 190,000, respectively.

"right" threshold, the law could appear superior in explaining Chinese city-size distributions.

The above results show that both the Pareto exponent and fit vary with sample thresholds, revealing non-Pareto behavior of the city-size

Table 2.5.  Regression Results on Non-Pareto Distributions: Chinese Cities (Dependent Variable: log $G$)

| Year | Variable | Coefficient | S.D. | Sample Size | Adj. $R^2$ Value |
|------|----------|-------------|------|-------------|------------------|
| 1991 | Constant | −9.6915 | 0.3380 | 479 | 0.9918 |
|      | log $P$ | 3.3465 | 0.0550 | | |
|      | $(\log P)^2$ | −0.1739 | 0.0022 | | |
| 1998 | Constant | −10.5614 | 0.4110 | 665 | 0.9896 |
|      | log $P$ | 3.6005 | 0.0659 | | |
|      | $(\log P)^2$ | −0.1863 | 0.0026 | | |

distribution. To confirm this non-Pareto behavior, we added a quadratic term to the basic logarithmic version of Eq. (1), giving Eq. (2):

$$\log G = a - \alpha(\log P) + \beta(\log P)^2 \qquad (2)$$

where $a = \log A$.

Table 2.5 shows the regression results. For both 1991 and 1998, we found that Chinese cities were not distributed according to the Pareto law (a linear regression model in logarithm). Non-Pareto behavior is evident by the significance of the quadratic term in the regression. Compared with the results in Table 2.3, Table 2.5 also shows that the quadratic model fits the actual distributions much better than the Pareto law, with the adjusted $R^2$ value rising from 0.89 to 0.99 for 1991 and from 0.91 to 0.99 for 1998. Figure 2.2 shows the fitted curves for both the Pareto and quadratic specifications. We observe that the quadratic curve fits the data points (i.e. the solid line) much better than the Pareto curve. The concave regression line implies that larger cities are more evenly distributed than smaller cities, confirming the rise in $\alpha$ as we restrict the sample to the larger cities used in Table 2.4 and Fig. 2.1.

## 5. Economic and Institutional Factors of China's Urbanization and City System

We have seen that China experienced rapid urbanization in the past two decades. A number of factors have promoted China's urbanization. One is

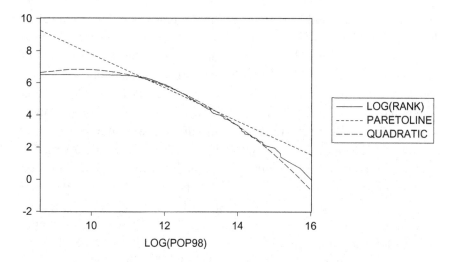

Figure 2.2.   Pareto and quadratic regression lines, 1998.

*Notes*: The solid line shows the data points; PARETOLINE is the fitted curve from the Pareto law; and QUADRATIC is the regression line from the quadratic model.

the relationship between industrialization and urbanization, as well demonstrated by the literature on urban growth (e.g. Henderson, 1988). Cities with a concentration of economic activities enjoy scale and agglomeration economies and continue to grow, primarily through rural-urban migration, until diseconomies become dominant. Since the economic reform started in the late 1970s, China has greatly upgraded its economic structure. In 1978, 70.5 percent of employed persons were in the agricultural (primary) sector, which contributed 28 percent to the national GDP (NBS, 2000, pp. 54 and 116). In 1999, these proportions decreased to 50 percent and 18 percent, respectively. Industrialization and upgrading of China's economic structure have created a great number of job opportunities in urban areas and absorbed a large amount of rural surplus workers, thus promoting China's urbanization.

Rural-urban migration in recent years is another important factor of city growth in China. Before urban reforms started in 1984, China long had a policy that strictly restricted rural-urban migration through a static urban household registration system. Under this system, rural people were not entitled to urban employment or to state subsidies for housing, food, fuel, medical care, and schooling. Without employment and state subsidies, rural workers could not survive in urban areas. The urban reforms since 1984 have relaxed restrictions on migration in many ways. For example, enterprises in urban areas have become more autonomous in hiring and firing their workers, and the former "iron-bowl" employment system has been replaced by a labor contract system. Hence, many enterprises prefer to hire rural workers because of the lower labor costs. Other institutional changes have also facilitated rural-urban migration. For instance, housing has been delinked from employment, rationing of food and fuel has been abandoned, and the urban household registration system is being gradually phased out. As a result, China has been experiencing a huge influx of rural workers into urban areas. In 1998, 44 million rural workers left their homeland to seek jobs somewhere else (NBS, 1999b). According to Liu (2000), between 2.3 and 2.7 million rural workers migrated to cities each year in the late 1990s. Chen and Parish (1996) found that about one fifth of the entrants in the urban labor force came from rural areas.[3]

China's open-door policy has also promoted China's urbanization. Specifically, foreign direct investment (FDI) has been a key force driving the recent coastal city growth and urbanization in East China. In the period of 1986–1998, China attracted over $260 billion in FDI, with 87.7 percent going to the coastal region. The role of FDI in urban economic development and thus urbanization can be observed in several aspects. First, FDI directly promotes exports. According to Zhang and Song (2000), the share of foreign-invested enterprises' (FIEs) exports in China's total exports increased from a negligible proportion (0.05 percent) in 1980 to 12.6 percent in 1990 and to 45.5 percent in 1999. Second, FDI indirectly affects exports because local domestic firms may increase their exports by observing the export activities of FIEs and FIEs improve the linkage between local and foreign firms. Third, FDI creates jobs. Song (2000) found that FDI has become a more important contributor to creating urban

---

[3] Generally, there are three types of rural migrants. The first are those who are officially permitted to move to cities. The second involves peasants who engage in industrial, commercial, and service activities in cities (the floating population). The third are the daily commuters who live in villages and go to nearby cities to work on a daily basis (the pendulum population).

employment. In 1985, FIEs employed 0.13 million workers, accounting for only 0.1 percent of the total urban employment. In 1998, FIEs' employment reached 5.9 million workers, accounting for 3.8 percent of the total urban employment. The experience of Shenzhen, the first special economic zone in China, is a good demonstration of the role of FDI in promoting China's urbanization. In the eight years between 1991 and 1998, the population of Shenzhen increased by 165 percent, from 432,000 to 1,146,000. Data used in this paper show that each year during this period, per capita FDI for Shenzhen was far greater than the average per capita FDI for all Chinese cities. It is evident that FDI has indeed promoted China's city growth and urbanization.

China's city system exhibits the profound impacts of institutional factors. One important institutional factor is the government development strategy. As several previous studies argued, Chinese leaders have always attempted to control the growth of the large cities and to limit severely rural-urban migration (Hsu, 1996; Fan, 1999). Before the economic reform, Chinese urban policy emphasized the growth of heavy industries. Cities were narrowly viewed as potential sites of industrial plants, and favored cities were assigned a number of large state-owned heavy industrial enterprises. Such an urban development strategy discouraged the growth of light and service industries in most cities, thus unnecessarily restricting their economic base and limiting employment growth. In addition, the Chinese government was very concerned about coastal security. Because of this concern, China carried out the "three-front" project in the 1950s and 1960s. Many strategic manufacturing plants were moved from the coastal region to the inland region. New industrial cities were built far from the coastal line and the government sent many workers and technical personnel to these new cities. Hsu (1996) analyzed city development in Luoyang and Guiyang and found a lasting impact of early government decisions on city growth. Hsu showed that government economic policies and urban directives of the 1950s were critical determinants of the development of Chinese cities, not just in that decade but also for many years beyond that period.

China's current urban policy still favors the development of small cities. The official urban policy is to "control large cities, develop medium-sized cities rationally, and actively develop small cities". This urban policy, however, has been challenged by scholars. For example, Zhao and Zhang (1995) showed a high positive correlation between city efficiency and city size, not only in economic measures but also in social and environmental measures. Hong and Chen (2000) studied cities in Jiangsu Province and found that small cities have a disadvantage in providing urban infrastructure. They argued that a certain consumption scale and population size are necessary conditions for promoting service industries and markets. Song (2001) used 1997 city-level data and showed that larger cities tend to have lower unemployment rates. As far as employment is concerned, job creation is associated with urban size. Product variety in production and consumption is related to urban size; variety, in turn, requires labor specialization, thus creating jobs (Abdel-Rahman and Fujita, 1990; Ogawa, 1998).

China's city system has been also affected by the migration policy. Until the late 1990s, China had strictly limited rural-to-urban migration, especially to large cities. Thus, the anti-migration policy had not only slowed down the pace of China's urbanization, but also affected the structure of China's city system because China limited migration to larger cities more strictly than to smaller cities.

## 6. Conclusion

China's urbanization has experienced three phases. The rate of urban growth during the first period, from 1952 to 1965, was fast. Anti-urbanization, however, prevailed during the Cultural Revolution and the urban population share stagnated at about 18 percent from 1965 to 1978. Rapid urbanization started with the economic reform in 1978 and has continued since then, with the urban population share steadily increasing to nearly 31 percent in 1999.

Based on 1991 and 1998 city-level data, we find that Chinese cities became more evenly distributed in the 1990s. We also find that the Pareto law fits Chinese data well, although China's city system exhibits some non-Pareto behavior statistically. The empirical results on the Pareto exponent are consistent with earlier findings that populous countries tend to have more evenly distributed cities.

Several major economic and institutional factors have contributed to the rapid urban growth and changes in urban systems in the past two decades. The recent industrialization of China's economy has created many job opportunities in cities. This, along with the relaxation of many rural-urban migration restrictions, has resulted in a huge influx of rural workers into cities. The open-door policy and FDI have also helped China to become more urbanized, especially in the coastal areas. All these changes have affected not only the total urban population but also the size distribution of Chinese cities.

## References

Abdel-Rahman, H.M. and Fujita, M. (1990). "Product Varieties, Marshallian Externalities, and City Size". *Journal of Regional Science*, 30, pp. 165–183.

Bureau of the Census (1993). *1990 Census of Population and Housing.* Washington DC: Bureau of Census, pp. 728–732.

Chen, X. and Parish, W.L. (1996). "Urbanization in China: Reassessing an Evolving Model". In J. Gugler (ed.), *The Urban Transformation of the Developing World.* New York: Oxford University Press, pp. 60–90.

Fan, C.C. (1988). "The Temporal and Spatial Dynamics of City-Size Distribution in China". *Population Research and Policy Review*, 7, pp. 123–157.

Fan, C.C. (1999). "The Vertical and Horizontal Expansions of China's City System". *Urban Geography*, 20, pp. 493–515.

Fujita, M., Krugman, P., and Venables, A.J. (1999). *The Spatial Economy*, Cambridge, MA: The MIT Press.

Gabaix, Xavier (1999). "Zipf's Law for Cities: An Explanation". *Quarterly Journal of Economics*, 114(3), pp. 739–767.

Guerin-Pace, F. (1995). "Rank-Size Distribution and the Process of Urban Growth". *Urban Studies*, 32(3), pp. 551–562.

Henderson, J.V. (1988). *Urban Development: Theory, Fact, and Illusion.* New York: Oxford University Press.

Hong, Y. and Chen, W. (2000). "The New Development of Urbanization Pattern". *Economic Research Journal*, 392, pp. 66–71.

Hsu, M.L. (1996). "China's Urban Development: A Case Study of Luoyang and Guiyang". *Urban Studies*, 33, pp. 895–910.

Liu, S. (2000). "The Current Conditions and Policies of China's Employment". In Y. Wang and A. Chen (eds.), *China's Labour Market and Problems of*

*Employment*. Chengdu, Sichuan: Southwestern University of Finance and Economics Press, pp. 22–29.

Mills, E.S. and Hamilton, B.W. (1994). *Urban Economics*, 5th edition. New York: HarperCollins College Publishers.

National Bureau of Statistics of the PRC (NBS) (1994, 2000). *China Statistical Yearbook*. Beijing: China Statistics Press.

National Bureau of Statistics of the PRC (NBS) (1992–1999a, various issues). *Urban Statistical Yearbook of China*. Beijing: China Statistics Press.

National Bureau of Statistics of the PRC (NBS) (1999b). *China Labor Statistical Yearbook*. Beijing: China Statistics Press.

Ogawa, H. (1998). "Preference for Product Variety and City Size". *Urban Studies*, 35, pp. 45–51.

Parr, J.B. (1985). "A Note on the Size Distribution of Cities Over Time". *Journal of Urban Economics*, 18, pp. 199–212.

Rosen, K.T. and Resnick, M. (1980). "The Size Distribution of Cities: An Examination of the Pareto Law and Primacy". *Journal of Urban Economics*, 8, pp. 165–186.

Song, F. and Timberlake, M. (1996). "Chinese Urbanization, State Policy, and the World Economy". *Journal of Urban Affairs*, 18(3), pp. 285–306.

Song, S. (2000). "Policy Issues of China's Urban Unemployment". EAI Working Paper No. 49, The National University of Singapore.

Song, S. (2001). "City Size and Urban Unemployment: Evidence from China". *World Economy & China*, 9(1), pp. 46–53.

Zhang, K. and Song, S. (2000). "Promoting Exports: The Role of Inward FDI in China". *China Economic Review*, 11, pp. 385–396.

Zhao, X. and Zhang, L. (1995). "Urban Performance and the Control of Urban Size in China". *Urban Studies*, 32(4–5), pp. 813–845.

# CHAPTER 3

# Evolution of China's Urban Development Strategy and Institutions

*Ding Lu*

In the six decades of the People's Republic of China, the country has followed a rather unusual path of urbanization and regional development under a changeful policy-institution environment. Especially in the last two decades of the 20th century, China's urban development strategy and institutions went through drastic changes as the economy was transformed from a centrally planned economy to a market-based economy. Since then the state urbanization strategy has evolved from the so-called small-town consensus to one that relies on megacities to play a central role in regional development. The state urbanization strategy has been increasingly influenced by local and regional interests in a more decentralized post-reform political-economy structure. Institutional changes in the urban real estate market, central-local fiscal relationship, and residential administration of migrants have made profound impacts on the process of urbanization.

## 1. Introduction

Wealth, urbanization, and geographic conditions vary across the vast territories of China. Roughly speaking, China consists of six types of regions.[1] The first is the metropolitan areas that include Beijing, Tianjin, and Shanghai, which are governed as province-level municipalities. These well-developed areas have over 70 percent of their densely populated residents living within 100 kilometers of the coast or navigable waters.

---

[1] We here follow the classification of major regions in China by [Démurger *et al.* (2002a and 2002b)].

The second is the northeast provinces of Heilongjiang, Jilin, and Liaoning, which constituted the traditional industrial heartland of China for nearly a century. In these provinces, the rich deposits of coal, iron, and other minerals and direct access to seaports are the geographic conditions for the cluster of a number of heavy-industry cities.

The third is the coastal provinces of Hebei, Shandong, Jiangsu, Zhejiang, Fujian, Guangdong, and Hainan, all with over 80 percent of the population living within 100 kilometers of the sea or navigable rivers, and which had the highest GDP per capita growth rate in the last two decades.

The fourth is the central provinces, including Shanxi, Henan, Anhui, Hubei, Hunan, and Jiangxi, which comprise the agricultural heartland of China. The two large rivers and their many tributaries endow 57 percent of the population with easy water transportation.

The fifth group is the northwest provinces of Inner Mongolia, Shaanxi, Ningxia, Gansu, Qinghai, Xinjiang, and Tibet. Largely arid, these provinces have the lowest population density in China, with only 8 percent of the land being arable.

The sixth group is the southwest provinces of Sichuan, Chongqing, Yunnan, Guizhou, and Guangxi, which have rainfall and temperature conditions that are suitable for crop cultivation, but suffer from being too mountainous, with 14 percent of the land on a slope greater than 10 degrees.

In terms of per capita GDP, the metropolitan, northeast, and coastal regions enjoy levels of development well above the national average. The regional disparity in incomes, however, is not fully matched by the regional differentiation in urbanization. For instance, the northeast provinces may be more urbanized than some coastal provinces but their per capita income is lower than the latter. The same applies when the northwest provinces are compared to the central ones.

The present regional differentiations in urbanization and levels of development across the country carry with them the imprints of drastic changes in state policies towards urbanization and regional development in the past decades. Indeed, since the founding of the People's Republic of China, the nation has followed a rather unusual path of urbanization and regional development under a changeful policy-institution environment. Few other countries in modern history have experienced so many changes in the way the government intervenes in the urbanization process. Few other places have seen regional development so profoundly affected by such interventions. The lessons of these policy changes are valuable to many other developing countries as well as the Chinese themselves. Reviewing the evolution of China's urbanization strategy and policy will not only help us understand better the past events and identify the roots of many current issues but also sharpen our vision for the trends of changes in the future.

## 2. China's Early Urbanization Experience

Urban areas, as venues of concentrated socioeconomic activities since ancient times, have been profoundly influenced by geographic conditions and socioeconomic changes. For more than 2,000 years during the agricultural age, China was one of the world's most developed centrally administered kingdoms due to the imperial court's control over an irrigation network that covered a vast territory. The central functions of Chinese cities at that time were of military strongholds or administration and control centers. For the most part of the centuries between the 9th and the mid-19th century, China had the world's largest city, the biggest share of top-sized cities, and the largest urban population (Chandler, 1987).

Compared to the United States, China has a geographic landscape less friendly to development. As the fourth-largest country by size on Earth, China has a vast territory of 9.6 million sq kilometers that stretches from the temperate to subtropical zones. If you superimpose a map of China on that of the US, you will find that the two countries have similar sizes and are located in about the same temperate zone. However, the two countries are quite different in topographic characteristics. As discussed in Démurger *et al.* (2002b), the most important difference being that the US has coastlines running the length of its eastern and western borders, whereas Western China is landlocked. China is also much higher, hillier, and drier, with plains at less than 500-meter elevation making up only 25 percent of the total land area, and mountains and plateaus accounting for 60 percent. Arable land accounts for only about 10 percent of the land size. These topographic features of China imply higher transportation costs and a greater requirement for physical infrastructure construction. These make the task of economic development in China more challenging than in the US.

Within China, the geographic conditions across regions are highly uneven. They have worked together with regional policy differences to increase the disparity in regional development in recent years.[2] Démurger *et al.* (2002b), provides a succint description of these conditions. Physically, China resembles a three-step staircase running downward from west to east. It begins with the 4,000-meter-high Qinghai-Tibet Plateau in the west, proceeds to the highlands and basins in the center which are about 1,000 to 2,000 meters above sea level, and ends with hilly regions and plains that are less than 1,000 meters high. The combination of higher precipitation, warmer climate, and access to navigable rivers and the sea have made the central and eastern provinces more conducive for farming and trade, and, hence, the population centers of China. The Qinghai-Tibet Plateau was traditionally the poorest region. The location of China's economic activity used to be centered in the Yellow River valley in the northwest (where Chinese civilization began in 2000 BC), which is about 1,000 kilometers away from the coast. This original location of the economic center was determined by the importance of high agricultural productivity and land-based trade in ancient times. The bulk of China's international trade at that time was conducted through the famous Silk Route, which passed through the northwest corner of China. Over time, the pressure of an expanding population and the frequent invasions by the northern tribes caused more of the population to move south and into the mid-coastal and southeast regions. By the 12th century, the Yangtze River valley had become well developed and densely populated. Meanwhile, manufacturing, trade, and commerce became increasingly important and so did the cities that emerged as manufacturing, trade, and commerce centers. Around 1500, for instance, of the ten largest cities of the world, China had four, with populations ranging from 147,000 (Nanjing) to 672,000 (Beijing). Cities like Hangzhou and Yangzhou in the Yangtze Delta served as splendid examples of manufacturing and trading centers for high-quality handicraft goods and precious artefacts (Chandler, 1987).

The economic importance of the coastal region increased dramatically after the Opium War in 1840 when the Western powers forced China to first open several coastal ports and then the whole country for trade. The advantages of coastal locations rose drastically thanks to their connections to the world shipping routes and increased linkage to the hinterland through navigable rivers, canals, and railways. With the setting up of foreign concessions and opening up of treaty ports, international trade expanded, foreign direct investments flowed in, and local industrialists made their appearances, especially in the mid-coastal and southeast regions. China's early modernization was thus characterized by a reorientation of the urban system towards the coastal regions in response to new trading and commercial opportunities. Despite the long chaotic period of protracted wars and famines through the second half of the 19th century to the mid-20th century, modern commercial and industrial activities brought booms to the coastal region and attracted a large number of migrants from the hinterland as well as abroad. This process of capitalist urbanization led to the emergence of large metropolises like Shanghai, Guangdong, and Tianjin, which became centers of growth and economic dynamism for nearly a century after China was forced to trade with the rest of the world.

## 3. Urbanization in the Centrally Planned Economy Period (1949–1977)

The founding of the People's Republic of China in 1949 by the Communist Party of China (CPC) marked the beginning of a three-decade-long period of a socialist centrally planned economy. Following the Soviet development strategy, China adopted two key sets of guiding principles: (a) the Marxist principles of public ownership with the state as trustee, and of generalized egalitarianism; and (b) the Stalinist practices of central planning for resource allocation, suppression of light industries and services in favor of heavy industries, and minimizing trade and financial linkages with the capitalist economies [Démurger *et al.* (2002b)].

### 3.1. *Socialist industrialization and anti-urbanism*

As China pursued industrialization under Soviet-style planning, its urbanization process was heavily influenced by the Marxist ideology of social equity, including the ideal of "abolition of the separation of town and country" (Engels, 1954, pp. 411–412). Like in other countries, effective industrialization logically led to urbanization and spatial concentration. To counter the trend of increasing spatial inequality, the Chinese central planners implemented Marxist "de-urbanism" and "anti-urbanism" in a bid to close the gap between the urban and rural sectors. Such an ideology was reinforced by the Chinese revolutionaries' hatred towards the large coastal cities as they were symbols of foreign capitalist occupation and domination. It was well received by the China observers that socialist China before economic reform was "wedded to a broad anti-urban strategy" (Kirkby, 1985, pp. 1–18). This strategy was well suited to the single-minded emphasis on full-scale national industrialization in the 1950s and 1960s.

The initial urban policy for implementing the strategy was the transformation of "consumer cities" to "producer cities". Cities in which manufacturing production was dominant were deemed "proletarian producers", while cities specializing in commercial, financial, and other non-manufacturing activities were categorized as "bourgeois consumers" (Zhu, J., 1999). The government prioritized planned investment in the "productive" activities (the primary and secondary sectors) of socialist cities while suppressing the growth of "non-productive" sectors (Kwok, 1988). Much state attention and capital were given to industrial and agricultural production while investment was largely neglected for intra-city infrastructure, amenities, and service sectors like housing, utilities, finance, and communications. Meanwhile, great efforts were made to mobilize housewives and other elements of the "leisure class" into the active labor force.

When new industrial bases were developed, the Chinese planners followed a policy of "production first, living conditions second". Urban development was characterized by the "discrimination in allocation of non-productive expenditures" and "discrimination in personal consumption" (Kirkby, 1985, pp. 156–159). Of state investment in capital construction, the portion that went to "non-productive" sectors declined from 33–34 percent for the period 1950–1957 to less than 20 percent for the period 1958–1975. Meanwhile, the portion for housing dropped from about 10 percent to only 4–7 percent.[3]

---

[3] The "non-productive" investment was devoted to urban utilities, cultural, educational, and social service installations, housing, public buildings, commercial enterprises, transport, and communications constructions.

## 3.2. *Regional self-sufficiency and inland investment*

All these measures were supposed to enhance the "productive" mode of socialist cities at the expense of their "consumptive" functions. The strategy later had a new dimension when Mao added the principle of regional economic self-sufficiency to China's economic policy-making. Based on this principle, a region should be self-sufficient not only in food production but also in industrial goods as well. This principle was justified by inter-regional egalitarianism and national security needs. Mao perceived regional economic self-sufficiency as the key to China's readiness to engage in a protracted defence of its territory. He and his generals envisaged three lines of defence (coastal, central, and inland west), and they decided in 1964 on a massive construction of military-industrial complexes in Western China, the so-called the Third Front.[4] Under this principle, guidelines for urban development stressed the rules of "strictly controlling the size of large cities and developing small cities and towns" and "no construction of concentrated cities" (Zhou, 1997, p. 306).

These guidelines caused the large amount of wastage that occurred in China's industrialization and urbanization process. First, it led to a large bulk of state investment capital going to the inland provinces, while the financing of the capital came from heavy "taxation" on coastal cities. In 1957, among China's Eastern, central, and western regions,[5] the ratio for the number of cities was 1.0:1.0:0.4 and the ratio for the urban population was 1.00:0.46:0.18. By 1978, these ratios had changed to 1.0:2.2:0.6 and 1.00:0.69:0.33 respectively (NBSC, 2009).

Second, many sets of capital equipment in Shanghai and other coastal cities were relocated to the mountainous areas in Guizhou, Sichuan, and Hubei. In those areas, basic infrastructure like transportation and electricity was in short supply, and the sources of raw materials were far away. The pouring of investment funds into the interior provinces was a clear violation

---

[4] For a detailed discussion on the rationale of this principle, see Démurger *et al.* (2002b).

[5] The eastern region includes Beijing, Tianjin, Hebei, Liaoning, Shanghai, Jiangsu, Zhejiang, Fujian, Shandong, Guangdong, and Hainan. The western region includes Inner Mongolia, Guangxi, Sichuan, Guizhou, Yunnan, Tibet, Shaanxi, Gansu, Qinghai, Ningxia, and Xinjiang. The central region includes Jilin, Heilongjiang, Anhui, Jiangxi, Henan, Hubei, and Hunan.

of the comparative advantage principle. Industrial productivity was inevitably compromised. Even though the interior provinces' share of fixed assets went from 28 percent in 1952 to 57 percent in 1983, their share of the gross value of industrial products only went up from 31 percent to 41 percent.

Third, at the urban level, the urban-regional development strategy led to the "wasteful quest for completeness regardless of the scale of operation" (Kirkby, 1985, p. 156). One of the consequences of this development was that the degree of specialization among China's small and medium-sized cities was unusually low as compared with other countries (Chang and Kwok, 1990). Even in the early 1980s, it was observed that most Chinese cities still tended to have similar industrial structures. Although a convergence of structures among megacities would conform to their functions of agglomeration and conglomeration, such a convergence among smaller cities, however, reflected the legacies of inefficient self-sufficiency (Zhou, 1997, p. 244). In the rural areas, the setup of the self-sufficient People's Communes suppressed the rural market towns. Traditional commercial connections between urban and rural areas as well as large and small cities were severed.

Fourth, such industrialization endeavors sacrificed the quality of life in new and old urban areas. A model of urbanization during the Mao era was the Daqing oilfield in Northeast China, which was built upon the principle of "production first, living conditions second". The industrial base was well known at that time as a physical convergence of city and countryside, industry and agriculture. "The only clear message [of Daqing] to city planners was that as little as possible should be spent on urban housing and utilities, in order to free funds for more productive and socialistic ends" (Kirkby, 1985, p. 206).

Finally, the growth of the interior provinces not only occurred at the expense of the coastal provinces, it also lowered the overall growth rate of the economy. The discrimination against the coastal region was so severe that although Shanghai provided more than 40 percent of the state revenue during the Cultural Revolution period, it was not even allowed to retain enough funds to cover the depreciation of its capital stock. The wastage that occurred with this discriminatory policy against coastal investments was further increased because of the poor planning, bad execution, and shoddy management of investments in the interior provinces (Démurger *et al.*, 2002b).

## 3.3. *State-compelled migration and strict control over urban population*

The single-minded emphasis on full-scale national industrialization and Mao's local self-reliance principle compounded the serious inefficiency problems in agricultural production. With rapid industrialization in the 1950s, China's grain output was under great pressure to support the increasing urban population. The socialist collectivization of the agricultural sector, however, limited the rate of growth of agricultural productivity and hence the availability of overall grain surplus for distribution to the non-agricultural population. Meanwhile, thanks to the "production first" policy, the deteriorating urban infrastructure limited the ability of large cities to provide employment and daily necessities for their growing population. To cope with this situation, a policy of "strictly control the development of large cities" was adopted (Zhu, Y., 1999, p. 190). The merits of metropolises were generally overshadowed by supply-side constraints and thus overlooked.

During the period of the Great Leap Forward (1958–1961), agricultural collectivization went to its extreme as rural households were organized into thousands of People's Communes, characterized by egalitarian distribution systems and a self-sufficient production mode with rural industrialization drives. The disastrous drop in agricultural output caused the starvation and death of millions of people during a three-year nationwide famine after the Great Leap Forward. The grain crisis prompted the central planners to impose more measures to tighten state control over the growth of all types of towns and cities in the early 1960s.

Kirkby (1985) divided the Chinese measures to control urban population into two categories. One category refers to the passive measures which include the *hukou* (household registration) system introduced in 1958 and the rationing system for basic consumer goods introduced in the mid-1950s. Under the household registration system, the entire population was divided into those with urban residence and those with rural residence. Food and other basic consumer goods were rationed according to household registration and the rationing was biased in favor of urban residents, who, unlike their rural counterparts, had little means to achieve self-sufficiency. Administratively, the state imposed strict criteria for achieving official town status in the 1960s and 1970s, which led to many

towns being demoted to commune status, both nominally and functionally. In Fujian Province alone, the number of towns was cut from 225 in
1956 to 127 in 1963 and further down to 98 in 1966 (Zhu, Y., 1999). These
arrangements segregated the Chinese population into rural residents and
urban residents, whose *hukou* statuses were largely determined by their
birthplace.

The other category relates to those active measures of state-compelled
migration. From the 1960s through the 1970s, the government launched
waves of *xia fang* ("sending down") campaigns to send millions of urban
workers, technicians, engineers, and their family members to interior
provinces, remote border regions, and rural areas. Between 1961 and 1965,
about 25 million urban employees and residents were sent to the countryside (NBSC, 2009). During the Cultural Revolution (1966–1976), such
campaigns were implemented in a more coercive manner towards purged
cadres/officials, intelligentsia, prisoners, and a large number of urban
youths. These campaigns were "held together by a common thread — the
necessity for the Party to maintain a stable and manageable urban polity in
a situation of severely constrained central investments in the non-productive
urban fabric and insufficiencies in grain supply" (Kirkby, 1985, p. 32).
Laquian (1997) detailed China's state-compelled migration during the
period into three types: the "settle-down campaign in rural areas", the
"border region settlement", and the "inland industrial shift". The first type
of migration, during the Cultural Revolution alone, involved 17 million
urban youths, amounting to more than one tenth of the urban population.
The second type led to the establishment of about 2,000 state-owned farms
in the border regions with 4.9 million workers and staff up to 1985. The
third type shifted approximately 10 million technicians and skilled workers from the eastern-coastal cities to the western region of China. All of
these had profound impacts on China's urbanization and city distribution.

### 3.4. *Industrialization without much urbanization*

Given the above institutions and policies, it is easy to understand the phenomenon of China's three-decade-long "industrialization without much
urbanization" from the 1950s to the late 1970s, which was observed by
many researchers. Thanks to the overall industrialization strategy and all

those passive and active measures to control the urban population, China's urbanization during the period was dominated by state planning and hence can be described as "state-compelled urbanization" (Zhu, Y., 1997). The overall urbanization process displayed a very unusual path.

As shown in Fig. 3.1, both the urban share of total population and the urban share of total employment rose in the 1950s due to industrialization and surged during the Great Leap Forward (1958–1960). In the "adjustment" period of 1961–1963 after the failure of the Great Leap Forward, both slumped due to the retrenchment of a large number of urban employees and mandatory urban-to-rural migration. The urban share of population continued to slide down through the 1960s till the mid-1970s, reflecting the effect of the *xia fang* campaign, the state-compelled urban-to-rural mass migration. During these years of de-urbanization, the urban share of population declined steadily despite the uneven economic growth. Meanwhile, the urban share of total employment inched up and overtook the urban share of population.

Figure 3.1.   Urbanization of population vs. urbanization of employment (1952–2000).

*Source*: *China Statistical Yearbook*, various issues.

*Note*: Urban population share = urban non-agricultural population/total population. Urban employment share = urban jobs/total jobs. Urban employment ratio = urban jobs/urban population.

The urbanization did not resume its upward movement till the start of the economic reform in 1978, a year when the urban share of population was still lower than its 1959 level. The gap between the urban share of jobs and the urban share of population kept growing till 1978. Along with these changes, the urban employment ratio (urban employment divided by urban population) rose whenever the urban employment share rose faster than the urban population share.

### 3.5. *Urban-rural segregation*

Under the household registration system and the rationing system, people with permanent urban residence were entitled to state-compelled allocation of food and other basic consumer goods. This resulted in a formidable urban-rural segregation, which effectively blocked non-state-compelled population mobility. "Although ideological bias and public pronouncement favored the countryside, in reality the extraction of resources from the rural sector and assistance to the urban sector widened both the agriculture-industry imbalance and rural-urban gap" (Kwok, 1992, p. 69).

This rural-urban dualism enforced by state planning contributed to the privileged status of urban permanent residents to receive state subsidies. Despite that, the negligence of "non-productive sector" development in the urban areas resulted in chronic deterioration of urban infrastructure in many cities and led to a severe shortage of consumer service supplies in the urban area. In particular, by the late 1970s, most of the Chinese cities experienced a "housing crisis" characterized by overcrowded living conditions and scarce housing facilities (Kirkby, 1985). The urban housing shortage persisted through the 1980s as over 6–7 million (about one third) of urban households did not have sufficient floor space according to official standards (Lee, 1997).

Figure 3.2 reflects the "industrialization without much urbanization" phenomenon before 1978. The urban share of total population followed the trend of structural change in GDP from the 1950s to the mid-1960s, but failed to do so from then to the end of the 1970s. The ratio of urban road length to highway length dropped from about 10 percent in the early 1950s to below 5 percent through the 1960s to the early 1980s, reflecting severe under-investment in urban infrastructure. Between 1959 and 1966,

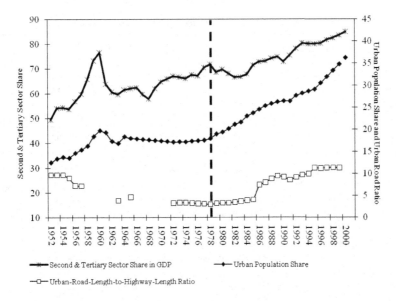

Figure 3.2.   Urban share in total population vs. secondary and tertiary sector share in GDP.
*Source: China Statistical Yearbook*, various issues.

even the total number of cities fell from 183 to 175 due to the demotion of some cities to county towns (Table 3.1).

Paradoxically, despite the anti-urban policies, the concentration of the urban population in very large cities had been a fact of life during the socialist centrally planned period. As shown in Table 3.2, the primacy of large cities from the 1950s to the early 1980s was not reduced. This was largely due to the overall de-urbanization policies that not only restricted the growth of large cities but also constrained the development of small cities and towns. For the two decades between the late 1950s and the end of the 1970s, the total number of cities and their distribution hardly changed (Table 3.1) except for a one-third drop in the number of cities with fewer than 100,000 residents. China's urbanization stagnated.

## 4.  Urbanization Policy in the Post-Reform Period (1978–2000)

At the end of 1978 a decisive political victory was won by the rehabilitated cadres, led by Deng Xiaoping, over the remnants of the Maoist establish-ment at the Third Plenum of the Eleventh Party Congress of the Chinese

Table 3.1.    Number of Cities Classified by Non-agricultural Population

|        | ≥2 mil | 1 mil to <2 mil | 0.5 to <1 mil | 0.2 to <0.5 mil | 0.1 to 0.2 mil | <0.1 mil | Total |
|--------|--------|-----------------|---------------|-----------------|----------------|----------|-------|
| 1953   | 3*     | 6**             | 16            | 28              | 49             | 18       | 120   |
| 1959   | 5      | 10              | 21            | 24              | 81             | 42       | 183   |
| 1966   | 5      | 8               | 20            | 22              | 78             | 42       | 175   |
| 1978   | 6      | 7               | 27            | 31              | 91             | 29       | 191   |
| 1984   | 8      | 12              | 30            | 39              | 137            | 69       | 295   |
| 1992   | 10     | 22              | 30            | 66              | 246            | 133      | 507   |
| 2000   | 13     | 25              | 54            | 220             | 241            | 111      | 664   |

*Source*: *China Urban Yearbook*, various issues. The 1953 data are from Sidney Goldstein (1985), *Urbanization in China: New Insights from the 1982 Census*, Honolulu: Papers of the East-West Population Institute No. 93.
*Note*: * Number of cities with population larger than 2.5 million; ** number of cities with population between 1 million and 2.5 million.

Table 3.2.    Percentage Shares of Urban Population Living in Different Size Classes of Cities (1952–2000)

| City Size        | 1952 | 1965 | 1982 | 1985 | 1992 | 1996 | 2000 |
|------------------|------|------|------|------|------|------|------|
| Over 1 million   | 40.1 | 43.0 | 43.3 | 39.4 | 39.6 | 35.2 | 37.7 |
| 0.5–1.0 million  | 19.0 | 20.5 | 20.5 | 19.3 | 13.1 | 14.8 | 13.9 |
| Others           | 40.9 | 36.5 | 36.2 | 41.3 | 47.3 | 50.0 | 48.4 |

*Source*: Data for 1952–1985 from Zong Lin (1988), "On the Scale, Structure and Development Strategy," *China City Planning Review*, (4), pp. 13–21; data for 1992–2000 compiled from *China Statistical Yearbook* and *China Urban Yearbook*, various issues.

Communist Party. The event marked the beginning of an era of market-oriented reform in China.[6] The strategy on the domestic front was the decollectivization of agricultural production, the decentralization of the fiscal system, and the deregulation of prices; the strategy on the international

---

[6] There was heated controversy over what the fundamental economic mechanisms in the rapid growth of China after 1978 are. Some economists (the experimentalist school) believed that the growth was enabled by the discovery of new non-standard economic mechanisms, such as collectively owned rural enterprises and fiscal contracting, whereas others (the convergence school) saw the growth as the result of moving toward a private market economy, wherein best international practices were adopted and modified according to local conditions. For a review of this debate, see Sachs and Woo (1994).

front was the open-door policy. All these reforms led to profound changes in urbanization policies and process.

In the first phase of reform, decollectivization restored agricultural production to household farming. The adoption of a "production responsibility system" allowed farmers to keep and sell products in excess of the state grain collection quotas. Linkages between the rural and urban areas were enlivened by non-planned market transactions for those freely-traded agricultural goods. Soon the People's Communes were abolished and their administrative functions were taken over by township governments and village committees. The traditional townships regained their status and those former economic centers of the communes with densely populated settlements were also designated as towns (Laquian, 1997; Zhu, Y., 1999).

## 4.1. *Reversion of Maoist migration policy*

Parallel to reform in the rural areas, during 1978–1982, the Party leaders reversed the Maoist policy of *xia fang* by allowing millions of previously rusticated urban youths and persecuted cadres/officials and intelligentsia to return to their city hometowns (Chan, 1992). In response to the employment problem of a suddenly enlarged urban labor force, the government in 1980 decided to develop various ways of creating jobs in urban service sectors, including support for the growth of the private economy (Lu, 1994, p. 122). With official encouragement, the new, private, and mostly "non-productive" (i.e. service) business development produced much-needed household services and created numerous jobs for the returned youths. This allowed the state to allocate more funds for investment in housing and urban infrastructure (Kwok, 1992).

## 4.2. *Rural industrialization and in situ transformation in rural areas*

The early success of the rural reform significantly raised agricultural productivity and released millions of rural laborers from crop cultivation. From 1978 to 1986, the proportion of rural crop-cultivation laborers in the total rural labor force decreased from 84 percent to 67 percent. An increasing pool of rural labor force became surplus and started seeking jobs outside the agricultural sector. It was estimated that in 1987, of the rural labor engaged in crop cultivation, more than 100 million were underemployed (Li, 1997, p. 38). Favorable conditions in the 1980s facilitated the shift of surplus labor force from agricultural to non-agricultural sectors, leading to a rapid growth of township and village enterprises (TVEs) in the rural areas. The expansion of these rural enterprises continued into the 1990s. By the end of the 1990s, the TVEs produced one third of China's total industrial output and hired more than 100 million rural residents.

There were two major policy objectives for developing TVEs in the Chinese government guidelines during the 1980s (Lee, 1992). One was "using industry to subsidize agriculture" (*yi gong bu nong*), expecting township and village authorities to use their revenue from these enterprises to maintain and improve conditions for agricultural production. The other was to help prevent excessive rural-to-urban migration, or in other words allowing peasants to "leave the land (farming) but not the rural areas" (*li tu bu li xiang*). Embedded in this policy was the fear that an outflow of rural laborers into the cities would add unbearable stress to the overstretched infrastructure, stressed job market, and tight grain supply in the urban areas.

It was against this background that Chinese central planners reached the so-called small-town consensus at a major national conference on urban development convened in October 1980, Beijing. The consensus settled the essence of the post-reform urbanization strategy in this guideline (Zhou, 1997, p. 307): "Strictly control the size of large cities, rationally develop medium-sized cities, and vigorously promote the development of small cities and towns".[7] Some scholars observed that this guideline was "ideologically based" and central-planning-oriented, reflecting the legacy of anti-urbanism in the pre-reform period (Kwok, 1992; Wen, 2002). It preferred scattered, small-scale, and decentralized urbanization in the rural areas and rejected large-scale and concentrated urbanization. The implication was that large-scale urbanization was considered to be socially degrading, environmentally undesirable, and economically costly. Others like Kirkby perceived the guideline to be mainly a pragmatic one to

---

[7] In China, large cities refer to those cities with a population of over 0.5 million; medium-sized cities refer to those with a population of between 0.2 and 0.5 million; small cities refer to those with a population below 0.2 million. Cities with a population of over 1 million are called super-sized cities.

"provide the country with a balanced and rational network of thriving urban-industrial centres" (Kirkby, 1985, p. 207). Some researchers, however, observed that "the strategy of emphasizing small town development and rural industrialization appeared almost concurrently with the market-oriented reform and was formulated on a sounder basis" than the strategy to "strictly control the size of large cities" (Zhu, Y., 1997, p. 191).

A milestone policy change occurred in 1984 when the State Council lowered the criteria for the designation of official town status and promoted the policies of "abolishing townships and establishing towns" (*che xiang jian zhen*) and "placing villages under town administration" (*zhen guan cun*).[8] The policy change led to the designation of 2,583 towns in the next two years and a total of 14,539 towns by 1992. Meanwhile, the State Council allowed peasants and their dependants to move to designated towns for permanent settlement, provided that they had permanent residence in the town's jurisdiction, were able to run a business or had a stable job in township enterprises, and could meet their own needs for basic food supply outside the food rationing system.[9] Although some studies showed that the move was more of an official sanction, than an initiative, of a *fait accompli* that had prevailed in some localities for several years, the legalization of rural-to-town migration opened the gates for a torrent of peasant migrants. In 1985, Hubei Province alone recorded 1.29 million peasant migrants (He, 1988). The influx of those migrants not only provided a major source of population growth in small towns but also became an important source of capital for small town development (Lee, 1992). Through building their own facilities and estates, contributing land use fees to the town governments, and joint investment in collective enterprises, these migrants were the driving force of the spontaneous "urbanization from below" in the post-reform era.[10] In addition to the

---

[8] *Guowuyuan Gongbao* (State Council Gazette) (1984), No. 30, pp. 1012–1014.

[9] *Guowuyuan Gongbao* (State Council Gazette) (1984), No. 26, pp. 919–920.

[10] In the mid-1980s, the national government authorized municipal and township governments to collect urban construction and maintenance levies from enterprises to finance urban infrastructure maintenance. Studies showed that such levies were merely enough for maintaining existing infrastructure. Urban development investment in small towns was mainly funded by county-level funds in addition to state investment. Revenues from township enterprises and levies on wealthy peasant in-migrants were the main sources of county-level funds (Lee, 1992).

pivotal role of the administrative sanction for such migration, the rapid business expansion of TVEs and the inflow of foreign capital to small-town industries were the two key developments that contributed to the *in situ* urbanization in the rural areas, as found by Zhu's case studies of the phenomenon in Fujian Province (Zhu, Y., 1999).

In 1986, the State Council also lowered the criteria for the designation of city status. The city definition was adjusted again in 1993. The local government administrative structure was reformed by "converting prefec-tures to cities (*che di jian shi*)" and "placing counties under city administration" (*shi guan xian*) (Niu, Yu, and Li, 2009). The status change helped raise the fiscal autonomy of many new urban areas as they offi-cially became small and medium-sized cities. The number as well as population of the small and medium-sized cities thus grew rapidly (Tables 3.1 and 3.2).

### 4.3. *Central role of large cities in opening to the world*

The small-town consensus, however, was challenged in the mid-1980s. There was evidence that firms in large cities performed more profitably and efficiently than those in small ones. Large cities in China have also been the main sources of fiscal revenues. Some Chinese scholars therefore advocated promoting the development of large cities. Others suggested that medium-sized cities should be given priority for growth (Zhou, 1997). In 1989, the Urban Planning Law of the People's Republic of China was nevertheless promulgated with only a modification of the earlier guideline in its fourth article: "The State follows the policy of strict control over the size of large cities and rational development of medium-sized cities and small cities with the purpose of promoting productivity and a rational distribution of the population" (Wang, 1996). The law upheld the restrictive policy towards the large cities but gave both the medium-sized cities and the small ones the same "rational" support on the basis of efficiency considerations.

In practice, the mid-1980s witnessed an increased role of central cities as China opened its door to foreign investors. This opening up initially was limited to two southern provinces (Guangdong and Fujian), with the establishment of several special economic zones (SEZs) in 1979–1980.

The open economic zones provided investors with various preferential tax treatments, and exemptions on duties and from labor regulations.[11] After the initial success of SEZs, 14 coastal cities were designated in 1984 the status of coastal open cities (COCs), which were entitled to set up their own economic and technological development zones (ETDZs) and given the right to approve foreign investment projects up to a limit.

Meanwhile, plans were mapped out to establish macro-regions with functionally defined boundaries and "key-point" cities as gravity centers. The Shanghai economic zone was officially created in 1983, which covers an area of 640,000 sq kilometers including the whole municipality of Shanghai and the provinces of Jiangsu, Zhenjiang, Anhui, Jiangxi, and Fujian. In the mid-1980s, it accounted for one third of China's GDP and one fifth of the nation's population. The Beijing-Tianjin-Tangshan development region was launched in 1984 to form another growth axis centered around the three megacities. The rationale for the development of these regions was to exploit the benefits of megacity agglomeration and its spread effects by following the models of Japan's Tokyo-Yokohama megalopolis or America's eastern seaboard megalopolis (Laquian, 1997). These planning initiatives were followed by the establishment of coastal open economic zones (COEZs) in 1985 and an open coastal belt (OCB) in 1988. In 1990, to revive foreign investors' confidence in the aftermath of the Tiananmen Incident, the central government announced a plan to develop the Shanghai Pudong New Area as a fresh zone for investment and businesses.

Despite the above initiatives, the decisive turning point in favor of metropolitan growth axes did not come till 1992, when the paramount leader Deng Xiaoping personally called for speedier reform and greater openness of the economy during his legendary South China Inspection Trip (*nanxun*). After that Shanghai became openly promoted as the "dragon head" of the vast inland territory along the Yangtze River and its Pudong area emerged as a new financial center dubbed the "oriental Manhattan" in less than a decade. In the first two years after Deng's *nanxun*, national and provincial governments launched hundreds of

---

[11] Details on the different preferential policies applied in these zones can be found in Yang (1997), Chapter 3; Ma (1999), Chapter 7; Wang and Hu (1999), Chapter 6; Chen (2000); and Démurger (2000).

various development zones, leading to a real estate development boom in coastal cities.

Implementing these coastal preferential policies required the delegation of authority to local officials to plan their open zones, to approve plans for infrastructure development, and to negotiate and license foreign investment projects. The municipal governments of the coastal cities were also delegated the authority to borrow from abroad for urban infrastructure development (Laquian, 1997). For those reasons, provincial capitals and a number of major cities were designated the special status of separate planning city (*jihua danlie shi*) or subprovince city with greater autonomy in local development planning and finance. On top of the four municipalities (Beijing, Shanghai, Tianjin, and Chongqing), 15 large cities have enjoyed such an administrative status.[12]

The greater role of central cities became increasingly eminent as the policy of being open to foreign investment was extended to all of China after 1992. In that year, the central government decided to extend the practice of 14 coastal open cities (designated in 1984) to five inland major cities along the Yangtze River, 13 border cities, and 11 inland provincial capitals.[13]

## 4.4. *Emergence of a floating population*

The booms in the large cities and the coastal regions attracted millions of "floating" or "mobile" people, another type of spontaneous rural-to-urban migration. In two decades from 1978 to 1998, the number of rural laborers who were employed in cities increased from fewer than two million to 65 million (Li and Lou, 2009). This phenomenon also reflected the fact that the rural industries and *in situ* development of small towns were no long able to keep rural surplus laborers in their homeland. However, since the *hukou* system made it difficult for rural migrant workers to gain permanent residence in major cities, this

---

[12] *China Statistical Yearbook* (2001) and "*jihua danlie shi*" (separate planning city) in Chinese online encyclopedia, Baidu Baike (http://baike.baidu.com/view/112105.htm).

[13] "*Yanhai kaifang chengshi*" (coastal open cities), in Chinese online encyclopedia, Baidu Baike, (http://baike.baidu.com/view/603394.htm).

in-migration was by the mid-1990s considered "temporary". The mobile rural migrant workers, officially estimated to be over 100 million by the end of the 1990s, have provided a huge source of cheap labor to the urban economy.[14] Their existence, however, has also imposed huge pressures on the urban services. By the early 1990s, the migrant population had already reached more than one tenth of the population of many large cities (Yeung, 2000). Nowadays, in most Chinese cities, migrant workers with rural *hukou* outnumber the workers holding urban *hukou* (Fan, 2010).

The spontaneous flow of rural migrant workers into cities happened against the small-town consensus and the government's policy to have *in situ* industrialization in the rural areas. It was therefore frowned upon and discouraged by the governments at all levels. In 1982, the State Council promulgated the Rules for Compulsory Deportation of the Homeless and Beggars in Urban Areas, which authorized the urban police to arrest and deport anyone who did not have a legal permit to live and work in the cities. The practice was not terminated until 2003, when the government introduced new rules to deal with the homeless and beggars after the widely reported Sun Zhigang incident.[15]

In the context of fiscal decentralization in the post-reform years, local municipal governments have taken diversified measures and local policies to cope with the influx of rural migrants. Generally the local authorities welcome the floating labor force to meet the needs of local development but usually take various measures to protect the privileges of the incumbent urban residents by keeping the in-migrants "temporary" and limiting their access to local public services such as healthcare and schooling. The rural migrants therefore constitute an underclass of marginally employable and disposable workers. In cities like Shenzhen, Guangzhou, and Shanghai, however, permanent residence and other related privileges have

---

[14] Wen Jiabao indicated that there were 120 million migrant rural workers in urban areas at the time he assumed his duty as China's premier (Xinhuanet.com, March 18, 2003).

[15] Sun Zhigang was a 27-year-old college graduate who visited Guangzhou without a permit to live and work in the city. He was tragically beaten to death on March 20, 2003, after he was arrested by the police for having no permit document. (See "The Sun Zhigang Incident and Reform of Household Registration System", www.rdyj.com.cn/2003/rdqk-12-10.html.)

been offered since the late 1990s to attract skilled laborers and wealthy in-migrants who can afford to invest in urban real estate over certain price thresholds. Notwithstanding that, the major portion of the floating population has yet to be entirely integrated into the urban sector.

### 4.5. *Emergence of urban property market and re-urbanization in cities*

Under the socialist legal framework, all urban land is owned by the state. In most Chinese cities before the late 1980s, urban land use rights were allocated free of charge to state-owned or state-controlled socioeconomic units (*danwei*) and there was no land market. Meanwhile, most of the urban residents lived in rented public housing estates, rationed and managed by *danwei*. The rent charged by *danwei* was often too low to cover the maintenance costs.

When China opened up for foreign investment in the early 1980s, it became obvious that land is a valuable resource and cities like Shenzhen pioneered the practice of levying fees for land use, first to foreign-invested firms and then to all land users. However, based on socialist ideology, China's 1982 Constitution forbade any organizations or individuals to "appropriate, buy, sell, or lease land, or unlawfully transfer it in any way". It was not until 1987 when the inhibition was broken in Shenzhen where the first deal leasing land use rights was sealed. Other special economic zones and coastal open cities soon followed suit to conduct trial land use rights transactions (Li, 2009). In this process, a pivotal institutional change was detaching land use rights from land ownership, which had been *de jure* a state monopoly. This made it possible for legal persons to own and transact land use rights. An amendment to China's Constitution in 1988 officially legalized the transfer of land use rights through leasing and subleasing transactions between users, developers, and local governments. With this change, the real estate sector has become an important component of the urban economy and property development a key business sector.

The emergence of a property market received a decisive boost in 1992, when the Communist Party's 14th National Congress reached the consensus to build a "socialist market economy" after Deng Xiaoping called for a comprehensive reform of the economic system. In the following nationwide boom of hundreds of development zones, the so-called rolling development approach was introduced: Local governments initiated real estate development plans by granting development rights of sites to local developers, which were usually government-linked companies. State banks would provide loans to the developers to "clear the land" for further development. This usually involved compensating the residents or farmers for their relocating costs. Once this was done, the indigenous developers would sublease and transfer the land use rights to foreign companies for real estate projects. Thus the local developers recovered the invested funds usually with hefty profits and would use the funds for the next round of rolling development (Lu and Tang, 1997, p. 83). Such schemes, though often involving bureaucratic rent-seeking, drastically sped up the construction of urban infrastructure and the growth of the real estate market in the 1990s. The initial years of real estate marketization provided a big push for urban expansion but also led to construction and investment bubbles.

Pilot housing reforms to privatize housing consumption and production started in some cities in the 1980s. After the State Council issued the Decision on Deepening Urban Housing Reform in July 1994, mass privatization of housing started. Most of the previously *danwei*-administered public housing units were sold to tenants at discounted prices. Numerous new housing projects were built by real estate developers and a housing market soon emerged. In July 1998, the State Council issued the Notice on Further Deepening Urban Housing Reform and Promoting Housing Construction to officially end the in-kind housing rationing in the state-owned sector. From then on, all housing subsidies or allowances have been paid in money. To help low-income households afford homes, welfare public housing projects were launched in the mid-1990s (Shang, 2009; Wu, Xu, and Yeh, 2007).

With the emergence of the property market, most Chinese cities underwent a re-urbanization process with massive urban reconstructions in the 1990s. In the central business districts of large cities, manufacturing sectors gave way to commercial and financial services almost immediately after the launch of the property market. Shanghai, for instance, witnessed an explosive growth in building construction in the

1990s when the number of properties completed was many times the number built over 30 years before 1980. In the mid-1990s Shanghai boasted "the world's biggest construction site" with 5,000 construction firms employing 1.4 million construction workers and a fifth of the world's cranes on 20,000 building sites (Zhu, J., 1999, p. 64). As the market became the dominant force in urban development, the decades-long transformation of "capitalist consumer cities" to "socialist producer cities" in the pre-reform era was quickly reversed in a matter of a few years.

### 4.6. *The "two-track urbanization"*

In the early 1990s, thanks to the greater role of the market in allocating resources, it was observed that "China's economic activity has already begun to change from supply-driven to demand-driven. But in urban planning, 'supply-driven' still has a strong influence" (Wang, 1992, p. 70). China's post-reform urbanization has been proceeding along two tracks: one is the "conventional urbanization" sponsored by the government and the other is the "spontaneous urbanization" driven by local economic development and market forces. In many places, "local economic activities and foreign investment have replaced the State as the dominant force in sponsoring and regulating the urbanization process" (Zhu, Y., 1999, p. 204). Case studies in Fujian Province illustrate the role of spontaneous urbanization in causing the *in situ* transformation of rural areas. Several local conditions were identified to be favorable for local urbanization in Fujian Province. They include the preliminary stage of industrialization in the area, high population density[16] with improved transport and communication, and the local industries' connections to overseas Chinese businessmen who were willing to contribute to their ancestor land (Zhu, Y., 1999, p. 160).

Such "urbanization from below" has also become increasingly important in the urbanization and re-urbanization for large cities and metropolises,

---

[16] In 1990, the coastal area of Fujian had a population density of 595 persons per sq kilometer, much higher than that of the most densely populated developed countries like Japan and Italy (197 persons per sq kilometer), England and Wales (192 persons per sq kilometer), and Belgium (206 persons per sq kilometer).

thanks to the development of the property market and the decentralization of fiscal authority. As happened in the cases of Huhehaote, Lanzhou, Nanjing, and Zhengzhou, the central-government-sanctioned plans for urban size were not effectively binding to real urban growth. The centrally planned urban sizes for a term of over five or even ten years were often outgrown by real development within a year after their approval (Zhou, 1997, p. 317).

As shown by Wu, Xu, and Yeh (2007), the late 1980s witnessed the emergence of a five-tiered land administration system, consisting of the central, provincial, city, county, and township governments. Local governments, especially at the city and county levels, gained much discretionary power on land income and land disposal.

As shown in Fig. 3.1, China entered an era of fast urbanization as well as economic growth after its market-oriented reform started. The quick increase of the urban population before 1983 was mainly of a recovery nature, when the Maoist state-compelled migration policy was abolished and reversed. After 1984, the year when economic reform was launched in the urban area, 14 coastal cities were opened to foreign investment, and more towns were designated and opened to in-migration. Urbanization consequently sped up. It is worth noting that the gap between urban population share and urban employment share quickly narrowed and finally closed by the end of the 1980s and, after 1992, the former surpassed the latter so that the two resumed a pattern of relationship which existed before the mid-1950s. This suggests a reversion from "producer cities" to "consumer cities".

Figure 3.2 shows that the urban share of population also quickly rose to match the change in economic structure in the post-reform years, in contrast to the path of "industrialization without much urbanization" before 1978. Meanwhile, the ratio between urban road length and highway length leapt up in the mid-1980s and continued to rise in the 1990s, reflecting heavy investment in urban infrastructure.

Tables 3.1 and 3.2 display the relative increases of cities in different size classes. Between 1982 and 2000, the total urban population more than doubled from 215 million to 456 million. Most of this increase, however, was generated in cities with populations less than half a million as the share of these cities (which are medium-sized and small, by Chinese definition) in the total urban population rose by more than 12 percentage points to 48.4 percent (Table 3.2). The rapid urbanization is also marked by the sharp increase in the number of cities from 191 in 1978 to 664 in 2000 (Table 3.1). Again, the cities with populations below 0.2 million shared the largest increment in numbers.

## 5. Urbanization and Regional Development into the 21st Century

Entering the 21st century, China's urbanization and regional development policies have continued to evolve on two major fronts. One is the rebalancing of regional development and the other is redefining the urbanization guideline.

### 5.1. *West China Development Program*

China's economic takeoff and rapid growth in the last two decades of the 20th century was mainly a coastal phenomenon. The process inadvertently enlarged the development gap between the coastal and inland regions. The per capita income of the western region was only about one third of that of the eastern region by the turn of the century. This development gap was also reflected in the process of urbanization (Fig. 3.3). At the turn of the century, the Chinese government launched the West China Development Program, aiming to reorient this economic vigor towards its western inland regions. A series of fiscal initiatives and institutional innovations have been proposed and implemented to boost the region's development prospects and close the income gap between the eastern coast and the inland provinces. By the end of 2002, the government had launched 36 megaprojects for infrastructure development worth about 600 billion yuan (US$70 billion) in these provinces.[17] These megaprojects include the 1,142-kilometer-long Qinghai-Tibet railway (completed in 2006), the 4,200-kilometer-long West-to-East natural gas pipeline, and the West-to-East power transmission system. The state has also pledged to build roads to connect all the counties in the region. To Chinese policy makers, the development of the western region is meant

---

[17] West China Development Office of State Council web site, http://www.chinawest.gov.cn/.

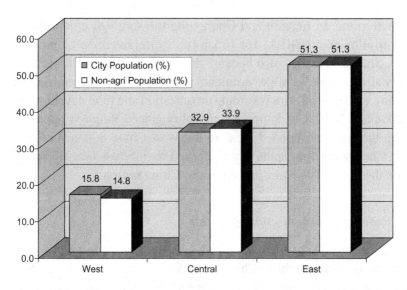

Figure 3.3. Share of total urban population by regions (1998).

*Source*: *China Statistical Yearbook*, various issues.

*Note*: The eastern region includes Beijing, Tianjin, Hebei, Liaoning, Shanghai, Jiangsu, Zhejiang, Fujian, Shandong, Guangdong, and Hainan. The western region includes Inner Mongolia, Guangxi, Sichuan, Guizhou, Yunnan, Tibet, Shaanxi, Gansu, Qinghai, Ningxia, and Xinjiang. The central region includes Jilin, Heilongjiang, Anhui, Jiangxi, Henan, Hubei, and Hunan.

to reduce interregional disparities and to meet both the environmental protection and national security goals.

An important element of the West China Development Program has been environmental protection. One of the main projects is the "reforestation of the cultivated land", which provides state subsidies to farmers reforesting their cultivated land. It targeted to invest 100 billion yuan and reforest 14.67 million hectares of land nationwide by 2010.[18] Most of the reforestation has been implemented in the upstream areas of China's largest rivers.

Since the launch of the West China Development Program, the central government has also extended some regional preferential policies that used to benefit the coastal cities. For instance, in 2007, the State

---

[18] "*Tui Geng Huan Lin Gongcheng*" (Reforesting Cultivated Land Project), Xinhuanet.com, Dec 29, 2009.

Council granted Chengdu and Chongqing the status of comprehensive reform pilot area (CRPA) for urban-rural integrated development. In 2010, Shanxi Province also became the largest CRPA in China. Such a status allowed the local governments much greater freedom in experimenting with new reforms regarding urbanization and rural development.[19] In 2008 and 2010, Chongqing Municipality gained Beijing's approval to set up the first two bonded areas in the West China region. In October 2010, Zhengzhou, the capital city of Henan Province, also was approved to set up the first bonded area in the Central China region.[20]

## 5.2. *Redefining urbanization guideline*

Through the 1980s to the early 1990s, despite the rising role of central cities and economic hubs in China's endeavor to open its economy to foreign trade and investment, the so-called small-town consensus remained the official guideline. The Urban Planning Law (1989) upheld the restrictive policy towards the large cities while sanctioning the growth of small and medium-sized cities.

After the hyper economic growth of the 1990s, which was largely a boom along the coastal line and central cities, the government gradually changed its tune on its urbanization policy. The 9th Five-Year Plan (1996–2000) emphasized the role of central cities and transportation trunk lines in regional development.[21] The 10th Five-Year Plan (2001–2005) moved further to outline the following principles of urbanization: (1) promote urbanization and transfer of rural population into cities; (2) coordinate development of cities of all sizes to form a rational cities-towns system; (3) develop small cities and towns with a focus on county capitals and major towns, actively develop small and medium-sized cities, improve the central cities' function as regional hubs and enhance the large

---

[19] *"Guojia zonghe peitao gaige shiyan qu"* (comprehensive reform pilot area), in Chinese online encyclopedia, Baidu Baike (http://baike.baidu.com/view/1302344.html).

[20] *"Baoshui Qu"* (bonded area), in Chinese online encyclopedia, Baidu Baike (http://baike.baidu.com/view/1302344.html).

[21] Li Peng (1996), "Report on the Ninth Five-Year Plan for National Economic and Social Development and the Long-Term Guideline for Goals to be Achieved in 2010," *People's Daily* (Beijing), March 19.

cities' role as centers of gravity; (4) avoid expanding urban areas blindly.[22] The guideline indicates a more balanced official approach towards developing cities of various sizes and a conscious drive to promote urbanization. However, it still imposes constraints on the expansion of urban areas.

On the other hand, as late as 1998, the Chinese Communist Party's Central Committee continued to promote the development of small cities and towns as a "big strategy" for rural economic and social development. In the following few years, the central government implemented this strategy by removing institutional barriers to rural residents' migration to small cities and towns. In 2001, the State Council made it clear that the rural residents who have jobs or homes in county-level cities and other designated towns should be allowed to register as permanent urban households in these places (Niu, Yu, and Li, 2009).

The emphasis on *in situ* urbanization at the county level reflects a profound institutional feature of the China's gradualist reform, i.e. making progress without leading to much pain and loss of vested interests. In the context of urbanization, the policy to continue focusing on the development of small cities and towns while refraining from allowing free migration to large cities bodes well for the vested interests of urban residents in large cities. The temporary residential status of rural migrant workers in large cities guarantees that these workers and their dependents will not compete with incumbents for healthcare, education, social security, and other local public goods. It also ensures that the rural migrant workers will continue to be a cheap labor force for urban employees.

It is worth noting that the debate about urbanization guidelines has driven the policy changes in the 2000s. For instance, the first white paper on national urban development published by the China Association of Mayors, an authoritative platform for urban research, was a project by about 100 of China's top urban specialists (China Association of Mayors, 2002). It proposed a long-term agenda for China's urbanization and regional development. According to this agenda, China should raise its urbanization rate (defined as share of urban residents in total population) from the then

---

[22] National People's Congress (2001), "Guidelines for the PRC's Tenth Five-Year Plan of Economic and Social Development," Xinhua News Agency, March 17.

36 percent to 75 percent in 50 years, making the nation's urban population reach about 1.0 to 1.1 billion by the year 2050. To fulfill this goal, the annual cost of urbanization should amount to about 4 percent of China's annual GDP. The report suggests that the government should support and promote the development of seven urban belts across the country and the formation of three city clusters, namely the Pearl River Delta cluster, Yangtze River Delta cluster, and Beijing-Tianjin-Tangshan Delta cluster.

The most interesting part of the report was its criticism of the "three myths" of urban planning: (1) urban development would inevitably result in the so-called urban disease; (2) the growth of large and megacities should be restricted; (3) cities and towns should be distributed evenly across regions. For many years, these myths have dominated and misguided China's urbanization policy making. Thanks to the influence of these myths, urbanization was "seriously lagging behind the level of industrialization and development", creating "a huge bottleneck" in China's further growth, according to the report.

By the end of 2002, the Chinese Communist Party's 16th National Congress acknowledged the "inevitable trend of industrialization and modernization for surplus rural labor to move to non-agricultural industries and to cities and towns". It defined "the path to urbanization with Chinese characteristics" as "to raise the level of urbanization gradually and persist in the coordinated development of large, medium and small cities and small towns".[23]

As the Chinese economy continued its hyper growth in the following years, it became increasingly obvious that relying on *in situ* urbanization at the county level was not enough to absorb the rural surplus labor and meet the demand for economic development. In 2007, the Chinese Communist Party's 17th National Congress proclaimed the following "path of urbanization with Chinese characteristics":

> We will promote balanced development of large, medium-sized and small cities and towns on the principle of balancing urban and rural development, ensuring rational distribution, saving land, providing a full range of functions and getting larger cities to help smaller ones. Focusing

---

[23] Jiang Zemin (2002), Political Report on the Chinese Communist Party's 16th National Congress, November 8 (http://news.xinhuanet.com, November 17).

on increasing the overall carrying capacity of cities, we will form city clusters with megacities as the core so that they can boost development in other areas and become new poles of economic growth.[24]

Accordingly, the Urban and Rural Planning Law, which took effect on January 2008, no longer regulates the control of the size of large cities.

The 2007 version of a "path of urbanization with Chinese characteristics" represents a watershed in China's urbanization guidelines. It is the first time that the central government has acknowledged the need to "form city clusters with megacities as the core". It may harbinger a new era of state strategy to answer the challenges of urbanization. In October 2010, the Central Committee of the Chinese Communist Party proposed the guideline for the 12th Five-Year Plan (2011–2015). The proposed guideline launched the "primary function area" strategy, which divides the country into several function areas according to population density and resource constraints. Based on the division of function areas, development of those urban areas with good economic potential will be given state priority and support. It supplements the 2007 version of a "path of urbanization with Chinese characteristics" with a call for "enforcing management of urbanization". The upshot is to raise the population density of urban built areas to prevent excessive urban sprawling. It upheld the policy to control population inflow to large cities while extending the policy that relaxes household registration to medium-sized cities as well as small cities and towns.[25] These policies indicate further cautious reform of migration administration and an urbanization strategy with more pro-megacity and pro-city-cluster features.

## Referensces

Chan, Kam Wing. (1992). "Post-1949 Urbanization Trends and Policies: An Overview". In Gregory E. Guildin (ed.), *Urbanizing China*. New York: Greenwood Press, pp. 41–63.

---

[24] Hu Jingtao (2007), Political Report on the Chinese Communist Party's 17th National Congress, October 24 (http://news.xinhuanet.com).

[25] Central Committee of the CPC (2010), "Proposal of Preparing the 12th Five-Year Plan of National Economic and Social Development," October 18 (news.xinhuanet.com, October 27, 2010).

Chandler, Tertius. (1987). *Four Thousand Years of Urban Growth*. New York: St. David's University Press.

Chang, S.D. and Kwok, R.Y. (1990). "The Urbanization of Rural China". In R.Y.W. Kwok, W. Parish, A.G.O. Yeh and X.Q. Xu (eds.), *Chinese Urban Reform: What Model Now?* Armonk, NY: M.E. Sharpe, pp. 140–157.

Chen, Yisheng. (2000). *On the Development of Economic and Technological Zones in China*. Beijing: Chinese Academy of Sciences.

China Association of Mayors (2002). *Zhongguo Chengshi Fazhan Baogao 2001–2002* (China Urban Development Report: 2001–2002). Beijing: Xiyuan Press.

Démurger, Sylvie, Sachs, Jeffrey D., Woo, Wing T., Bao, Shuming and Chang, Gene. (2002a). "The Relative Contributions of Location and Preferential Policies in China's Regional Development". *China Economic Review*, 13(4), pp. 444–465.

Démurger, Sylvie, Sachs, Jeffrey D., Woo, Wing T., Bao, Shuming, Chang, Gene and Mellinger, Andrew. (2002b). "Geography, Economic Policy and Regional Development in China". *Asian Economic Papers* 1(1), pp. 146–197.

Démurger, Sylvie. (2000). *Economic Opening and Growth in China*. Paris: OECD Development Centre Studies.

Engels, Friedrich. (1954). *Anti-Duhring 1876–78*. Moscow: Foreign Language Publishing House.

Fan, Gang. (2010). "Urbanizing China". www.project-syndicate.org, accessed on Dec. 30.

He, Yan. (1988). *"Dui weilaide nongcun shengyu laodongli de shuliang fenxi"* (A quantitative analysis of the future of the rural surplus laborers). *Renkou Yanjiu* (Population Research), 4, pp. 34–37.

Kirkby, R.J.R. (1985). *Urbanization in China: Town and Country in a Developing Economy 1949–2000 AD*. New York: Columbia University Press.

Kwok, R., Yin-wang. (1988). "Metropolitan Development in China: A Struggle between Contradictions". *Habitat International*, 12(4), 195–207.

Kwok, R., Yin-wang. (1992). "Urbanization under Economic Reform". In Gregory E. Guildin (ed.), *Urbanizing China*. New York: Greenwood Press.

Laquian, Aprodicio A. (1997). "The Effects of National Urban Strategy and Regional Development Policy on Patterns of Urban Growth in China". In Gavin W. Jones and Pravin Visaria (eds.), *Urbanization in Large Developing Countries: China, Indonesia, Brazil, and India*. Oxford: Clarendon Press, pp. 52–68.

Lee, Yok-shiu F. (1992). "Rural Transformation and Decentralized Urban Growth in China". In Gregory E. Guildin (ed.), *Urbanizing China*. New York: Greenwood Press, pp. 89–118.

Lee, Yok-shiu F. (1997). "Urban Housing Reforms in China, 1979–89". In Gavin, W. Jones and Pravin Visaria (eds.), *Urbanization in Large Developing Countries: China, Indonesia, Brazil, and India*. Oxford: Clarendon Press, pp. 86–107.

Li, Enping. (2009). "Reform of Chinese Urban Land Regime". In Niu Fengrui, Pan Jiahua, and Liu Zhiyan (eds.), *Zhongguo Chengshi Fazhan 30 Nian* (Urban Development in China: 30 Years 1978–2008). Beijing: Social Sciences Academic Press.

Li, Jing Neng. (1997). "Structural and Spatial Economic Changes and Their Effects on Recent Urbanization in China". In Gavin W. Jones and Pravin Visaria (eds.), *Urbanization in Large Developing Countries: China, Indonesia, Brazil, and India*. Oxford: Clarendon Press.

Li, Meng and Lou, Wei. (2009). "Social Security System of Peasant Labor Rights in China". In Niu Fengrui, Pan Jiahua, and Liu Zhiyan (eds.), *Zhongguo Chengshi Fazhan 30 Nian* (Urban Development in China: 30 Years 1978–2008). Beijing: Social Sciences Academic Press.

Lu, Ding and Tang, Zhimin. (1997). *State Intervention and Business in China: The Role of Preferential Policies*. London: Edward Elgar.

Lu, Ding. (1994). *Entrepreneurship in Suppressed Markets: Private-sector Experience in China*. New York and London: Garland Publishing, Inc.

Ma, Jun. (1999). *The Chinese Economy in the 1990s*. Basingstoke: Palgrave Publishers Ltd.

National Bureau of Statistics of China (NBSC). (2009). *Sixty Years of Social Economic Achievements of People's Republic of China* — Series Report No. 10.

Niu Fengrui, Yu, Meiren, and Li, Feifei. (2009). "The Road to Urbanization with Chinese Characteristics". In Niu Fengrui, Pan Jiahua, and Liu Zhiyan (eds.), *Zhongguo Chengshi Fazhan 30 Nian* (Urban Development in China: 30 Years 1978–2008). Beijing: Social Sciences Academic Press.

Sachs, Jeffrey D. and Woo, Wing Thye. (1994). "Structural Factors in the Economic Reforms of China, Eastern Europe, and the Former Soviet Union". *Economic Policy*, 18, pp. 101–145.

Shang, Jiaowei. (2009). "Urban Housing Construction in China". In Niu Fengrui, Pan Jiahua, and Liu Zhiyan (eds.), *Zhongguo Chengshi Fazhan 30 Nian* (Urban Development in China: 30 Years 1978–2008). Beijing: Social Sciences Academic Press.

Wang, Shanjun. (1996). "On Current Large City Development in China". *Chinese Journal of Population Science*, 8(2), pp. 193–203.

Wang, Yukun. (1992). *Zhongguo: Shiji Zhijiao de Chengshi Fazhan* (China: Urban Development at the Turn of the Century). Shenyang: Liaoning People's Press.

Wang, Shaoguang and Hu, Angang. (1999). *The Political Economy of Uneven Development: The Case of China.* Armonk, New York: M.E. Sharpe.

Wen, G. James. (2002). "WTO Accession and China's Urbanization and Population Relocation?" Paper presented at the ASSA meeting, Atlanta, Jan. 4, 2002.

Wu, Fulong, Xu, Jiang and Yeh, Anthony Gar-On. (2007). *Urban Development in Post-reform China: State, Market and Space.* London and New York: Routledge.

Yang, Dali L. (1997). *Beyond Beijing — Liberalization and the Regions in China.* London: Routledge.

Yeung, Yue-man. (2000). *Globalization and Networked Societies: Urban-regional Change in Pacific Asia.* Honolulu: University of Hawaii Press.

Zhou, Yixing. (1997). *Chengshi Dilixue* (Urban Geography). Beijing: Commerce Press.

Zhu, Jieming. (1999). *The Transition of China's Urban Development: From Plan-Controlled To Market-Led.* Westport, Connecticut: Praeger.

Zhu, Yu. (1999). *New Paths to Urbanization in China: Seeking More Balanced Patterns.* New York: Nova Science Publications, Inc.

# CHAPTER 4

# Urban Planning for Local Development*

*Jieming Zhu*

Urban planning should be an effective tool for maintaining status quo interests and establishing order in the land market. Planning as a positive instrument for socioeconomic change is demonstrated in the exercise of plan-making. However, there are no mechanisms in the planning system to generate positive actions and thus to guarantee positive implementation of plans. China's developmental planning paradigm emerges from its unique historical circumstances. The post-1978 deliberate urbanization results from the pre-1978 suppressed urbanization which created great shortages of urban land and premises. The huge demand for physical expansion to accommodate rural-urban migrants has led to a planning system which should fulfill the aspirations of a growing economy. Both instruments of strategic concept plans and the flexible development control regime enlisted by the local developmental state cannot be ignored as two of the important contributing factors to the spectacular economic growth. The essence of the developmental planning is threefold. Preference is given to newly emerging interests over status quo interests, land revenues are mobilized to develop quality infrastructure and public facilities, and planning is made responsive to market change. Nevertheless, real long-term sustainable growth, which is not promised by the existing planning practice, requires further institutional change to the transitional paradigm of China's urban planning.

* Reprinted with the author's permission from "China's Developmental Planning in Rapid Urbanization," in Thomas L. Harper, Anthony Gar-On Yeh, Heloisa Coata (eds.) (2008), *Dialogues in Urban and Regional Planning*, New York: Routledge, pp. 76–105.

## 1. Introduction

Though interrelated, urbanization, socioeconomic transformation and urban planning are in three different domains, having their own logic. Urbanization as a result of trading and industrialization has improved the welfare of mankind tremendously, but it has also created malicious urban problems that degrade people's lives. It is commonly known that urban planning aims to mitigate the negative impact of uncontrolled urban growth and to manage the development of urban settlements according to pre-set goals with environmental sustainability and social justice embedded. In the market economy, economic growth and land use planning have independent research agendas which seldom converge, and the views and ideological standing of economists and planners often epitomize the binary confrontation between the state and the market. Conventionally, economic efficiency concerns economists, while social equity and environmental sustainability matter to planners.

Modern urban planning started as an exercise of producing physical plans to be followed in building urban settlements, or to be used for land development control. Ebenezer Howard's *To-Morrow: A Peaceful Path to Real Reform* (1898) and his garden cities Letchworth (1903) and Welwyn (1920) are duly considered to mark the onset of modern urban planning, though there were a few planned cities or settlements (Beijing of the Ming and Qing Dynasties, Washington, DC, British model industrial villages such as New Lanark and Port Sunlight, to cite a few) prior to the Howard era. The very English term "town planning" was allegedly coined by the Birmingham councilor John Sutton Nettlefold in 1905 (Sutcliffe, 1981).

This paper explores and analyzes an emerging nouveau practice in China's developmental planning. By looking into the nature of urban planning, the author scrutinizes the issue of how urban planning can promote socioeconomic transformation in the context of rapid urbanization. Without the capacity for mobilizing economic resources and consensual social support, urban planning can hardly achieve the developmental goals actively and directly. Derived from the preceding central economic planning system in which urbanization was effectively planned and controlled, and against the background of a unique institution of the local developmental state arising from the economic transition, the model of

China's developmental planning is generated by the rapid urbanization driven by endogenous industrialization and exogenous globalization. The developmental planning is composed of two elements, i.e. land use plans, especially the strategic concept plan, and flexible development control. Recognizing its path-dependent rationality and short-term achievements in the historical circumstances, the author believes that the developmental planning should be a transitional paradigm. It will evolve further to become an institution responsible for long-term sustainable growth.

## 2. A Conceptual Framework: Linking Urban Planning with Local Transformation

There is broad consensus that the general objectives of urban planning are to help achieve economic efficiency, social equity and environmental sustainability in the shaping and reshaping of the built environment. However, there is no consensus that urban planning is able to successfully achieve those noble aims. The role of urban planning needs to be scrutinized.

### 2.1. *The role of urban planning: Passive regulations and governance*

According to a definition widely cited in the 1960s and 1970s, urban planning is "the art and the science of ordering the use of land and the character and siting of buildings and communication routes so as to secure the maximum practicable degree of economy, convenience and beauty" (Keeble, 1969, p. 1). There are two generic categories of urban planning regarding land use: land use plans — both long-term for the future and short-term for the present; and development control — managing land development according to land use plans. Land use planning serves the purposes of spatial coordination of land use and provision of supportive infrastructure for local growth, while development control based on master plans or zoning maintains order in the development of the urban built environment through internalizing externalities according to the system of land owners' property rights.

Planning should be effective in maintaining status quo interests and establishing order in the land market, if the planning machinery has the statutory status. Land use plans and development control bring order and certainty to the land development market, which is deemed favorable to local communities. However, development control is intended to maintain the existing order rather than to initiate radical changes: "The control was exercised by the full force of *the law* and was very largely negative in effect, i.e. the schemes and their implementation were concerned with what should not occur rather than what should come about" (McLoughlin, 1973, pp. 15–16).

Planning as a positive instrument for socioeconomic change is actually demonstrated in the exercise of plan-making. Well-known classic plans such as Garden City, Radiant City, City Beautiful and Neighborhood Unit have been inspirational exemplars to the planners. However, in the market economy where developers primarily make development decisions, there are no mechanisms in the planning system to generate initiatives and thus to guarantee positive implementation of the plan, except when the development market is buoyant (so that planners can take up those development proposals in accord with the plan and reject those which are not) or when developers are public agencies (such as New Town Corporations, governments of Brasilia, Canberra, Singapore).[1] As a matter of fact, planners' positive influence in effecting change has been in recession in many developed countries where economic growth has slowed down considerably (Peiser, 1990). Urban planning is increasingly becoming a tool of urban governance mediating various interests in pluralist societies, instead of a statement of visions and missions.

## 2.2. *Urban planning to promote local transformation: Active initiatives*

Can urban planning achieve the objective of actively promoting local change? In many developing countries with adopted mixed economic systems in the 1960s, planning was given the task of facilitating economic growth, and it was termed development planning. According to Waterston

---

[1] Or private developers who are philanthropists committed to social reform such as Robert Owen who built New Lanark, Scotland, and who are concerned with social welfare like James W. Rouse who built Columbia, Maryland, in the US.

(1965), urban planning and development planning are planning activities classified into two different categories. Waterston (1965, p. 27) further explains the definition of development planning: "countries were considered to be engaged in development planning if their governments were making a conscious and continuing attempt to increase their rate of economic and social progress and to alter those institutional arrangements which were considered to be obstacles to the achievement of this aim". The outputs of development planning are often in the form of five-year economic development plans at the national or regional level.

Regional planning in developed counties tends to coordinate balanced regional development either by allocating to designated deprived areas more than their fair share of public resources or by restricting development in prosperous locales, thus allowing the former to have a chance of receiving investments which might otherwise not come about without development controls exerted in the latter (Wannop, 1995).[2] The normative concept of "growth poles" gained currency in the mid-20th century to address unequal regional development against the positive theory of polarized development (Friedmann and Weaver, 1979), but it lacked empirical evaluation supportive of its experiments. Regional economic development mediated by the planning-coordinated redistribution of development activities within the region is not necessarily a positive-sum.

Local development has become one of the top priorities on the agenda of municipal governments of many Western industrial cities that have been experiencing structural change in their economies and suffering from tremendous job losses. Market failures are obvious in inner

---

[2] The 1947 Town and Country Planning Act introduced Industrial Development Certificates (IDCs), and industrialists wishing to build new factories of 5,000 sq ft or more in size were required to apply for IDCs (Hall, 1999). IDCs were intended to divert industrial expansion to designated "development areas". Turok (1989) claims that the shortage of factory space in London in the 1950s and 1960s was one of the reasons that surrounding new towns grew quickly — by absorbing those industrial firms that otherwise had been settled in London. Since late 1964, an Office Development Permit was needed for developers to build offices larger than a specified size in London, upon provision of sufficient evidence of the necessity for the proposed office development in the restricted areas. Office decentralization was facilitated through rigid planning controls and conducive financial subsidies. Up to 1977, a total of 170,000–250,000 office jobs were relocated from central London (Alexander, 1979, p. 65), though as much as 44.5 percent of the decentralized jobs moved a distance of less than 15 miles from their original location (Daniels, 1975).

cities that should draw investments to where land and property costs are lower than that in other locales. Urban planning as a tool of public intervention is logically tasked to formulate courses of action for positive socioeconomic change. To promote economic transformation, local governments must take on "an initiating rather than a passive role" (Blakely, 1994, p. 52). Economic growth and public-private partnership have replaced welfare provision, and the government has somehow become an "enterprise state" (Cochrane, 1991). Place marketing is actively engaged, aiming to develop economic confidence and to attract inward investment, especially mobile international capital. City governments have shifted their role from conventional regulators to entrepreneurial developers (Jessop, 1998). The link between local economic development strategies and urban planning is that those strategies are often property-led, such as "development of high-profile prestige property projects and investment in city place promotion or boosterist activities, geared at enhancing the economic position of a city in relation to other urban centres" (Loftman and Nevin, 1998, p. 129).[3] Either privately owned or autonomous, firms as growth engines are not subject to government planning, and are footloose following market fundamentals. What local governments or communities can engage in to stimulate or to maintain economic activity is thus limited, and what city planning departments can marshal are often the land-related resources which are one way or another under the control of governments. However, urban renewal practices have not shown that property-led regeneration is a convincing model leading to sustainable local regeneration (Turok, 1992). Not a proven solution, urban planning as a means of promoting local transformation remains a tough challenge.

---

[3] Birmingham is an example of the transition in the role of local government from providing city residents with services and welfare to managing city affairs with entrepreneurial approaches. Over the years, the urban physical fabric has been substantially transformed by the construction of the International Convention Centre, National Indoor Arena, Hyatt Hotel, Brindley Place and Centenary Square (Loftman and Nevin, 1998). Besides business development, community-based improvement schemes and training of labor skills, Blakely (1994) suggested land-related programs to regenerate cities such as land banking, physical infrastructure development on industrial and commercial land, speculative buildings, flexible zoning, regulatory improvement through simplification, development of a detailed physical improvement plan for tourism, and townscaping.

## 2.3. *Background: Transition from socialist central planning to local development*

The economic reform launched in 1979 aimed at a grand dream of national advancement. It was determined to raise productivity which had been in a dire situation under the rigid central planning system. Decentralization of economic management set off an unprecedented transformation which gradually replaced central directives with material incentives to the agents at local levels. The state is transforming itself from a producer and social- ist welfare provider to an advocate for marketization. The socialist authoritarian state is changing from its preoccupation with political cor- rectness to the pursuit of economic development in order to legitimize itself by improving the livelihood of its citizens, with progressive reforms that are gradually phasing out unsustainable socialist welfarism and letting the market take over its role of provision. The socialist political state is clearly changing to a socialist developmental state (Oi, 1996). Public opin- ion maintains that popular acceptance of the government should be established by its successful management of economic development, because economic progress is the sole goal capable of uniting China's cit- izens after 30 years of perennial political upheavals. There are "developmental coalitions deriving political legitimacy from what can be called the nation's collective aspirations" (Bardhan, 1990, p. 5).

Empowered with autonomy, China's local governments have changed from passive agents of the central state to active developers responsible for local prosperity, which results in competition between the center and locales (Solinger, 1992; Wang, 1994; Nolan, 1995; Oi, 1995; Unger and Chan, 1995; Wong, Heady and Woo, 1995; Huang, 1996). Advancing development strate- gies that can stimulate local change and expanding fiscal capacity have become two indispensable goals of local governments (Wong, 1987, 1992), resulting in the re-emergence of localism in China's national politics.[4] As a result, autonomous local governments are highly motivated to maximize local revenues (Breslin, 1996; Lin, 2000). From its origins in the socialist

---

[4] In the late 1980s and early 1990s, local governments bargained for the retention of more fiscal income and pushed the central state to the limit in granting special policies to localities for offering preferential measures in order to attract foreign investment (Reich, 1991; Nolan, 1995). The central state's role in national development has been undermined owing to insufficient central fiscal funds

state in the centrally controlled economy, China's local governments has become an economic interest group with its own policy agenda and preferences, and thus have become the local developmental state.

The local developmental state tends to play an active and facilitative role in guiding market forces to achieve the goal of local transformation. As the state is no longer the principal of most urban economic organizations, it is a great challenge for the local government to take a leading role in local development, since the urban economy is market-driven to a large extent and economic organizations are autonomous. What the local developmental state can command is the state-owned land assets within its territorial jurisdiction, riding on the land reform which has been carried out as an important component of the economic reform. Public land leasing has replaced free land allocation which was practised as a socialist doctrine during the period between 1949 and 1988, and state-owned urban land has been restored as an economic asset to the owner. Market-driven land and property development responded promptly to the price signals derived from interactions between demand and supply. Land assets have become a substantial source of local revenues. Consequently, land use planning has become a tool of local governments for resource mobilization.

## 2.4. *Developmental planning: China's response to rapid urbanization during transition*

Urban planning is an effective tool for maintaining spatial order in the physical environment, coordinating development with an orderly structure of land uses which contain sufficient public and merit goods, and managing

---

(Wang, 1994). The declining capacity of the central government in redistributing budgetary funds between regions inevitably revives competition between localities (Goetz and Clarke, 1993). On March 2, 2003, a report on the competitiveness of Chinese cities was published by the China Academy of Social Sciences, which ranked cities according to their achievements in science and technology, economic growth rates, etc. Hong Kong was ranked first, followed by Shanghai and Shenzhen (http://finance.sina.com.cn/g/20030303/0751316063.shtml, accessed on July 16, 2003). Seeing Guangzhou ranked sixth, behind Shenzhen in the same province, the mayor of Guangzhou complained and doubted whether the ranking was fairly done (http://news.sina.com.cn/c/2003-03-09/1402939281.shtml, accessed on July 16, 2003). After Beijing had won the 2008 Olympic Games, and Shanghai the 2010 Expo, Guangzhou felt left behind by these competitors and decided to bid for the 2010 Asian Games. It won the bidding.

the landed interests of diverse urban communities. But urban planning is not able to shape the new physical landscape according to pre-set goals and socioeconomic policies without the capacity for mobilizing economic resources and social support. In the context of globalization and the consequent fierce competition for wealth creation, cities, whether in developed or in developing countries, are expected to lead their nations in the battle for prosperity. Competitiveness and local change have become the central themes for those cities not economically well-off: "The language of welfare has been replaced by the language of growth … in urban areas" (Cochrane, 1991, p. 298). Cities in the developing countries, nevertheless, have no choice other than to promote development. In those cities where public policies intend to participate in the "game", not letting the "invisible hand" dominate the competition, two questions remain: What is the link between urban planning and urban transformation? How can urban planning be made a tool for the active pursuit of local change? China's developmental planning has been evolving in the contexts of grand social change and the transition from socialist land rights towards a system in favor of market competition.

From the property rights perspective, the land reform has brought about changes in land rights. Property rights are primarily a bundle of rights associated with ownership which consists of the right to use an asset, the right to derive income from it, the right to change its form and substance, and the right to alienate the rights mentioned above to another party at a price mutually agreed upon (Pejovich, 1990). The system of property rights is concerned with economic efficiency and distributive justice, which places limits on the actions of individuals and governments (Paul, Miller and Paul, 1994). Determined by social norms as constraints for human interactions, property rights are deemed essential in the governance of land markets (Fischel, 1985; North, 1990; Webster and Lai, 2003). Land use planning and development control are essential in defining land rights by stipulating land uses and prescribing conditions for land development. The land rights regime, to a large extent, determines the mode of land development.

Land use planning which manipulates rights over land use and development is logically marshaled by the local developmental state as a means of promoting local development. As an institution, land use planning is transforming itself from a tool of central economic planning to an instrument regulated by property rights for the management of market-driven land development. The old informal socialist institution — users' land use rights which allow urban land to be held by its users without any rental payment — is dealt with in order to tackle rigidity in land resource reallocation which has constituted an immediate obstacle to the initiation of urban land markets. The land development right — a new institution — is granted to existing land users to unlock the redevelopment process hampered by the socialist legacy of land use rights.

In view of the great potential of progressive urbanization and upcoming urban physical change, China's local governments have taken on urban planning as a strategic tool for growth management. Planning a visionary urban structure for the future seems closely connected with drawing up prospective changes for the city. Unprecedented rapid urbanization and economic growth driven by the exogenous globalized investments and endogenous fast industrialization as well as real estate development have provided a historical opportunity for mayors to have their visionary urban plans accomplished within their tenures. Under the new land rights regime, urban planning is able to mobilize land resources and social support by prescribing the highest and best uses to both rural and urban land. Besides, development control, which defines land development rights, is given sufficient leeway for flexibility in order to be responsive to capricious market change. Because of the gradualism adopted due to political constraints, a pragmatic approach of trial and error has prevailed in the implementation of new initiatives. Market circumstances are hardly predictable for two reasons: rapid change and a land market that is in the making. Planning in its conventional mode is passive, and tends to align itself with the status quo interests. Developmental planning tends to be in favor of progressive new interests, responsive to market changes and conducive to local growth in the context of rapid urbanization and economic transition.

## 3. Rapid Urbanization under Capricious Market Change and Land Resource Dissipation

China's economic reforms have brought about tremendous changes in the country. The national economy has been growing remarkably at a rate of about 9 percent per annum on average in GDP since 1978. China's cities are undergoing rapid social, economic and physical transformations. The transition from central planning to market orientation is the key factor underpinning the transformations. Opening up to the world economy and market-mediated production and consumption have fundamentally changed how the economy and society are managed. Managing constant and unpredictable change, because of the emerging market forces, has been a tremendous challenge to a country that is used to top-down control. The unprecedented economic reform, however, has been managed under the framework of gradual institutional change. Control mechanisms are relaxed gradually, and economic factors are incrementally freed from the control of outgoing institutions. In order to complement the emerging market economy, the new institution of land leasing makes land resources available in the land market, but land parcels held under the old socialist institutions are still kept from the "highest and best uses".

## 3.1. *Rapid urbanization*

Urbanization was suppressed during the centrally controlled period of 1949–1978, as the leadership tried "to achieve industrialization without a high level of urbanization" (Ma, 1981, p. 2). Urban residents accounted for 12.5 percent of the total population in 1950; the figure rose merely to 19.4 percent in 1980. Rapid urbanization has ensued since 1978. Within 18 years, 250 million people were urbanized (see Table 4.1). Cities, especially those in the coastal region, have been seeing dynamic physical expansion (see Tables 4.2 and 4.3).

It took England and Wales 100 years (1801–1901) to have their urbanization level increase by 44 percentage points (0.4 percentage points per annum), and Western Europe 50 years (1950–2000) for an increase of

Table 4.1.    Urbanization and Increase of Urban Population

| Year | 1950 | 1980 | 1982 | 2000 |
|---|---|---|---|---|
| Urbanization level (urban pop. as % of total) | 12.5 | 19.4 | 21.4 | 36.2 |
| Net increase in urban population (million) | | 93.4 | | 253.9 |

*Sources*: NBSC (1999c); Shen (2005).

Table 4.2.    Urban Physical Expansion in Regions

| Year | 1981 | 1986 | 1991 | 1996 | 2001 | 2004 |
|---|---|---|---|---|---|---|
| Urban Built-up Area (sq km) | | | | | | |
| Mainland China | 7,438.0 | 10,127.3 | 14,011.1 | 20,214.2 | 24,026.6 | 30,406.2 |
| East Region | — | 4393.7 | 6200.4 | 10303.7 | 11987.0 | 16414.5 |
| Central Region | — | 4094.2 | 5666.7 | 6962.6 | 8244.8 | 9288.6 |
| West Region | — | 1639.4 | 2143.0 | 2947.9 | 3794.8 | 4703.1 |
| Urban Built-up Area as % of the Total Area | | | | | | |
| Mainland China | 0.77 | 1.05 | 1.46 | 2.11 | 2.50 | 3.17 |
| East Region | — | 3.38 | 4.77 | 7.93 | 9.22 | 12.63 |
| Central Region | — | 1.46 | 2.02 | 2.49 | 2.94 | 3.32 |
| West Region | — | 0.30 | 0.39 | 0.54 | 0.69 | 0.86 |

*Sources*: NBSC (1982b, 1987b, 1992b, 1997b, 2002b, 2005b).

Table 4.3.    Expansion of Urban Built-up Area (sq km, 1986–2004)

| Year | Tianjing | Nanjing | Chengdu | Hangzhou | Shenyang |
|---|---|---|---|---|---|
| 1986 | 282 | 121 | 87 | 61 | 164 |
| 1995 | 339 | 150 | 97 | 96 | 194 |
| 2004 | 487 | 447 | 386 | 275 | 261 |

*Sources*: NBSC (1987b, 1996b, 2005b).
*Note*: These five cities were among the largest ten cities in 2004.

15 percentage points (0.3 percentage points per annum). While East Asia (excluding mainland China) took 50 years (1950–2000) for an increase of 36 percentage points (0.7 percentage points per annum), during the period 1980–2004, China's urbanization rose from 19.4 percent to 41.8 percent (0.9 percentage points per annum) (see Table 4.4). It is a recognized phenomenon that late developers tend to have faster growth rates than early developers in urbanization (Davis and Golden, 1954; Zelinsky, 1971). China is in times of rapid urbanization.

Rapid urbanization has been driven by the two engines of industrialization and real estate development. Drastic urban changes in the coastal cities are also accounted for by the release of the enormous pent-up demand for urban space which was suppressed by the previous policy of "industrialization without urbanization". Shanghai is a case in illustration. The land and property development at such a substantial scale since 1980,

Table 4.4. Estimated Urbanization Level (Urban Population as Percentage of the Total) in China, East Asia and Western Europe (1950–2000); and in England and Wales (1650–1951)

| Year | 1950 | 1960 | 1970 | 1980 | 1990 | 2000 | 2004 |
|------|------|------|------|------|------|------|------|
| Mainland China[1] | 12.5 | 19.8 | 17.4 | 19.4 | 26.4 | 36.2 | 41.8 |
| East Asia[2] (excluding mainland China) | 33.1 | 41.0 | 51.6 | 59.6 | 66.0 | 69.1 | — |
| Western Europe[3] | 65.3 | 69.7 | 74.3 | 76.6 | 78.6 | 80.5 | — |
| Year | 1650 | 1750 | 1800 | | 1801 | 1901 | 1951 |
| England and Wales[4] | 8.8 | 16.7 | 20.3 | | 33.8 | 78.0 | 80.8 |

*Sources*: 1. NBSC (2005a); 2. United Nations (2004); East Asia includes China (inclusive of Taiwan, Hong Kong and Macao), North Korea, South Korea, Japan and Mongolia; 3. United Nations (2004); Western Europe is composed of Austria, Belgium, France, Germany, Liechtenstein, Luxembourg, Monaco, the Netherlands and Switzerland; 4. de Vries (1984, p. 39) for 1650–1800 data, urban population of all cities with at least 10,000 inhabitants; Law (1967) for 1801–1901 data; and Champion (1975) for 1951 data.

particularly since 1990, could be attributed to the fact that the city was severely underinvested in during 1950–1980 (see Table 4.5).

### 3.2. *Capricious market change*

Capricious change and uncertainty are, first and foremost, caused by the opening up to the global economy. Only 3 percent of total retail sales in China were transacted at market prices in 1978 (Naughton, 1995, p. 14). By the late 1990s, 60–70 percent of goods and services had their prices determined in the market (Zhao, 1999). Imports and exports as percentages of GDP suggest how open an economy is to the world economy. Imports and exports only accounted for 5.2 and 4.6 percent of China's GDP in 1978 respectively. The percentages rose to 21.2 (imports) and 23.3 (exports) in 2002 (NBSC, 2003a), whereas the sum of exports and imports as a percentage of GDP is about 30 percent in America, Japan, India and Brazil (Woodall, 2004, p. 8).

Unpredictable change is exacerbated by the rising degree of marketization. The economy is increasingly dominated by the sectors responding to market demand rather than planning order, evidenced by how the non-state-owned sectors have grown and become an indispensable component of the economy. State-owned and collective-owned enterprises accounted for 77.6 and 22.4 percent of the total industrial output in 1978 respectively.

Table 4.5.   Economic and Physical Growths of Shanghai (1950–2004)

| | 1950 | 1980 | 1990 | 2004 | Increment (1951–1980) | Increment (1981–1990) | Increment (1991–2004) |
|---|---|---|---|---|---|---|---|
| GDP (billion ¥) | 2.2 | 31.2 | 75.6 | 745.0 | 29.0 | 44.4 | 669.4 |
| Population (million) | 4.6 | 7.0 | 8.6 | 11.0 | 2.4 | 1.6 | 2.4 |
| Housing stock (million sq m) | 23.6 | 44.0 | 89.0 | 352.1 | 20.4 | 45.0 | 263.1 |
| Office stock (million sq m) | 2.3 | 3.4 | 6.0 | 40.1 | 1.1 | 2.6 | 34.1 |
| Shop stock (million sq m) | 3.3 | 2.4 | 4.0 | 28.6 | −0.9 | 1.6 | 24.6 |

| Period | Investment in Fixed Assets as % of GDP | Investment in Housing as % of GDP | Housing Supply (million sq m) |
|---|---|---|---|
| 1953–1978 | 8.6 | 0.4 | 17.56 |
| 1981–2004 | 44.6 | 10.5 | 269.02 |

*Source*: SMBS (2005a).

There were no private-owned industries then. In 1999, state-owned and collective-owned enterprises contributed 28.2 and 35.4 percent respectively and the remaining 36.4 percent was produced mainly by private-owned industrial firms (NBSC, 2000a).

The increasing degree of marketization with little guidance by state policies further contributes to capriciousness in the emerging market. The rapid process of housing commoditization demonstrates how substantially the market forces have affected the changing mode of housing provision from public to private. In a span of 20 years, the sole responsibility for urban housing provision has been transferred from the state to the market (see Table 4.6). Housing reforms have effectively privatized the existing housing stock and commercialized new housing provision. Withdrawal of the state from urban housing provision has been striking.[5]

---

[5] It should be considered as a significant change in China which still regards itself a socialist country. In the nominally capitalist Britain, one in five housing units were public and social rental housing in England and Wales, according to its 2001 population census. The share of public housing in the housing stock of Scotland was 26 percent in 2004, declining from 38 percent a decade earlier.

Table 4.6.  Housing Provision in Shanghai (1982–2004)

| Year | Annual Housing Supply in Floor Area (1,000 sq m) | | | | |
|------|-------|------------------|--------------|---------------------------------|--------------|
| | Total | Public Housing | As % of Total | Commodity Housing (Private) | As % of Total |
| 1982–1983 | 7456.1 | 7456.1 | 100.0 | 0.0 | 0.0 |
| 1984–1987 | 17750.5 | 17361.4 | 97.8 | 389.1 | 2.2 |
| 1988–1991 | 16755.1 | 14065.3 | 83.9 | 2689.8 | 16.1 |
| 1992–1995 | 32050.2 | 21059.2 | 65.7 | 10991.0 | 34.3 |
| 1996–1999 | 62294.2 | 15897.5 | 25.5 | 46396.7 | 74.5 |
| 2000–2004 | 108996.4 | 10631.3 | 9.8 | 98365.1 | 90.2 |

*Sources*: SMBS (1990a–2005a; 1989b–2005b).

## 3.3. *Dissipation of land resources*

Under the centrally controlled system (1949–1978), land was excluded from economic transactions, following the dogma of Marxism and the socialist principle of public land ownership. Urban land was virtually a free good. Use and allocation of land were determined by central plans. Once a land plot had been allocated, it was very difficult in practice for the state to retrieve it from the user, because the state-owned enterprises were the basic units of the socialist state economy and "the people" were the "masters" of the socialist society. Users' entitlement to land use rights became a unique socialist institution which was incorporated in the formation of socialist cities.

An amendment to the 1982 Constitution in 1988 legalized the commoditization and marketization of urban land so that urban land could be leased to developers or users for a fixed period after a payment of rent in a lump sum to the state. However, redevelopment of urban built-up areas was hampered by the sitting land users. As a legacy of the pre-reform era of socialist industrialization when urban land was a free means of production and the industrialists' demand overtook that of others in land allocation (Fung, 1981), quite a number of manufacturing factories occupied central locations in downtowns. In 1985, it was estimated that 30 percent of the land area in the central city of Shanghai was occupied by factories and warehouses (Fung, Yan and Ning, 1992). Up to 1991, there was still

1.74 million sq meters of factory space in the downtown district which at the same time only had 1.39 million sq meters of office space (SMBS, 1992b). Urban land occupied by the existing users was prevented from being allocated to the "highest and best uses", and land rent opportunities dissipated.

According to the China's Constitution (1998), urban land is owned by the state, and rural land is collectively owned by rural communities. Collective land ownership vests land rights in three entities: township (*xiang/zhen*), administrative villages (*xingzhengcun*) and natural villages (*zirancun*). Collective land ownership is, however, ambiguous regarding its nominal owners. There is a phrase describing the owners of the collective ownership: *sanji suoyou, dui wei jichu* (collective ownership by three entities — the commune, the brigade, and the team, of which the team is the basic holder). Ownership of rural land is vested in the collective entities at three levels. How much each entity is entitled to has never been clearly delineated. Ambiguously delineated and incomplete collective land rights generate disorderly competition for land resources. Collective rural land is inappropriately appropriated for *in situ* urbanization as a result of competition for land rent in the public domain, and land rent dissipates during competition.

## 4. China's Developmental Planning

Rapid industrialization and economic growth, the influx of migrants to cities, and the zeal of the local developmental state for urban growth in particular have constituted tremendous challenges to an urban planning system molded under the centrally controlled economy. Blue print plans based on top-down economic projection clearly could not cope with market-oriented urban development. Unpredictable market changes made land use plans irrelevant and useless often within a few years of their existence. Although the nominally statutory land use master plan was updated periodically to reflect current situations, the role of its guidance for urban physical growth was seriously in doubt.

According to the Urban Planning Act (1989), a Master Plan is statutorily required for urban land development. The Master Plan formulates the city's spatial structure of land uses with due consideration for its environmental capacity and infrastructural provision. Its goal is to create a sustainable environment with balanced economic and social development. Nevertheless, it does not show positive guidance towards achievement of the planning objectives, nor does it have flexibility in accommodating unexpected socioeconomic changes. Its regulatory character does not help to accomplish the ambitious agendas of the local developmental state.

### 4.1. *Land use planning: Promotion and mobilization*

The strategic concept plan, a non-statutorily required plan, emerged spontaneously initially from the cities experiencing rapid urbanization to envision urban physical expansion into the future. The dynamic growth of urban economies needs a spatial structure to coordinate numerous private housing estates, industrial zones, shopping centers, and other land development activities initiated by developers whose number has mushroomed since the 1990s. The strategic concept plan serves the local developmental state to advance the transformation led by urbanization on one hand. It is reported that about 50-odd cities had built new university districts[6] by 2005;[7] 36 cities were pursuing new central business districts in 2003, instead of consolidating the existing city centers,[8] and there were 3,837 industrial development zones in 2003, occupying 36,000 sq kilometers of land[9] in total nationwide.[10] On the other hand, the strategic concept plan enables the municipal government to appropriate land resources and thus to expand local revenue sources. Local funding is becoming increasingly critical to local growth because of decentralization.

---

[6] The university district is a sizable zone in the urban periphery where a cluster of universities and student accommodation facilities is located. These universities were scattered in the central area which was cramped for space.

[7] http://www.landscapecn.com/news/html/news/detail.asp?id=29730, accessed on July 11, 2006.

[8] http://news.soufun.com/2003-04-16/150448.htm, accessed on July 11, 2006.

[9] http://www.people.com.cn/GB/14857/22238/28463/28464/2015058.html, accessed on June 21, 2004.

[10] Those large-scale urban expansion projects are deemed out of proportion compared with the actual demand. In 2003, there were 174 cities with populations exceeding one million; 33 cities with populations of over two million (NBSC, 2005b). New CBDs and university districts are only justified for those large cities with millions of people. The amount of land (36,000 sq kilometers) occupied by 3,837 newly planned industrial development zones even exceeds the total existing urban built-up area of 30,406 sq kilometers in the country (2004) (NBSC, 2005b).

In the newly initiated urban land market, land use planning has the unimpeded right to prescribe land use (zoning and rezoning), as urban land is owned by the state, and the landed interests are not well established yet as the property rights of existing land users are not unambiguously and legally defined. Though agricultural land is collectively owned by the rural community, the right to develop rural land for urban uses is owned by the urban state exclusively. Zoning and rezoning unimpeded by status quo interests would make land available for the highest and best uses. Because of the city-centered land management system, the local municipal government is in the best position as the agent of the state to capture the land rent[11] generated from rezoning for higher and better uses. Since the 1988 land reform, land leasing has been a major source of municipal revenues. Land use planning therefore becomes a two-prong pro-growth instrument: making land available for urban development/redevelopment and mobilizing land revenues to be used for the improvement of infrastructure and amenities. As a result, government-led investment in urban infrastructure has escalated since the 1990s (see Table 4.7; Shanghai and Guangzhou are cited as examples because data are available).

Table 4.7.   Investment in Urban Infrastructure and as Percentage of City GDP, Shanghai and Guangzhou

| | 1950–1978 | | 1979–1990 | | 1991–2000 | | 2001–2004 | |
|---|---|---|---|---|---|---|---|---|
| | billion ¥ | % of GDP | billion ¥ | % of GDP | billion ¥ | % of GDP | billion ¥ | % of GDP |
| Shanghai | 6.0 | 1.7 | 25.0 | 4.5 | 310.0 | 11.7 | 237.2 | 9.9 |
| Guangzhou | — | — | 3.1 | 1.8 | 74.1 | 5.6 | 63.1 | 4.6 |

*Sources*: SMBS (2005a); GMBS (2005).

---

[11] Land rent is the value of land appropriated in economic transactions, for the market price of land is interpreted as capitalized land rent. The rent of a land plot is largely determined by its designated use (agricultural, residential, commercial and so on) by zoning and the equilibrium of demand for and supply of land as commodity. The potential land rent represents the amount of rent that can be capitalized under the land's "highest and best use". The gap between the potential land rent and actual land rent capitalized under the present land use creates the land rent difference (Smith, 1979).

Two cities, Nanchang and Jing'an in Shanghai, are chosen here to illustrate the practice of developmental planning. Shanghai has been experiencing drastic growth in the booming coastal region. Jing'an is one of the districts in central Shanghai. Nanchang is one of the ordinary provincial capital cities in the central region which is less dynamic than the eastern region. Nanchang drafted a grand strategic plan to develop a new town as big as its existing old town across the River Gan in the mid-1990s (see Fig. 4.1). It plans to make the two towns into one entity with the 1,000-meter-wide River Gan running in between. The new Nanchang airport, Bayi Bridge (the second bridge crossing the River Gan) and the industrial zone were built in the late 1990s. In order to demonstrate its commitment, the municipal government and other key government departments relocated their offices to the other side of the river to form a new civic center in 2001, followed by the construction of a new university district in 2003.

A more ambitious scheme is to make a new CBD in the new territory, which has to rely on market forces. It is yet to be seen whether the

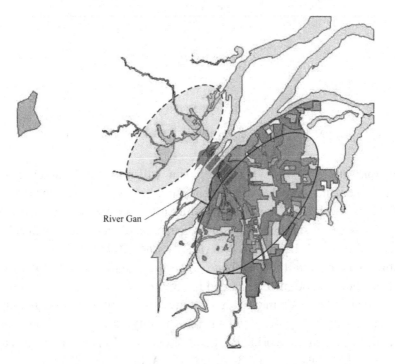

River Gan

Figure 4.1. The proposal for new town development in Nanchang.

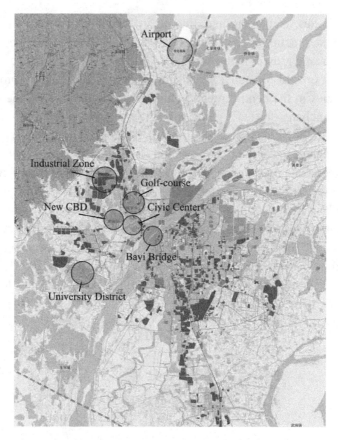

Figure 4.2.   Major projects built in the late 1990s and early 2000s in Nanchang.

government-led new town development will stimulate market investments. For the purpose of inducing market responses, government-
affiliated developers have been building a leisure complex containing a
golf course, five-star hotels, business centers, and an international school
next to the site of the proposed new CBD since 2003 (see Fig. 4.2). As a
publicity campaign, the Nanchang government built the world's highest
Ferris wheel at 160 meters, named the Star of Nanchang, in 2006 on the
River Gan. The city's marketing strategy has seemed to work. It caught
the attention of *Newsweek* which put the city as one of the ten most
dynamic cities in the world, along with London, Munich, Las Vegas, and
Moscow (*Newsweek*, July 3–10, 2006). A total of 4,856 hectares of

agricultural land has been acquired for the new town program, and 3,080 hectares leased to developers and users by now. The land rent captured is a main source of funding for the development of infrastructure and public amenities.

Media reports claimed that Shanghai was the world's largest construction site in the 1990s (*The Straits Times*, January 15, 1998). It was probably not an exaggeration. Between 1993 and 2000, building construction and demolition in the whole city of Shanghai were undertaken at an unprecedented scale: 131.2 million sq meters constructed and 30.5 million sq meters demolished (SMBS, 1994b–2001b). In all, 17.7 percent of the total building stock (172.6 million sq meters) that had existed in Shanghai Municipality before 1990 was demolished during the period 1993–2000. During the same period in its Jing'an District, 4.81 million sq meters of building floor area were constructed, while 2.49 million sq meters of deteriorated structures were demolished (SMBS, 1994b–2001b). The total building stock by 1990 was 9.08 million sq meters (SMBS, 1991b). This suggests that a quarter of the stock was demolished and 53 percent more was added during the period. A survey by the author reveals that during the period 1992–2000, land redevelopment carried out amounted to 237 projects on land parcels adding up to a total area of 135.7 hectares, accounting for 17.8 percent of the total area of the district (762 hectares). Out of 135.7 hectares, 88.5 hectares (65.2 percent) were residential land; 11.5 hectares (8.5 percent) were institutional land, and 35.7 hectares (26.3 percent) were industrial land (see Fig. 4.3). A substantial amount of land has been made available to be redeveloped for higher and better uses, transforming the district significantly.

City governments have to rely increasingly on local funding because of decentralization. Decentralization has also diminished the desire for regional cooperation, and resulted in competition among cities in the region.[12] In rapidly growing regions, a city has to compete with others in

---

[12] A report on the competitiveness of Chinese cities was published by the China Academy of Social Sciences in 2003, which ranked cities according to their achievements in science and technology, economic growth rates, etc. Hong Kong was ranked first, followed by Shanghai and Shenzhen (http://finance.sina.com.cn/g/20030303/0751316063.shtml, accessed on July 16, 2003). Seeing Guangzhou ranked sixth, behind Shenzhen in the same province, the mayor of Guangzhou complained and doubted whether the ranking was fairly done (http://news.sina.com.cn/c/2003-03-09/1402939281.shtml, accessed on July 16, 2003). After Beijing had won the 2008 Olympic Games, and Shanghai

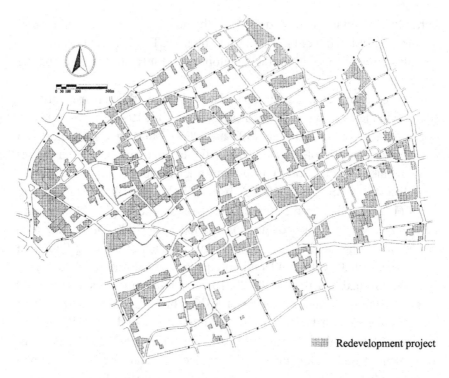

Redevelopment project

Figure 4.3.   Land redevelopment projects in Jing'an District, Shanghai, 1992–2000.

order to maintain its position or move upward in a new regional hierarchy under restructuring. For instance, cities in one of the most dynamic regions — the Pearl River Delta region — saw their positions moving up and down during the period 1990–2003. Shenzhen and Dongguan rose significantly, while Guangzhou, Jiangmen and Zhaoqin declined relatively (see Fig. 4.4 and Table 4.8).

---

the 2010 Expo, Guangzhou felt left behind by these competitors and decided to bid for the 2010 Asian Games. It won the bidding. The saga has become a classic of city rivalry. Since 2003, a survey team from the National Bureau of Statistics has been publishing annually the league of the top 100 most competitive Chinese cities. Competitiveness is measured mostly by economic strength and social development. In the "Competitiveness of China's Cities 2004" blue paper published by the China Academy of Social Sciences, Zhengzhou, a provincial capital in the central region, was ranked 50th. In 2006, the blue paper "Competitiveness of China's Cities 2005" ranked Zhengzhou 37th. The progress in ranking was much celebrated by the city (http://www.zhengzhou.org.cn/phpweb/ShowContent.php?aid=48669&tid=2, accessed on April 4, 2006).

Figure 4.4.  Nine cities in the Pearl River Delta city region.

Table 4.8.  City's GDP as a Percentage of the City Grouping in Pearl River Delta Region

| City in Pearl River Delta Region | 1990 | 2003 |
| --- | --- | --- |
| Guangzhou | 33.1 | 30.4 |
| Shenzhen | 14.1 | 25.2 |
| Zhuhai | 4.3 | 4.1 |
| Foshan | 13.0 | 12.0 |
| Jiangmen | 9.7 | 6.4 |
| Dongguan | 6.7 | 8.3 |
| Zhongshan | 4.5 | 4.4 |
| Huizhou | 5.1 | 5.1 |
| Zhaoqin | 9.6 | 4.1 |
| Total (billion ¥) | 96.5 | 1148.4 |

*Source*: NBSC (2004b; 1991b).

Strategic concept plans provide visions which enable the local developmental state to marshal social support. The gist of a strategic concept plan is often represented by a succinct slogan which is easily understood by the general public. Guangzhou simply puts the aim of its future as "small change in a year, moderate change in three years, and great change in five years". Zhuhai proposes that the city should have "large ports, great industries and grand development". Shenyang declares, "Shenyang in the north as Guangzhou in the south", with connotations that Shenyang should be as dynamic and prosperous as Guangzhou. The Shanghai Urban Planning Exhibition Hall, the first in the country, has attracted many citizens to view its exhibits of achievements and visionary developments for the future. It has aroused civic pride and inspiration among local residents. Though not every resident benefits from substantial urban change, the majority and new arrivals should have their welfare linked with growth and expansion. The government earns its legitimacy by garnering social support. Taking it as a good city marketing project, many other cities have followed suit.

### 4.2. Development control: Responsive to market change

A new development control system has been established by the Urban Planning Act (1989). It stipulates that prior permissions are required for land and building developments. Development applications are evaluated by the planning authority against the urban land use plans. Thereafter, a Land Use Planning Note will be issued with land use planning parameters attached such as land use, plot ratio, site coverage and building height. When all the formalities for land transaction are cleared and land site details finalized, a Land Development Permit is issued. With the permit, the developer can proceed to commission architects to design the building. After an examination of the building designs by the planning bureau, a Building Permit is granted and the project can proceed to the construction stage. This process of development control is the so-called one-note-and-two-permits system.

However, empirical investigations reveal that planning authorities have much flexibility in handling development projects, and thus development control is highly discretionary without necessary transparency.

While inward investments are keenly pursued by the local developmental state, cajoling developers into committing their investments to the city, instead of other places, usually results in the government yielding to developers' short-term interests. Accommodating developers' requests in their land development proposals seems more important than abiding by pre-determined land use particulars set by the urban master plan. Zhu (2004) has elaborated through a case study of Shanghai's redevelopment that up to 53 percent of cases are overwhelmed by discrepancies between what are required by the land use plans and the final completed projects in terms of the planning parameters of land use, plot ratio, site coverage, and building height.

State regulatory intervention in the land market is well recognized as necessary in order to deal with market failures such as externalities and underproduction of public goods. Those market failures are more or less caused by uncertainty in the market, while coercive development control provides the land market with certainty and order which are essential for maintaining market confidence (Pigou, 1932; Nelson, 1977; Brabant, 1991; Lai, 1999). Certainty and order are essentially related to the stability of the status quo interests. The dilemma that China's local developmental state faces is that uncertainty is embedded in the gradual transition when the market-oriented economy is evolving and market mechanisms are in the making. In the context of rapid urbanization, the status quo interests in the city may be a minority, compared with that of a large volume of immigrants. Likewise, the land development market is in a continual flux, and uncertainty is the norm. Thus, the priority of land use plans during the gradual transition is to be responsive to market change. Flexibility, instead of rigidity, is one of the properties the land use plans should possess.

A philosophy seems to be embedded in the development control practice that if planning cannot lead the market, planning should follow the market. The flexible development control regime suits the needs of the local developmental state to unconditionally pursue urban transformation. This highly discretionary tool is inherited from the pre-1978 centrally controlled economy which did not need an independent mechanism serving as a medium between the state and the market. The development control regime is used as a mechanism by which the local developmental state negotiates with developers for the purpose of urban growth.

A case of the formation of Shanghai office centers is a good illustration of planning being led by market-driven development. According to the strategic plan drafted in the late 1980s, Jing'an and Huaihai Road were not designated as office centers (see Fig. 4.5).

Nevertheless, these two office centers had emerged by the late 1990s (see Fig. 4.6). Out of four prime office centers in the early 2000s, two (Hongqiao and Lujiazui) were planned and the other two (Jing'an and Huaihai Road) were initiated and built jointly by local district governments and largely private developers. The latter two are rated by real estate agents and perceived by office users to be of better quality than the former two, which suggests that market-led development with responsive planning control is not without merit in this specific circumstance. The development of the 9 million sq ft Huaihai Road office center without orchestration at the municipal level demonstrates the capacity of the local developmental state and unleashed market forces (see Fig. 4.7).

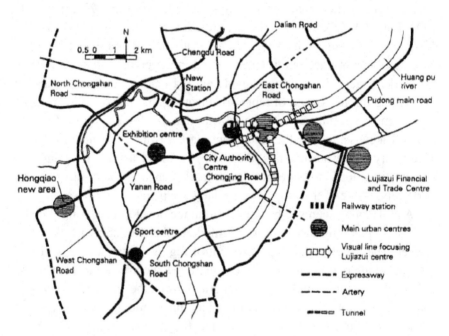

Figure 4.5.   Shanghai's strategic plan in the 1980s.

*Source*: Huang (1991, p. 92).

Figure 4.6.   Four prime office centers in Shanghai central city by the late 1990s.
*Note*: H — Hongqiao; L — Huaihai Road; J — Jing'an; P — Lujiazui.

This case of the market-oriented planning process is not an exception. Instead, it has become commonplace in China's cities nowadays. Reflecting the merits of market initiatives, the Huaihai Road office center is a successful redevelopment project which has produced a well-known showcase, Xintiandi, and benefited many stakeholders — local communities, local and municipal governments, developers, customers, and tourists (He and Wu, 2005; *The Economist*, September 25, 2004, p. 76).

Figure 4.7.   Huaihai road office center.

*Note*: Skyscrapers in the background are the office buildings developed in the 1990s along Huaihai Road where low-rise structures like those in the foreground used to dominate.

## 5. Conclusion: Developmental Planning and Sustainable Development

Urban planning to advance socioeconomic transformation is not an isolated issue concerning only a developing China. It is interesting to find that the issue is also debated in developed countries. Focusing on the link between urban planning and urban change, an independent review of British land use planning is under way. In the context of intensified international competition caused by globalization, the review intends to find ways of making land use planning deliver economic growth without compromising social equity and environmental sustainability (Barker, 2006). The interim report of the Barker Review highlights that delays in development control, certainty in the market, and planning responsiveness to social and economic change, as well as to market demand and supply, are at issue.

The Chinese economy has performed spectacularly since 1978 when the reforms started, improving the welfare of a nation which used to be one of the poorest in the world. Although this economic miracle is largely attributed to the rapid industrialization and globalization which are driven by decentralized business activities responsive to demand and supply, the land use planning system, providing the right site at the right place to the right user, cannot be ignored as one of the important contributing factors. Rapid socioeconomic change cannot be achieved without an urban planning system conducive to development.

China's developmental planning has been very responsive to market change. Responsiveness means making resources available for development and lowering transaction costs to businesses,[13] which explains how China's urban planning facilitates growth. It makes sense that land resources locked and underutilized by the centrally controlled system have to be released, and the scarce land resources have to be utilized in the most productive way. Strategic concept plans have played a critical role in the mobilization during the gradual transition when ambiguity prevailed. The flexibility in planning control is not so unreasonable for a market emerging from a transitional economy that is highly volatile and erratic without perceivable patterns to trace.

Nevertheless, China's developmental planning is not sustainable over the long term. It is a transitional paradigm. Ambitious spatial structuring as a forward-looking vision does have a marketing effect on the business community, but that alone does not necessarily stimulate market investment. The power of leverage by public investment in land and infrastructure is more determined by market fundamentals than by government ambitions, as evidenced by the diminishing "leverage ratio" from dynamic to marginal regions. Many new CBDs and industrial zones fail in attracting sufficient office and factory projects to stand on their own feet. Too much flexibility in planning compromises certainty in the land development market, which is harmful to urban communities.

The more harmful consequence is that, lacking established rules for market transactions, the emerging land development market is hampered in its evolution towards maturity. Inadequate rules lead to chaos and disorder in coordination. There is a danger that the land market will become

---

[13] There was a debate over whether the removal or streamlining of some planning controls would encourage entrepreneurs to expand their businesses. An explanation from the perspective of institutional economics is that streamlining of planning controls is meant to reduce the transaction cost for businesses. The other major business cost is production cost which is increasingly declining owning to technological innovations.

the commons where negative externalities are uncontrolled — a commonplace in developing cities. Urban planning as an institution is the rules of the "game" of market-driven urban development. In view of the fact that China's urbanization has been carried out without the same tradition and foundation of market-based development control system as many developed economies were (such as the British pre-1909 development control system),[14] clear and firm rules for the land market need to be established, so that there is rule-based fairness in urban development. Rules are needed to install certainty to counter too much flexibility in the market. Long-term sustainable growth requires a regime of well-defined property rights and market order that provides certainty and internalization of externalities. In the context of a majority of China's urban residents being property owners and with many more to come, well-defined property rights protect owners' interests, and thus help to mitigate social and environmental woes.

As discussed, China's developmental planning has bolstered dynamic economic growth for a quarter of a century. However, excessive responsiveness to whimsical markets has achieved what was intended at the great expense of building a solid foundation for long-term sustainable growth. Transparent rules with clear land rights are essential for good development, as well as for social equity and environmental protection to a certain extent, in a market economy. To an urban regime led by the local developmental state, building rules and order seem only to play a passive role. What China's urban planning system needs to shore up for is marshalling resources for development by positive planning (Adams, 1994). Through a development program of public and merit goods provision, public land ownership should allow city governments to engage in leverage planning to achieve developmental planning goals (Brindley, Rydin and Stoker, 1996). Nevertheless,

---

[14] The first Republic of China was established in 1911 after the Qing Dynasty collapsed. It was followed by either civil wars or foreign invasions until 1949 when the People's Republic of China was born. A centrally controlled economic system was adopted immediately until 1978 when the economic reform towards a market-oriented economy commenced. Thus, China as a nation with a claimed 5,000-year civilization has never had its economy and society run fully based on market rules. The transition from central planning to a market economy is under way.

it poses a tall order to China's local government which has to be both accountable and entrepreneurial. Market order has to be maintained by the government which at the same time is a market player. There are no successful precedents yet.

## References

Adams, D. (1994). *Urban Planning and the Development Process*. London: UCL Press.

Alexander, I. (1979). *Office Location and Public Policy*. London: Longman.

Bardhan, P. (1990). "Symposium on the State and Economic Development". *Journal of Economic Perspectives*, 4(3), pp. 3–7.

Barker, K. (2006). *Barker Review of Land Use Planning: Interim Report — Analysis*. Norwich: HMSO.

Blakely, E.J. (1994). *Planning Local Economic Development: Theory and Practice*, 2nd edition. Thousand Oaks, California: SAGE.

Brabant, J.M. (1991). "Property Rights' Reform, Macroeconomic Performance, and Welfare". In H. Blommestein and M. Marrese (eds.), *Transformation of Planned Economies: Property Rights Reform and Macroeconomic Stability*. Paris: OECD.

Breslin, S.G. (1996). "China: Developmental State or Dysfunctional Development?" *Third World Quarterly*, 17(4), pp. 689–706.

Brindley, T., Rydin, Y., and Stoker, G. (1996). *Remaking Planning: The Politics of Urban Change*. London: Routledge.

Champion, A.G. (1975). "The United Kingdom". In R. Jones (ed.), *Essays on World Urbanization*. London: George Philip and Son, pp. 47–66.

Cochrane, A. (1991). "The Changing State of Local Government in the UK". *Public Administration*, 69, pp. 281–302.

Daniels, P.W. (1975). *Office Location: An Urban and Regional Study*. London: G. Bell and Sons.

Davis, K. and Golden, H. (1954). "Urbanization and the Development of Pre-Industrial Areas". *Economic Development and Cultural Change*, 3, pp. 6–26.

de Vries, J. (1984). *European Urbanization 1500–1800*. London: Methuen and Co.

Fischel, W.A. (1985). *The Economics of Zoning Laws: A Property Rights Approach to American Land Use Controls*. Baltimore: The Johns Hopkins University Press.

Friedmann, J. and Weaver, C. (1979). *Territory and Function: The Evolution of Regional Planning*. Berkeley: University of California Press.

Fung, K.I. (1981). "Urban Sprawl in China: Some Causative Factors". In L.J.C. Ma and E.W. Hanten (eds.), *Urban Development in Modern China*. Boulder, CO: Westview Press, pp. 194–221.

Fung, K.I., Yan, Z.M., and Ning, Y.M. (1992). "Shanghai: China's World City". In Y.M. Yeung and X.W. Hu (eds.), *China's Coastal Cities: Catalysts for Modernization*. Honolulu: University of Hawaii Press, pp. 124–152.

Goetz, E.G. and Clarke, S.E. (1993). *The New Localism: Comparative Urban Politics in a Global Era*. Newbury Park, CA: SAGE.

Guangzhou Municipal Bureau of Statistics (GMBS) (2005). *Guangzhou Statistical Yearbook*. Beijing: China Statistics Publishing.

Hall, P. (1999). "The Regional Dimension". In B. Cullingworth (ed.), *British Planning: 50 Years of Urban and Regional Policy*. London: The Athlone Press.

He, S.J. and Wu, F.L. (2005). "Property-led Redevelopment in Post-reform China: A Case Study of Xintiandi Redevelopment Project in Shanghai". *Journal of Urban Affairs*, 27(1), pp. 1–23.

Huang, F.X. (1991). "Planning in Shanghai". *Habitat International*, 15(3), pp. 87–98.

Huang, Y. (1996). *Inflation and Investment Controls in China*. Cambridge: Cambridge University Press.

Jessop, B. (1998). "The Narrative of Enterprise and the Enterprise of Narrative: Place Marketing and the Entrepreneurial City". In T. Hall and P. Hubbard (eds.), *The Entrepreneurial City: Geographies of Politics, Regime and Representation*. Chichester, West Sussex: John Wiley & Sons, pp. 77–99.

Keeble, L. (1969). *Principles and Practice of Town and Country Planning*. London: Estates Gazette.

Lai, L.W.C. (1999). "Hayek and Town Planning: A Note on Hayek's Views towards Town Planning in *The Constitution of Liberty*". *Environment and Planning A*, 31, pp. 1567–1582.

Law, C.M. (1967). "The Growth of the Urban Population in England and Wales, 1801–1911. *Transactions of the Institute of British Geographers*, 41, pp. 125–143.

Lin, S. (2000). "Too Many Fees and Too Many Charges: China Streamlines Its Fiscal System". Background Brief No. 66, East Asian Institute, National University of Singapore.

Loftman, P. and Nevin, B. (1998). "Pro-growth Local Economic Development Strategies: Civic Promotion and Local Needs in Britain's Second City, 1981–1996". In T. Hall and P. Hubbard (eds.), *The Entrepreneurial City: Geographies of Politics, Regime and Representation*. Chichester, West Sussex: John Wiley & Sons, pp. 129–148.

Ma, L.J.C. (1981). "Introduction: The City in Modern China". In L.J.C. Ma and E.W. Hanten (eds.), *Urban Development in Modern China*. Boulder, CO: Westview, pp. 1–18.

McLoughlin, J.B. (1973). *Control and Urban Planning*. London: Faber and Faber.

National Bureau of Statistics of China (NBSC) (2000a; 2003a; 2005a). *China Statistical Yearbook*. Beijing: China Statistics Press.

National Bureau of Statistics of China (NBSC) (1982b; 1987b; 1991b; 1992b; 1996b; 1997b; 2002b; 2004b; 2005b). *Statistical Yearbook of Chinese Cities*. Beijing: China Statistics Press.

National Bureau of Statistics of China (NBSC) (1999c). *Comprehensive Statistical Data and Materials on 50 Years of New China*. Beijing: China Statistics Press.

Naughton, B. (1995). *Growing Out of the Plan: Chinese Economic Reform, 1978–1993*. Cambridge: Cambridge University Press.

Nelson, R.H. (1977). *Zoning and Property Rights: An Analysis of the American System of Land-Use Regulation*. Cambridge, MA: MIT Press.

Nolan, P. (1995). "Politics, Planning, and the Transition from Stalinism: The Case of China". In H.J. Chang and R. Rowthorn (eds.), *The Role of the State in Economic Change*. Oxford: Clarendon, pp. 237–261.

North, D.C. (1990). *Institutions, Institutional Change and Economic Performance*. Cambridge: Cambridge University Press.

Oi, J.C. (1996). "The Role of the Local State in China's Transitional Economy". In A.G. Walder (ed.), *China's Transitional Economy*. Oxford: Oxford University Press, pp. 170–187.

Oi, J.C. (1995). "The Role of the Local State in China's Transitional Economy". *The China Quarterly*, 144, pp. 1132–1149.

Paul, E.F., Miller, F.D., Jr., and Paul, J. (1994). *Property Rights*. Cambridge: Cambridge University Press.

Peiser, R. (1990). "Who Plans America? Planners or Developers?" *Journal of the American Planning Association*, 56(4), pp. 496–503.

Pejovich, S. (1990). *The Economics of Property Rights: Towards a Theory of Comparative Systems*. Dordrecht, Netherlands: Kluwer Academic Publishers.

Pigou, A.C. (1932). *The Economics of Welfare*, 4th edition. London: Macmillan. Shanghai Municipal Bureau of Statistics (SMBS) (1990a–2005a). *Shanghai Statistical Yearbook*. Beijing: China Statistics Publishing.

Shanghai Municipal Bureau of Statistics (SMBS) (1989b–2005b). *Shanghai Real Estate Market*. Beijing: China Statistics Publishing.

Shen, J. (2005). "Counting Urban Population in Chinese Censuses 1953–2000: Changing Definitions, Problems and Solutions". *Population, Space and Place*, 11(5), pp. 381–400.

Smith, N. (1979). "Toward a Theory of Gentrification: A Back to the City Movement by Capital Not People". *Journal of the American Planning Association*, 45, pp. 538–548.

Solinger, D.J. (1992). "Urban Entrepreneurs and the State: The Merger of State and Society". In A.L. Rosenbaum (ed.), *State & Society in China: The Consequences of Reform*. Boulder, CO: Westview, pp. 121–142.

Sutcliffe, A. (1981). "Introduction: British Town Planning and the Historian". In A. Sutcliffe (ed.), *British Town Planning: The Formative Years*. Leicester: Leicester University Press, pp. 2–14.

Turok, I. (1992). "Property-led Urban Regeneration: Panacea or Placebo". *Environment and Planning A*, 24(3), pp. 361–379.

Turok, I. (1989). "Development Planning and Local Economic Growth: A Study of Process and Policy in Bracknell New Town". *Progress in Planning*, 31, pp. 59–150.

Unger, J. and Chan, A. (1995). "China, Corporatism, and the East Asian Model". *The Australian Journal of Chinese Affairs*, 33, pp. 29–53.

United Nations (2004). *World Urbanization Prospects: The 2003 Revision*. New York: United Nations.

Wang, H. (1994). *The Gradual Revolution*. New Brunswick, NJ: Transaction.

Wannop, U.A. (1995). *The Regional Imperative: Regional Planning and Governance in Britain, Europe and the United States*. London: Jessica Kingsley Publishers.

Waterston, A. (1965). *Development Planning: Lessons of Experience*. Baltimore: The Johns Hopkins Press.

Webster, C. and Lai, L.W.C. (2003). *Property Rights, Planning and Markets: Managing Spontaneous Cities*. Cheltenham, UK, and Northampton, MA, USA: Edward Elgar.

Wong, C.P.W., Heady, C., and Woo, W.T. (1995). *Fiscal Management and Economic Reform in the People's Republic of China*. Hong Kong: Oxford University Press.

Wong, C.P.W. (1992). "Fiscal Reform and Local Industrialization: The Problematic Sequencing of Reform in Post-Mao China. *Modern China*, 18(2), pp. 197–227.

Wong, C.P.W. (1987). "Between Plan and Market: The Role of the Local Sector in Post-Mao China". *Journal of Comparative Economics*, 11, pp. 385–398.

Woodall, P. (2004). "The Dragon and the Eagle: A Survey of the World Economy". *The Economist*, October 2–8, pp. 1–24.

Zelinsky, W. (1971). "The Hypothesis of the Mobility Transition". *Geographical Review*, 61, pp. 219–249.

Zhao, R. (1999). "Review of Economic Reform in China: Features, Experiences and Challenges". In R. Garnaut and L. Song (eds.), *China: Twenty Years of Economic Reform*. Canberra: Asia Pacific Press, pp. 185–199.

Zhu, J.M. (2004). "From Land Use Right to Land Development Right: Institutional Change in China's Urban Development". *Urban Studies*, 41(7), pp. 1249–1267.

CHAPTER 5

# Industrialization, Urbanization, and Land Use in China*

*Xiaobo Zhang, Timothy D. Mount and Richard N. Boisvert*

Rapid industrial development and urbanization transfer more and more land away from agricultural production and affect the patterns of land use intensity. This paper analyzes the determinants of land use by modeling arable land and sown area separately. An inverse U-shaped relationship between land use intensity and industrialization is explored both theoretically and empirically. The findings highlight the conflict between the two policy goals of industrialization and grain self-sufficiency in the end. Several policy recommendations are offered to reconcile the conflict.

## 1. Introduction

Land scarcity has become an increasingly important issue in China. Because of rapid industrial development, urbanization, and population growth, the land base for agricultural production has been shrinking steadily. Since 1952, more than 13 million hectares of arable land have been lost.[1] In contrast to the decline of arable land, the sown area, the

---

\* Reprinted with the authors' permission from *Journal of Chinese Economic and Business Studies*, 2(3), pp. 207–224. The authors gratefully acknowledge helpful comments from Shenggen Fan, Junich Ito, Peter Hazell, and Scott Rozelle.

[1] Arable land is land that can be farmed even if it is not. Sown area or cropping area is equal to the product of the arable land area and the multiple-cropping index. It has been noted from the recent agricultural census that the previous official arable land area has been under-reported (SSB, 1997, p. 368; Ash and Edmonds, 1998; Smil, 1999). The debate in the literature focuses on the magnitude of under-reporting. In spite of the shortcomings of the official statistics, they are the only source on land stock

product of the arable land area and the multiple-cropping index, has increased by more than 13 million hectares since 1952. Understanding the driving forces behind the change in the multiple-cropping index (land use intensity) is not only crucial for analyzing China's future grain production and trade situation, but also for shedding light on the fundamental shift in production methods facing many developing countries as they industrialize and become more urban.

Although converting land from low productive use (e.g. farming) to high productive use (e.g. manufacturing) may be a good thing in many cases, many countries still use strict regulations to govern land conversions, due to either farmer lobbies or the ideology of food security. Therefore, for many developing countries, maintaining or increasing land intensification is more realistic than expanding cultivated area in the process of agricultural development.

Along with industrialization, land use intensity usually undergoes a dramatic change as shown in the newly industrialized Asian (NIA) countries. In the case of Taiwan, the multiple-cropping index rose from 1.2 in 1921 to around 1.6 in the 1960s and 1970s, when rapid industrialization took place. However, by the 1990s, it declined to 1.4 as the opportunity cost of labor in farming had steadily increased (Mao and Schive, 1995). Is China's land use intensity going to follow the same patterns of the NIA countries and start declining? Are there any tensions between industrialization and the grain self-sufficiency policy? The rapid economic growth and large regional variations in China provide us with an opportunity to examine these issues quantitatively.

We develop an analytical framework based on policy and historical details. Compared with previous studies of China's land use, this study has at least two unique features. First, land intensity is modeled separately from arable land area. Most previous studies (Heilig, 1997; Li and Sun, 1997; Fischer, Chen, and Sun, 1998) have just focused on arable land area,

---

at the provincial level readily available and consistently compiled over a long period. The trends of land use may not be severely affected by this problem since most of the under-reporting of arable land occurs in the hilly and mountainous regions (Ash and Edmonds, 1998). Considering that the ratio of under-reporting is rather constant over time, by taking advantage of the availability of a panel data set, we can use regional dummies to largely reduce the systematic measurement errors in our econometric analysis.

thus understating China's grain production capacity. In China, local governments have much authority to procure land for non-agricultural use, whereas the central government responds to the overall food situation by setting policy guidelines for local governments and farmers. Since land is nominally owned by the collective, individual farm households are not allowed to convert their land for non-agricultural use, but they do have the right to cultivate their land and use multiple cropping. Therefore, it is sensible to model the different decision processes separately.

Second, using a 33-year (1965–1997) panel data set at the provincial level, we can quantify the driving forces behind the changes in arable land area and land use intensity separately. This is also an improvement over previous studies on land use, which generally are qualitative or just based on time series data (Brown, 1995; Heilig, 1997; Zhang, Huang, and Rozelle, 1997; Ash and Edmonds, 1998). Using the panel data set, we can also study the interaction between governments and farmers.

The paper is organized as follows: We provide a historical review of Chinese agricultural land use policy in Section 2. Then, in Section 3 we develop an analytical framework to model arable land area and land use intensity. Section 4 presents the econometric results based on a panel data set. The conclusions and policy implications are provided in Section 5. A detailed description of the data is presented in the appendix.

## 2. An Historical Review of China's Agricultural Land Use

Arable land area per capita in China is now less than 0.08 hectares (SSB, 1998), which ranks among the lowest in the world. From the data in Table 5.1, we can obtain more critical impressions about the relationship among land use (arable land and sown area), industrialization, urbanization, and grain trade balance.

Three features are apparent. To begin, it appears that there is a negative relationship between arable land area and industrialization and urbanization. During the period 1952–1997, the arable land area declined by 12 percent, from 108 million hectares to 95 million hectares, while population more than doubled, from less than 0.6 billion to more than 1.2 billion. The ratio of non-agricultural GDP to agricultural GDP, an indicator of industrialization, increased fourfold and the share of

Table 5.1. Basic Information: Land, Urbanization, Industrialization, and Grain Net Export

| Period | Arable Land (million ha) | Sown Area (million ha) | Urbanization (Urban/Total Population) | Industrialization (Non-agr GDP/agr. GDP) | Net Grain Export (million metric tons) |
|---|---|---|---|---|---|
| 1952 | 107.9 | 141.3 | 0.14 | 0.98 | 1.53 |
| 1960 | 104.9 | 150.6 | 0.21 | 3.27 | 1.81 |
| 1961 | 103.3 | 143.2 | 0.19 | 1.76 | 1.68 |
| 1965 | 103.6 | 143.3 | 0.17 | 1.64 | -3.99 |
| 1966 | 103.0 | 146.8 | 0.17 | 1.66 | -3.55 |
| 1967 | 102.6 | 144.9 | 0.17 | 1.48 | -1.71 |
| 1968 | 101.6 | 139.8 | 0.16 | 1.37 | -1.99 |
| 1969 | 101.5 | 140.9 | 0.15 | 1.63 | -1.55 |
| 1970 | 101.1 | 143.5 | 0.15 | 1.84 | -3.24 |
| 1971 | 100.9 | 145.7 | 0.16 | 1.93 | -0.56 |
| 1972 | 100.6 | 147.9 | 0.16 | 2.04 | -1.83 |
| 1973 | 100.2 | 148.5 | 0.16 | 1.99 | -4.23 |
| 1974 | 99.9 | 148.6 | 0.15 | 1.95 | -4.48 |
| 1975 | 99.7 | 149.5 | 0.15 | 2.09 | -0.93 |
| 1976 | 99.4 | 149.7 | 0.15 | 2.05 | -0.60 |
| 1977 | 99.2 | 149.3 | 0.15 | 2.40 | -5.69 |
| 1978 | 99.4 | 150.1 | 0.16 | 2.56 | -6.96 |
| 1979 | 99.5 | 148.5 | 0.17 | 2.21 | -10.70 |
| 1980 | 99.3 | 146.4 | 0.17 | 2.32 | -11.81 |
| 1981 | 99.0 | 145.2 | 0.17 | 2.14 | -13.55 |
| 1982 | 98.6 | 144.8 | 0.18 | 2.00 | -14.87 |

(Continued)

Table 5.1. *(Continued)*

| Period | Arable Land (million ha) | Sown Area (million ha) | Urbanization (Urban/Total Population) | Industrialization (Non-agr GDP/agr. GDP) | Net Grain Export (million metric tons) |
|---|---|---|---|---|---|
| 1983 | 98.4 | 144.0 | 0.18 | 2.03 | −12.10 |
| 1984 | 97.9 | 143.6 | 0.19 | 2.13 | −7.22 |
| 1985 | 96.8 | 143.6 | 0.20 | 2.52 | 3.36 |
| 1986 | 96.2 | 144.2 | 0.20 | 2.69 | 2.10 |
| 1987 | 95.9 | 145.0 | 0.21 | 2.73 | −9.20 |
| 1988 | 95.7 | 144.9 | 0.21 | 2.89 | −8.15 |
| 1989 | 95.7 | 146.6 | 0.21 | 3.00 | −10.01 |
| 1990 | 95.7 | 148.4 | 0.22 | 2.70 | −7.89 |
| 1991 | 95.7 | 149.6 | 0.22 | 3.08 | −2.59 |
| 1992 | 95.4 | 149.0 | 0.23 | 3.59 | 0.39 |
| 1993 | 95.1 | 147.7 | 0.24 | 4.03 | 7.83 |
| 1994 | 94.9 | 149.9 | 0.25 | 3.95 | 4.26 |
| 1995 | 95.0 | 152.4 | 0.26 | 3.88 | −18.67 |
| 1996 | 95.0 | 154.0 | 0.26 | 3.95 | −10.25 |
| 1997 | 95.0 | 154.0 | 0.26 | 4.35 | 4.16 |
| Annual growth rate | | | | | |
| 1952–65 | −0.31 | 0.11 | 1.14 | 4.03 | −21.57 |
| 1966–78 | −0.29 | 0.18 | −0.38 | 3.67 | −7.98 |
| 1979–97 | −0.26 | 0.20 | 2.48 | 3.84 | 1.41 |
| 1952–97 | −0.31 | 0.21 | 1.43 | 3.70 | 5.76 |

*Sources*: Various SSB publications.

urban population rose from 14 percent to about 26 percent. It appears that industrialization and urbanization are among the most important factors explaining the decline of China's agricultural land use.

The second feature is that the intensity of cultivation is on the rise. Figure 5.1 shows that the sown area increased by about 9 percent from 1952 to 1997. The multiple-cropping index (calculated by the authors using the sown and arable areas) increased from 1.3 in 1952 to 1.6 in 1997, indicating that land is being more intensively cultivated. Clearly, the increase in grain production over this same period stems largely from

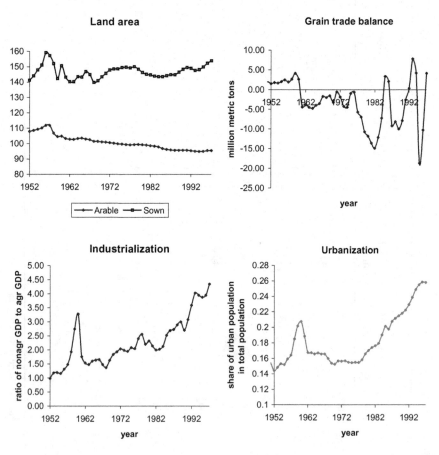

Figure 5.1.   Land use, grain trade, industrialization, and urbanization.

*Source*: Table 5.1.

increased reliance on multiple cropping, higher yields, or some combination of the two.

Third, there seems to be some relationship between the cycles in the grain trade balance and fluctuations in the sown area. Tang (1984) observed that Chinese agriculture had been marked by persistent cycles in grain trade in response to the central government's policies, but it is not clear how various factors play out by just looking at the data in Fig. 5.1. To gain a better understanding of the observed trends, it is necessary to review the history of China's development and agricultural policies.

### 2.1. Land reforms (1949–1955)

Following the establishment of the People's Republic of China in 1949, the state confiscated land from landlords and distributed it equally to peasants in order to improve both equity and efficiency. At that time, China faced a hostile international environment with political isolation and economic embargos. The political leaders adopted two important development strategies — heavy industrial development to catch up with the developed Western countries and a grain self-sufficiency policy to reduce its reliance on international markets (Lin, Cai, and Li, 1996). However, these two policies were not complementary over time.

### 2.2. The Great Leap Forward and the Great Famine (1956–1961)

With net grain exports continuing to rise during this period, the focus of national policy shifted from agricultural to industrial development. The Great Leap Forward boosted steel and other heavy industrial output at the expense of agricultural production in order to catch up with the industrialized nations. The ratio of industrial GDP to agricultural GDP rose threefold in four years, from 0.63 in 1956 to 1.9 in 1960. There was an accompanying sharp decline in arable land and sown area as land and labor were diverted from agricultural production. The sharp decline in the agricultural land base, together with the collectivization movement, resulted in a serious food shortage, triggering the greatest famine in human history (Lin, 1990). During the early 1960s, China had to import up to four million metric tons of grain annually, although it hesitated to do so initially.

## 2.3. Pre-reform (1962–1978)

In reaction to the Great Famine and the increasing reliance on international grain markets, the central government was forced to reconsider its industrialization policy. Grain self-sufficiency emerged as a priority of governmental policy. The slogan "*Yi liang wei gang, gang ju mu zhang*" (Food must be taken as a core; once it is grasped, everything falls into place) reflected the spirit of this policy. One way to reconcile the conflict between the two policies was to reduce the urban population and increase the rural population. Between 1961 and 1964, 20 million state workers and 17 million urban high school students were sent to the countryside for "re-education" by participating in agricultural production. Furthermore, the household registration system, in conjunction with elaborate rationing mechanisms, made migration from rural to urban areas virtually impossible (Chan, 1995). Hence, the share of the urban population kept dwindling until the late 1970s, which kept the demand for land for non-agricultural purposes under control.

By the early 1970s, the potential for boosting sown area through reductions of the urban population was almost exhausted. Therefore, from the early 1970s, all collectives were mobilized to learn from Dazhai (a model village in Shanxi Province) how to claim more land from marginal areas such as hillsides and lakes. During the 1960s and 1970s, grain self-sufficiency was barely achieved, primarily through keeping a large base of rural population and by cultivating more marginal land. The share of grain imports relative to total grain production was controlled at a level of less than 4 percent during this pre-reform period.

## 2.4. Rural reform and afterwards (1979 till present)

With the end of the Cultural Revolution, the Chinese economy was on the verge of collapse. The potential for increasing grain production through developing more marginal land and increasing land utilization under the old collective system was nearly exhausted. By the late 1970s, China had to import 10 million metric tons of grain annually from the world market. In response to the agricultural crisis, the government started to give more flexibility in decision making to individual household producers by officially promoting the household responsibility system nationwide. Thanks to the success of rural reform, agricultural output and grain production (measured at constant prices) grew 7.4 percent and 4.8 percent annually from 1978 to 1984, respectively (SSB, 1998). Because of the rapid agricultural growth, the share of agricultural GDP in total GDP increased from 0.28 to 0.32 during this period. Although there was little change in sown area during this period, a spectacular growth in agricultural output was generated.

The rural reforms released a large amount of labor from agriculture and provided a base for industrial development. Since the mid-1980s, the town and village enterprises (TVEs) in rural areas have experienced phenomenal growth, making it possible to absorb much of the surplus labor in rural areas. Developing the rural industry became a major objective for many local governments (Rozelle and Boisvert, 1995).

The development of the TVEs has not been distributed evenly. The TVEs developed much more rapidly in the coastal provinces than in the inland provinces largely because the coastal areas had better access to capital and new technologies. Meanwhile, localized migration from rural areas to nearby towns was much easier although many institutional barriers still existed for cross-regional migration (Kanbur and Zhang, 1999). As a result, the industrialization level in the coastal provinces was of a different magnitude from that in the inland provinces. In many of the industrialized coastal provinces, farmers faced more opportunities for higher pay from non-farm work. Thus, farmers had less incentive to continue intensive cropping. Accordingly, the multiple-cropping index for many coastal provinces, such as Jiangsu Province, began to fall from their historical highs of the late 1980s (see Fig. 5.2). For China as a whole, there appears to be an inverse U-shaped relationship between cultivation intensity and industrialization, as shown in Fig. 5.3.

For the inland provinces, the dual economy, characterized by lower levels of industrial development and large surpluses of rural labor, was still dominant. Most farmers had to stay on their land because of limited local non-farm opportunities and the potential cost of migration across regions. Thanks to cheaper fertilizers and other land-saving technologies resulting from industrialization throughout China, farmers were able to intensify cropping on their land. As a result, many inland provinces, such as Sichuan Province, experienced an increase in the multiple-cropping index over this period (see Fig. 5.2).

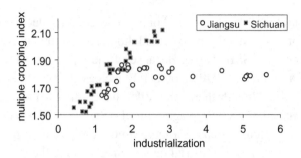

Figure 5.2.    Land use intensity and industrialization in Jiangsu and Sichuan.

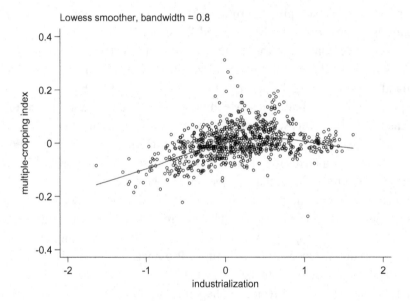

Figure 5.3.    Land use intensity and industrialization for all the provinces.

*Note*: Both industrialization and the multiple-cropping index are expressed in logarithmic form. To eliminate the effect of provincial specific factors, such as weather and soil conditions, on cultivation intensity, we have removed the provincial means from each observation on the multiple-cropping index. The solid line represents the locally weighted regression of the multiple-cropping index on industrialization with a bandwidth at 0.8.

In 1991, a much more open reform policy was advocated in an effort to stimulate the sluggish Chinese economy. The experience of special economic zones in Shenzhen and other coastal cities was regarded as a successful development pathway for others to follow. Many local governmental officials were sent to the South or the East to gain experience. Through this learning experience and in an effort to compete for foreign direct investment, special economic zones were established throughout China. Thousands of acres of arable land were converted to special zones and roads, but many of them were left idle due to the lack of foreign investment. From 1991 to 1996, 0.69 million hectares of arable land were converted for non-agricultural use, among which 0.08 million hectares for use by special zones or real estate development were idle (MOA, 1998).

With the decline in agricultural land area and a lack of attention to agricultural issues, China had to import nearly 20 million metric tons of grain from the international market in 1995 (SSB, 1996). This record high level of imports sent a strong alarm to policy makers. In an attempt to reduce food imports and regain grain self-sufficiency, the central government implemented two measures. First, an administrative decree was issued in April 1997 (MOA, 1998) to keep farmland loss under control. Under this decree, all arable land converted for non-agricultural use during the period 1991–1995 was to be re-examined and the additional conversion of arable land for non-agricultural use was frozen for one year. Second, since provincial governors were responsible for the *mi dai zi* (rice bag) (Crook, 1997), the national self-sufficiency policy became a policy of local self-sufficiency (Huang, Lin, and Rozelle, 1999). Mandatory targets for acreage plans were assigned to lower levels of government. Because of these efforts, both arable land and sown area were stabilized and grain imports were reduced.

Our review of the history of China's agricultural policy reveals that balancing industrial development, urbanization, and food security has been a persistent challenge for the central government. From time to time, the government has had to adopt mandatory administrative means to manage the problem. Urbanization and industrialization are important driving forces behind the conversion of farmland. Nevertheless, the relationship between industrialization and land intensification is more complicated. Total grain production depends on total sown area, which in turn, is determined by the availability of arable land area and land use intensity.

## 3. Conceptual Framework

Ideally, one should analyze land use with a structural model, which takes into account both demand and supply factors. Simply using reduced-form estimation will obscure the underlying process. However, due to the lack of data for land price, labor wage, and agricultural output and input price, it is impractical to do so. Here we adopt an alternative way by modeling arable land area and land use intensity separately as they are determined by different factors. First, we present a model of arable land use for a local government because it has the authority to convert farmland for non-agricultural use. For simplicity, we assume that the total arable land area in each province is fixed, and the land can be used for either agricultural or non-agricultural purposes.[2]

As discussed in the previous section, the demand for agricultural land is likely to be associated with industrialization, urbanization, and national policy. Therefore, the arable land function can be expressed as follows:

$$A_t = F(ind_{t-1}, urb_{t-1}, pop_{t-1}, p_{t-1}, \theta_{t-1}),    (1)$$

where $A_t$ is the arable land area at time $t$; $ind_{t-1}$ refers to the industrialization level at time $t-1$, defined as the ratio of industrial GDP to agricultural GDP; $urb_{t-1}$ is the share of urban population; $pop_{t-1}$ refers to the population growth rate at year $t-1$; $p_{t-1}$ represents the terms of trade, the relative price of agricultural products to the price of non-agricultural products; and $\theta_{t-1}$ is the national grain trade deficit, which we use as a proxy for the overall national policy for land use in year $t-1$.[3]

Generally, one would think that the demand for non-agricultural land use is positively related to industrialization and urbanization. Because the total endowment of land is fixed, if more land is used for industrial and

---

[2] Because most of China is already heavily populated, there are few opportunities to claim marginal land. Arable land may also be lost due to environmental changes caused by soil erosion and salinity (Ash and Edmonds, 1998). Because environmental changes are mostly related to population growth, increase in agricultural inputs, and development of rural enterprises, they can partly be captured by the population and industrialization variables in the model. The data needed for a more complete analysis were not available.

[3] Although rapid change in grain trade positions often has an important impact on the tightness of land use policy, other factors may also affect land policy.

urban development, then less land is left for agricultural use. Therefore, we expect a negative relationship between agricultural land use and industrialization and urbanization. Population pressure might be another factor behind the reduction in arable land. If the terms of trade are favorable to the agricultural sector, then arable land is less likely to be transformed for non-agricultural use. Since the demand for arable land cannot exceed a region's natural limit, it is sensible to model the share of arable land as an aggregate logit model so that a prediction based on the model will not exceed its natural endowment. The model can be written explicitly as

$$\frac{A_t}{\overline{A}} = f(ind_{t-1}, urb_{t-1}, pop_{t-1}, p_{t-1}, \theta_{t-1}), \qquad (2)$$

$$(-) \quad (-) \quad (-) \quad (+) \quad (+)$$

where $f$ is a logit function of the form $\frac{1}{1+\exp(-\beta X)}$ and all the independent variables in $X = \{ind_{t-1}, urb_{t-1}, pop_{t-1}, p_{t-1}, \theta_{t-1}\}$ are in logarithmic form and $\beta$ is a vector of the corresponding coefficients. The hypothesized signs of the coefficients in $\beta$ are shown in parentheses under expression (2). A negative sign for industrialization suggests a conflict between the objectives of the industrialization and grain self-sufficiency policies. Since the total land area $\overline{A}$ and land allocations for non-agricultural uses are generally unknown, we cannot estimate (2) directly. By multiplying through by $\overline{A}$ and taking the logarithm of both sides, the following equation is obtained for estimation:

$$\ln(A_t) = \ln(\overline{A}) - \ln(1 + \exp(-\beta X)). \qquad (3)$$

Since $\ln(\overline{A})$ is fixed for each province, a dummy variable for each province is an appropriate proxy. The dummy variable may also help to eliminate some systematic measurement errors of arable land. Accordingly, Eq. (3) can be estimated by a nonlinear regression procedure.

We also need to model land use intensity. In China, each household is assigned a fixed amount of land by the government; the physical land area is not a decision variable for a farmer. But farmers can influence total output through their decisions on land use patterns and intensity.[4] Farmers base their

---

[4] For one rationale for treating area allocations and yield separately in estimating an agricultural supply function, see McGuirk and Mundlak (1991).

farming decision largely on the economic context and available technologies. Farm-gate product prices, labor wage rate, and the availability of technologies are among the major factors of consideration. To a large extent, the information is exogenous to farmers. For simplicity, but without loss of generality, we assume each farmer has one unit of land. Let us further assume that there are only two production seasons with technologies $F_1$ and $F_2$, respectively, and the price of output is equal to $P$ in both seasons.[5] Moreover, we assume constant returns to scale in agricultural production. If farmers do not have a non-farm working opportunity, they would determine the land use intensity to maximize the total profit from agricultural production as follows:

$$\text{Max } \pi = PF_1(l_1|\Phi) + P\alpha F_2(l_2|\Phi) - w(l_2 + \alpha l_2) - gc(\alpha) \qquad (4)$$
$$\{l_1, l_2, \alpha\}$$

where $l_1$ and $l_2$ are the amounts of labor used in the first (major) season and second season of production, respectively; $\Phi$ is a vector of public investments such as irrigation and agricultural research (R&D); $\alpha$ represents the proportion of the land used for cropping in the second season ($1 + \alpha$ can therefore be regarded as a multiple-cropping index); $c(\alpha)$ is the non-labor cost incurred in second season of production (it is assumed to be convex in $\alpha$); $w$ stands for the agricultural wage; and $g$ is an indicator representing the reduction in non-labor input costs due to cost-reducing technological changes in the industrial sector (an indirect benefit of industrialization).[6] Since we assume that farmers use all their land for production in the main season, the non-labor cost is fixed for the main season and therefore it does not appear in Eq. (4). The first-order conditions for (4) are

$$PF_1'(l_1|\Phi) = w, \qquad (5)$$

$$PF_2'(l_2|\Phi) = w, \qquad (6)$$

$$PF_2(l_2|\Phi) = l_2 w + gc'(\alpha). \qquad (7)$$

---

[5] For simplicity, the subscript for each observation is omitted. In fact, the levels of output price, wage rate, and technology development may vary across regions.

[6] Under the assumption of constant returns to scale for production, the cost neutrality technology in (4) is equivalent to a profit-neutral or Hicks neutral technical change (Chambers, 1988).

A reduced-form solution for the multiple-cropping equation can be expressed as

$$\hat{\alpha} = \hat{\alpha}(P, w, \Phi, g).$$ (8)

From (7), we can conduct a standard comparative static analysis for $\hat{\alpha}$ with respect to $w$, $\Phi$, and $g$:

$$\frac{d\hat{\alpha}}{dP} = \frac{F_2(l_2 \mid \Phi)}{gc''(\hat{\alpha})} > 0$$ (9)

$$\frac{d\hat{\alpha}}{dw} = -\frac{l_2}{gc''(\hat{\alpha})} < 0$$ (10)

$$\frac{d\hat{\alpha}}{d\Phi} = -\frac{P(\partial F_2(l_2 \mid \Phi)/\partial\Phi)}{gc''(\hat{\alpha})} > 0$$ (11)

$$\frac{d\hat{\alpha}}{dg} = -\frac{c'(\hat{\alpha})}{gc''(\hat{\alpha})} < 0.$$ (12)

Since $c$ is convex, the denominators in the above equations are positive. Therefore, a higher agricultural price increases the multiple-cropping index; an increase in the wage lowers the multiple-cropping index, while technical progress in the industrial sector, represented as a decrease in $g$, promotes multiple cropping. Since an increase in public investment generally has a positive impact on production, the numerator in (11) is positive, implying that public investment increases land use intensity.

Unfortunately, we have no usable data on the technology and wage variables for empirical analysis. Hence we develop an argument for using the rate of industrialization and urbanization as proxies for the wage $w$ and technical progress $g$ in the empirical specification of the model (8).

In a dual economy, with limited non-farm opportunities and abundant surplus labor, the agricultural wage is fixed at a subsistence level (Lewis, 1954). With the expansion of the industrial sector and reductions of surplus labor in the rural sector, the agricultural wage will eventually be bid up to a higher level. Writing it more formally, we have

$$\frac{\partial w}{\partial ind} \begin{cases} = 0 & if \ ind \leq ind^* \\ > 0 & if \ ind > ind^* \end{cases},$$ (13)

where *ind\** is the turning point for an economy to increased industrialization from a traditional dual economy.

Another consequence of industrialization is that the unit costs of non-labor inputs generally fall thanks to technological innovations. This is exactly what happened in China where the real prices of fertilizers and pesticides have declined and the quality has increased over the last several decades (SSB, 1998). This leads to the following relation:

$$\frac{\partial g}{\partial ind} < 0. \tag{14}$$

Using these conditions, we can derive the relationship between multiple cropping and industrialization:

$$\frac{d\hat{\alpha}}{dind} = \frac{\partial \hat{\alpha}}{\partial w} \frac{\partial w}{\partial ind} + \frac{\partial \hat{\alpha}}{\partial g} \frac{\partial g}{\partial ind}. \tag{15}$$
$$(-) \quad (0 \text{ or } +) \ (-) \ (-)$$

The signs of the changes in the arguments on the corresponding variables are shown in parentheses. The third and fourth parentheses in (15) reveal that industrialization increases land use intensity by lowering non-labor input costs. When industrialization is low, represented by surplus labor, the effect of industrialization on the agricultural wage is zero or negligible, and the first part of (15) is close to zero. Under these conditions, the net effect of industrialization on land use intensity is positive. However, when industrialization develops to a certain stage, the tighter labor market will put upward pressure on the agricultural wage rate. As the first part of (15) becomes negative and dominant, the multiple-cropping index would begin to decline. Overall, the model suggests an inverse U-shaped relationship between cultivation intensity and industrialization. This is an important hypothesis that is tested empirically below.

Similarly, we can derive the argument for urbanization. In general, urbanization absorbs surplus labor and makes wages higher. Unlike industrialization, urbanization may not provide technology innovations in the farming sector. Therefore, the total effect of urbanization can be expressed as

$$\frac{d\hat{\alpha}}{dind} = \frac{\partial \hat{\alpha}}{\partial w} \frac{\partial w}{\partial urb} + \frac{\partial \hat{\alpha}}{\partial g} \frac{\partial g}{\partial urb}. \tag{16}$$
$$(-) \quad (0 \text{ or } +) \ (-) \ (0)$$

The model suggests a negative relationship between the multiple-cropping index and urbanization.

## 4. Results

To test the above hypotheses empirically, we use a panel data set for 25 provinces that includes land use, industrialization, urbanization, population, and the price ratio for grain procurement to the consumer price index for the years 1965–1997. This dataset includes the earliest year for which systematic data for sown area and terms of trade for each province are available. After taking a one-year lag for all the independent variables, we have 800 observations in total. A detailed description of the data is provided in the appendix.

Table 5.2 gives the estimated model for the arable land area (3). Provincial dummies are used as a proxy for total land area $\bar{A}$ for all the regressions. To capture the effect of regime changes, we create regime dummies by dividing the whole period of 1966–1997 into three periods: pre-reform (1966–1978), reform (1979–1985), and post-reform (1986–1997). The first regression (R1) does not include any regime dummies. In the second (R2), we add a dummy variable for the pre-reform period to check whether there is a systemic difference between the pre-reform period and the rest of the years. The third regression (R3) includes not only the dummy variable for the pre-reform period but also a dummy variable for the post-reform period.

In general, the results are similar across the three specifications. The negative and statistically significant coefficients for industrialization, urbanization, and population growth suggest that these variables are indeed driving forces behind the conversion of farmland for non-farm use. The coefficients on these variables are robust across the three specifications. The coefficients for the grain deficit price ratio have the expected positive signs, but they are poorly determined.

Next, we model land use intensity and test the curvature of the land use intensity with respect to industrialization. Specifically, we want to show that the second derivative is negative. Thus, the model needs to include both a linear and a quadratic term for industrialization.[7] In addition, we use

---

[7] Other functional forms, such as an inverse function, were also tried and the results are similar.

Table 5.2.  Estimated Results for Arable Land Area

|                            | R1         | R2         | R3         |
|----------------------------|------------|------------|------------|
| Industrialization          | −0.106**   | −0.104**   | −0.115**   |
|                            | (0.032)    | (0.036)    | (0.037)    |
| Urbanization               | −0.621**   | −0.615**   | −0.702**   |
|                            | (0.103)    | (0.107)    | (0.115)    |
| Grain trade deficit        | 0.169      | 0.194      | 0.608*     |
|                            | (0.334)    | (0.338)    | (0.364)    |
| Population growth          | −0.424**   | −0.432**   | −0.485**   |
|                            | (0.174)    | (0.175)    | (0.176)    |
| Price ratio                | 0.010      | 0.011      | 0.022      |
|                            | (0.053)    | (0.053)    | (0.052)    |
| Pre-reform (1965–1978)     |            | 0.003      | −0.031     |
|                            |            | (0.018)    | (0.020)    |
| Reform (1979–1985)         |            |            | −0.047     |
|                            |            |            | (0.028)    |
| Log likelihood             | 1648.15    | 1648.17    | 1650.21    |

*Notes*:
1. Results are obtained using the logit equation (3). Province dummies are included but not reported here. One and two asterisks indicate that estimates are at the 10 percent and 5 percent significance levels, respectively. Figures in parentheses are standard errors.
2. The dependent variable is the logarithm of arable land area. All the independent variables are in logarithms and have a one-year lag. The industrialization variable is defined as the ratio of non-agricultural GDP to agricultural GDP; the urbanization variable is represented as the share of urban population in total population; the price ratio variable is the ratio of the grain procurement price index relative to the overall consumer price index.

a quadratic function of urbanization to partly capture the effect of the agricultural wage rate and technical progress. The multiple-cropping index can be estimated as a function of the following variables:

$$\hat{\alpha}_t = \hat{\alpha}(ind_{t-1},\ ind_{t-1}^2,\ urb_{t-1},\ urb_{t-1}^2, pop_{t-1}, p_{t-1},$$
$$irrigation_{t-1},\ R\&D_{t-1}), \qquad (17)$$

where *ind* measures industrialization, expressed as the ratio of non-agricultural GDP to agricultural GDP; *urb* is the share of urban population in total population; *pop* represents the population growth rate, *p* is defined as the ratio of the grain procurement price index to the consumer price index;

*irrigation* is the share of irrigated area relative to total arable area; and *R&D* is the logarithm of total expenditure on agricultural research. To account for possible endogeneity problems, all the variables have a one-year lag.

Table 5.3 presents the estimated results for four different specifications. In all the four specifications, we include provincial dummies to capture the difference in land use intensity due to region-specific factors, such as weather conditions and soil quality. The first regression R1 does not includes regime or year dummies. The second regression (R2) includes two dummies in the intercept, one for the pre-reform period and one for the reform period, to capture the possible effect of policy changes. In the third specification (R3), we replace regime dummies with year dummies, which can capture more year-specific effects. The fourth specification allows coefficients to vary across the three periods by including interaction terms of the independent variables with the regime dummies. The corresponding coefficients for the three different periods are presented in columns 5, 6, and 7.

The positive coefficients for IND and the significant negative sign on $IND^2$ across all the specifications confirm our model's prediction of an inverse U-shaped relationship between land use intensity and industrialization. The coefficients for urbanization are significantly negative, implying that urbanization may absorb labor from the farming sector and reduce land use intensity. The two public inputs — irrigation and R&D — have significant positive effects on land use intensity, which is consistent with the theoretical prediction given by (11). In contrast to the model for arable land area, the coefficient for the reform period is highly significant, confirming the importance of institutional change on cropping intensity.

The results in Table 5.3 can be used to calculate the turning points of land intensity in terms of industrialization. Using the most recent 1997 data and the R4 model in the post-reform period, we find that the multiple-cropping index reaches a maximum when the ratio of agricultural GDP relative to total GDP reaches 24.9 percent. In 1997, all the coastal provinces, except Guangxi Province, surpassed the turning point, while the ten inland provinces did not. Clearly, the potential for future growth in grain output exists primarily in the inland provinces. It may take a long time for all

Table 5.3.    Estimated Results for Land Use Intensity

| | R1 | R2 | R3 | R4 | | |
|---|---|---|---|---|---|---|
| | | | | Pre-reform | Reform | Post-reform |
| IND | 0.224** | 0.224** | 0.165* | 0.206** | 0.307** | 0.515** |
| | (0.022) | (0.021) | (0.023) | (0.025) | (0.065) | (0.073) |
| $IND^2$ | −0.092** | −0.108** | −0.122** | −0.132** | −0.144** | −0.234** |
| | (0.012) | (0.011) | (0.011) | (0.019) | (0.039) | (0.032) |
| URB | −0.250** | −0.391** | −0.706** | −0.487** | −0.058 | −0.521** |
| | (0.114) | (0.113) | (0.108) | (0.194) | (0.234) | (0.251) |
| $URB^2$ | −0.064 | −0.094** | −0.158** | −0.108** | 0.001 | −0.118** |
| | (0.028) | (0.027) | (0.025) | (0.047) | (0.063) | (0.075) |
| Irrigation | 0.072** | 0.083** | 0.031* | 0.069** | 0.131** | 0.092** |
| | (0.018) | (0.017) | (0.018) | (0.020) | (0.025) | (0.025) |
| R&D | 0.008 | 0.050** | 0.037** | 0.075** | 0.016 | 0.048** |
| | (0.011) | (0.012) | (0.016) | (0.015) | (0.019) | (0.013) |
| Population | 0.069 | −0.098 | −0.087 | −0.117 | −3.140** | 0.132 |
| growth | (0.163) | (0.154) | (0.145) | (0.162) | (1.374) | (0.424) |
| Price ratio | −0.098** | −0.028 | −0.047 | −0.024 | 0.016 | −0.140* |
| | (0.032) | (0.030) | (0.041) | (0.042) | (0.051) | (0.078) |
| Pre-reform | | 0.038 | | −0.057 | | |
| (1965–1978) | | (0.015) | | (0.222) | | |
| Reform | | −0.059** | | | 0.874** | |
| (1979–1985) | | (0.010) | | | (0.283) | |
| Year dummies | No | No | Yes** | | | |
| Log likelihood | 764.6 | 810.0 | 803.6 | 806.2 | | |
| AIC | 763.6 | 809.0 | 802.6 | 805.2 | | |

*Notes*:
1. One and two asterisks indicate that estimates are at the 10 percent and 5 percent significance levels, respectively. Figures in parentheses are standard errors.
2. The dependent variable is the multiple-cropping index. All the independent variables, except the regime and provincial dummies, are in logarithms and lagged by one year. IND (industrialization) is represented by the ratio of non-agricultural GDP to agricultural GDP; URB (urbanization) is measured as the share of urban population in total population; Irrigation is the share of irrigated area relative to total arable area; and R&D is the total expenditure on agricultural research.
3. Province dummies are included but not reported here.

provinces to reach or exceed the turning point. However, as provinces become more industrialized, the growth of land use intensity will decrease. Increasing public investment in R&D and irrigation will help improve land use intensity.

## 5. Conclusions and Policy Implications

This paper develops a framework for identifying the determinants of land use in China based on policy and historical events. Separate models for arable land area and multiple cropping are specified to reflect the different decision processes that determine each of them. A panel data set at the provincial level for the years 1965–1997 is constructed from various governmental sources for the empirical analysis. In spite of the complexity of modeling land use, the results are quite encouraging, and they provide us with a better understanding of the driving forces behind the changes in China's grain production.

It is not surprising that the empirical evidence reinforces our hypotheses that industrialization and urbanization are important contributory factors to the conversion of farmland for other uses. These results also underscore the fact that the industrialization and grain self-sufficiency policies, both proposed in the 1950s, are inherently in conflict. Prior to the economic reform in the 1980s, these two objectives were enforced through the household registration system that kept the large rural population in place. Since the reform, the two goals have become more balanced, largely by increasing land productivity through the practice of multiple cropping.

The empirical results show that an inverse U-shaped relationship exists between land use intensity and industrialization. On one hand, industrialization brings down non-labor input costs for agricultural production, promoting the practice of multiple cropping. On the other hand, industrialization, especially the rapid development of rural enterprises, offers more non-farm job opportunities, raising wages and making intensive farming unattractive as surplus labor is exhausted. The results also show a strong negative link between urbanization and land use intensity. Initially the total sown area in a province may expand slightly due to greater cropping intensity. Eventually, as the province further industrializes and urbanizes, the total sown area will shrink, undermining the objective of grain self-sufficiency.

Until recently, the primary way for the government to control farmland loss and increase sown area was through administrative orders, but the efficiency loss from doing so may have been high (Rozelle and Huang, 1999). However, there are several better ways to deal with the potential decline in sown area. First, encouraging freer labor movement across regions will delay the slowdown of cropping intensity in economically advanced provinces. Second, long-term investment in agricultural research should be expanded in order to further increase yields. If the growth rate of yield surpasses the rate of loss in sown area, total grain output will not fall. Third, China should make more use of international trade to exploit its comparative advantage by augmenting the import of land-intensive crops, such as grain, and paying for these with additional exports of labor-intensive commodities. Considering the inherent tensions between the industrialization and grain self-sufficiency policies, raising rural income is a more appropriate national policy.

## Appendix: On Data Sources

Sown area and arable land area are widely used as indictors of agricultural land use. However, it is generally believed that the official statistics for cultivated land area are significantly biased (Ash and Edmonds, 1998; Ministry of Agriculture, 1998). Sown area statistics are a more policy-responsive and consistent indicator.

The sown areas for each province from the period from 1979 to 1997 were obtained from various issues of *China Agricultural Yearbook, China Rural Statistical Yearbook*, and *China Statistical Yearbook*. For earlier years, the data for sown area were taken from *National Agricultural Statistical Materials for 30 Years, 1949–1979*. Some missing observations were supplemented by data in provincial yearbooks. The arable areas from 1980 to 1997 were taken from various issues of *China Agricultural Yearbook* and *China Rural Statistical Yearbook*. For earlier years, the information was taken from *National Water Resource Statistical Materials for 30 Years, 1949–1979*. However, the sown area and arable land data for most provinces only go back to the early 1960s. Therefore, the dataset used in our estimation only covers the period from 1965 to 1997. Tibet, Hainan, and Ningxia are excluded due to lack of consistent data. The three direct administrative cities — Beijing, Shanghai, and Tianjin — are also not included because of their relatively small shares of agricultural production. As a result, the dataset contains 24 provinces.

The total and rural population data for each province for the period from 1982 to 1997 were taken from various issues of *China Agricultural Statistical Yearbook*. Prior to 1982, the data were taken from *China Provincial Historical Statistical Materials, 1949–1989*. Some missing data were estimated based on provincial yearbooks and *National Water Resource Statistical Materials for 30 Years, 1949–1979*. The urban population was estimated by subtracting the rural population from total population. Urban and rural residencies are determined by the household registration system. Generally speaking, rural and urban residents are supposed to specialize in farm work and non-farm work in their registration areas, respectively. The ratio of the urban-to-total-population is used as a proxy for urbanization. However, with the success of the rural reform, many workers have been freed from agricultural activities and have moved to urban areas, especially in big cities, to seek opportunities without any entitlement to subsidies like other urban residents. Consequently, there may be possible biases resulting from using the official registered numbers of rural and urban residents.

Nominal GDP and the annual growth rates of real GDP for industrial, agricultural, and service sectors are available from SSB's *The Gross Domestic Product of China*. The ratio of non-agricultural GDP to the GDP in the agricultural sector is used to measure the level of industrialization. The ratio of industrial GDP to total GDP is not used as a measurement because it would give a declining trend of industrialization due to an increasing share of GDP in the service sector. The previous year's growth rates of real GDP are used as a criterion to select the best neighbor province to imitate.

Total grain import and export data from 1950 to 1991 were downloaded from the USDA/ERS database. The information after 1991 was obtained from various issues of *China Statistical Yearbook*. The Ministry of Foreign Economic Relations and Trade (MOFERT) were responsible for compiling the grain trade statistics prior to 1985. Since 1985, the Customs Department started reporting the trade statistics as well. There are slight differences between the two sources but their trends are similar. As the Customs Department statistics are more reliable (Colby, Crook, and Webb, 1992), we use the data from this source after 1985. Annual aggregate grain production is available from the same sources as the grain trade statistics.

The irrigated area data were taken from various issues of *China Statistical Yearbook*. The agricultural R&D expenditure data for the years following 1986 were taken from various issues of *Statistical Materials on Agricultural Science and Technology* (MOA, 1987–1997). Data for earlier years were obtained from the provincial academies of agricultural sciences. The nominal research expenditure data were deflated to constant 1980 yuan using the national retail price index taken from *China Statistical Yearbook* and transformed to a stock variable following the method outlined in Fan and Pardey (1997).

The agricultural procurement price index and general consumer price index are from *Comprehensive Statistical Data and Materials on 50 Years of New China* (SSB, 1999).

## References

Ash, R.F. and Edmonds, R.L. (1998). "China's Land Resources, Environment and Agricultural Production". *China Quarterly*, 156, pp. 836–879.

Brown, L. (1995). *Who Will Feed China: Wake-Up Call for a Small Planet.* New York: W.W. Norton & Company.

Chambers, R.G. (1998). *Applied Production Analysis.* New York: Cambridge University Press.

Chan, K.W. (1995). "Migration Controls and Urban Society in Post-Mao China". Seattle Population Research Center Working Paper, No. 95–2.

Colby, W.H., Crook, F.W., and Webb, S-E.H. (1992). "Agricultural Statistics of the People's Republic of China, 1949–1990". Economic Research Service, United States Department of Agriculture, 1192. More recent data can be found at http://usda.mannlib.cornell.edu/.

Crook, F.W. (1997). "How Will China's 'Rice Bag' Policy Affect Grain Production, Distribution, Prices, and International Trade?" In *Agricultural Polices in China*. Paris: OECD Publications.

Fan, S. and Pardey, P. (1997). "Research, Productivity, and Output Growth in Chinese Agriculture". *Journal of Development Economics*, 53, pp. 115–137.

Fischer, G., Chen, Y., and Sun, L. (1998). "The Balance of Cultivated Land in China during 1988–1995". International Institute for Applied Systems Analysis (IIASA), Interim Report 98–047.

Heilig, G.K. (1997). "Anthropogenic Factors in Land Use in China". *Population and Development Review*, 23(1), pp. 139–168.

Huang, J., Lin, J., and Rozelle, S. (1999). "What Will Make Chinese Agriculture More Productive?" Paper presented at Conference on Policy Reform in China, November 18–20, Stanford University.

Kanbur, R. and Zhang, X. (1999). "Which Regional Inequality? The Evolution of Rural-Urban and Inland-Coastal Inequality in China, 1983–1995". *Journal of Comparative Economics*, 27, pp. 686–701.

Lewis, W.A. (1954). "Economic Development with Unlimited Supplies of Labor". *Manchester School*, 28, pp. 139–191.

Li, X. and Sun, L. (1997). "Driving Forces of Arable Land Conversion in China". International Institute for Applied Systems Analysis (IIASA), Interim Report 97–076.

Lin, J.Y. (1990). "Collectivization and China's Agricultural Crisis in 1959–1961". *Journal of Political Economy*, 98(6), pp. 1228–1252.

Lin, J.Y., Cai, F., and Li, Z. (1996). *The China Miracle: Development Strategy and Economic Reform*. Hong Kong: The Chinese University Press.

Mao, Yu-Kang and Schive, Chi (1995). "Agricultural and Industrial Development in Taiwan". In John W. Mellor (ed.), *Agriculture on the Road to Industrialization*. Baltimore: Johns Hopkins University Press, pp. 23–66.

McGuirk, A. and Mundlak, Y. (1991). *Incentives and Constraints in the Transformation of Punjab Agriculture*. Washington, DC: International Food Policy Research Institute Report No. 87.

Ministry of Agriculture (MOA). (Various issues). *China Agricultural Yearbook*. Beijing: China Statistical Publishing House.

Ministry of Agriculture (MOA). (Various issues). *Statistical Materials on Agricultural Science and Technology*. Beijing: China Statistical Publishing House.

Rozelle, S. and Boisvert, R.N. (1995). "Control in a Dynamic Village Economy: The Reforms and Unbalanced Development in China's Rural Economy". *Journal of Development Economics*, 46, pp. 233–252.

Rozelle, S. and Huang, J. (1999). "Grain Market Reform, Stage? A Review of Performance and Policy". Paper presented in the Annual American Agricultural Economics Association Meetings at Nashville, TN, August 8–11, 1999.

Smil, V. (1994). "China's Agricultural Land". *China Quarterly*, 158, pp. 414–429.

State Statistical Bureau (SSB). (Various Years). *China Price Statistical Yearbook*. Beijing: China Statistical Publishing House.

State Statistical Bureau (SSB). (Various years). *China Rural Statistical Yearbook*. Beijing: China Statistical Publishing House.

State Statistical Bureau (SSB) (Various years). *China Statistical Yearbook.* Beijing: China Statistical Publishing House.

State Statistical Bureau (SSB) (1990). *National Water Resource Statistical Materials for 30 Years, 1949–1979.* Beijing: China Statistical Publishing House.

State Statistical Bureau (SSB) (1998). *The Gross Domestic Product of China (1952–1995).* Dalian: Dongbei University of Finance and Economics Press.

State Statistical Bureau (SSB) (1998). *Historical Statistical Materials for Provinces, Autonomous Regions and Municipalities (1949–1989).* Beijing: China Statistical Publishing House.

State Statistical Bureau (SSB) (1999). *Comprehensive Statistical Data and Materials on 50 Years of New China.* Beijing: China Statistical Publishing House.

Tang, A.M. (1984). "An Analytical and Empirical Investigation of Agricultural in Mainland China, 1952–1978". Chung-Hua Institution for Economic Research, Taiwan.

Zhang, L., Huang, J., and Rozelle, S. (1997) "Land Policy and Land Use in China". In *Agricultural Policies in China.* Paris: OECD Publications.

# CHAPTER 6

# Assessing Urban Spatial Growth Patterns in China during Rapid Urbanization*

*Chengri Ding and Xingshuo Zhao*

This paper examines three trendy urban spatial development patterns in China: special economic zones, university towns, and central business districts, as compared to mixed land use. The findings suggest the potential negative consequences and associated efficiency losses that may affect the long-term sustainable growth of cities. Some of the issues and problems generated by these patterns resemble urban sprawl but others represent disconnection between urban functions and forms in terms of efficiency in land use and development. It is unlikely that these patterns can be avoided, even with emerging market forces, without substantial reforms in planning and administration that govern and influence the behavior of local government officials. Meanwhile, the current city development and urban spatial form across Chinese cities suggest that the model of mixed land use may not be as desirable as in the US. Therefore, urban development should be focused on the creation and development of employment (sub)centers and urban spatial development in conjunction with these (sub)centers through the integration of land use and transportation.

## 1. Introduction

The recent increase in energy prices and heightened consciousness of the contribution of urban energy use to global climate change has renewed interest in issues of urban form. The economic, environmental, social, and

---

* Reprinted by the author's permission from *The Chinese Economy*, 44(1): 45–71.

health-related costs of inefficient spatial development have emerged as the focus of attention. Perhaps the most studied and documented urban spatial deficiency is sprawl. Characterized by low-density, discontinuous, and/or homogenous land development, urban sprawl leads to greater dependency on automobiles, raising commuting distance and time (Soule, 2006; Sierra Club, 1998). In addition to decreasing the effective size of the labor market (Prud'homme, 2000), this leads directly to increased energy consumption and environmental pollution. There have been a number of estimates of the costs of urban sprawl in the US: avoidable costs of time and fuel were computed to be $78 billion in 2000 (Smart Growth America); incremental costs of infrastructure services were, on average, $1.13 for every dollar of revenue generated; and development costs were calculated to be 7 percent more compared to compact and mixed land use alternatives (Green, 2006). Other negative impacts of urban sprawl cited include farmland loss, rising tax burden, increasing social and income segregation, and deteriorating public health (Soule, 2006, Sierra Club, 1998; Victoria Transport Policy Institute, 2008).

Driven by the unprecedented urbanization and industrialization in general and by the massive fixed asset investment and transport development, particularly since the early 1990s, Chinese cities have witnessed remarkable spatial expansion and fundamental reshaping of their landscapes.[1] The total built-up area of cities and towns, for instance, has increased from 7,438 sq kilometers to 25,973 sq kilometers between 1981 and 2002.[2] The growth rate for big cities (prefecture-level cities) is even greater. Their share of total built-up area increased from 68.6 percent to 76.4 percent in just four years between 1998 and 2002, implying that their growth outpaced that of medium and small urban

---

[1] For instance, the urbanization rate increased from 18 percent in 1978 to 40 percent in 2007 while per capita income rose from $300 in 1978 to $2,482 in 2007. Fixed asset investments jumped from $61.63 billion in 1988 to $1960.56 billion in 2007 while total investments in housing and real estate increased from $44.58 billion in 1986 to $470.25 billion in 2000. All figures in this paper are converted into dollars at the exchange rate of $1 = 7RMB, although it was around $1 = 8.2 RMB in the period of 1998–2004. Data sources: http://www.tecn.org/data/detail.php?id = 25401; http://kfq.ce.cn/tj/200810/07/t20081007_16990732.shtml; and http://tjsj.baidu.com/pages/jxyd/14/3/97b28adee5eaefe23103f6d7703f3a7c_0.html.

[2] *Source*: http://tjsj.baidu.com/pages/jxyd/26/72/a26bcebda9a261a9ef5f9a72c926a326_0.html.

settlements.[3] The reshaping of urban spatial structure is manifested mainly in changes of land use patterns and increases in land use intensity. Along with the land market development, low-value-added activities such as industrial warehouses in central locations have been relocated to urban fringes and their original sites allocated to high-value-added commercial and retail activities instead (Ding, 2004). The rapid erection of skyscrapers in old cities indicates increases in land use intensity.

Although emerging market forces and pricing mechanisms have begun to influence land development and urban form (Ding, 2004), the ways they are occurring across Chinese cities point to the still predominant roles of non-market factors such as officials behavior and institutional modalities of planning. Therefore, this paper will focus on the investigation, assessment, and evaluation of the emerging urban spatial development patterns in the light of the existing theory. We will limit ourselves to focus on patterns that are typical, prevalent, and/or sizable across Chinese cities and whose negative effects would be enormous. Some of the issues and problems generated by these patterns resemble urban sprawl but others represent disconnection between urban functions and forms in terms of efficiency in land use and development. The most egregious drivers of inefficient spatial expansion are the construction of special economic zones (SEZs), the development of university towns, and the trend towards new central business districts (CBDs). The paper will also look at the implications of promoting mixed land use in China under the aegis of the smart growth platform. These investigations are important for China because of the unprecedented scale and scope of spatial expansion in an era of high energy prices and greater awareness of

---

[3] Again, this resulted from faster economic growth in the non-agricultural economy in big cities compared to small cities. The total GDP of the tertiary sector produced by prefecture-level cities was $229.2 billion and accounted for 63.74 percent of the total national GDP of the tertiary sector in 1998. Both the total GDP of the tertiary sector and its share jumped to $855.5 billion and 71.50 percent in 2006, respectively. The increase in concentration of industrial activities in big cities is in even more striking. The secondary industry's GDP produced by prefecture-level cities was $259.4 billion and accounted for 47 percent of the total GDP in that sector. These numbers increased to $946.1 billion and 65.07 percent in 2006, respectively (Note: (1) Here we refer to GDP by non-primary economies in *shixiaqu* (city districts) instead of *quanshi* (city administrative territories) are used; (2) Figures are calculated from data from 1999 and 2007 statistical yearbooks of China.)

environmental consequences. The importance is also magnified by the irreversible and long-lasting impacts of urban spatial development. The paper is organized as follows: Section 2 reviews the theory and empirical evidence with regard to urban spatial form. Section 3 identifies emerging urban spatial patterns in China and carries out primary assessment. We mainly focus on special economic zones (SEZs), university towns, and CBDs. Section 4 discusses mixed land use which has been proposed as one of smart growth urban forms in the US and its implications in China. Section 5 concludes.

## 2. Why Does Urban Form Matter?

### 2.1. *Urban spatial form*

Urban spatial form can be characterized by type and intensity of land use; typical measures of intensity are population density, employment density, and capital density.[4] Agglomeration economies, positive externalities, and spillover effects attract firms and businesses to locate together, creating clustering patterns of employment centers or nodes. A central business district is one such kind of employment center. Urban spatial structure or form appears the simplest in a monocentric city where the majority of jobs are assumed to be located in the CBD. Employment density, population density, land use intensity, and land prices all decline away from the CBD while commuters travel between the CBD jobs and suburban homes. Although both employment and population densities decay, the slope of population density is much flatter than that of employment density. When there are multiple employment (sub)centers, the urban spatial form becomes more complicated and so do spatial traffic flows. However, in general, the fundamentals of the monocentric city such as declining land prices, population density, and building density away from the (sub)center(s) remain unchanged.

Urban spatial form evolves over time, even though it shows a high degree of resilience and a slow rate of change in most cases. Rising car

---

[4] Due to data issues population density distribution is far more studied than employment density distribution. Building height and building density can be used as a proxy for capital density (total capital investment on a unit of land).

ownership and increased accessibility due to improvements in transportation not only encourage job decentralization and population suburbanization but also cause flattening of the land price and population density gradients. The fact that employment distribution has a steeper curve than population distribution has not changed over time, at least in the preceding 200 years.[5]

## 2.2. *Urban form and urban growth*

The linkage between urban form and urban economic growth is mediated by agglomeration economies that facilitate labor pooling, reduce costs of production in manufacturing and transportation, and promote spillovers in technology and management (Ciccone and Hall, 1996; Sedgley and Elmslie, 2004; Gabe, 2004). Clustered employment and non-residential activities are beneficial to the creation, transfer, and use of knowledge (Lorenzen and Maskell, 2004; Jaffe *et al.*, 1993; Phelps, 2004).[6] The increasing size and concentration of the population and workers promotes the chances of face-to-face contact, which "is an efficient communication technology, can help solve incentive problems, can facilitate socialization and learning, and provides psychological motivation" (Storper and Venables, 2004). By facilitating face-to-face contact, clustering of firms and workers increases localized interactions that promote technological innovation. Face-to-face contact also plays important roles in business development and social networking. Therefore, cities are hubs for innovation in the production of ideas and knowledge and in their commercialization (Feldman and Audretsch, 1999; Jaffe, Trachtenberg and Henderson, 1993).

Urban density is an important determinant of increasing economic returns to scale which facilitates the growth of a city due to positive feedback. Ciccone and Hall (1996) provide empirical evidence of the

---

[5] On average, the population density within 0–5 miles from the CBD is 7,700 persons per sq mile across American cities while the employment density is 24,000 persons per sq mile (Glaeser, undated).

[6] Increases in travel distance and time are measured against a hypothetical and unrealistic model of mixed land use in which jobs and housing are balanced.

connection between urban density and labor productivity. They conclude that doubling employment density in a county will increase average labor productivity by 6 percent. Henderson, Kuncoro, and Turner (1995) find that the concentration of employment is correlated with high employment opportunity while Gabe (2004) reveals a strong association between industrial concentration and industrial outputs. Sedgley and Elmslie (2004) find that population density has a positive and significant relationship with the extent of innovation.

### 2.3. *Urban form and transportation*

The linkage of urban form and transportation is complex and the literature presents mixed conclusions. One school of thought argues that centralized employment with decentralized population distribution enjoys many advantages in urban transportation such as low transportation cost, high percentage of public transit ridership, and low percentage of auto usage (Bertaud, 2003). Rising income, improving transportation accessibility, and higher car ownership, however, lead to urban sprawl which results in increased commuting time over longer distances. This casts doubts on the unequivocal transportation cost advantage of the monocentric city by suggesting that jobs and housing can be better balanced in subregions or along corridors by job decentralization and population suburbanization to reduce the overall transport demand (Gordon and Richardson, 1997).

The view that job decentralization and the emergence of subcenters of employment concentration, characterizing the development of a polycentric city, result in lower total travel demand has been challenged both theoretically and empirically (Cervero and Wu, 1998; McMillen, 2003; McDonald and Prather, 1994). McMillen (2003) reveals that a positive correlation exists between population and commuting costs as dependent variables and with subcenters as the independent variable. This conclusion is also supported by Cervero and Wu (1998), whose study concludes that the decentralization of employment centers does not lead to decreased commuting times. Cervero and Wu (1998) find that increases in the number of employment centers and the size and density of these employment centers are accompanied by increases in average commute vehicle miles traveled (VMT) per worker, decreases in the public transit share, and increases in the share of commutes by drive-alone automobiles.[7] Other studies conclude that the lowest transportation demand is produced by having centrally located businesses where employees use public transit rather than having people work in peripheral locations (Naess and Sandberg, 1996; Lahti, 1994). In theory, job heterogeneity and a high percentage of two-income households make it less likely that job decentralization will shorten commuting distances (Naess and Sandberg, 1996; Cervero and Wu, 1998). This is of particular importance since Chinese cities have a high percentage of two-income households.

For Chinese cities, particularly many small and medium-sized ones, the existing literature implies that job decentralization may not help to reduce urban travel demand as expected mainly because of a lack of spatial concentration of employment due to the wide spread of mixed land use. Since 1949, Chinese cities have been shaped by the growth of *danwei*-type development compounds that are distinguished by a high degree of mixed land use (Ding, 2009; Gaubatz, 1995). The *danwei*-type development compounds disperse jobs widely over urban built-up areas. Therefore, the development of employment clustering nodes can be constructive to urban agglomeration economies and a transit-friendly urban built-up environment. This is empirically supported by international evidence of the advantages of centralized employment with respect to travel demand. Studies in Norwegian regions suggest that the advantages of having workplaces in urban areas or central locations include (1) decreased average commuting distance; (2) increased share of public transit usage and decreased single-driver motor usage; and (3) lower energy consumption (Naess and Sandberg, 1996).

---

[7] The combined effects of the growth of employment (sub)centers in terms of number, size, and density of employment are that average commute VTM per employee rose from 7.1 to 8.7 while the public transit share declined from 19.3 percent to 15.4 percent during the period of 1980–1990, respectively (Cervero and Wu, 1998).

## 3. Emerging Urban Spatial Patterns in Chinese Cities and Assessments

We focus on three typical urban spatial development forms: special economic zones, university towns, and central business districts. They are identified mainly because they are prevalent and sizable so that any impacts would be substantial. It is recognized that qualitative assessment of urban spatial patterns requires extensive data in disaggregated form. This kind of data is not readily available. Therefore, this paper takes a different approach in its assessment, mainly through theoretical inquiry and international references and comparisons.

### 3.1. *Special economic zones*

### 3.1.1. *Development*

A special economic zone is an administratively established geographic region that offers more liberal economic and/or legal incentives than others. It is usually established to attract foreign investment and to promote international trade.[8] Following the great success of SEZs, they have spread widely into many other cities. In 2004, there were 6,866 SEZs of all levels (national, provincial, and municipal).[9] Given the total of 665 cities in China (prefecture-level and county-level cities combined), this implies over ten SEZs per city on average regardless of city size, development potential, or economic status.

Some SEZs have emerged as important hubs in terms of industrial output, employment concentration, and FDI. A survey of 54 national SEZs in 2007, for instance, revealed that they (1) contributed $181.37 billion to the GDP produced industrial added value of $131.42 billion and industrial output of $548.95 billion; (2) generated tax revenues of $203.68 billion; (3) engaged in international trade worth $330.88 billion; and (4) attracted

---

[8] There are free trade zones, export processing zones, industrial estates, urban enterprise zones, high-tech industrial parks, science and technology parks, economic exploitation zones, and others.

[9] The majority of SEZs are approved by subnational government. For instance, in 2008, there were 1,568 SEZs approved by the State Council. Among them 222 were national-level SEZs and 1,346 were provincial- and city-level ones.

FDI of \$17.32 billion. The growth rates of these macroeconomic indicators were significantly higher than the national averages. For instance, the growth rate of GDP in these 54 SEZs in 2007 was 25.5 percent, more than double the national average for the same period. In addition, land productivity is very high. These 54 SEZs accounted for 0.1 percent of total SEZ land but contributed 5.15 percent of the national GDP, 4.1 percent of national tax revenues, and 23.2 percent of total FDI.[10] SEZs are also distinguished by high employment concentration. The average employment size is almost 100,000 workers per SEZ, giving 5.35 million jobs on the total developed land of 664 sq kilometers. The average employment density is 8,000 per sq kilometer; in some it exceeds 20,000 workers per sq kilometer (such as the Hongqiao SEZ in Shanghai) while others are exceptional in terms of employment size. For instance, the Shenzhen SEZ in 2005 provided more than 422,500 jobs on 70 sq kilometers of land.

### 3.1.2. *Assessment*

Notwithstanding their outstanding contributions to economic success, the ways in which SEZs are developed in China create two prominent spatial problems.[11] The first is related to excessive land conversion. Over-designation of SEZs and lack of capital investment cause much converted land to remain idle and undeveloped. The 6,866 SEZs occupied more than 38,000 sq kilometers of land in 2004. The estimated cost of fully serving 1 sq kilometer with infrastructure such as roads, sewers,

---

[10] *Source*: http://www.qetdz.com.cn/zhengcefazhiju/xxdt_content.asp?news_id=12197.

[11] The development of SEZs motivated by fiscal and economic decentralization results in local competition and contributes to overheating of the economy manifested in overinvestment that leads to excess industrial capacity. Almost all major manufacturing sectors in China are characterized by excess production capacity. The value of warehoused manufacturing goods, for instance, was estimated at \$200 billion in 2006. Steel production capacity in 2005 was estimated at 470 million tons against an actual demand of 370 million tons. The ratio of automobile production capacity to market absorption was 1.47:1 in 2005. Other industrial sectors with significant excess capacities include electrolytic aluminum, ferroalloy, coke, calcium carbide, automobile, copper smelting, cement, electric power, coal, and textile goods. The petrochemical, paper box, chemical fertilizer, domestic electric appliance, micro-computer, and shipbuilding industries are also characterized by excess production capacity.

water, and electricity is over $28.6 million.[12] It is therefore not surprising to observe significant amounts of idle and wasted land resources in SEZs due to the lack of capital and actual demand for production. Along with the concerns over rising social unrest due to land requisition from farmers, farmland depletion and food security, overheating of the economy and the risk of high inflation, this realization triggered the central government to take aggressive measures against the SEZ fever; more than 4,800 SEZs were cancelled in the summer of 2004 and 24,900 sq kilometers of land was eliminated as a result (accounting for 64.5 percent of total SEZ land). Out of this, over 1,300 sq kilometers have been forced to be returned for agricultural use (Cao, 2004).

The second problem is related to the satellite type of SEZ development. Many SEZs are located at the urban fringe and are home to both the jobs and the residents. These create multiple satellite towns even in small and medium-sized cities. For instance, Langfang, which is located between Beijing and Tianjin, is a city of slightly over 4 million on a territory of 6,429 sq kilometers. Langfang is a medium-sized city since the total urban population in 2005 was 400,000 in the central built-up areas. Its administrative areas include one city and eight districts, and each of them has one provincial-level SEZ (Fig. 6.1).[13] By 2008, the total planned area of these SEZs amounted to 208 sq kilometers (Table 6.1).[14]

This kind of dispersed SEZ is common across Chinese cities. Kunshan, located between Shanghai and Suzhou, is one such medium-sized city with a population of 600,000 with Kunshan *hukou* in 2007. In 2007, 12 SEZs spread over the entire 921 sq kilometers of Kunshan's territory provided jobs for a floating population of 1.4 million that worked as *nongmingong* (so-called rural migrant workers). Lacking skills, *nongmingong* most often end up in low-paid jobs and their shelter needs are accommodated through workplace housing, rental housing, or enclaves around their workplaces

---

[12] It costs 200 million RMB to serve 1 sq kilometer.

[13] There are nine provincial-level SEZs in the city and one of them, located in the city proper, is developed in two spatially separate locations: one is Langfang SEZ and the other is Longhe SEZ.

[14] In 2005, more than 5,000 hectares of land development was completed and these nine SEZs contributed 35.1 percent and 45.5 percent to the total GDP and fiscal revenues, respectively.

Figure 6.1.    Locations of Langfang's SEZs.

Table 6.1.    Planned Areas of Langfang's SEZs

| SEZs | Planned Land (sq km) |
| --- | --- |
| Langfang | 38 |
| Yanjiao | 42 |
| Xianghe | 6 |
| Bazhou | 8.6 |
| Gu'an | 10 |
| Yongqing | 16 |
| Wenan | 30 |
| Dacheng | 20 |
| Dachang | 10 |
| Longhe | 28 |

(Mobrand, 2004). Each SEZ thus emerges as a spatial development node or nucleus in which jobs and housing are balanced but there is little integration of labor markets in the city. The dispersal of SEZs decreases labor mobility and negatively affects agglomeration economies in production, labor pooling, and spillover effects.

The development of satellite towns proves inefficient in a number of ways. First, the jobs-housing imbalance increases, particularly between permanent and non-*nongmingong* residents, as evidenced in other countries (Cervero, 1998; Jacquemin, 1999; Dupont, 2004; Richardson, Bae and Jun, 2002). Workplace housing provides temporary solutions for *nongmingong* but alternative housing options should be sought to better serve the needs of the enormous number of rural-urban migrants projected during rapid urbanization and industrialization in the future. Job accessibility, urban service provision, and affordable housing for these low-income individuals and households will be among the top issues that would be better addressed in large, comprehensive, and heterogeneous job markets such as those in metropolitan areas rather than in satellite towns.

Second, the increasing jobs-housing imbalance inevitably causes commuting time and distance to rise. Levine (1990) provides empirical evidence that low-income households commute longer distances during employment decentralization while Jun and Hur (2001) conclude that having an industrial town outside Seoul increased the total vehicle kilometers traveled per worker by 1,510 kilometers per year. Furthermore, spreading out SEZs in the urban fringes creates auto dependency and a transit-unfriendly built-up environment.

Third, satellite town development has also resulted in inequality and class segregation. The cost of living and lack of public transportation creates exclusionary conditions in which only the middle and upper classes can afford to live in the newly developed towns in the urban fringes. Finally, the spreading of SEZs implies high costs in transportation provision for travelers as well. Enlarged burdens in infrastructure provision may indirectly increase the costs of business development. In sum, it is desirable to cluster these employment activities spatially as they can benefit greatly from internal scale economies and agglomeration economies in production.

## 3.2.  University towns

### 3.2.1.  Development

The development of university towns is one of the most striking urban spatial developments in terms of scale.[15] By the beginning of this decade, over 50 university towns were developed across the country. Each is a large-scale land development initiative accommodating multiple universities clustered in a concentrated geographic region (Table 6.2). The average size of these university towns is just less than 20 sq kilometers with almost 12 universities each. These university towns share many features and we will examine one of them: Guangzhou University Town.

Guangzhou University Town, one of largest of its kind, started construction in 2001. It is located about 17 kilometers from the center of Guangzhou City and planned on 43.3 sq kilometers of land with a target enrollment of 300,000 to 350,000 students. The completion of the university town

Table 6.2.    University Towns

| Name | City | Area (sq km) | No. of Universities | Current Enrollment |
|------|------|--------------|---------------------|--------------------|
| Shahe | Beijing | 8 | 36 | 80,000 (by 2010) |
| Liangxiang | Beijing | 6.5 | 5 | |
| Yuelushan | Changsha | 3.33 | 13 | 72,000 |
| Changzhou | Changzhou | 13.33 | 6 | 54,000 |
| Chongqing | Chongqing | 33 | 14 | 80,000 |
| Guangzhou | Guangzhou | 43.3 | 10 | 100,000 |
| Hainan | Haikou | 6.67 | 3 | 22,000 |
| Xiasha | Hangzhou | 10 | 14 | 40,000 |
| Dongfang | Langfang | 13.3 | 27 | 40,000 |
| Xianlin | Nanjing | 70 | 11 | 110,000 |
| Songjiang | Shanghai | 4.83 | 7 | 80,000 |
| Shenzhen | Shenzhen | 2 | 5 | 10,000 |
| Jimei | Xiamen | 31.32 | 10 | 200,000 (planned) |
| Longzihu | Zhengzhou | 22 | 5 | 117,000 (planned) |

---

[15] This is driven partly by rapid increases in the enrollment of higher education institutes and partly by the national policy to promote a knowledge-based economy. The growth rates of college enrollment in 1999 and 2001 were 48 percent and 44 percent, respectively.

development involves multiple phases of construction. The first phase is the construction of Xiaoguwei Island of 18 sq kilometers, which will house ten universities. The physical layout of the university town deserves attention: It features three ring roads that separate different land uses in the town (Fig. 6.2). The land surrounded by the innermost ring road is used for a big central stadium, physical recreation facilities, and open/green space. The land between the first and second ring roads is used for student dormitories while classrooms, offices, and administrative buildings are constructed between the second and third ring roads. The third ring road serves as a

Figure 6.2.   Guangzhou University Town.

A: Guangdong University of Technology
B: Southern China University of Technology
C: Guangzhou Medical University
D: Guangzhou University of Chinese Medicine
E: Guangzhou University of Foreign Language and Trade

F: Sun Yat-Sen University
G: Xinghai Conservatory
H: Southern China Normal University
I: Guangzhou University
J: Guangzhou College of Fine Arts

*Source*: http://www.gzuc.net/zhinan/ucmap.html.

buffer on the river shore, separating the town from the off-campus communities and neighborhoods.

### 3.2.2. Assessment

The preliminary assessment of university towns indicates that there are three main issues. First, clustering of universities may help to build inter-university connections and intellectual resource sharing but they create physical barriers to intra-university communication. This is because the majority of universities relocate some colleges and programs into newly established universities towns while their central administrative units and other colleges remain on old campuses. Shenzhen University Town has only graduate programs for several colleges while Zhejiang University has moved its undergraduates into Zijingang University Town. There is no evidence that inter-campus collaboration has more added value compared to intra-campus linkages. Therefore, the opportunity costs of physical separation within universities may well exceed any gains from clustering different universities.

Second, the size and spatial arrangement in some cases diminishes the potential of resource sharing between or among universities. For instance, it is difficult, if not impossible, for students to take classes at other universities in Guangzhou University Town. Since ten universities have their classrooms built along the outside ring on the island, the average distance between department buildings on the opposite side of the island is 4.5–5 kilometers. Unless school buses are provided, sharing classes will be a real issue. This creates a dilemma for school administrations. The provision of school buses will have cost implications while inter-university class sharing will be impossible without school buses. If students cannot benefit from the presence of other nearby universities, the rationale for the clustering becomes questionable.

Third, there are no documented advantages or benefits of creating a university compound that is home to ten universities and 200,000–400,000 students. Conventional wisdom is that this is too big. Big is not always good if the returns to scale are not commensurate. Certainly there seems to be no economic justification to build a dining hall with a capacity to feed 20,000 people at the same time as is the case at Zhejiang University Town in Hangzhou. Dinners or lunches would be less crowded if there are many small restaurants spread over the entire compound. The size is impressive, but the induced trips are unnecessary and undesirable.

Fourth, university towns are developed in the urban fringes and in many cases in the middle of nowhere (for instance in Shenzhen). The isolated and remote locations of university towns raise doubts about their spillover effects in general and their impacts on the local knowledge-based economy in particular. Their long-term impacts remain to be seen, but the short-term impacts appear minimal, if any.

Finally, the clustering of universities in a spatially compact fashion also has long-term consequences. It is anticipated that income will continue to grow along with industrialization and urbanization in China over the next couple of decades. The demand for higher education, therefore, will increase accordingly, which will inevitably require university expansion. However, each campus in a university town is so packed that there is little space left for additional construction. This implies that any expansion will have to take place on other sites or in other locations, creating multiple campuses for a university.

### 3.3. *Central business districts*

### 3.3.1. *Development*

Since the 1990s, many large cities (with populations exceeding 1 million) in China began to construct new CBDs. By 2002, 36 cities (such as Beijing, Shanghai, Guangzhou, Shenzhen, Zhengzhou, etc.) had planned or established a new CBD. As the economy continues to grow and living standards rise, non-manufacturing jobs become increasingly important. Therefore, building CBDs for non-manufacturing jobs such as commercial, retail, service jobs (e.g. in the finance and banking sectors) to be concentrated in compact geographic areas is a vital development strategy. In addition, rising energy prices and growing concerns over global warming and the environment make it extremely critical to promote mass transit and to limit and restrict the usage of private cars. The high density in and around CBDs for both employment and the population will help to encourage non-motorized trips and increase the share of ridership of mass transit alternatives.

A CBD is distinguished by a high employment concentration, commercial and retail-oriented activities, skyscrapers, and high traffic congestion.

An international comparison reveals that the average employment density is more than 30,000 workers per sq kilometer (Table 6.3) in selected cities. The highest density is in New York with more than 238,000 jobs per sq kilometer in its small and well-defined CBD with an area of 3.11 sq kilometers. By contrast, Tokyo's three inner wards are treated as one of its CBDs in which 2,434,200 jobs were offered in 2001 in an area of 42.2 sq kilometers, yielding an average employment density of 57,683 jobs per sq kilometer. The average employment density in Tokyo appears much lower than New York's but this is a misleading comparison since the respective land usages are very different. New York's CBD is comprised of commercial (including office space) and retail activities while there are many non-CBD-type land uses in Tokyo's three wards. If similar criteria are used to delineate Tokyo's CBD, the two cities may have a much closer employment density than shown in Table 6.3.[16]

Another striking physical feature that makes a CBD stand out in the city landscape is the clustering of commercial skyscrapers. The average FAR in the core of Seoul's CBD is over 10 while the rest of the CBD and subcenters have a FAR of 8. Land development for residential uses, has FAR values ranging between 0.5 and 4, much lower than those in Seoul's CBD and other subcenters. The striking contrast between the CBD's commercial development and other predominantly residential uses is similar in many other cities. For instance, the FAR value in Singapore's CBD ranges between 8 and 25 while land for residential uses have FARs between 1.5 and 4. Residential development close to the CBD has a higher density with the FAR going up to 6.

CBDs in Chinese cities have similar physical features as those observed in Western cities. Land values are high, and skyscrapers are concentrated.[17] But unlike Western cities, CBDs in China have low land use

---

[16] This leads to the question of how CBDs should be defined and delineated. Different indexes such as population density, employment density, floor area ratio (FAR), land value, and land use have been used to delineate CBDs and all of them have deficiencies in one way or another (see Murphy [1972] for more detailed discussions).

[17] Land in Chongqing's CBD was sold at the price of more than $3,214 per sq meter (15 million RMB per *mu*) in 2009. *Source*: http://office.sz.focus.cn/news/2009-05-05/670144.html.

Table 6.3.    Employment Density in CBDs: International Comparison

| City | Area (sq km) | Employment (10,000) | Year | Employment Density (job/sq km) |
|---|---|---|---|---|
| Boston | 8.54 | 25.82 | 1990 | 30,227 |
| Calgary | 2.85 | 8.67 | 1990 | 30,445 |
| Houston | 3.88 | 11.89 | 1990 | 30,615 |
| Vancouver | 3.37 | 10.40 | 1990 | 30,901 |
| Osaka | 37.28 | 131.79 | 2001 | 35,352 |
| Chicago | 16.05 | 59.23 | 1990 | 36,901 |
| Portland | 2.85 | 10.84 | 1990 | 38,055 |
| London | 29.77 | 126.05 | 1990 | 42,338 |
| Sydney | 4.14 | 17.56 | 1990 | 42,398 |
| Ottawa | 1.81 | 8.23 | 1990 | 45,418 |
| Los Angeles | 3.62 | 16.73 | 1990 | 46,158 |
| Brussels | 3.11 | 14.49 | 1990 | 46,644 |
| Melbourne | 2.33 | 12.63 | 1990 | 54,200 |
| Seattle | 1.81 | 9.86 | 1990 | 54,420 |
| Tokyo | 42.20 | 243.42 | 2001 | 57,683 |
| Seoul | 21.23 | 122.68 | 1990 | 57,791 |
| Washington | 4.66 | 31.67 | 1990 | 67,967 |
| San Francisco | 3.88 | 29.10 | 1990 | 74,945 |
| Toronto | 1.81 | 14.37 | 1990 | 79,268 |
| Paris | 1.55 | 14.00 | 2000 | 90,129 |
| Hong Kong | 1.04 | 19.35 | 1990 | 186,876 |
| New York | 3.11 | 73.95 | 1990 | 238,022 |

Source: http://www.demographia.com/db-intlcbddensa.htm.

intensity manifested in low FARs and low building density. For instance, Beijing's CBD (located in Chaoyang district) was planned in 2001 on an area of 3.99 sq kilometers (Fig. 6.3). It is divided into 125 lots with a total area of 2.46 sq kilometers (excluding roads). Discounting the 28 existing uses, 97 lots are planned for seven different land uses that include commercial, mixed, residential, school, cultural and recreational, public infrastructure, and open/green space. Excluding open/green space, the average building density (the ratio of land used for building over the total land in each lot) is 32.81 percent and the average FAR is 5.3. Land use intensity varies significantly between types, as expected. Commercial use

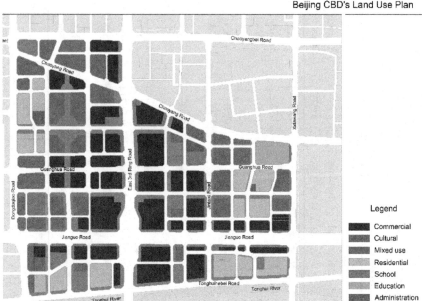

Figure 6.3.   Mixed land use in Beijing's CBD.

has the highest FAR of 5.67, followed by mixed use with 3.95 FAR, and residential use with 3.5 FAR. Other types have FARs that range from 0.5 to 2. The variation of building density between land uses is quite small. Land used for schools have the lowest building density of 20 percent while cultural and recreational uses have the highest value of 40 percent. These general features of low building density, high portion of green space in each lot as well as in the entire CBD areas, and presence of low-value-added and use types such as school and public utility in Beijing's CBD are widely shared by CBDs in other Chinese cities (Table 6.4 and Fig. 6.4)

### 3.3.2. *Assessment*

A comparison of CBDs in Chinese cities, whose spatial configuration of land use patterns is similar to that of the CBD in Beijing, with international

Table 6.4.   Land Uses in CBDs

**Beijing Chaoyang's CBD**

| Land Use | Lot | | Area | | Land for Construction (ha) | Building Density (%) | FAR | Green Space (%) |
|---|---|---|---|---|---|---|---|---|
| | Num | % | Hectare | % | | | | |
| Commercial | 36 | 37.11 | 84.21 | 42.50 | 29.47 | 35.00 | 5.67 | NA |
| Mixed | 30 | 30.93 | 58.54 | 29.54 | 17.63 | 30.17 | 3.95 | NA |
| Residential | 14 | 14.43 | 30.84 | 15.56 | 7.71 | 25.00 | 3.50 | NA |
| Open/Green | 6 | 6.19 | 10.61 | 5.35 | | | | |
| School | 4 | 4.12 | 7.20 | 3.63 | 1.44 | 20.00 | 0.50 | NA |
| Cultural & recreational | 4 | 4.12 | 4.13 | 2.08 | 1.65 | 40.00 | 1.75 | NA |
| Public utility | 3 | 3.09 | 2.62 | 1.32 | 0.77 | 28.33 | 0.97 | NA |
| **Chongqing's CBD** | | | | | | | | |
| Commercial | 60 | 40.54 | 61.67 | 34.72 | 21.41 | 45.18 | 6.71536 | 19.73 |
| Mixed | 7 | 4.73 | 9.33 | 5.25 | 0.49 | 34.29 | 4.85714 | 32.86 |
| Residential | 8 | 5.41 | 27.46 | 15.46 | 4.25 | 41.25 | 5.85625 | 15.00 |
| Green space | 41 | 27.70 | 69.88 | 39.34 | NA | NA | NA | NA |
| Public square | 19 | 12.84 | 4.55 | 2.56 | NA | NA | NA | NA |
| Public utility | 13 | 8.78 | 4.72 | 2.66 | NA | NA | NA | NA |

(Continued)

Table 6.4. *(Continued)*

Beijing Chaoyang's CBD

| Land Use | Lot Num | Lot % | Area Hectare | Area % | Land for Construction (ha) | Building Density (%) | FAR | Green Space (%) |
|---|---|---|---|---|---|---|---|---|
| **Shenzhen Futian's CBD** | | | | | | | | |
| Commercial and office | 40 | 41.24 | 34.12 | 17.22 | NA | NA | 7.16 | 11.67 |
| Commercial and Park | 2 | 2.06 | 5.80 | 2.93 | NA | NA | 0.95 | 42.50 |
| Tourism | 6 | 6.19 | 6.06 | 3.06 | NA | NA | 7 | 14.17 |
| Office | 12 | 12.37 | 20.24 | 10.21 | NA | NA | 4.7 | 24.00 |
| Recreational | 11 | 11.34 | 26.60 | 13.43 | NA | NA | 1.6 | 19.55 |
| Residential | 12 | 12.37 | 30.45 | 15.37 | NA | NA | 2.5 | 23.64 |
| Mixed (commercial, residential, office) | 1 | 1.03 | 3.28 | 1.66 | NA | NA | 2.8 | 25.00 |
| Other | 4 | 4.12 | 12.42 | 6.27 | NA | NA | 1.8875 | 18.33 |
| Public utility | 7 | 7.22 | 5.42 | 2.74 | NA | NA | NA | NA |
| Green space | 13 | 13.40 | 55.95 | 28.24 | | | | |

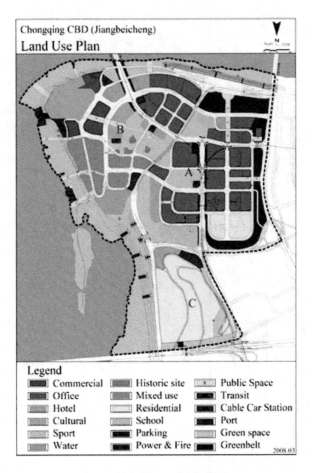

Figure 6.4.   Chongqing's CBD.

norms suggests the following six characteristics (Table 6.5). First, build-ing density is low, particularly compared to other international cities. The mid-town CBD in Manhattan, for instance, has 36 lots in an area of 35.26 hectares. The average building density is 85.89 percent (the maximum is 100 percent while the minimum is 63 percent). Second, the FAR is low. The average FAR in New York is 14.26, nearly three times as high as in Beijing while the maximum is 26.21, almost four times as high as the highest FAR in Beijing.

Table 6.5.   International Comparison of CBD Development: Beijing vs. New York

|  | Beijing | New York |
|---|---|---|
| Land use | Mixed land use: | Predominantly |
|  | • Commercial | • Commercial |
|  | • Retail | • Retails |
|  | • Residential |  |
|  | • Public utility |  |
|  | • School |  |
|  | • Cultural and recreational |  |
|  | • Green space |  |
| Building height | High | High |
| FAR | Low | High |
| Building density | Low | High |
| Green space in each lot | Significant portion | None |

Third, CBDs in Chinese cities commonly include land use types that should not belong to a CBD's activities. According to Murphy (1972), non-CBD land uses include (1) permanent residences (including apartment buildings and rooming houses); (2) government and public property (including parks and public schools as well as establishments carrying out administrative functions); (3) organization establishments (churches, colleges, etc.); (4) industrial establishments (except newspapers); (5) wholesaling and commercial storage; and (6) railroads and switching yards.[18] A location or site in the CBD is just too valuable for these types of less intensive use. In fact, these types of land development in Beijing's CBD have low FARs even though land values are very high. Fourth, mixed land use in a CBD mainly refers to a mixture of commercial and retail activities in the CBDs of Western cities while in Beijing the mix also includes residential uses. It is usually planned to have up to 60 percent of building space for residential purposes.

Fifth, land is developed or planned following a standard template. For instance, building density has little variation across different land uses. Conventional wisdom suggests that residential development and schools

---

[18] He also included vacant buildings and lots.

need a lot of open/green space so that building density will be substantially lower than that for commercial activities. However, the building density among different uses in Beijing's CBD is not sufficiently varied. Finally, there are too many open/green spaces and many of them are fragmented resulting from open/green space construction around sky-rise buildings.

There is little dispute about the need to develop CBDs in Chinese cities. What is at issue are the ways in which CBDs have been designed, planned, and constructed. Primary assessment reveals that potential or forgone economic costs are high. Economic losses are manifest in the fact that both land use types and land use intensity are at odds with high land values. It is against market principles and general trends to plan less intensive land uses such as schools and cultural facilities in CBDs. Economic potential is also negatively affected when the urban physical environment is not friendly to face-to-face contact as well as to pedestrians and shopping, as is the case when fragmented open/green space surrounds buildings. Hence, the ways in which open/green space has been constructed contributes little to the improvement of the urban physical environment and serves no purpose other than city beautification. Fiscal impacts cannot be overlooked either. There have been serious discussions and studies on the introduction of property tax. If it is not implemented, revenue loss from low building density will be huge. The likelihood for low building density both to incur an above-average cost in infrastructure provision and to encourage motorization rather than mass transit ridership will be high.

It should be pointed out that there is a general perception that CBDs in Chinese cities have high land development intensity by looking at the heights of buildings. This would be true if building height were the sole measure of intensity. In fact, building heights in Chinese CBDs are comparable to those in Western cities' CBDs while there are significant differences in FARs because of variations in building density. Assuming that the 36 commercial uses in Beijing's CBD have the same average value of building density as that in Manhattan, the existing building heights would imply an average FAR of 13.93 instead of 5.67 (and a maximum FAR of 17.2). This would have given both cities a comparable average FAR. Low building density is the direct outcome of Chinese planners widely accepting the belief that it would make the urban environment "better", without fully understanding the opportunity costs and overall impacts.

## 4. Mixed Land Use

One of the most prominent policy and planning elements to promote efficient urban spatial form in general and to combat urban sprawl in particular in the US is associated with mixed land use. Advocates of Smart growth propose mixed land use at the community level as one of the countermeasures for urban sprawl. The anticipated benefits from mixed land use include reduction in autodependency, reduction in travel demand, development of public spaces and pedestrian-oriented retail, and increases in dense and compact development (Victoria Transport Policy Institute, 2008). They also include positive impacts on property values from commercial uses in close proximity to residential areas. The capitalization of improved community quality through property taxes helps raise local tax revenues (Knaap, 2008).

Chinese cities are distinguished by their high degree of mixed land use. Homes, shops, offices, and recreation facilities can be found in many compounds usually separated from the outside by walls. Therefore, Chinese cities are already practising smart growth if they are simply judged in terms of the degree to which land use is mixed. But the answer to the question of whether Chinese cities exhibit smart growth may be much more complicated.

### 4.1. *Development*

In the pre-reform period, *danwei* was a socioeconomic unit that served multiple functions by providing workplaces, housing, and other services not only to employees but also to their immediate families. Thus *danwei* became the basic unit in which both different land use types and socioeconomic functions were mixed. Subsequently, urban spatial expansion was planned and developed around the establishment of *danwei* in the planned economy. This *danwei*-based urban spatial expansion caused the spreading of mixed-use compounds across built-up areas and created the so-called cellular structure in the urban fabric (Gaubatz, 1995). The size of *danwei* in terms of total employment determined the geographic scale of mixed land use patterns. It can range from a small lot of a few hectares to several dozen sq kilometers. If the *danwei* are big, a city or town can be developed out of them. Shanghai Baoshan, for instance, is developed along with Shanghai Baoshan Steel Corporation.

Although emerging land markets have begun to influence urban land use and spatial structure (Ding, 2004), mixed land use patterns continue to persist at least from a micro-level perspective. This is mainly because (1) balance is one of the most distinguished features of Chinese architecture and (2) urban planning has been deeply rooted in the practice of architecture design and the clustering of different land uses in one location is considered to achieve balance.

Consequently, mixed land uses across Chinese cities are developed at two different levels: city vs. community. At the city level, urban spatial development is often organized and planned through the so-called dispersed clustering model (*fensan zutuan moshi*). For instance, Zunyi City of Guizhou Province has a built-up area of 478 sq kilometers, with a population of 800,000 in 2007. It is planned (2008–2020) that future spatial growth will be organized around nine development areas (one center, two subcenters, and six development nodes) to accommodate a net population increase of 900,000 (Fig. 6.5). Each of these nine development areas has mixed land uses: commercial, institutional, and residential. This type of dispersed clustering land development model is widely practised across Chinese cities. At the community or neighborhood level, the idea of placing housing geographically close to jobs is deeply rooted in the minds of policy and plan makers, although reforms (housing and economic privatization) have forced *danwei* to focus on the workplace. Development and/or planning patterns similar to Zunyi's dispersed clustering model can be found on much smaller scales such as neighborhoods or communities. For instance, the development of Beijing's CBD illustrates the planning of mixed land uses at the neighborhood level. The CBD has land for commercial, residential, public, education, cultural, recreational, and green space uses in an area of less than 4 sq kilometers (Fig. 6.5).[19]

---

[19] The area of the constructed land exclusive of roads is 2.46 sq kilometers.

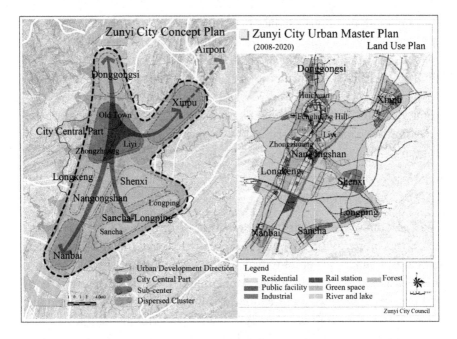

Figure 6.5.   Dispersed clustering of land development model.

## 4.2. Assessment

### 4.2.1. Employment distribution

Employment density decreases with the degree to which non-residential and residential uses are mixed. Unlike the high population density across Chinese cities, employment density is quite low. The highest employment density in Beijing, for instance, was 13,000–15,000 jobs per sq kilometer (Ding, Knaap and Song, 2004). In comparison, the average employment density of CBDs in cities like New York, Tokyo, Hong Kong, Seoul, Washington DC, and Chicago was over 50,000 jobs per sq kilometer in 1990 (Table 6.3).

The cellular type of urban spatial structure due to spatial spreading of mixed land uses causes the employment density curve to flatten, lowering the employment concentration. Low employment concentration and density negatively affect labor productivity, technology spillovers, agglomeration economies, and the development of business networks and connections (Lorenzen and Maskell, 2004; Phelps, 2004; Ciccone and Hall, 1996; Henderson, Kuncoro, and Turner, 1995; Sedgley and Elmslie, 2004). Spatially scattered workplaces also negatively affect the city's economic growth by fragmenting urban labor markets and decreasing job accessibility, particularly for the low-income population and rural-urban migrants.

### 4.2.2. *Urban transportation*

The flat employment distribution resulting from mixed land use affects urban transportation in two ways. First, the average travel distance may increase. Centralized employment distribution has the lowest average travel distance given a declining population density toward the city edge and can have the lowest per capita travel demand (e.g. VMT) (Bertaud, 2003, 2004). Although the pattern of centralized employment may cause enormous congestion, particularly in the city center, it produces orderly spatial traffic flows that are friendly and conducive to traffic management measures and policies such as congestion pricing, public transit, high-occupancy vehicle lanes, and reversible lanes that are possible only for traffic patterns that have congestions at different times in different directions. In contrast, spreading out jobs across Chinese cities due to mixed residential and non-residential uses impedes the effectiveness of such measures and policies.

Second, the spreading out of mixed land uses more likely generates chaotic and stochastic traffic flows that augment traffic interferences (Fig. 6.3). The co-existence of multiple transport modes (walking, bicycling, motorcycling, and buses) increases traffic interferences that can significantly slow down traffic and create mental stress for drivers (Ding, 2009). The vulnerability of non-motor users would also increase and traffic safety would be a serious issue.

In the context of Chinese city development, mixed land use may affect urban transportation differently in different time periods. In the pre-reform period, the combination of the dual roles of *danwei* in housing and economic production, labor immobility, and the dominance of walking and bicycling enabled mixed land use to serve socioeconomic functions well, even though the urban infrastructure and transportation was far less adequate. In the post-reform period, however, changes and growth have been profound and dramatic. They are reflected in the following areas: (1) increasing job mobility; (2) relocation of manufacturing from central locations to the outskirts; (3) increasing accessibility in the urban fringes due to massive transportation investments; and (4) rising car ownership and motor usage. Because of these changes, the share of bicycling declined from 58 percent in 1986 to 40 percent in 2000, as did bus ridership from 31 percent to 22 percent during the same period (Liu and Guan, 2005). These reductions in bicycling and mass transit were matched by the corresponding increases in automobile usage; private car owner-ship increased by 20 to 30 percent between 2000 and 2005.

Combined with the fact that it is very common to have more than one worker per household, the implication of these changes is that it is very unlikely that both workers from the same household would have a common workplace when employment is scattered over entire metropolitan areas. Some, if not all, household members would have to commute longer com-pared to the case of concentrated employment distribution. In sum, the development of employment nodes or subcenters would at least help to maintain non-motorized trips or slow down the decline of their shares.

### 4.2.3. *Efficiency in public finance*

Theory suggests that homogeneity in preferences enables local govern-ments to operate efficiently by offering public services and goods at the prices that residents within their jurisdictions are willing to pay. "Voting with their feet" means that residents relocate to the local jurisdiction whose supplies of public goods best matches their preferences. The practice of zoning provides local governments with a tool to keep free-riders out of their community.[20] This Tiebout-type of hypothesis of public finance effi-ciency was proved empirically. Gramlich and Rubinfeld (1982) reveal that regions with greater numbers of jurisdictions to choose from show greater homogeneity in the demand for local public goods within each jurisdiction

---

[20] Free-riders refer to residents who pay less than what they are served in public goods and services.

than do regions with fewer jurisdictions. Although homogenous land use alone cannot yield efficiency in public finance, the urban cellular structure makes it difficult and costly for local governments to provide goods and services that can best match local needs.

### 4.2.4. *Is smart growth an appropriate strategy for China?*

Mixed land use has been promoted as one of the key ingredients or principles to promote smart growth in US cities where motorization is predominant and built-up areas are sprawling. It is believed at least among smart growth proponents and advocates that mixed land use can help to reduce auto dependency and travel demand (VMT). Even though there is a lack of empirical evidence for the effectiveness of smart growth programs (Knaap, 2008), the principle of the mixed land development strategy may sound attractive and fit the urban reality in the US for two reasons. First, their impacts on urban agglomeration economies and labor productivity would be negligible, if any. Market-driven developments have already forged major employment (sub)centers including CBDs while the proposed strategy of mixed land development primarily focuses on mixing residential uses with shopping, commercial, and retail development. Therefore, this proposed mixed land development has little impact on job concentration and citywide employment distribution profiles.

Second, mixed land use affects non-work-related trips more than home-based work trips in US cities (Victoria Transportation Policy Institute, 2008). In addition, the shares of home-based work trips in both rush hours and total trips have declined over the past couple of decades in the US. On average in the US, home-based work trips account for about 35 percent and slightly over 26 percent during the morning and afternoon rush hours, respectively.[21] Because of the inelasticity of home-based work trips, the use of mixed land use as a policy measure to reduce urban travel demand would only be effective if both non-work-related trips and auto usage are dominant, as is the case in US cities.

---

[21] Other trip types include (1) home-based work trips; (2) home-based school trips; (3) home-based shopping trips; (4) home-based other trips; (5) non-home-based work trips; and (6) non-home-based other trips (Nair and Bhat, 2003).

That mixed land use may appear a sound and economically and socially justifiable smart growth strategy in the US does not mean, however, that it can work well in other countries, particularly in China, for a number of reasons. First, due to the *danwei*-based urban development and expansion, employment density distribution tends to be flat in Chinese cities in which strong and dominant CBDs are often absent. Second, as in the cities of developing countries where, on average, the share of home-based work trips can be high as 75 percent, work-related trips account for the majority of the urban transportation demand. This can trivialize the potential gains from mixed land use on urban motorization because of the low elasticity of home-based work trips. Finally, a lack of spatial traffic patterns has caused serious congestion problems for cities like Beijing. The prevalence of mixed land use is certainly one of the causes. The introduction of demand-side management for urban traffic congestion rather than supply-side solutions would be more effective if there were spatial traffic flow patterns. The development of employment (sub)centers for non-manufacturing jobs in cities is essential. Because land uses throughout Chinese cities are already mixed, any gains of future development of mixed land use may be marginal if the principle of diminishing return holds. Therefore, we should be cautious in promoting mixed land use development as a smart growth strategy in Chinese cities.

## 5. Final Remarks

Through primary assessment of the urban spatial development patterns of SEZs, university towns, CBDs, and mixed land use, this paper suggests that their potential negative consequences and associated efficiency losses can be substantial, affecting the long-term sustainable growth of cities. It is unlikely that these patterns can be avoided, even with emerging market forces, without substantial reforms in planning and administration that govern and influence the behavior of local government officials. It is important to point out that efficient urban forms should be assessed along with city or country situations. For instance, mixed land use is widely proposed as an important policy and planning measure to counter urban sprawl in the US. But the current city development and urban spatial form across Chinese cities suggest that it may not be as desirable as in the US since (1) Chinese cities are characterized by a high degree of mixed land use; (2) job opportunities are spread over entire cities proper with a lack of concentration of non-manufacturing jobs; (3) the dominance of two-income households; and (4) the dominance of non-motorized trips. Given these, urban development should be focused on the creation and development of employment (sub)centers and urban spatial development in conjunction with these (sub)centers through the integration of land use and transportation. Efficiency gains would be substantial if the principles of urban agglomeration economies, scale economies, mobilities, and externalities are taken into account in the planning and development of urban spatial expansion.

It is important to plan urban spatial expansion carefully in countries urbanizing rapidly partly because of the irreversibility or costly adjustment of urban land development and partly because of the impacts of urban form on agglomeration economies, transportation, the environment, and social development (World Bank, 2009). What makes planning even more challenging and complicated in China are the profound and extraordinary institutional changes that have both cause and effect relationships with economic growth during the rapid urbanization and industrialization which are taking place at the same time as the country's transition to a market economy. Challenges in planning are reflected not only in the urgent need to reposition the country to better align the division of labor between planning regulations and emerging market forces but also in how best to play an active role in envisioning, guiding, and directing future spatial development for sustainability.

There are no correct answers to these challenges. The challenges, however, should be addressed first by fully recognizing the emerging forces underlining urban spatial growth and then by co-opting them into the planning process. Effective implementation mechanisms that both recognize China's administrative system and have helped to achieve economic success in the past decades can make planning play an important role in reshaping the urban fabric and landscape in order to create efficient development forms and patterns during the process of rapid urbanization.

## References

Beardsell, Mark and Henderson, Vernon. (1999). "Spatial Evolution of the Computer Industry in the USA". *European Economic Review*: 43, pp. 431–456.

Bertaru, A. and Malpezzi, S. (1999). "The Spatial Distribution of Population in 35 World Cities: The Role of Markets, Planning and Topography". Paper presented to the American Real Estate and Urban Economics Association, New York, January.

Bertaud, A. (2003). "The Spatial Organization of Cities: Deliberate Outcome or Unforeseen Consequence", World Development Report, World Bank.

Bertaud, A. (2004). "The Spatial Organization of Cities: Deliberate Outcome or Unforeseen Consequence?" http://alain-bertaud.com/images/AB_The_spatial_organization_of_cities_Version_3.pdf.

Bertaud, A. (2007). "Urbanization in China: Land Use Efficiency Issues". http://alain-bertaud.com/AB_Files/AB_China_land_use_report_6.pdf.

Black, Duncan and Henderson, Vernon. (1999) "Spatial Evolution of Population and Industry in the United States". *The American Economic Review*, 89(2), pp. 321–327.

Borrego, C., Martins, H., Tchepel, O., *et al.* (2006). "How Urban Structure Can Affect City Sustainability from an Air Quality Perspective". *Environmental Modeling and Software*, 21: pp. 461–467.

Cervero, R. (1998). "The Master Planned Transit Metropolis: Singapore". In *The Transit Metropolis: A Global Inquiry*. Washington DC: Island Press, pp. 155–180.

Cervero, R. and Wu, K.L. (1998). "Sub-centering and Commuting: Evidence from the San Francisco Bay Area, 1980–1990". *Urban Studies*, 35(7), pp. 1059–1076.

Ciccone, A. and Hall, R. (1996). "Productivity and the Density of Economic Activity". *The American Economic Review*, 86(1), pp. 54–70.

Crane, R. and Chatman, D.G. (2003). "As Jobs Sprawl, Whither the Commute?" *Access*, 23, pp. 14–19.

Ding, C. (2009). "Policy and Planning Challenges to Promote Efficient Urban Spatial Development during the Emerging Rapid Transformation in China". *Sustainability*. 1, pp. 384–408.

Ding, C. (2004). "Urban Spatial Development in the Land Policy Reform Era: Evidence from Beijing". *Urban Studies*, 41(10), pp. 1889–1907.

Ding, C., Knaap, G. and Song, Y. (2004). "Envisioning Beijing 2020". Technical Report for the Revision of Beijing's Comprehensive Plan 2020, Working Paper, Lincoln Institute of Land Policy.

Dupont, V. (2004). "Urban Development and Population Redistribution in Delhi: Implications for Categorizing Population". In Tony Champio and Graeme Hugo (eds.), *New Forms of Urbanization: Beyond the Urban-Rural Dichotomy.* Burlington, VT: Ashgate Publishing Company, pp. 171–190.

Feldman, M.P. and Audretsch, D.B. (1999). "Innovation in Cities: Science-Based Diversity Specialization, and Localization Competition". *European Economic Review*, 43, pp. 409–429.

Gabe, Todd M. (2004). "Establishment Growth in Small Cities and Towns". *International Regional Science Review*, 27(2), pp. 164–186.

Gaubatz, P.R. (1995). "Urban Transformation in Post-Mao China: Impacts of the Reform Era on China's Urban Form". In D.S. Davis, R. Kraus, B. Naughton, and E.J. Perry (eds.), *Urban Spaces in Contemporary China: The Potential for Autonomy and Community in Post-Mao China*. Washington, DC: Woodrow Wilson Center Press; Cambridge University Press, pp. 28–60.

Glaeser, E. (undated). "Sprawl and Urban Growth". NBER 9733. http://www.owlnet.rice.edu/~econ461/notes/lecture14c.doc.

Glaeser, E.L., Kallal, H.D., Scheinkman, J.A., and Shleifer, A. (1992). "Growth in Cities". *Journal of Political Economy*, 100, pp. 1126–1152.

Gordon, Harry and Richardson, Peter. (1997). "Are Compact Cities a Desirable Planning Goal?" *Journal of the American Planning Association*, 63(1), pp. 95–106.

Green, H. (2006). "Urban Sprawl Costs: Why We Do Not Have More Affordable Housing". *Santa Barbara News-Press*. http://www.populareconomics.com/documents/urbanSprawlCosts.pdf.

Gramlich, E.M. and Rubinfeld, D.L. (1982). "Micro Estimates of Public Spending Demand Functions and Tests of the Tiebout and Median Voter Hypothesis". *Journal of Political Economy*, 90(3), pp. 536–560.

Henderson, J.V., Kuncoro, A. and Turner, M. (1995). "Industrial Development in Cities". *Journal of Political Economy*, 103(5), pp. 1067–1085.

Jacquemin, A.R.A. (1999). *Urban Development and New Towns in the Third World: Lessons from the New Bombay Experience*. Brookfield, VT: Ashgate Publishing Company.

Jaffe, Adam B, Manuel Trajtenberg and Rebecca, Henderson. (1993). "Geographic Localization of Knowledge Spillovers as Evidenced by Patent Citations," *The Quarterly Journal of Economics*, MIT Press, vol. 108(3), pp. 577–598, August.

Jun, M. and Hur, J. (2001). "Commuting Costs of 'Leap-frog' Newtown Development in Seoul". *Cities*, 18(3), pp. 151–158.

Knaap, G. (2008). "The Sprawl of Economics: a Response to Jan Brueckner". Working paper, Lincoln Institute of Land Policy.

Knaap, G., Ding, C. and Hopkins, L.D. (2001). "Managing Urban Growth for Efficiency in Public Infrastructure: Toward a Theory of Concurrency". *International Regional Science Review*, 24(3), pp. 328–343.

Lahti, P. (1994). "Ecology, Economy, Energy and Other Elements in Urban Future". Paper for a Nordic research workshop in Espoo, Finland, February 17–18.

Leong, C.K. (2007). "A Tale of Two Countries: Openness and Growth in China and India". Dynamics, Economic Growth, and International Trade (DEGIT) Conference Paper.

Levine, J. (1990). "Employment Suburbanization and the Journey to Work". PhD Dissertation, Department of City and Regional Planning, UC Berkeley.

Liu, R.R. and Guan, C.Q. (2005). "Mode Biases of Urban Transportation Policies in China and their Implications". *Journal of Urban Planning and Development*, 131(2), pp. 58–70.

Lorenzen, Mark and Peter Maskell. (2004). "The Cluster as a Nexus of Knowledge Creation". In Cooke and Piccaluga (eds.), *Regional Economies as Knowledge Laboratories*. Cheltenham: Edward Elgar, pp. 77–92.

McDonald, John F. and Prather, Paul. (1994). "Suburban Employment Centers: The Case of Chicago". *Urban Studies*: 31(2), p. 201.

McMillen, Daniel, P. (2003). "Employment Subcenters in Chicago: Past, Present, and Future". *Economic Perspectives*, 27, pp. 2–14.

Meng, Xi and Li, Y. (2005). "Urban Land Supply in the Chinese Transitional Economy: Case Studies in Beijing and Shenzhen". In C. Ding and Y. Song (eds.), *Emerging Land and Housing Markets in China*. Cambridge, MA: Lincoln Institute of Land Policy.

Murphy, R. (1972). *The Central Business District*. London: Longman Publisher.

Naess, Petter and Sandberg, Synnove Lyssand. (1996). "Workplace Location, Modal Split and Energy Use for Commuting Trips". *Urban Studies*, 33(3), pp. 557–580.

Nair, Harikesh S. and Bhat, Chandra R. (2003). "Modeling Trip Duration for Mobile Source Emissions Forecasting". *Journal of Transportation and Statistics*, 6(1), pp. 17–30.

Phelps, N. A. (2004). "Clusters, dispersion and the spaces in between: for an economic geography of the banal." *Urban Studies* 41(5/6): 971–989.

Prud'homme, R. (2000). "Patterns and Prospects in China's Urbanization Strategy". Workshop on China's Urbanization Strategy: Opportunities, Issues and Policy Options, Beijing, May 8–10.

Richardson, H.W., Bae, C.C., and Jun, M. (2002). "Migration and the Urban System of South Korea". In H.S. Geyer (ed.), *International Handbook of Urban Systems: Studies of Urbanization and Migration in Advanced and Developing Countries*. Cheltenham, UK: Edward Elgar, pp. 503–524.

Sierra Club. (1998). "The Dark Side of the American Dream: The Costs and Consequences of Suburban Sprawl". http://www.sierraclub.org/sprawl/report98/.

Sedgley, Norman and Elmslie, Bruce. (2004). "The Geographic Concentration of Knowledge: Scale, Agglomeration, and Congestion in Innovation Across U.S. States". *International Regional Science Review*, 27(2), pp. 111–137.

Soule, D. (2006). *Urban Sprawl: A Comprehensive Reference Guide*. Westport, CT: Greenwood Press.

World Bank. (2009). "Reshaping Economic Geography". World Development Report.

Yusak, O.S.E. and Maat, K. (2007). "The Influence of Built Environment to the Trends in Commuting Journeys in the Netherlands". *Transportation*, 34, pp. 589–609.

Victoria Transport Policy Institute (2008). *TDM Encyclopedia: Smart Growth*. http://www.vtpi.org/tdm/tdm38.htm.

## CHAPTER 7

# Land Use Reform, Land Markets, and Urban Land Use in Beijing*

*Chengri Ding*

This paper outlines how the public (land) leasing system (i.e. land use rights system) was introduced as the foundation of today's urban land market. The land transaction data of Beijing in 1997–1999 is used to examine the effects of the urban land market on land use patterns. The results provide evidence that market forces and prices have significant influences on the determination of urban land use and land development.

## 1. Introduction

The open-door policy adopted by the Chinese central government in 1978 marked the beginning of a series of socioeconomic reforms that were distinguished by their gradualism. Since then, there has been great socioeconomic progress in China. Gross domestic product, fixed capital investments, and foreign trade have all had double-digit increases since the 1980s. Simultaneously, China has witnessed rapid urbanization.[1]

This trend of economic growth will continue to fuel the process of urbanization for decades to come. Consequently, urban spatial expansion

---

\* This research has been supported by a grant from the Lincoln Institute of Land Policy. We wish to acknowledge the assistance provided by Xin He in data entry, digitizing, and primary data management and organization. Any errors belong to the author.
[1] There were 666 cities in 1996, which was 3.6 times that in 1982 (182), and twice that in 1985 (324), respectively. The total urban population grew from 106 million in 1957 to 347.5 million in 1995 (*China Statistical Yearbook*, various issues). The average growth rate was 227 percent, far more than the 86.8 percent for the total population in the same period. The urban population reached nearly 30 percent in 1996. Some cities grew by 200 percent in the period of 1985–1995.

will occur at a high rate in anticipation of this economic growth which will require land not only for settlement but also to provide substantial improvements to infrastructure. With rapid urbanization, it is a challenging task to provide housing for this urban population growth.

A survey using satellite images (TM images) shows that urbanized areas in 31 of the largest cities expanded by 50–200 percent in 1986–1996 due to population and economic growth (Li, 1997). The urbanized area in Beijing doubled during 1985–1992. The urbanized area in Guangzhou City in 1990 was 182.3 sq miles, which is less than half of its planned size in 2010 (Yang and Wu, 1996).

The other challenge faced by the Chinese government is associated with social stability which is dependent on self-reliance for food. The onus lies on officials and scholars to meet the demand for land and to simultaneously protect farmlands, each of which has a different goal, one being economic and the other more or less political and social. In addition, many of these urbanized areas lack adequate basic infrastructure such as sewers, drainage facilities, electricity, and transportation, and are overcrowded and contain numerous unstable structures. The local governments face an increasing financial burden as a result of decreasing inter-governmental grants. They are actively seeking financial sources to provide better urban services and demanding reforms in urban policies.

It has not taken the Chinese officials and scholars very long to realize that land reforms hold the key to many of these challenges. Therefore, since the mid-1980s, these have become the central theme of urban reform policies. They also help to strengthen the financial conditions of local governments, to provide urban infrastructure and services, to improve land use through rationing land allocation, to institutionalize arbitration over land use conflicts, to improve land management, to coordinate socioeconomic development with comprehensive plans, and to address environmental needs.

China has undertaken a series of land reforms, with the Land Administration Law passed in 1986 being the first attempt to establish land markets which had not existed in China for nearly 40 years since 1949. The law establishes the land use rights system (public land leasing system) by separating land use rights and land ownership. While the state still maintains its ownership of land, individuals and private and public entities are allowed to lease the state-owned land. The maximum leases vary from 40 to 70 years, depending upon the type of land use and land development. Even though public land leasing has been experimental in the special economic development zones (SEDZs), the law institutionalizes public land leasing throughout the country. Since the law challenged the Constitution (passed in 1982) that banned any transaction of land use rights, the Constitution was amended in 1988 to enable land-related laws to be consistent with each other. Other major land policies include the 1989 Provisional Act of Land Use Taxation on State-Owned Urban Land, the 1990 Provisional Regulation of Land Use Rights Granting and Transferring of State-Owned Land in Cities and Towns, the 1993 Provisional Act of Land Value Increment Tax on State-Owned Land of 1993, and the 1995 Urban Housing and Real Estate Management Act (Ding, 2003).

These laws and regulations have introduced market principles and price mechanisms into land use determination and the rationalization of land allocation. They have also empowered urban planning and land use controls. Primary assessment of the land reforms of the 1980s and early 1990s yields mixed results (Ding, 2003). Land reforms produce both desirable and undesirable effects. On the positive side, land reforms are given credit for the emerging land markets, increase in revenues for local governments, rapid development of the housing and real estate sectors, and improving land use efficiency and land management. On the negative side, land reforms have also created chaotic and uncoordinated development patterns, government corruption, an invisible or black market for land transactions, and increasing social injustice (Ding, 2003).

The impact of land policy on urban land use and land use efficiency is an interesting issue for planners in particular and policy makers in general. Much attention has been given to this impact in the past decade. Dowall (1992a) examines the impact of urban policies on land and housing development in developing countries. Using data from the Karachi Development Authority, Dowall (1991) concludes that the substantial price difference between that of land produced and allocated by the public sector to citizens at below-market prices and the developed market value of plots "creates an enormous incentive for speculation, and merely transfers the benefits of development gain from the public sector to private individuals, and financially constrains the Karachi Development Authority, limiting its ability to build much-needed infrastructure" (p. 470). Dowall and Leaf (1991) examine the influence of infrastructure and tenure on land price determination and the spatial variation of land prices. Dowall (1994) further suggests that Chinese cities should reform the ways in which urban redevelopment projects are financed in order to make redevelopment projects financially sound and feasible.

In addition, even though developing countries have their own unique industrialization and urbanization trajectories that do not exactly replicate the ones experienced in developed cities, the urban spatial structure of developing and developed countries is remarkably similar (Dowall and Leaf, 1991; Dowall and Treffeisen, 1991; Dowall, 1992). Land values, population density, and land use intensity tend to decrease away from the urban centers, resulting in a tradeoff between accessibility and housing and/or land prices in a maximization of the residents' satisfaction. There is also evidence supporting the notion of land-capital substitution in land markets that are emerging (Dowall and Treffeisen, 1991).

The purpose of this paper is to examine the impact of land reforms on urban spatial land use patterns in Beijing. The basic research questions it addresses include

- What are the spatial patterns of land prices in the post-reform period?
- To what extent are land use patterns correlated with the spatial variation of land prices?
- Does land use intensity (or capital density) variance correspond to changes in land prices?

## 2. Historical Review of Land Policies

Before 1979, there were two kinds of land ownership: state-owned vs. collectively owned (Zhang, 1997; Zhao, Bao, and Hou, 1998).[2] There was virtually no private land ownership and the Constitution banned land transactions. A land market did not exist and land was neither a commodity nor

---

[2] There are exceptions such as natural resources, for instance forestry, water bodies, and minerals, which are owned by the state.

had value attached to it. In urban areas, the state owned land and allocated land use rights free of charge to socioeconomic units, called *danwei,* for an indefinite period of time. A *danwei* was a basic unit of the social fabric that had dual functions as an administrative structure for organizing the society and the economy as well as a political tool for inculcating a socialist collective ethic. A *danwei* was responsible for both the production and housing of all of its members. Since the public owned *danwei,* land use rights and land ownership were legally inseparable. In other words, the state owned the land and granted land use rights to *danwei,* which were legally prevented from transferring their land use rights to a third party. Although laws required that *danwei* should return unused land to the state, this seldom happened because land had no value and there was no economic incentive to do so.

Land allocation depended largely upon the political powers to which a *danwei* was connected as well as the political atmosphere in which the industrial sector plans were determined (Wong and Zhao, 1999; Li, 1999; Badcock, 1986). Under the planned economy system, economic efficiency was not a primary concern in site determination, nor was the principle of the highest and best use considered in the process of land development. Therefore, land development could not be explained in a model based on the assumption of rational behavior from an economic standpoint.

Land supply to accommodate the needs of urban growth was provided through land acquisition that required the conversion of land ownership from the collective to the state. Municipal governments might or might not be involved in these land acquisitions. Since there was no land market, farmers who gave up land could be compensated for their losses and provided means for a livelihood according to the Constitution. Compensation packages usually included jobs, resettlement compensations, compensations for the loss of crops and attached structures on the land, and granting of an urban residency permit (*hukou*). A *hukou* was a locality residency license that enabled its holder to access public services attached to a locality. For instance, an urban *hukou* enabled its holder to access a far better transportation system than rural *hukou* holders in a remote area. Although monetary compensations were not substantial, the farmers were willing to give their land for urban projects because an urban *hukou* was highly desirable. An urban *hukou* allowed farmers to access social welfare (retirement benefits, medical insurance that were provided only to workers in public-owned enterprises) and public services (schools, recreational and entertainment facilities, and transportation) that had been denied to them before. There were wide variations in the provision of public goods and services in a geographic context. Moreover, the state price policy in the pre-reform era further exacerbated the difference in living standards between urban and rural residents. Through monopolizing the agricultural and industrial sectors, the government set low prices for agricultural goods and high prices for industrial goods (a practice called *jian dao cha*). In doing so, urban residents were subsidized by the price policy and the peasants suffered from it. The price policy helped to achieve rapid industrialization while a strict control on migration through the *hukou* system slowed down urbanization. Generally speaking, urban residents (with an urban *hukou*) enjoyed a higher standard of living than rural residents so there was less resistance from farmers negotiating land acquisitions.

Industrial growth was a primary target for the government. Under the Chinese planned system, the government first worked out short-range (one-year plans) and/or middle-range socioeconomic development plans (five-year plans). These plans laid out specific economic growth goals that were measured by industrial output. Capital investments would be made after gauging the differences between existing capacities and the need to accommodate planned economic development. Because of the ways in which political and administrative systems were set up, the governments did not usually have any problems in acquiring land. Land was commonly exchanged for cash, taking advantage of the fact that land had no market value.

Under the restrictive influence of these land policies, the following aspects characterized the urban spatial patterns in Chinese cities:

- Spatial distribution of urban population: The urban population was highly concentrated around the center (Bertaud, 1992). This pattern allowed Chinese cities to function with minimal investments in urban infrastructure.
- Spatial distribution pattern of built-up area: The compactness of built-up urban areas left virtually no green spaces for a high population

density even though capital density was substantially lower than their counterparts in other countries (Bertaud, 1992). It was not surprising to observe a low rate of floor space per capita across Chinese cities.

- Population density gradient: Even though the urban population density declined outward, urban population patterns were striking in that the density gradient curve was relatively flat and dropped sharply at the urban edges (Bertaud, 1992).

- Land use structure: In general, the share of residential land was not as big in China as in developed countries whereas industrial use accounted for a substantial portion of urban land. Industrial and residential land uses accounted for 20–30 percent and no more than 50 percent, respectively (Ding, 2003). Land in the industrial sector was clearly over-allocated compared to most market economy cities (Hong Kong, 5.3 percent; Seoul, 6 percent; and Paris, 5 percent) (Bertaud and Renaud, 1992).

- Land use deficiency: Land use deficiency was reflected in the low and flat density, the presence of low-value-added sectors in the urban cores, and the co-existence of excessive supply and demand (Dowall, 1993; Bertaud and Renaud, 1992; Li, 1999).

## 3. Public Land Leasing (Land Use Rights System) and Urban Land Markets

Driven by a surge of foreign direct investments, one of the primary goals of economic reforms, the Chinese public land leasing system was developed in special economic development zones to provide them with access to land. Under this system, land use rights and land ownership were separated so that land use rights could be transferred or sold while the state kept its ownership. Leasing terms varied from 40 to 70 years, depending upon the type of land use, and leasing fees were paid up front. The development of public land leasing in these SEDZs improved land use efficiency, generated extra-governmental revenues to finance much-needed urban infrastructure, and contributed to the rapid development of real estate and housing sectors (Chan, 1999). Revenues from the sale of land use rights (or public land leasing fees) accounted for 25–50 percent of the local municipal governments' budgets, resulting in improved urban infrastructure and housing conditions (Yang and Wu, 1996).

These initial successes partially contributed to further land policy reforms and the spread of the land use rights system throughout the country. Following the first Land Administration Law passed (1986) and the amendment of the Constitution (1988), the State Council announced The Provisional Regulation of Land Use Rights Granting and Transferring of State-owned Land in Cities and Towns in 1990 to provide concrete implementation guidelines. According to the regulation, "granting" land use rights meant local governments leased land to land users whereas "transferring" land use rights meant subleasing or leasing transfers between users and local governments. The former defined the primary land markets while the latter defined the secondary land markets. Governments were usually not involved in the secondary land markets except for performing legal and administrative duties (Liu and Xie, 1994). Since the total amount of land that could be leased from users other than governments depended on the cumulative volume of land leased from governments, the local governments monopolized the primary land markets and indirectly influenced the secondary land markets. The law also stipulated that land leased from the governments could be rented and mortgaged to a third party.

The public leasing system (land use rights system) has had a profound impact on the socioeconomic and urban development, and is viewed as the first revolutionary land policy in the post-reform era. The improvements in land use efficiency, formation of land markets, increased financial capacities of the local governments, rapid development of the housing and real estate sectors, and improved urban infrastructure are some of the tangible benefits. However, it also brings unwanted consequences such as black markets, corruption, rising social injustice, and uncoordinated urban land development. In addition, since there are no rental adjustments to reflect land price increments over time, the local governments lack effective tools to capture value increases provided by the installation of urban infrastructure. Hence the potential losses to government revenues are enormous. An initial assessment of the land use rights system shows that it has at least partially achieved its objectives and goals (Ding, 2003).

Since land markets had not existed for nearly 40 years after 1949, the major challenge facing officials in implementing public land leasing was to determine land prices. The benchmark land use rights price system was developed in the early 1990s to overcome the lack of market data for comparisons. The benchmark land use rights prices were used as a reference to guide transactions. Accordingly, land prices (or the lump sum of the total land rents of land use rights leasing) depended on the land grade (determined by the accessibility and the locality's amenities and prosperity), land use, floor area ratio, and land improvement (Hu, 1990; Zhang and Li, 1997). Critics say that benchmark prices reflect government behavior (Li and Walker, 1996) whereas others argue that benchmark prices reflect market conditions since they actively guide land transactions and serve as price references (Hu, 2000).

According to the formula for benchmark land prices, there are two types of land price: one for raw land and the other for improved land. For improved land, governments have provided urban infrastructure such as gas, electricity, water and sewer services and finished land leveling. Improved land is called *shudi* whereas raw land without urban infrastructure and land leveling is called *shengdi*. Issues related to tenant resettlement on improved land have also been resolved. Thus, improved land is ready for investment.

## 4. Study Area

Beijing has been the capital of China for six dynasties, or the past 500 years, and is well known for its rich cultural heritage. The population in Beijing in 1995 was 10.7 million and was expected to reach 11.6 million by 2000. The urbanized area covered 600 sq kilometers in 1990 and was expected to reach 750 sq kilometers over the following ten years. This area is made up of eight districts containing the most urbanized areas in Beijing. Amongst them, four are located in the inner city, called *nei qu* or the inner district and the other districts are called *wai qu* or the outer district.

The spatial development is characterized by ring patterns (see Fig. 7.1). Ring 1, not shown on the map, is located around the walls that encircle the emperor's residence, called *Huang Cheng*. Inside the Huang Cheng is the Forbidden City. The old city is located between ring 1 and ring 2. Highway ring 2 is located along the defence walls, most of which were destroyed

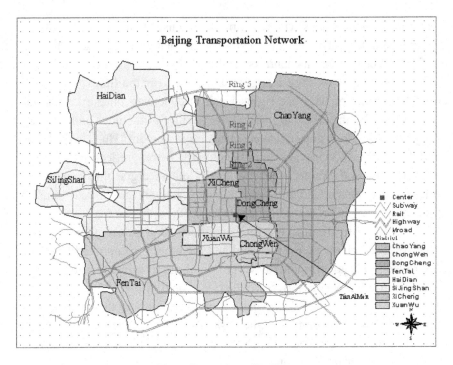

Figure 7.1.    Map of Beijing.

during the Cultural Revolution. In general, the development of highway rings 2 through 5 reflects the sequence of land development. Southern Beijing, however, did not see rapid development until the late 1990s. Land development occurred between rings 2 and 3 in the 1970s and 1980s, particularly in the west and north. Since 1980, the urban area has rapidly expanded into the west, north, and east. The Asian Olympic village is located in the north and northeast between rings 3 and 4. The village was developed in the mid and late 1980s for the 1990 Summer Asian Olympic Games. Because of this, the area became one of the fastest growing areas in Beijing in the 1990s. The state promoted science and technology research as a way to drive the economy forward. In implementing the economic development strategy, massive construction was undertaken in the 1990s in both Zhongguancun, located in the northwest between rings 3 and 4, and Dewai, located between rings 4 and 5. Both areas have a high concentration of educational and research institutions. The famous foreign embassy district is located in the east between rings 2 and 3. The presence of foreign embassies accounts for the rapid development of high-quality office buildings, four- and five-star hotels, and retail and entertainment establishments.

Information on public land leased from the municipal government to users or developers was collected for this study. This data represents all transactions between the second half of 1997 to the first half of 1999. After data cleaning (deleting incomplete records and industrial and public projects),[3] 863 observations remained. The data included land prices (for *shudi* and *shengdi*), floor area ratios, land grades, types of land use (mixed, commercial, office space, residential, etc.), and lot sizes.[4] Although the prices were appraised values, we believe these appraised data are representative of the market values because

- the lack of transaction data made the benchmark land prices (or appraised values) valuable in determining land leasing fees or land use rights prices;
- the appraised values were determined by a group of leading independent experts who knew land development in Beijing very well and so took market influences into account;
- these data recorded public land leasing in the primary land market which was monopolized by the governments that set up the benchmark land prices. So the actual transaction prices would fluctuate around the benchmark prices without substantial deviation on average (Hu, 2000).

Other data collected included base maps (transportation network systems, green space, rivers, and political boundaries). Transportation network data included highways, major roads, subways, and railroads. A GIS database was developed by geocoding land transactions and integrating land transactions and base maps (Fig. 7.2). GIS tools such as overlay and buffer were used to create spatial variables such as distance to the city

---

[3] Industrial and public developments were subsidized so that their land prices were not representative of true values.

[4] There are 9 land grades with grade 1 being the top grade and grade 9 the lowest grade.

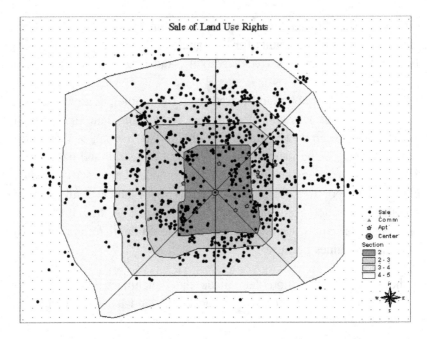

Figure 7.2.    Map showing sale of land use rights.

center and highways, and other landmarks. Tables 7.1 and 7.2 list the variables, definitions, and descriptive statistics.

Although there is no CBD in Beijing by Western definition (this is
true throughout Chinese cities), roads and economic activities are organized and/or developed around or connected to Tiananmen Square, the
political and cultural center. Tiananmen Square is also close to the geo-
metric center of the built-up areas. Thus, the distance to Tiananmen
Square is used to examine the spatial variation of land prices. The average
distance to the city center is 12.63 kilometers.

The average price of *shudi* was over 9,400 RMB per sq meter, almost
three times as much as that of *shengdi*. Most of the lots were sold for residential development which accounted for more than two thirds of all land
transactions. Among the eight districts, Chaoyang had the most active
land market, and more than one third of the sales occurred there. This
might be partly due to the fact that the Beijing municipal government has
designated a new CBD in that district. The newly designated CBD is
located in the east between rings 2 and 3.

Table 7.1. Variables and Definitions

| Variable | Definition |
| --- | --- |
| PRICE1 | Shudi price of land use rights |
| PRICE2 | Shengdi price of land use rights |
| F_RATIO | Floor area ratio |
| GRADE | Dummy variable indicating the land grade is 1 |
| MIXED | Dummy variable indicating mixed land use |
| OFF | Dummy variable indicating official land use |
| COM | Dummy variable indicating commercial land use |
| RES | Dummy variable indicating residential land use |
| DIST_CNT | Distance to the city center — Tiananmen Square |
| DIST_HW | Distance to highways |
| DIST_MROAD | Distance to major street roads |
| DIST_RAIL | Distance to railroads |
| DIST_SUB | Distance to subways |
| HW_BUF | Dummy variable indicating if land is located within 500 m buffer zone of highways |
| GREEN_BUF | Dummy variable indicating if land is located within 1000 m buffer zone of green space |
| SUB_BUF | Dummy variable indicating if land is located within 500 m buffer zone of subways |
| XICHENG | Dummy variable indicating if land is located in Xicheng District |
| DONGCHENG | Dummy variable indicating if land is located in Dongcheng District |
| XUANWU | Dummy variable indicating if land is located in Xuanwu District |
| CHONGWEN | Dummy variable indicating if land is located in Chongwen District |
| HAIDIAN | Dummy variable indicating if land is located in Haidian District |
| CHAOYANG | Dummy variable indicating if land is located in Chaoyang District |
| FENGTAI | Dummy variable indicating if land is located in Fengtai District |
| SHIJINGSHAN | Dummy variable indicating if land is located in Shijingshan District |

## 5. Urban Spatial Patterns in the Post-reform Period

To explore the relationship between land prices and locational attributes, we used the following hedonic equation:

$$\log P = \beta_0 + \beta_1 \log(\text{Floor\_Area\_Ratio}) + \beta_2 \text{Grade}$$
$$+ \beta_3 \text{LandUse} + \beta_4 \log X_1 + \beta_5 X_2 + e \qquad (1)$$

where $P$ = land prices; $X_1$ = vector of continuous locational or transportation variables; $X_2$ = vector of dummy locational or transportation variables; $\beta$ = coefficients; and $e$ = random error.

Table 7.2.    Descriptive Statistics

| Variable | Mean | Median | Maximum | Minimum |
|---|---|---|---|---|
| PRICE1 | 9463.9860 | 7257 | 78060 | 473 |
| PRICE2 | 3260.3270 | 2247 | 41735 | 173 |
| F_RATIO | 3.5653 | 3.09 | 20.34 | 0.38 |
| GRADE | 4.499421 | 5 | 9 | 1 |
| MIXED | 0.1425 | 0 | 1 | 0 |
| OFF | 0.0962 | 0 | 1 | 0 |
| COM | 0.0788 | 0 | 1 | 0 |
| RES | 0.6825 | 1 | 1 | 0 |
| DIST_CNT | 2.6330 | 2.4745 | 6.2278 | 0.4896 |
| DIST_HW | 0.2204 | 0.1947 | 0.733 | 0.0006 |
| DIST_MROAD | 0.1362 | 0.0971 | 0.6857 | 0.0007 |
| DIST_RAIL | 0.7724 | 0.6135 | 2.3323 | 0.0001 |
| DIST_SUB | 1.0973 | 0.9917 | 3.9909 | 0.0012 |
| HW_BUF | 0.5805 | 1 | 1 | 0 |
| GREEN_BUF | 0.1298 | 0 | 1 | 0 |
| SUB_BUF500 | 0.1657 | 0 | 1 | 0 |
| XICHENG | 0.0637 | 0 | 1 | 0 |
| DONGCHENG | 0.0892 | 0 | 1 | 0 |
| XUANWU | 0.0811 | 0 | 1 | 0 |
| CHONGWEN | 0.0336 | 0 | 1 | 0 |
| HAIDIAN | 0.1611 | 0 | 1 | 0 |
| CHAOYANG | 0.3523 | 0 | 1 | 0 |
| FENGTAI | 0.1356 | 0 | 1 | 0 |
| SHIJINGSHAN | 0.0510 | 0 | 1 | 0 |

Factors or variables representing elements such as topography, trees, etc. are also expected to affect land prices. These were not available for this analysis, but we believe the omission of these factors would not affect the coefficient estimates of (1) if the omitted variables were not correlated with the explanatory variables (Hushak, 1975). Other function forms such as linear and log-linear were estimated. However, the model reported in this paper represented the best results based on the following criteria of multiple correlation coefficient, mean percentage error, mean absolute percentage error, and root mean square error (Dunford, Marti, and Mittelhammer, 1985).

If the emerging land markets begin to influence urban land use, land close to employment opportunities and transportation nodes that provide accessibility will be expected to be higher-priced and have a high capital density. Different types of land uses are expected to have different residuals which are dependent upon productivity, technology, competitive markets, and factor substitution (O'Sullivan, 1996). It is thus expected that land use will influence land prices. It is expected that the coefficient $\beta_1$ is significantly positive while the coefficient $\beta_2$ is significantly negative. The coefficients $\beta_3$, $\beta_4$, and $\beta_5$ are significant, their signs depending on the way the variables are measured. Equation (1) is estimated by applying econometric techniques such as the Box–Cox transformation, the Ramsey RESET test, and the White test so that both the best function forms and appropriate variables are chosen. Results show that the model fits the data well and enables us to answer the questions mentioned earlier.

## 5.1. *Descriptive patterns*

Descriptive analysis shows some interesting results. Figures 7.3 and 7.4 illustrate the land value variation across land grades. Both figures reveal that

- The sale price decreases dramatically between grade 1 and grade 2, and then the curve becomes flat. For instance, a residential project of grade 1 requires 17,000 RMB more per sq meter than that of grade 2. The margin drops to slightly over 4,100 RMB from grade 2 to grade 3, and to 2,100 RMB from grade 3 to grade 4. After grade 3, the marginal decrease with respect to land grade becomes quite small.
- Land is cheaper for residential development than for commercial, office, and mixed development.
- The price gap between *shudi* and *shengdi* also decreases with land grade. For instance, *shudi* costs 16,670 RMB more per sq meter than *shengdi* for residential projects in grade 1. The difference drops to only 600 RMB in grade 10.

An examination the relationship between floor area ratio and price yields similar conclusions (see Figs. 7.5 and 7.6). These figures suggest

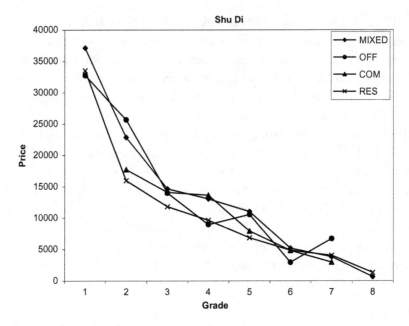

Figure 7.3.  Average *shudi* sale price variation with land grade.

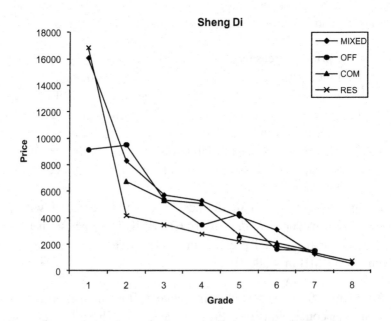

Figure 7.4.  Average *shengdi* sale price variation with land grade.

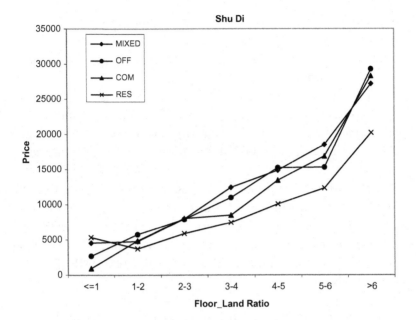

Figure 7.5.    Average *shudi* sale price variation with floor area ratio.

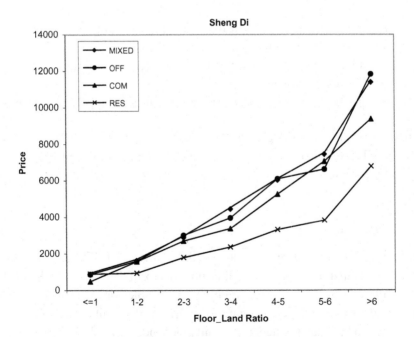

Figure 7.6.    Average *shengdi* sale price variation with floor area ratio.

- *Shudi* and *shengdi* land prices increase with the floor area ratio in approximately an exponential form. This pattern is at odds with the one shown in the benchmark price in which prices and floor area ratio are linearly correlated.
- The price gap between *shudi* and *shengdi* increases with the floor area ratio. A developer will pay over 13,000 RMB more per sq meter for *shudi* than for *shengdi* if the floor area ratio is larger than 6. The margin drops to 2,000–4,000 RMB if the floor land ratio is less than 3.
- The price difference across land uses increases with the floor area ratio. In other words, the price difference between mixed and residential projects increases. For instance, it costs almost 7,000 RMB more for mixed land use than residential development if the floor land ratio is over 6. The gap drops to only 1,000–2,000 RMB if the floor area ratio is less than 3.

Interesting results are also found from spatial or location analyses (see Figs. 7.7 and 7.8). It is found that

- Land rent curves of different land uses have a negative slope. This is commonly observed in a free market economy.
- Mixed land use has the steepest land rent gradient and residential use has the lowest slope.
- As expected, price differences between land uses diminish over distance.

Figures 7.9 and 7.10 depict the land price variations across districts. Districts located near the center have higher land prices than those districts farther away.

### 5.2. Statistical analysis

Before estimating (1), we conducted the Ramsey RESET test and the Box–Cox transformation to test the function form. The Ramsey RESET test will be significant if there are omitted variables or the model is misspecified. Box-Cox transformations help to determine the form of relationship between the dependent and independent variables. The results

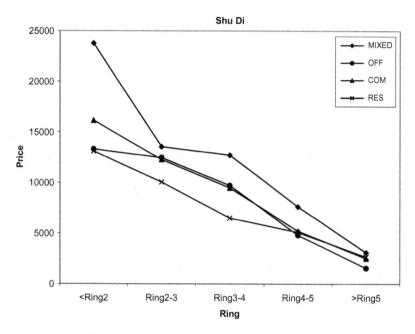

Figure 7.7.   Average *shudi* sale price variation by highway ring.

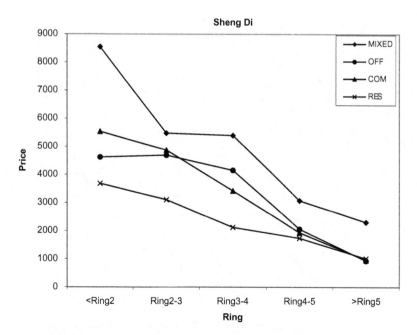

Figure 7.8.   Average *shengdi* sale price variation by highway ring.

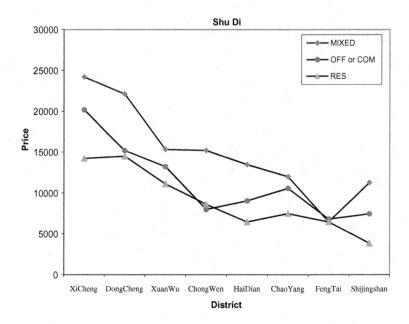

Figure 7.9.   Average *shudi* sale price variation by district.

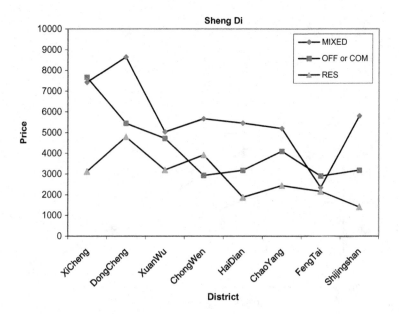

Figure 7.10.   Average *shengdi* sale price variation by district.

of the Ramsey RESET test strongly support the notion that a log-linear form is superior to other forms such as linear and semi-log.[5] This is true for both *shudi* and *shengdi* prices.

This conclusion was also confirmed by using the Box–Cox transformation technique.[6] Simulations suggest that $\lambda = 0.2$ and $\lambda \approx 0$ yield the best results in terms of goodness-of-fit for *shudi* and *shengdi* sales, respectively.[7] Thus in the following discussions, we will focus only on the results of (1), a transcendental model. The advantages of the transcendental model, expressed in (1), are

- it is easy to interpret results;
- it captures the nonlinear relationship suggested from the outcomes of Box–Cox transformation analysis; and
- it fits the data well in terms of goodness-of-fit.

Table 7.3 presents estimates of (1).[8] As expected, the results are interesting. First, the floor area ratio plays a dominant role in land price determination. The coefficient indicates that a unit increase in the floor area ratio raises prices by more than 2,000 RMB and 800 RMB per sq meter for *shudi* and *shengdi*, respectively. Both coefficients exhibit unit elasticity or close to unit elasticity. Land prices increase with land class. The coefficients show that land sale prices decrease by around 35 percent if the grade of land goes down by one. Thus, compared to residential development, non-residential developments such as commercial, office

---

[5] In the Ramsey tests, the null hypothesis is denied for both the linear and semi-linear forms of *shudi* sales, and for the linear form of *shengdi* sales. However, the null hypothesis cannot be rejected if a log-linear form is used.

[6] After the Box–Cox transformation on the dependent and independent variables, the model becomes $(y^\lambda - 1)/\lambda = \alpha + \beta (x^\lambda - 1)/\lambda$. If $\lambda$ is close to one, it becomes a linear form of $y = \alpha + \beta x$. If $\lambda$ is approaching zero, it is a log-linear form of $\ln y = \alpha + \beta \ln x$.

[7] These results are not reported here for the sake of space, but are available upon request. Moreover, null hypothesis cannot be rejected when $\lambda = 0.2$ and $\lambda \approx 0$ for *shudi* and *shengdi*, respectively, in the Ramsey RESET tests.

[8] The White test is conducted to test heteroskedasticity. Usually, heteroskedasticity is very common in cross-section data. Our results show no sign of heteroskedasticity at all for both *shudi* and *shengdi*. The Ramsey RESET test yields mixed results. The F-test is not significant for *shengdi* but is significant for *shudi* although the magnitude is moderate (only significant at the 90 percent level).

*C. Ding*

Table 7.3.   Estimated Results of (1)

| Variable | Shudi | | Shengdi | |
| --- | --- | --- | --- | --- |
| | Coefficient | *t*-Statistic | Coefficient | *t*-Statistic |
| Constant | 8.3819 | 68.3190 | 6.9758 | 67.6994 |
| LOG(F_RATIO) | 0.8880**** | 36.1203 | 1.0319**** | 49.9742 |
| LOG(GRADE) | −0.3403**** | −6.0620 | −0.3566**** | −7.5624 |
| MIXED | 0.2266**** | 5.7227 | 0.4868**** | 14.6424 |
| OFF | 0.1906**** | 4.2115 | 0.4697**** | 12.3589 |
| COM | 0.1543**** | 3.1170 | 0.3531**** | 8.4935 |
| LOG(DIST_CNT) | −0.4248**** | −7.3831 | −0.2223**** | −4.6003 |
| LOG(DIST_HW) | 0.0256 | 1.2768 | −0.0156 | −0.9252 |
| LOG(DIST_MROAD) | −0.0318** | −2.5118 | −0.0028 | −0.2622 |
| LOG(DIST_RAIL) | 0.0565**** | 3.9699 | 0.0248* | 2.0717 |
| LOG(DIST_SUB) | −0.0548* | −2.0985 | −0.0027 | −0.1241 |
| HW_BUF | 0.0862** | 2.4522 | 0.0274 | 0.9265 |
| GREEN_BUF | −0.0877* | −2.1906 | −0.0131 | −0.3900 |
| SUB_BUF | −0.0925 | −1.5392 | −0.0170 | −0.3372 |
| XICHENG | 0.5273**** | 6.4462 | 0.3087**** | 4.4934 |
| DONGCHENG | 0.2672**** | 3.4059 | 0.2428**** | 3.6854 |
| XUANWU | 0.2527**** | 3.0466 | 0.1633** | 2.3437 |
| CHONGWEN | 0.1569 | 1.5699 | 0.2404**** | 2.8633 |
| HAIDIAN | 0.3786**** | 6.4103 | 0.1601**** | 3.2275 |
| CHAOYANG | 0.2449**** | 4.4177 | 0.1739**** | 3.7356 |
| FENGTAI | 0.1255 | 1.8284 | 0.1059 | 1.8368 |
| *R*-squared | 0.781011 | | 0.848496 | |
| Adjusted *R*-squared | 0.775809 | | 0.844898 | |

*Notes*:
**** stands for significance at the 1 percent level.
** stands for significance at the 5 percent level.
* stands for significance at the 10 percent level.

space, and mixed use have significantly higher sale prices. Among all land use categories, mixed use development has the highest land value. This result is also consistent with the previous analysis.

Table 7.3 also reveals the existence of a negatively sloped land price gradient. The coefficient on distance to the city center is negative and significant at the 0.01 level. This indicates that land prices decrease by 42 and 22 percent for *shudi* and *shengdi*, respectively, if the lot is located one kilometer away from the city center. For *shudi*, land will be sold at higher prices if it is located closer to major roads and subways. Land will be more expensive if it is located farther away from railroads. Although distance to highways is not significant, the highway buffer is significantly positive. The coefficient indicates that land located within 500 meters of highways will sell for 9 percent more. For *shengdi*, however, transportation variables are not significant except for distance to railroads. District variables show that land in the inner districts has higher values than in the outer districts.[9] This indirectly supports the notion that the land rent curve has a negative slope. Demand for land in Haidian and Chaoyang Districts is high for the reasons discussed above.

Overall, the models explain more than 78 and 84 percent of the land price variation for *shudi* and *shengdi*, respectively, suggesting that the models fit the data well. Only 4 out of the 20 independent variables are insignificant for *shudi*. Among the 16 significant variables, there are 12 variables significant at the 1 percent level. For *shengdi*, the model yields a high degree of explanatory power with fewer significant variables. This suggests that each significant variable has a stronger explanatory power.

Urban theory states that higher land use density has a steeper land price gradient and is located closer to the city center. Thus, if the emerging land markets begin to influence urban land use, land price gradients can be expected to vary, depending upon land use and land use densities. To examine issues such as whether or not land prices have begun to influence land use and land use allocation and to what extent, we extended the model of (1) by introducing interactive terms.[10] Coefficients using these interactive terms will capture the difference in land price gradient across land use densities.

The results are reported in Table 7.4 (*shudi* price).[11] Comparing Tables 7.3 and 7.4, The results illustrate that the coefficients are robust

---

[9] The default variable is Shijingshan located in the western edge of the urbanized area.

[10] FLRLOW, FLRMID, and FLRHIGH are dummy variables, which group floor area ratio into three types: low, middle, and high floor area ratio, respectively. FLRLOW is set to 1 if floor area ratio is less than or equal to 4. FLRMID is set to 1 if it is between 4 and 6.5; FLRHIGH is set to 1 if floor area ratio is large than 6.5. Its kernel density distribution is used.

[11] *Shengdi* price has similar patterns. The results are not reported here to save space, but will be provided if requested.

*C. Ding*

Table 7.4.   Land Rent Gradient for Different Land Use Densities

| Variable | Coefficient | | t-Statistic |
|---|---|---|---|
| C | 8.414718 | | 66.43087 |
| LOG(F_RATIO) | 0.864375 | **** | 25.58346 |
| LOG(GRADE) | −0.341791 | **** | −6.08113 |
| MIXED | 0.222211 | **** | 5.563688 |
| OFF | 0.186105 | **** | 4.095999 |
| COM | 0.152078 | **** | 3.069492 |
| LOG(DIST_CNT)*FLOORLOW | −0.438888 | **** | −7.47325 |
| LOG(DIST_CNT)*FLOORMID | −0.385384 | **** | −5.90319 |
| LOG(DIST_CNT)*FLOORHIGH | −0.404256 | **** | −4.52646 |
| LOG(DIST_HW) | 0.025868 | | 1.289219 |
| LOG(DIST_MROAD) | −0.031564 | ** | −2.49332 |
| LOG(DIST_RAIL) | 0.055891 | **** | 3.924336 |
| LOG(DIST_SUB) | −0.054248 | * | −2.07009 |
| HW_BUF | 0.088012 | ** | 2.497645 |
| GREEN_BUF | −0.087611 | * | −2.18763 |
| SUB_BUF | −0.092572 | | −1.53692 |
| XICHENG | 0.524459 | **** | 6.405453 |
| DONGCHENG | 0.265347 | **** | 3.378955 |
| XUANWU | 0.246672 | **** | 2.96788 |
| CHONGWEN | 0.158319 | | 1.583375 |
| HAIDIAN | 0.374778 | **** | 6.333671 |
| CHAOYANG | 0.242389 | **** | 4.364012 |
| FENGTAI | 0.120197 | | 1.74764 |
| *R*-squared | 0.781438 | | |
| Adjusted *R*-squared | 0.775713 | | |

and the model is stable. Thus our discussion will focus only on these interactive terms. As expected, all of these interactive terms have negative and significant coefficients (at the 0.01 level), strongly suggesting the existence of negative land price gradients. It is, however, unexpected that low land use density has the steepest land price gradient and medium land use density has the flattest land price curve. These results indicate that low land use density is located closer to the city center, medium land use density is located farther away, and high land use density is located in between. This land use pattern contradicts urban economic theory.

Table 7.5 lists the results of (1), broken down by land uses. For non-residential use, the high floor area ratio has the steepest land price gradient whereas the difference between low and medium floor area ratio is marginal. Although the coefficients do not show much difference, they show signs of market influence, particularly when compared to residential use. It is expected that the gap in the land price gradient for different land uses and/or land use densities will increase with the maturing of land markets in China and the forming of input markets (such as capital and labor markets). The relationship between land density and distance is better illustrated in Fig. 7.11 derived from Table 7.5.

For residential use, the order of coefficients from high to low (in terms of absolute value) corresponds to low, medium, and high land use density. This suggests that low-density residential use is located centrally whereas high-density residential use is located farther away. Medium-density residential use is located in between (Fig. 7.11). This pattern can be explained thus even though it is at odds with urban economic theory. The residences of the highest officials of the central government are located right next to the Forbidden City which is just north of the city center. The municipal government has imposed strict building height restrictions to prevent anyone from looking into these residential areas from the tops of other buildings. This regulation explains the low density in Qianmen which is one of the biggest commercial and retail centers in Beijing (Qianmen is located to the south of Tiananmen Square). Building height restrictions are less strictly enforced as one moves away from the city center so that height gradually increases with distance from the center. This may explain the positive slope of the land use density curve, at least in limited geographical areas. In addition, one of the challenges in urban planning in Beijing is the balance between economic development and historic preservation. With Beijing's long history as a capital city for more than 500 years, it has many historical relics in the inner city that have been protected by restricting building height in the surrounding areas.

## 6. Conclusion

As opposed to land transactions being banned for many years and land being owned and allocated by the government, major land reforms have

Table 7.5.   Land Rent Gradient for Different Land Use Densities and Different Land Uses

| Variable | Non-residential | | | Residential | | |
|---|---|---|---|---|---|---|
| | Coefficient | | t-Statistic | Coefficient | | t-Statistic |
| C | 8.481167 | | 39.75964 | 8.533849 | | 51.4818 |
| LOG(F_RATIO) | 0.895252 | **** | 16.12672 | 0.861992 | **** | 19.13725 |
| LOG(GRADE) | -0.266441 | **** | -3.03371 | -0.430086 | **** | -5.53904 |
| LOG(DIST_CNT)*FLOORLOW | -0.384553 | **** | -3.50047 | -0.41672 | **** | -5.7359 |
| LOG(DIST_CNT)*FLOORMID | -0.381095 | **** | -3.23916 | -0.352499 | **** | -4.3174 |
| LOG(DIST_CNT)*FLOORHIGH | -0.465177 | **** | -3.4248 | -0.2948 | ** | -2.34004 |
| LOG(DIST_HW) | 0.029806 | | 0.765018 | 0.025323 | | 1.07069 |
| LOG(DIST_MROAD) | -0.028894 | | -1.17871 | -0.032288 | * | -2.15691 |
| LOG(DIST_RAIL) | 0.039805 | | 1.236792 | 0.055581 | **** | 3.442745 |
| LOG(DIST_SUB) | -0.026892 | | -0.56778 | -0.081566 | ** | -2.52647 |
| HW_BUF | 0.109698 | | 1.693162 | 0.079707 | | 1.871941 |
| GREEN_BUF | -0.069639 | | -0.97818 | -0.102525 | * | -2.07222 |
| SUB_BUF | -0.003993 | | -0.03852 | -0.174254 | ** | -2.31405 |
| XICHENG | 0.378774 | ** | 2.709614 | 0.589159 | **** | 5.643274 |
| DONGCHENG | 0.292214 | * | 2.156942 | 0.223634 | * | 2.148929 |
| XUANWU | 0.228679 | | 1.399307 | 0.235176 | ** | 2.357795 |
| CHONGWEN | 0.075043 | | 0.400042 | 0.180631 | | 1.492954 |
| HAIDIAN | 0.364652 | **** | 3.044932 | 0.352934 | **** | 5.056851 |
| CHAOYANG | 0.168488 | | 1.459476 | 0.246688 | **** | 3.776558 |
| FENGTAI | 0.043723 | | 0.313154 | 0.135209 | | 1.65222 |
| R-squared | 0.78807 | | | 0.758195 | | |
| Adjusted R-squared | 0.772217 | | | 0.75012 | | |

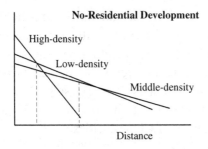

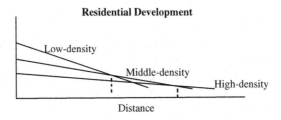

Figure 7.11.  Land price gradient.

caused markets to develop quickly and influence the urban landscape. The observation of a significant correlation between land price and land use density indicates the influences of market forces and prices on the determination of urban land use and land development. Land prices are also influenced by grade, access to transportation networks, and type of land use. This leads to the conclusion that the same parameters determine land prices in China as in market economy cities. Even though the patterns are the same, the processes by which one determines land prices may be different. For instance, it is very likely that the benchmark land prices have already taken these parameters into account and influenced market behavior. Hence, we believe this study gives strong evidence indicating the presence of market forces in determining urban land development in Beijing. Land designated for mixed use appears to exhibit a steeper land price gradient than one would expect to find in more mature urban land markets. Further, non-residential uses exhibit a variation of land price gradients across land use densities as expected in open land markets. The difference in the spatial behavior of land prices for residential and non-residential uses suggests an uneven development of land markets in

China. Less government involvement and influence will facilitate the development of land markets, which in turn will have a significant impact on urban land use. Finally, the value of land for residential use appears to vary significantly by district, perhaps reflecting the capitalization of differences in the quality of amenities. These results suggest that land markets and prices might soon play an important role in allocating land resources and shaping the form of Chinese cities.

# References

Badcock, B. (1986). "Land and Housing Policy in Chinese Urban Development". *Planning Perspectives*, 1(2), pp. 147–170.

Bertaud, A. (1992). "China-Urban Land Use Issues". "Unpublished paper".

Bertaud, A. and Renaud, B. (1992). "Cities Without Land Markets". World Bank Discussion Paper No. 227, Washington, DC.

Chan, N. (1999). "Land-Use Rights in Mainland China: Problems and Recommendations for Improvement". *Journal of Real Estate Literature*, 7, pp. 53–63.

Chicoine, D. (1981). "Farmland Values at the Urban Fringe: An Analysis of Sale Prices". *Land Economics*, 57(3), pp. 333–362.

Colwell, P.F. and Sirmans, C.F. (1980). "Nonlinear Urban Land Prices". *Urban Geography*, 1(2), pp. 141–152.

Ding, C. (2003). "Land Policy Reform in China: Assessment and Prospects". *Land Use Policy*, 20(2), pp. 109–120.

Dowall, D.E. (1991). "The Karachi Development Authority: Failing to Get the Price Right". *Land Economics*, 67(4), pp. 462–471.

Dowall, D.E. and Leaf, M. (1991). "The Price of Land for Housing in Jakarta", *Urban Studies*, 28, pp. 707–722.

Dowall, D.E. (1992a). "Benefits of Minimal Land-Use Regulations in Developing Countries". *Cato Journal*, 12(2), pp. 413–423.

Dowall, D.E. (1992b). "A Second Look at the Bangkok Land and Housing Market". *Urban Studies*, 29(1), pp. 25–38.

Dowall, D.E. and Treffeisen, P.A. (1991). "Spatial Transformation in Cities of the, Developing World: Multinucleation and Land-Capital Substitution in Bogota, Colombia". *Regional Science and Urban Economics*, 21(2), pp. 201–224.

Dowall, D.E. (1993a). "Urban Redevelopment in the People's Republic of China". *Housing Finance International*, 7(3), pp. 25–35.

Dowall, D.E. (1993b) "Establishing Urban Land Market in the People's Republic of China". *Journal of the American Planning Association*, 12, pp. 182–192.

Dunford, R.W., Marti, C.E., and Mittelhammer, R.C. (1985). "A Case Study of Rural Land Prices at the Urban Fringe Including Subjective Buyer Expectations". *Land Economics*, 61(1), pp. 10–16.

Hu, C.Z. (1990). "On the Development, Methodology and Management of Land Value Appraisal System". Internal Report, State Land Administration, Beijing.

Hu, C.Z. (2000). "Land Market, Land Price, and Land Policy", Presented at 5th Asian Real Estate Annual Conference, Beijing, China.

Hushak, L.J. (1975). "The Urban Demand for Urban-Rural Fringe Land". *Land Economics*, 51, pp. 112–123.

Kau, J.B. and Sirmans, C.F. (1979). "Urban Land Value Functions and the Price Elasticity of Demand for Housing". *Journal of Urban Economics*, 6, pp. 112–121.

Li, Y., (1997). *Sheng Cun Yu Fa Zhan: Zhong Guo Bao Hu Geng Di Wen Ti De Yan Ju Yu Si Kao*. Beijing: ZhongGuo Da Di.

Li, L.H. (1999). *Urban Land Reform in China*. St. Martin's Press, Inc.

Li, L.H. and Walker, A. (1996). "Benchmark Pricing Behavior of Land in China's Reform". *Journal of Property Research*, (13), pp. 183–196.

Li, G.Y. (1992). *Real Estate Development and Investment in China*. Tianjin: Tianjin Technical Translation Publisher.

Liu, W. and Xie, J. (1994). *Zhong Guo Tu Di Zhu Shui Fei Ti Xi Yi Ju*, Zhongguo Da Di.

Mills, E.W. (1972). *Urban Economics*. Glenview, IL: Scott, Foresman and Co.

Mills, E.S. (1969). "The Value of Urban Land". In H.S. Pearloff, (ed.), *The Quality of the Urban Environment*. Baltimore: Resources for the Future.

Muth, R. (1961). "Economic Change and Rural-Urban Conversions". *Econometrics*, 29, pp. 1–23.

Peiser, R. (1987). "The Determinants of Nonresidential Urban Land Values". *Journal of Urban Economics*, 22, pp. 340–360.

O'Sullivan, A. (1996). *Urban Economics*. Chicago: Irwin.

Walker, A. and Li, L.H. (1994). "Land Use Rights Reform and Real Estate Market in China". *Journal of Real Estate Literature*, 2(2), pp. 199–211.

Wong, K.K. and Zhao, X.B. (1999). "The Influence of Bureaucratic Behavior on Land Appointment in China: Informal Process". *Environment and Planning C: Government and Policy*, 17, pp. 113–126.

Wu, F. (1997). "Urban Restructuring in China's Emerging Market Economy: Towards a Framework for Analysis". *International Journal of Urban and Regional Research*, 21, pp. 640–663.

Xue, J. (1994). "The Development Trend of the Chinese Land Market". *Real Estate Market Review*, October, pp. 12–15.

Yang, C. and Wu, C. (1996). *Ten-Year Reform of Land Use System in China*. Beijing: Zhongguo Da Di.

Yeh, A.G.O. and Wu, F.L. (1995). "Internal Structure of Chinese Cities in the Midst of Economic Reform". *Urban Geography*, 16(6), pp. 521–554.

Zhang, X.Q. (1997). "Urban Land Reform in China". *Land Use Policy*, 14(3), pp. 187–199.

Zhang, X.H. and Li, Y. (1997). *Zhong Guo Tu Di Guang Li Shi Wu Qiu Shu*. Beijing: Zhongguo Da Di.

Zhao, M., Bao, G., and Hou, L. (1998). *Land Use System Reform and Urban and Rural Development*. Dong Ji.

Zhou, Z.P., Chen, Z.X., and Chau, Z.J. (1992). *A Perspective of the Chinese Property Market*. Hong Kong: Joint Publishing.

Zhu, J. (1994). "Changing Land Policy and Its Impact on Local Growth: The Experience of the Shenzhen Special Economic Zone, China, in the 1980s". *Urban Studies*, 31(10), pp. 1611–1623.

CHAPTER 8

# From Land Use Rights to Land Development Rights: Institutional Change in China's Urban Development*

*Jieming Zhu*

There has been a fundamental institutional change during the transformation from the centrally controlled system to a market-oriented economy in China since the early 1980s. The socialist land use right as an institution of the outgoing central planning system became an obstacle to the emerging land market for urban redevelopment, although land leasing as a new institution had created a real estate market primarily for the development of greenfield sites. From a case study of a district in Shanghai, it is discovered that rapid urban land redevelopment since 1992 has been greatly facilitated by the informal institution of the land development right. The land development right unlocks the process of land redevelopment in the central city, while the existing land user's land use right is taken care of during the gradual transition. Land use efficiency is improved to a great extent through land redevelopment for uses of higher productivity. However, the informal and insecure institution of the land development right induces hasty land redevelopment. Assisted by a capricious land use planning regime, the land development right yields suboptimal development. Clarification of property rights is the goal for further institutional change.

* Reprinted with the author's permission from *Urban Studies*, 41(7), pp. 1249–1267.

## 1. Introduction

Urban land in China was considered a means of production rather than an asset by the socialist state as the landlord in the era of centrally controlled planning. In the urban economy, dominated by state-owned enterprises which were strictly controlled by the state, land was not allowed to change hands. It was not easy for the state to retrieve land from its users either. The land use right became a distinctive socialist institution. It could also be found in other former socialist countries, as Marcuse observed: "*in socialist systems, the right of use ... was accorded a higher position than the rights of ownership*" (Marcuse, 1996, p. 135; emphasis in the original). China's rapid urban development in its coastal and central regions has been phenomenal since the 1980s (Lin, 2002). Economic reforms have unleashed a strong demand for urban physical construction which had been firmly controlled by the central planning system for 30 years. The physical development has been largely driven by emerging market mechanisms where commoditization and marketization of land and buildings are the principal factors. In the process of this transformation, there has been a fundamental institutional change.

The economic reforms since 1980 set up market orientation as the goal for systemic changes to the economy. Rigidity in land resource allocation constituted an immediate obstacle to the initiation of urban land markets. Although land leasing has evolved as a new institution since 1988, initially it only led primarily to a development market of greenfield sites, which was a process of urbanization — conversion of land from agricultural uses to urban occupation (Yeh and Wu, 1996). Potential redevelopment of brownfield sites remained hampered. Using a methodology of institutional analysis for the market of urban land development, this paper, through an in-depth case study of a district in Shanghai, elaborates on an institutional change in the emerging market for land redevelopment. A new institution — the land development right — has been created to unlock the redevelopment process by eliminating supply-side constraints upheld by the old institution of the socialist land use right. However, through an examination of the implications of the new institution for the emerging land market, it is found that the present informal and insecure land development right induces hasty capitalization of land rent. Facilitated by land use planning controls engaged with extensive bargaining, the land development right leads to a suboptimal utilization of scarce land resources. Further institutional change is expected, driven by market competition and the clarification of property rights.

## 2. Institutional Change in the Emerging Market of Land Development

Social and economic entities are bound by institutions which are "the humanly devised constraints that structure political, economic, and social interactions" (North, 1991, p. 97). The functioning of an economic system depends on a whole set of institutional conditions. For instance, these four general conditions are considered essential for economic systems: organization of decision making, mechanisms for coordination, property rights and incentives (Gregory and Stuart, 1992). Institutions are considered critical for economic growth, as institutions define a set of incentives and constraints for organizations and individuals who are actors in the economy. To achieve a more productive economy is intrinsically a matter of developing institutions conducive to growth. Organizations and individuals behave and invest in what will pay off within a framework defined by a matrix of formal and informal rules (North, 1993).

In the same vein, the land market is structured by institutions as well (Healey and Barrett, 1990; Ball, 1998). As land is a special commodity in the market because of its heterogeneity, low liquidity, high transaction cost and location fixity, the land market tends to be inherently less efficient than is assumed by neoclassical economics. Thus, institutions should be considered crucial to the understanding of the mechanisms and dynamics of an immobile property market (Guy and Henneberry, 2002). The subject of real estate transactions is not the land and buildings *per se* but essentially the interest in rights over them. Land property rights therefore matter for the performance of the real estate market (Fischel, 1985). Property rights are primarily a bundle of rights associated with ownership which consists of the right to use, the right to derive income and the right to alienate the rights mentioned above. These rights are arranged and allocated by institutions. The Coase theorem specifies that free exchange with costless transactions tends to move resources to the highest-valued uses, independent of the prior allocation of rights (Coase, 1960). However, in reality, transaction costs are always positive. Assignment of property rights is thus crucial for the achievement of efficiency.

Significant changes with the single goal of developing the national economy have occurred since 1978 in China, where a social transformation is being spearheaded by economic reforms. It has been decided to carry out reform to raise economic productivity, this having been far from satisfactory under the central planning system. Decentralization is being carried out to change centralized control to a system where decisions are made at local levels (Oksenberg and Tong, 1991; Huang, 1996; Qian, 2000). Marketization is intended to be incorporated into the management of urban state-owned enterprises to make economic production market-oriented. Hence, China's urban economy has been in the process of transformation from being plan-controlled to market-led. Commoditization and marketization of urban land are implemented at the same time as constituents of the urban reform programme (Yeh and Wu, 1996). As opposed to the drastic "big bang" approach adopted by former East European socialist countries, China's economic reforms are incremental. Because of political constraints, gradualism prevails and leads to an approach of trial and error in the implementation of new initiatives (Wang, 1994). Gradualism means a co-existence of new and old institutions. It is understood that the old institutions, which formerly played a principal role in the outgoing planning system, have a vested interest in maintaining the status quo. As a result, institutional change is conditioned by confrontations and compromises between the outgoing system and the incoming one.

The structural change of land property rights has been driven by the economic reforms. While institutional change is constrained by gradualism, the gradual reforms in the spirit of trial and error tend to generate new measures informally for testing before final formalization. Informal property rights without their definitions unambiguously understood by the whole community are not sufficient to provide order in the absence of formal institutions where the community is diverse and heterogeneous (World Bank, 2002). Informality also makes the newly structured property rights on trial insecure. Insecurity does not encourage behavior for the long term. Insecure property rights in the land market tend to induce short-term investments.

## 3. A Socialist Institution: The Land Use Right

Under the socialist system of the planned economy, property rights over natural resources and production means were virtually nationalized soon after the Chinese Communist Party came into power in 1949, although the nationalization of urban land was not officially finalized until the promulgation of the Constitution of 1982 (IFTE/CASS and IPA, 1994). Urban land has been entrusted to and controlled by the state which is held accountable to the public. The ownership is officially termed *shehui zhuyi quanmin suoyouzi* (socialist people's ownership). As the representative of "all the people", theoretically, the state had full ownership enabling it to handle resources and assets in the interest of the public. Following the dogma of Marxism and the socialist principle of public land ownership, land was excluded from economic transactions in China. The central planning system allocated land plots to users (agents of the state) through administration channels which did not charge users for land occupation and land users had no rights to transfer land. Urban land was virtually a free good. However, once state-owned enterprises and "the people" had been allocated land for their use and occupation, it was very difficult in practice for the state to retrieve land from the users, because the state-owned enterprises were the basic units of the socialist state economy and "the people" were the "masters" of the socialist society. Tenants' entitlement to a land use right became a unique socialist institution which was incorporated in the formation of socialist cities. The dramatically different structures of socialist cities from those of capitalist counterparts attest to the effect of this institution (French and Hamilton, 1979; Bertaud and Renaud, 1994).

The socialist land use right was strengthened by the practice of land being excluded from market transactions, following Clause 4, Article 10, of the Constitution of 1982: "No organization or individual may appropriate, buy, sell, or lease land, or unlawfully transfer it in other ways". There were no market mechanisms with which land users could exchange land use rights for other benefits in case of relocation. As there were no incentives to relinquish occupied land, there being no compensation, land users held on to their land plots firmly.

Although officially there were no land markets in China's cities, there was an active informal market where residents exchanged their state-owned housing. There seemed to be an explicit value for a housing use right, when a unit in a good location could be traded for a larger one in a not-so-good location (Tang, 1986). When there were occasional land use changes in the built-up area, governments had to offer land in other locations as replacements to displaced tenants. This was equivalent to the transfer of a tenant's land use right to the new sites. A survey of six residential land redevelopment projects in Shanghai in the 1980s indicated that the cost of new housing, to which the affected residents' use rights over the demolished apartments were transferred, was between 30 and 70 percent of the total redevelopment costs (World Bank, 1993).

This institution of the land use right was very firmly rooted in residents' minds. Even before urban housing was formally privatized, residents openly traded their public housing (with use right only) in the market under the auspices of housing commoditization (see Table 8.1).[1] Buyers' willingness to pay clearly showed their confidence in the security of housing with only a use right attached, while the government's tacit approval of the transactions verified this faith.[2] According to statistics relating to the Shanghai real estate market, it seemed that the price differences between housing with full property rights and with use right only were insignificant (SMBS, 1999a–2001a).

Table 8.1.  Housing Transactions in the Secondary Market, Shanghai

| Year | Total (Floor Area in sq meters | Housing with Full Property Rights (Floor Area in sq meters) | Housing with Use Right Only (Floor Area in sq meters) | Housing Transactions with Use Right Only as Percentage of Total |
|---|---|---|---|---|
| 1998 | 2,141,906 | 1,975,561 | 166,345 | 7.8 |
| 1999 | 3,796,961 | 3,366,940 | 430,021 | 11.3 |
| 2000 | 7,164,430 | 6,482,277 | 682,153 | 9.5 |

Source: SMBS (1999a–2001a).

---

[1] See http://www.peopledaily.com.cn/GB/jinji/32/177/20010816/536670.html, accessed on August 17, 2001.

[2] Beijing Youth, April 28, 2001, cited by http://www.realestate.cei.gov.cn, accessed on October 14, 2002.

After a ten-year trial in the Shenzhen Special Economic Zone, the commoditization and marketization of urban land have formally replaced the free allocation of land since 1988 when an amendment to the 1982 Constitution was approved by the National People's Congress that states: "the right of land use can be transferred in accordance with the law" (Zhu, 1999a). Public land leasing has been legalized so that urban land can be leased to developers or users for a fixed period after a payment of rent in lump sum to the state. Land leaseholds can be acquired through tender, auction or negotiation. The new institution of land leasing has been invented to complement the emerging market economy.

Land leasing and consequent building commoditization have generated a new organization — the market-driven property development industry — and have provided a powerful incentive to local governments for land development. The property development industry has been since motivated by the pursuit of development profits. A robust demand for buildings, stimulated by the emerging mechanism of market demand and supply, indicative of acute shortages of urban premises (resulting from suppressed building construction in the previous era of centrally controlled urbanization), has greatly facilitated the development of new urban areas in many booming coastal cities. During the period 1987–1999 in Shenzhen, 3,669 hectares of land were leased to developers and the city built-up area expanded from 58.0 to 132.7 sq kilometers (SZBS, 2000).

The physical growth of Shanghai was much greater than that of Shenzhen (see Fig. 8.1). In all, 10,224 hectares of land were leased (1988–2000) and 26.3 million sq meters of buildings have been constructed (1993–2000) in the Pudong area of Shanghai (SMBS, 2001b). It may be noted, however, that between 1988 and 1992, land leasing to developers/users was mainly the leasing of greenfield sites. Together with several small industrial zones, there were two sizable development projects in Shanghai — the Hongqiao Development Zone (since 1988) and the Pudong Development Zone (since 1990). All were greenfield sites where the leasing of agricultural land was coordinated by the municipal government (SMBS, 1992a).

There was hardly any leasing of brownfield sites for redevelopment in Shanghai before 1992. Redevelopment of the old central city was hampered by the sitting land users. After recovery from the political turmoil

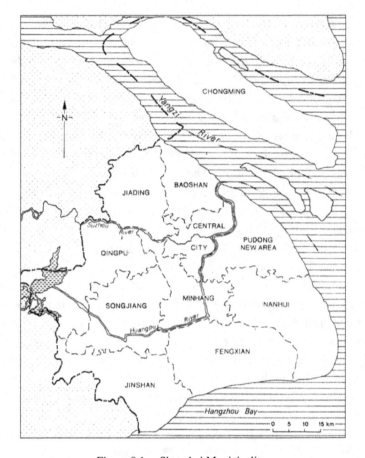

Figure 8.1.    Shanghai Municipality.

Source: Yeung and Sung (1996, p. 6).

demonstrated in Tiananmen Square in 1989, the economic reforms were pushed forward by Deng Xiaoping in his symbolic tour to the cities of Southern China in 1992. Inward foreign investment inundated coastal cities, looking for low-cost production sites and expecting to penetrate into a potentially huge market. The demands for offices and housing were shown strongly and clearly in Shanghai (see Table 8.2).

The potential value of brownfield sites was pushed up by the emerging market forces which favored locations in the central city over those in the outskirts. The widening gap between the potential capital value of "the

Table 8.2. Commodity Housing Price Index and Office Rental Index, Shanghai (1985 = 100)

| | Year | | | |
|---|---|---|---|---|
| | 1985 | 1990 | 1992 | 1995 |
| High-rise housing | 100 | 235 | 774 | 1015 |
| Multistorey housing | 100 | 291 | 742 | 1029 |
| Office rental | 100 | 148 | 264 | 497 |

*Source*: SMBS (1996a).

highest and best land use" and the present capital value[3] of the existing land use constituted a powerful incentive for land redevelopment where many existing structures had been built before 1949. However, capitalization of the land capital value gap had a supply-side constraint: the tenants' land use rights had become *de facto* ownership rights.

As a legacy of the pre-reform era of socialist industrialization when urban land was a free means of production and industrialists' demand overtook that of others in land allocation (Fung, 1981), it was not unusual to see factories located in the central business district. Quite a number of manufacturing factories occupied central locations in downtown Shanghai. In 1985, 56.7 percent of all factories in Shanghai Municipality were in its central city where it was estimated that 30 percent of the land area was occupied by factories and warehouses (Fung *et al.*, 1992). Between 1985 and 1990, only 103 plants were relocated from the central city where there were a total of 5,600 factories occupying land a totaling 430 hectares (World Bank, 1993, p. 19). Up to 1991, there was still 1.74 million sq meters of factory space in downtown Huangpu District which at the same time only had 1.39 million sq meters of office space (SMBS, 1992b).

## 4. Institutional Change: The Land Development Right

Gradualism reflected in the changing urban land system is shown in the form of the co-existence of two categories of land stock: those sites

---

[3] The present capital value of land is "net returns expected to be earned in future years" (Harvey, 1987, p. 97).

acquired previously through administrative allocation under the old system and held thereafter by users, and those plots acquired through the newly invented land leasing. The former are in the urban built-up area, whereas the latter consist mainly of agricultural land on the fringes of the city that have been converted for urban uses. A survey showed that 96 percent of development in terms of land area occurred on the outskirts and in the suburbs between 1980 and 1990 in Shanghai (Sun and Deng, 1997).

Driven by a formidable market demand for premises in the central locations, institutional change is called for to remove supply-side constraints by offering incentives to various actors participating in land redevelopment. The Shanghai Municipal Ordinances on Urban Land Management promulgated in 1992 paved the way for land redevelopment in the built-up central city through land leasing by making a clear distribution of revenues from land sales among parties with vested interests. According to the ordinances, 70 percent of the revenues should be used for compensation to displaced sitting tenants, for demolition and for redevelopment of infrastructure on the site. The remaining 30 percent is split among *de jure* owners of the central (5 percent), municipal (12.5 percent) and district (12.5 percent) governments. Compensation for relinquishing land use rights has been formalized since then, although it is not clear how much compensation land users should be entitled to. It was not finally made explicit until October 2001 when the Management of Housing Demolition and Tenant Relocation ordinance was issued by Shanghai Municipal Government; this stated that for residential areas, evicted tenants should receive compensation at 80 percent of the prevalent market value of the demolished housing, while the "owner" or "provider" (an organization or a *danwei*)[4] received the remaining 20 percent.[5] Residents with only the socialist land use right to their state-owned housing claiming

---

[4] *Danwei* refers to a variety of state-owned enterprises, non-profit institutions and governmental bureaus where most urban residents were employed during China's centralized system. A *danwei* is a work unit that has such attributes as personnel administration, communal facilities, urban or non-agricultural purview and public sector (Lü and Perry, 1997, pp. 5–6). It is an instrument with which the government exerts political and social control over citizens and it is also a provider through which the state distributes socialist welfare to workers.

[5] http://www.shanghai.gov.cn, accessed on November 1, 2002.

at least 80 percent of its prevalent market value reflects an informal process of housing privatization which gives sitting tenants benefits in-kind as compensation for their many years of working in state-owned enterprises for low salaries. However, for those land plots controlled by the *danwei* land users, compensation for demolished premises only is not considered an incentive strong enough for them to give up their *de facto* ownership rights.

Informal entitlements attached to land use rights are varied among different users, although legally these users are only tenants who have not paid for land occupation. Private residents are entitled to proper compensation for their lost accommodation when requested to leave, but the *danwei* land users are entitled to more than compensation. The higher in the hierarchy a *danwei* is, the more secure the amount that the *danwei* land user could claim for its land use right (see Table 8.3).[6]

In short, private residents do not have bargaining power, whereas *danwei* land users do. The higher level a *danwei* land user is, the more

Table 8.3.   Hierarchy of Land Users

| Category of Land User | Supervising Authority | Level in Hierarchy |
|---|---|---|
| *Danwei* land users | Central government — ministries | 1 (Highest) |
| | Municipal government — bureaus | 2 |
| | District government — offices | 3 |
| | *Jiedao* office[a] | 4 |
| Individual residents | District government | 5 (Lowest) |

*Note*: [a] A *jiedao* office is a representative or an agency of district government; it provides basic social welfare and health care for those who are unemployed (Wu, 2002).

---

[6] In large cities like Shanghai, there has been a hierarchy of central state-owned enterprises (*zhongyang qiye*) and local state-owned enterprises (municipal-affiliated (*shishu qiye*), district-affiliated (*qushu qiye*) and *jiedao*-office-affiliated (*jiedao qiye*)). Almost all state-owned enterprises were managed by the central government before 1957 when the reform of the industrial management system was initiated to increase the power of local governments. The decentralization reduced the number of enterprises under central control and changed vertical control into horizontal management. Thus local state-owned enterprises emerged. In 1990, there were 52,058 central state-owned enterprises with 9.93 million employees and 276,758 local state-owned enterprises with 53.85 million employees (Lü and Perry, 1997, p. 8; SBS, 1995).

bargaining power it has. A *danwei* is controlled by a supervising authority of the same level, but it is beyond the control of the authorities of lower levels. Since 1992, the enacted Shanghai Municipal Ordinances on Urban Land Management have decentralized the administration of land development from the municipal authority to district governments. Thereafter, district governments are able to control the land users of level 3 and downwards. The land users of levels 1 and 2 are not managed by the district government and their land use rights virtually cannot be taken away by the district authorities.

Before the initiation of land redevelopment to capture the land capital value gap, a *danwei*'s property rights over the present land capital value have to be defined and clarified, and the property rights of the local government (one of the *de jure* landowners) over the potential land capital value have to be manifested. A new institution, the land development right (LDR), for the *danwei* land users has been invented in this context. The institution is intended to unlock the supply of land for redevelopment while accommodating the existing institution of the *danwei*'s land use right. The land development right is what a sitting *danwei* can claim, based on its land use right, to redevelop the site occupied by itself and, if necessary, neighboring sites occupied by other *danwei* land users or residents.

A district named District A (see Fig. 8.2) with an area about 8 sq kilometers in Shanghai central city was chosen for an intensive investigation to probe how urban redevelopment unfolds within the new institutional structure of a dual land development mode (land leasing and LDR). The survey was also intended to find out how the LDR is acquired and defined. During 1992–2000, only 36 sites, amounting to 30.7 hectares, where previous land users were in the categories of levels 3, 4 and 5, were offered through land leasing for land redevelopment, while 260 sites were acquired under the LDR where land was occupied by land users affiliated to the central and municipal governments (levels 1 and 2) as well as other users of levels 3, 4 and 5. A total of 6.4 million sq meters of building floor area, or 77.6 percent of the total, were developed by either *danwei* land users or developers under the LDR, while 1.8 million sq meters, or 22.4 percent of the total, were developed on the sites through land leasing (see Table 8.4). A dual property rights regime has therefore been

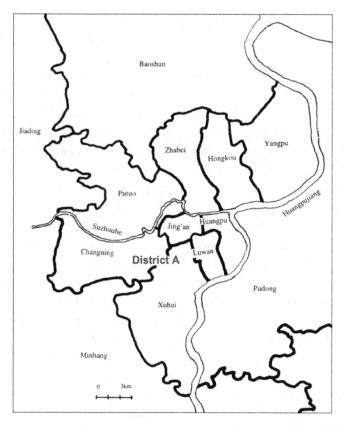

Figure 8.2.   The location of District A within Shanghai's central city.

Table 8.4.   Dual Land Acquisition in District A, Shanghai, 1992–2000

| Land Acquisition | Developer | Number of Projects | Amount of Building Floor Area Built (sq meters) | Building Floor Area as Percentage of Total |
|---|---|---|---|---|
| Land leasing | Foreign developers | 36 | 1,849,043 | 22.4 |
| Land acquired under LDR | Local developers and *danwei* users | 260 | 6,415,399 | 77.6 |
| Total | | 296 | 8,264,442 | 100.0 |

*Source*: Author's survey.

formulated in such a fashion for the brownfield redevelopment in Shanghai: one market where land is acquired through land leasing and another market where land is obtained through LDR.

While the acquisition of land leasehold is through public auction, tendering and negotiation, acquisition of the LDR depends on the hierarchical order and financial capacity of *danwei* land users who intend to conduct redevelopment, as well as the blessing of the local government. In an old, high-density district, redevelopment often involves multiple land users and thus gives rise to land assembly. Acquisition of the LDR thereby entails competition among land users whose sites are concerned. To win the LDR depends very much on the bidder's financial strength and whether they can compensate sitting land users for alienating their use rights. Usually, either those *danwei* in higher hierarchical positions or those *danwei* with better financial capacities win the bid, as they can buy out other land users who are often residents and small *danwei* tenants. In the cases of redevelopment of residential land and sites where none of the land users is capable of undertaking redevelopment, local developers would be appointed for the task. What is given to the developers in the first place is a development option. Given a development option, the developers should proceed to acquire the LDR (buying the land use right from occupants) before the option expires (see Table 8.5). One of the developers of each of the two cases D34 and E04 (Table 8.5) had to give up their development options to their partners when they could not raise enough capital for their share of the cost of buying out.

As an informal institution, the LDR is not formally tradable in the market, although it is valuable. While holders of LDRs do not possess full property rights, land assets are not secured and ownership remains ambiguous. However, once land plots are redeveloped, developed buildings with titles are tradable at market prices and thus development profits materialize, subject to a prior fee payable to the municipal government to certify the land transfer. The value of the LDR can be realized only by pushing the redevelopment project through until the building is ready for sale or rent, and then the land capital value gap captured. If in funding difficulties, those holders of LDRs have to seek and woo development

Table 8.5.    Cases of LDR Acquisition

| Project | Supervising Authority of the Developer | Site Area (ha) | Compensation for Other Land Users' Alienation of Use Right |
|---------|----------------------------------------|----------------|------------------------------------------------------------|
| B08 | District Bureau of Finance and Commerce | 0.33 | 11 *danwei* land users; 136 households |
| B25 | District Bureau of Finance and Commerce | 1.20 | 29 *danwei* land users; 146 households |
| C01 | Municipal Bureau of Economic Planning | 3.87 | No other land users |
| C25 | Municipal Bureau of Electronic Products and Instruments | 2.38 | No other land users |
| D17 | District Bureau of Construction | 1.24 | 18 *danwei* land users; 580 households |
| D18 | District Bureau of Construction | 0.24 | 5 *danwei* land users; 91 households |
| D31 | District Bureau of Construction | 0.61 | 6 *danwei* land users; 160 households |
| D34 | District Bureau of Construction | 0.51 | 20 *danwei* land users; 250 households |
| E04 | District Bureau of Construction | 0.86 | 22.13 million to district government |
| E11 | District Bureau of Construction | 0.14 | 9 *danwei* land users; 100 households |
| G03 | Municipal government | 0.03 | No other land users |
| G10 | District Bureau of Construction | 0.41 | 121 households |
| H01 | District Bureau of Construction | 1.77 | 40 *danwei* land users; 1,106 households |
| H04 | District Bureau of Finance and Commerce | 1.24 | 3 *danwei* land users; 540 households |
| H17 | District Bureau of Construction | 1.50 | 18 *danwei* land users; 460 households |
| H31 | District Bureau of Construction | 0.36 | 4 *danwei* land users; 165 households |
| I03 | District Bureau of Public Health | 0.23 | No other land users |
| J02 | District Bureau of Construction | 0.22 | 1 *danwei* land user; 7 households |

*Source*: Author's survey.

capital to form a partnership.[7] A common form of partnership between the LDR and development capital has been that where one party contributes land with the LDR and another party is responsible for financing the building construction. Out of 23 samples investigated, 14 cases involve collaboration of this type: 4 overseas, 7 SOE and 3 private partners. The completed projects are split in ownership between the two partners. The share to the party contributing the land reflects the value of the LDR to the project (see Table 8.6). This partnership also provides a channel through which private capital participates in urban construction. This provides an opportunity for developers in the private sector to grow, as real estate development in the mode of land leasing requires a large outlay of funds which are usually not available to emerging private businesses in China. Partners from the private sector are found in 32 projects (12.3 percent of the total).

The definition of the LDR has another dimension: What is allowed to be developed? What can be developed based on the LDR is defined by land use planning which is a system of regulating mechanisms determining how land parcels should be developed. As an essential factor shaping the land and property market, land use planning stabilizes the land market through increased certainty with respect to the future character of a place and reduces or internalizes the impact of negative externalities (Jud, 1980). According to the Urban Planning Act 1989, prior permission is required for

---

[7] Shanghai Dianbiaochang (SD), a state-owned manufacturer of electrical apparatus since 1954, occupied a site of 6.1 hectares for its manufacturing. The potential value of the factory site had been enhanced significantly by the concentration of residential and commercial activities in the area over the years. Once the LDR was recognized, SD had been in active pursuit of redevelopment opportunities, with the blessing of the district government which allowed the change in land use from industrial to commercial and residential. The establishment of a joint venture to carry out commodity housing and office real estate development was planned and it was expected that, with SD's land and the investor's capital, SD could diversify into the real estate business. Since 1993, SD has conducted a few marketing seminars overseas aiming to persuade foreign capital to invest in this proposed project. At one time, a deal was nearly closed with a Hong Kong developer who was about to join the partnership when he received another offer in a better location and decided to pull out (Wang and Hung, 1997). It was observed by the author that in the Shanghai Real Estate Fair held in Singapore, Sydney and Melbourne in 1997, 38 land sites in the tiny Huangpu District were keenly promoted to potential foreign investors for redevelopment on behalf of *danwei* land holders.

Table 8.6. Examples of Partnership between LDR and Development Capital

| Case | Area of Land Plot Contributed by the Land Party (ha) | Building Floor Area Built (sq meters) | Value of LDR: Share to the Land Party |
|------|------|------|------|
| C25 | 2.38 | 81,200 | 36,540 sq meters (45 percent of the total) plus 5 million yuan as relocation expenses |
| G03 | 0.03 | 1,638 | 655 sq meters (40 percent of the total) |
| H04 | 1.24 | 62,434 | 18,730 sq meters (30 percent of the total) |
| I03 | 0.23 | 18,044 | 9,022 sq meters (50 percent of the total) |

*Source*: Author's survey.

land and property developments. Development applications are evaluated by the planning authority against the non-statutory Land Use Master Plan. Thereafter, a Land Use Planning Note will be issued with land use planning parameters attached such as land use, plot ratio, site coverage and building height. When all the formalities for the land transaction are cleared and the land site details finalized, a Land Development Permit is issued. With the permit, the developer can proceed to commission architects to design the building. After an examination of the building designs by the planning bureau, a Building Permit is granted and the project can proceed to the construction stage. This process of development control is the so-called one-note-and-two-permits system.

It has been discovered that discrepancies are overwhelming between what is required by land use planning and the final completed buildings in terms of the planning parameters of land use, plot ratio, site coverage and building height. As the Land Use Master Plan is not statutory, it is not unlawful for the Land Use Planning Note to deviate from what is stipulated in the Master Plan.[8] The Land Use Master Plan is to a very great extent made irrelevant by these discrepancies (see Table 8.7). However,

---

[8] The land use planning system in post-reform China has been elaborated on thoroughly by Xu (2001), Ng and Xu (2000) and Xu and Ng (1998). An illustrious story about the workings of the planning system is provided by Xu (2001). During the period 1992–1996, the mayor of Guangzhou sent at least 2,000 memos to the city planning department to request planners to follow his suggestions in dealing with development applications.

Table 8.7.   Discrepancies in Planning Requirements between the Land Use Master Plan and Land Use Planning Notes

| Requirement | Cases with Discrepancies | Cases without Discrepancies | Not Known |
|---|---|---|---|
| Land use | 8 | 15 | — |
| Building coverage | 14 | 1 | 8 |
| Plot ratio | 14 | 1 | 8 |
| Building height | 13 | 3 | 7 |

*Source*: Author's survey.
*Note*: A sample of 23 cases was selected from a census of 260 real estate projects developed during the period 1992–2000.

Table 8.8.   Discrepancies in Planning Parameters between Land Use Planning Notes and Completed Projects

| Requirement Category | Cases with Discrepancies | Cases without Discrepancies | Not Known |
|---|---|---|---|
| Land use | 2 | 21 | — |
| Site coverage | 2 | 12 | 9 |
| Plot ratio | 12 | 3 | 8 |
| Building height | 7 | 9 | 7 |

*Source*: Author's survey.
*Note*: A sample of 23 cases was selected from a census of 260 real estate projects developed during the period 1992–2000.

planning parameters in the Land Use Planning Note are supposedly relevant and should be considered as statutory. Vast discrepancies in plot ratio and building height reveal the consequences of the LDR (see Table 8.8).

There are even two cases of land use change after the Land Use Planning Notes have been issued. An in-depth investigation unveils that development projects of the land leasing type observe planning requirements, or developers have to pay monetary penalties for building more than what is allowed. The developer of the case A01 paid US$135,694 for building an extra 307 sq meters of floor area which resulted from a misunderstanding of local building codes. Nevertheless, there are no penalties to the developers of cases violating planning requirements in the LDR mode.

## 5. Implications of the Land Development Right for the Emerging Land Market

Large-scale redevelopment has taken place since the early 1990s for the first time in Shanghai central city where old industrial structures have been demolished and new office buildings erected. Many industrial tenants and residents have been relocated to the suburbs. Restructuring of urban land uses has occurred. Between 1993 and 1997, the floor area of industrial buildings in two central districts decreased by 13 and 42 percent, and office space increased by 21 and 273 percent respectively (SMBS, 1994b, 1998b). Central districts favored by the service and financial sectors see a higher intensity of investment than those districts on the periphery and in the suburbs. Investment in the built environment begins to follow the land rent gradient. Driven by market demand, land use efficiency in the central city has been improved significantly.

Sensational media coverage of the city reported that Shanghai was the world's biggest construction market in the 1990s (*Straits Times*, January 15, 1998). Between 1993 and 2000 in District A, 4.81 million sq meters of building floor area were constructed, while 2.49 million sq meters of old structures were demolished (SMBS,1994b–2001b). The total building stock by 1990 was 9.08 million sq meters (SMBS, 1991b). This suggests that a quarter of the stock was demolished and 53 percent more was added during the period. Similarly, during the same period, building construction and demolition in the whole city of Shanghai were undertaken at an unprecedented scale: 131.2 million sq meters constructed and 30.5 million sq meters demolished (SMBS, 1994b–2001b). In all, 17.7 percent of the total building stock of 172.6 million sq meters that had existed in Shanghai Municipality in 1990 was demolished during the 1993–2000 period. Given that development under the LDR accounted for 77.6 percent of the total (see Table 8.4), rapid land redevelopment must be attributed to the institution of the LDR. It should be regarded as effective in unshackling the land redevelopment that had been hampered by old institutions during the transition. However, because of its informality and insecurity, the LDR induces hasty redevelopment to capitalize the land capital value gap, whereas land leasing projects can wait for the best moment to begin. The LDR was one of the main causes of the large oversupply of property in the late 1990s (Zhao *et al.*, 1998).[9] High vacancy rates seemed to be a feature of LDR projects. A separate survey done by the author confirmed that by the end of 2002, office buildings developed under land leasing had a vacancy rate of 7.1 percent (based on 19 samples) and those developed under the LDR had a vacancy rate of 14.1 percent (based on 8 samples).

In the category of redevelopment under the LDR, the district government had the option of land leasing but did not take it for 122 projects upon which 2.74 million sq meters of floor area were built, accounting for 42.7 percent of the total. A total of 52 district-affiliated *danwei* land users were allowed to claim the LDR from their land use rights, and one municipality-affiliated developer and 69 district-affiliated developers were offered the LDR over 70 sites which were mainly in residential use (see Table 8.9). This is explained by the politics of China's market-driven, property-led urban development in the 1990s. Transparent land leasing is supposedly the best way to maximize revenues from land sales in the interests of owners, but it has not been used as often as it should have been. Three layers of land ownership bring about competition in the distribution of revenues among the central, municipal and district governments. The LDR gives a clear incentive to land holders to redevelop land. The district government also has an incentive to transfer land under the LDR. The LDR only requires a nominal payment to the municipal government besides appropriate compensation to the sitting tenants,[10] and non-competitive LDR land acquisition ensures that the key actors are local district *danwei* and district developers. Local growth coalitions are shaped in the context of political legitimacy, decentralization and regional competition (Zhu, 1999a, 1999b).

---

[9] It has been estimated that the office vacancy rate reached about 40 percent in December 1997 (Jackson, 1997).

[10] Initially, the LDR did not require any payment to governments. Since 1995, in order to strengthen its position as one of the landowners, the municipal government has required that a payment must be made to itself to validate the land transfer. The payment is equivalent to a five-year land use fee at a rate charged to foreign tenants who use land for production and business. This rate is only a fraction of the prevalent land leasing prices.

Table 8.9.   Land Redevelopment under LDR in District A, Shanghai, 1992–2000

| LDR | Developer | Number of Projects | Amount of Building Floor Area Built (sq meters) | Building Floor Area as Percentage of Total |
|---|---|---|---|---|
| Derived from land use rights | Municipality-affiliated *danwei* | 138 | 3,674,677 | 57.3 |
| Transferred from district | Municipality-affiliated developer | 1 | 13,500 | 0.2 |
| government | District-affiliated developers | 69 | 1,709,494 | 26.6 |
| | District-affiliated *danwei* | 52 | 1,017,728 | 15.9 |
| | Subtotal | 122 | 2,740,722 | 42.7 |
| Total | | 260 | 6,415,399 | 100.0 |

*Source*: Author's survey.

Under the umbrella of growth coalitions, the local government and local developers cooperate in a fashion of reciprocity. The district government allows its subordinate development firms and *danwei* land users to carry out land redevelopment in the LDR mode. Land rent derived from underpriced land acquisition, which should otherwise go to the government coffers, is taken by the developers. In return, the beneficiaries have a responsibility to help the government for the benefit of community. Therefore, LDR land transfer is regarded as being more beneficial than land leasing in certain circumstances to the locality. This practice is obviously not to the superior central and municipal governments' advantage. Its currency is, however, buttressed by a tacit consent based on a new pro-development ideology which binds governments at all levels together. Land leasing has only been used so far for land plots on important locations which are jointly managed by both municipal and district governments, and mainly applied to foreign developers.

The new development ideology adopted since the economic reforms has transformed China's local governments into the developmental state responsible for local growth. The performance of the developmental state is predominantly gauged by economic and physical growth. For the old built-up District A, large-scale upgrading of dilapidated structures and relocation of residents from substandard housing after many decades of negligence and deterioration to decent apartments are the tasks at the top of the local government's agenda. The local government's tight budget is nevertheless grossly inadequate for this ambitious development program (Wang and Hu, 2001; Lin, 2000). The emerging real estate market initiated by the commoditization of land and buildings provides a key instrument drawing market capital into urban redevelopment. Different from policy-led government actions, redevelopment decisions by the developers are market-driven since the selling prices of new developments are determined by the demand and supply in the market.

A redevelopment project would not be justified if cost-benefit analysis does not anticipate profitability. The cost of acquiring the LDR is determined more or less by the amount of compensation to the sitting tenants for their relocation. Many districts, especially residential quarters in the central city of Shanghai, are of very high density — 80,000 habitants per sq kilometer on average in the 1980s. One neighborhood reached a density of 230,000 residents per sq kilometer — one of the highest in the world (Fung *et al.*, 1992). High density and thus the high cost of resident relocation make redevelopment costly. These residential quarters would not be considered ripe for redevelopment under current market conditions without government subsidies. In order to push for redevelopment, negotiations between developers and government often lead to alteration of planning parameters under the auspices of a flexible land use planning system in the interests of individual projects. Planning controls are used as a mechanism by which the developmental state negotiates with developers for mutual benefits (Zhu, 1999a, 1999b). It was found from the survey that one third of land use control items were not observed and revised after the release of the Land Use Planning Notes (see Table 8.8). The local government's receptive stance to demands for higher density makes land use planning a collaborative mechanism. As one of the defining elements of the LDR, the collaborative planning control is an important tool of the local growth coalition. It is noticeable that the other party of this collaboration is usually the district-affiliated *danwei* and developers. A quarter of the total redeveloped building floor area

(6.4 million sq meters) is undertaken by those local developers on the sites where current land use densities are probably high.

Individual projects may thus become financially feasible, but a capricious planning organization undermines certainty in the land market. A development control system open to bargaining creates additional uncertainty in the land market. Uncertainty leads to the absence of a predictable and transparent environment which is essential for market activities. There are rents generated from changing land use and increasing land use density without internalizing related externalities.[11] Externalities are pronounced in the urban land market (Bowers, 1992). When individuals make decisions to maximize utility, the costs and benefits of the decisions have to be internalized if the whole community is to be sustainable. Bargaining for increases in land use density without bearing arising social costs is thus a pursuit of rent-seeking: the capture of unearned profits with cost in the form of congestion and strained infrastructure borne by neighbors and the community. Unchecked rent-seeking facilitated by the authority's collaborative reception further breeds rent-seeking. Aggregation of externalities with no internalization brings the land market to the brink of the commons where land use planning is not observed. A quality built environment is collectively produced and maintained by order. When market order maintained by land use planning does not exist, market actors do not have a long-term perspective. Developers would choose to maximize returns within a short time frame. Building at a higher density seems feasible and sensible to recover redevelopment costs sooner than otherwise, knowing that other fellow developers would do the same.

In the development market structured by the LDR, it is observed that developers tend to engage more often in lengthy bargaining for favorable land use terms than in pursuing quality development (see Table 8.10).

---

[11] When there is relative land scarcity, land use zoning often determines the price of a piece of land by regulating its use and use intensity. A change to a more productive use and/or a higher density gives rise to a higher land price, other things being equal. In public land leasing, the price of land leasehold is determined by its land use and density. While zoning takes into consideration the community's environmental and infrastructural capacities, changing land use and raising land use density directly impact the community. Having higher land use density without paying for it means that these negative externalities are not internalized. Rents are created when individuals gain at the expense of the community.

Table 8.10.   Cases of Bargaining for Increasing Plot Ratio

| Project | Land Use Planning Note | Building Permit | Building Completed |
|---|---|---|---|
| B08 | | | |
| Date | November 1992 | June 1996 | NA |
| Plot ratio | 7.0 | 9.4 | — |
| B25 | | | |
| Date | May 1992 | May 1996 | March 1998 |
| Plot ratio | 6.0 | 8.6 | 8.6 |
| D18 | | | |
| Date | July 1993 | March 1995 | October 1998 |
| Plot ratio | 6.5 | 6.57 | 6.9 |
| D31 | | | |
| Date | June 1994 | March 1998 | December 1999 |
| Plot ratio | 5.5 | 6.4 | 6.75 |
| E11 | | | |
| Date | February 1994 | January 1996 | NA |
| Plot ratio | 1.0 | 2.3 | — |
| H04 | | | |
| Date | July 1994 | July 1997 | April 1999 |
| Plot ratio | 6.0 | 6.0 | 6.2 |
| H17 | | | |
| Date | June 1991 | August 1995 | April 1998 |
| Plot ratio | 3.5 | 3.7 | 4.2 |
| H31 | | | |
| Date | April 1994 | August 1996 | NA |
| Plot ratio | 5.0 | 5.3 | — |

*Source*: Author's survey.

The survey of application processes from initiation to the commencement of construction reveals that land acquisition is not time-consuming thanks to the institutions of land leasing and the LDR.[12] Finalization of site and building designs for projects under land leasing takes 12.5 months on average, but it takes an average of 29.3 months for projects under the LDR

---

[12] In a case of site clearance, it took 11 months to settle the relocation of 281 households and 16 *danwei* land users on a site of 1.53 hectares.

(see Table 8.11). LDR projects tend to have problems in raising development finance in time and in sufficient amounts. It is evident that the developers are engaged in intensive negotiations with authorities and state-owned banks for favorable terms. Suboptimal developments ensue as a result of cutting costs in architectural design and construction due to cost pressure. A comparison between two compatible groups of redevelopments (in similar locations) shows that projects are overall of higher quality in the land leasing mode than those in the LDR mode (see Table 8.12). Developers who have acquired land through land leasing at market prices are under cost pressure to distinguish their products from the competition of low-priced

Table 8.11.  Time Consumed in the Application Process

| Cases | Date Land Use Planning Note Issued (a) | Date Land Development Permit Issued (b) | Date Building Permit Issued (c) | Time-Gap between (a) and (b) (months) | Time-Gap between (b) and (c) (months) |
|---|---|---|---|---|---|
| **Land leasing** | | | | | |
| A01 | June 1993 | February 1994 | July 1995 | 8 | 17 |
| A11 | April 1993 | January 1994 | September 1994 | 9 | 8 |
| Average | | | | 8.5 | 12.5 |
| **LDR** | | | | | |
| B08 | September 1992 | March 1993 | June 1996 | 6 | 39 |
| B25 | November 1992 | March 1993 | May 1996 | 4 | 38 |
| C01 | August 1993 | December 1993 | July 1996 | 4 | 31 |
| C25 | December 1995 | January 1997 | July 1999 | 13 | 30 |
| D18 | July 1993 | May 1994 | May 1995 | 10 | 12 |
| D31 | October 1993 | June 1994 | March 1998 | 8 | 45 |
| D34 | September 1994 | March 1996 | July 1998 | 18 | 28 |
| H01 | August 1994 | September 1994 | May 1997 | 1 | 32 |
| H04 | July 1994 | November 1994 | July 1997 | 4 | 32 |
| H17 | June 1991 | March 1994 | August 1995 | 33 | 17 |
| H31 | April 1994 | December 1994 | August 1996 | 8 | 20 |
| I03 | March 1993 | November 1993 | March 1996 | 8 | 28 |
| Average | | | | 9.8 | 29.3 |

*Source*: Author's survey.

*Note*: A sample of 16 cases was selected from a census of 296 real estate projects developed during the period 1992–2000. Two cases were dropped due to incomplete data while the remaining 14 cases are presented herewith.

Table 8.12.   Comparison of the Quality of Office Property Developments

|  | Class A as Percentage of Total | Class B as Percentage of Total | Class C as Percentage of Total |
|---|---|---|---|
| Developments under land leasing | 74 | 26 | 0 |
| Developments under LDR | 23 | 62 | 15 |

*Source*: Author's survey.
*Note*: Classification of office property is done by the local real estate consultants based on building quality. Class A is the highest and Class C the lowest among the three classes, while Class B is in between. These statistics are based on a sample of 36 cases.

alternatives. A submarket is created where tenants pay rentals 30–40 percent higher than the alternatives developed in the LDR mode.

## 6. Conclusion

The LDR has eliminated the supply-side constraint and thus land redevelopment can be carried out in response to market demand. The institutional change is steered by a compelling desire to capture the land capital value gap created by a released pent-up demand for premises. However, under the auspices of the local growth coalition, the LDR is characterized as non-competitive land acquisition with flexible land use planning parameters on the basis of bargaining. In the local growth coalition buttressed by the LDR, a reciprocal relationship is demonstrated by a unique market provision of public goods (less profitable redevelopments pushed for, to the benefit of the local developmental state) and the state provision of private goods (rent-seeking allowed, to the benefit of local developers). A very flexible land use planning system subject to bargaining inevitably brings about rent-seeking, and prevalent rent-seeking makes the land market the commons. Planners' discretionary powers are understandable in the present era of rapid change when inflexible rules often seem too rigid. The balance between discretion and rules is, however, crucial; as Booth (1996, p. 110) states, "discretion and rules are not merely opposites, they are interdependent". In the transitional Chinese city of Shanghai, the quasi-commons in the land market and lack of competition in land acquisition often give rise to suboptimal urban construction.

Institutional change is fundamentally caused by competition towards a more efficient and productive system. North's notion of path dependence is obvious during incremental change from the socialist central planning system to an economy with market orientation, as the LDR evolves from the socialist land use right. It is meant to create a land market where land use efficiency can be improved through market mechanisms, while the old organizations of the *danwei* are still taken care of during the transition. The LDR is, however, deemed a transitional institution because it more often than not brings about a suboptimal utilization of land resources. The LDR cannot survive the circumstance of severe premise shortages. When building shortages have been alleviated considerably to the extent of over-supply, rapid quantitative growth is no longer warranted as a strategy or goal for the state to pursue. When given a choice, the customers weed out the inferior goods. This is demonstrated by the unsold and vacant buildings. Suboptimal utilization of land assets does not add positively to the credibility of the state. Rent-seeking breeds corruption. Finally, the central government, as a remote principal whose property rights over urban land have been attenuated by the institution of the LDR, has to strengthen its ownership. Since May 2001, the central government has strengthened its control of urban land ownership by issuing a directive demanding land transfer through land leasing. Land transfer through the LDR for property development is ruled out.[13] Clarification of property rights, a pre-condition for efficient resource utilization and optimal production, is therefore the goal for path-dependent institutional change.

## References

Ball, M. (1998). "Institutions in British Property Research: A Review". *Urban Studies*, 35(9), pp. 1501–1517.

Bertaud, A. and Renaud, B. (1994). *Cities without Land Markets: Lessons of the Failed Socialist Experiment*. Washington, DC: World Bank.

Booth, P. (1996). *Controlling Development: Certainty and Discretion in Europe, the USA and Hong Kong*. London: UCL Press.

---

[13] The Ministry of Land Resources has finalized regulations governing public land leasing in its Decree No. 11 issued on May 9, 2002 (http://www.people.com.cn/GB/14857/15305/25695/25909/25914/1974602.html, accessed on July 24, 2003).

Bowers, J. (1992). "The Economics of Planning Gain: A Re-Appraisal". *Urban Studies*, 29(8), pp. 1329–1339.

Coase, R.H. (1960). "The Problem of Social Cost". *The Journal of Law and Economics,* 3, pp. 1–44.

Fischel, W.A. (1985). *The Economics of Zoning Laws: A Property Rights Approach to American Land Use Controls*. Baltimore, MD: The Johns Hopkins University Press.

French, R.A. and Hamilton, F.E.I. (eds.) (1979). *The Socialist City: Spatial Structure and Urban Policy*. Chichester: John Wiley & Sons.

Fung, K.I. (1981). "Urban Sprawl in China: Some Causative Factors". In L.J.C. Ma and E.W. Hanten (eds.), *Urban Development in Modern China*, Boulder, CO: Westview Press, pp. 194–221.

Fung, K.I., Yan, Z.M. and Ning, Y.M. (1992). "Shanghai: China's World City". In Y.M. Yeung and X.W. Hu (eds.), *China's Coastal Cities: Catalysts for Modernization*, Honolulu: University of Hawaii Press, pp. 124–152.

Gregory, P.R. and Stuart, R.C. (1992). *Comparative Economic Systems*, 4th ed. Boston, MA: Houghton Mifflin.

Guy, S. and Henneberry, J. (Eds.) (2002). *Development and Developers: Perspectives on Property*. Oxford: Blackwell Science.

Harvey, J. (1987). *Urban Land Economics*. London: Macmillan.

Healey, P. and Barrett, S.M. (1990). Structure and Agency in Land and Property Development Processes: Some Ideas for Research". *Urban Studies*, 27(1), pp. 89–104.

Huang, Y. (1996). *Inflation and Investment Controls in China*. Cambridge: Cambridge Univerity Press.

IFTE/CASS (Institute of Finance and Trade Economics, Chinese Academy of Social Sciences) and IPA (Institute of Public Adminis-Institutional Change in China Ration) (1994). *Urban Land Use and Management in China*. Beijing: Jingji Publishing House [in Chinese].

Jackson, D.G. (1997). *Asia Pacific Property Trends: Conditions and Forecasts*. New York: McGraw-Hill Books.

Jud, G.D. (1980). "The Effects of Zoning on Single-Family Residential Property Values". *Land Economics*, 56, pp. 142–154.

Lin, G.C.S. (2002). "The Growth and Structural Change of Chinese Cities: A Contextual and Geographic Analysis". *Cities*, 19(5), pp. 299–316.

Lin, S. (2000). "Too Many Fees and Too Many Charges: China Streamlines Its Fiscal System". Background Brief No. 66, East Asian Institute, National University of Singapore.

Lü, X. and Perry, E.J. (1997). "Introduction" In X. Lü and E.J. Perry (eds.), *Danwei: The Changing Chinese Workplace in Historical and Comparative Perspective*, Armonk, NY: M.E. Sharpe, pp. 3–17.

Marcuse, P. (1996). "Privatization and Its Discontents: Property Rights in Land and Housing in the Transition in Eastern Europe". In G. Andrusz, M. Harloe and I. Szelenyi (eds.), *Cities after Socialism: Urban and Regional Change and Conflict in Post-socialist Societies*, Oxford: Blackwell, pp. 119–191.

Ng, M.K. and Xu, J. (2000). "Development Control in Post-reform China: The Case of Liuhua Lake Park". *Cities*, 17(6), pp. 409–418.

North, D.C. (1991). "Institutions". *Journal of Economic Perspectives*, 5(4), pp. 97–112.

North, D.C. (1993). "Institutional Change: A Framework of Analysis". In S.E. Sjostrand (ed.), *Institutional Change: Theory and Empirical Findings* Armonk, NY: M.E., Sharpe, pp. 35–46.

Oksenberg, M. and Tong, J. (1991). "The Evolution of Central-Provincial Fiscal Relations in China, 1971–1984: The Formal System". *The China Quarterly*, 125, pp. 1–32.

Qian, Y.Y. (2000). "The Process of China's Market Transition (1978–1998): The Evolutionary, Historical, and Comparative Perspectives". *Journal of Institutional and Theoretical Economics*, 156(1), pp. 151–171.

SBS (State Bureau of Statistics) (1995). *China Yearbook of Statistics*. Beijing: China Statistical Publishing [in Chinese].

SMBS (Shanghai Municipal Bureau of Statistics) (1991a–2001a). *Shanghai Real Estate Market*. Beijing: China Statistical Publishing [in Chinese].

SMBS (1991b–2001b). *Statistical Yearbook of Shanghai*. Beijing: China Statistical Publishing House [in Chinese].

*Straits Times* (Singapore) (1998). "Shanghai Stops Granting Land for Projects". January 15.

Sun, S.W. and Deng, Y.C. (1997). "A Study of the Role of Urban Planning in Shanghai". *Urban Planning Forum*, 2, pp. 31–39 [in Chinese].

SZBS (Shenzhen Bureau of Statistics) (2000). *Shenzhen Yearbook of Statistics*. Beijing: China Statistical Publishing [in Chinese].

Tang, Z.L. (1986). "Resident Relocation in Shanghai Central City". *Urban Planning Forum*, 41, pp. 12–21 [in Chinese].

Wang, H. (1994). *The Gradual Revolution*. New Brunswick, NJ: Transaction Books.

Wang, H.K. and Hung, C.T. (1997). "Shanghai's industrial relocation under land marketization: A case study on Shanghai electrical instrument works". Paper presented at the *International Symposium on Marketization of Land and Housing in Socialist China*, organized by Hong Kong Baptist University, October/November [in Chinese].

Wang, S. and Hu, A. (2001). *The Chinese Economy in Crisis: State Capacity and Tax Reform*. Armonk, NY: M.E. Sharpe.

World Bank (1993). *China: Urban Land Management in an Emerging Market Economy*. Washington, DC: The World Bank.

World Bank (2002). *Building Institutions for Markets: World Development Report 2002*. New York: Oxford University Press.

Wu, F.L. (2002). "China's Changing Urban Governance in the Transition Towards a More Market-Oriented Economy", *Urban Studies*, 39(7), pp. 1071–1093.

Xu, J. (2001) "The Changing Role of Land-use Planning in the Land-development Process in Chinese Cities: The Case of Guangzhou". *Third World Planning Review,* 23(3), pp. 229–248.

Xu, J. and NG, M.K. (1998). "Socialist Urban Planning in Transition: The Case of Guangzhou, China". *Third World Planning Review*, 20(1), pp. 35–51.

Yeh, A.G.O. and Wu, F.L. (1996). "The New Land Development Process and Urban Development in Chinese Cities". *International Journal of Urban and Regional Research*, 20(2), pp. 330–353.

Yeung, Y.M. and Sung, Y.W. (eds.) (1996). *Shanghai: Transformation and Modernisation under China's Open Policy*. Hong Kong: The Chinese University Press.

Zhao, M., Bao, G.L. and Hou, L. (1998). *Reforms of Land Use System and Development of Cities and the Country*. Shanghai: Tongji University Press [in Chinese].

Zhu, J.M. (1999a). "The Formation of a Market-oriented Local Property Development Industry in Transitional China: A Shenzhen Case Study". *Environment and Planning A*, 31(10), pp. 1839– 1856.

Zhu, J.M. (1999b). "Local Growth Coalition: The Context and Implications of China's Gradualist Urban Land Reforms". *International Journal of Urban and Regional Research*, 23(3), pp. 534–548.

CHAPTER 9

# A Transitional Institution for the Emerging Land Market in Urban China*

*Jieming Zhu*

Chinese economic reforms since 1978 have been a continuous process of fundamental institutional change. The new institution of ambiguous property rights over state-owned urban land evolves from the socialist institution of people's land ownership. This institutional change is driven by the changing economic system and by two new organizations — the local developmental state and *danwei*-enterprises. The new institution facilitates the formation of an emerging land market. This land market, structured by ambiguous property rights, has accounted for the dynamic urban physical growth in many of China's coastal cities in the 1980s and 1990s. Nevertheless, massive rent dissipation induced by the new institution does not provide market certainty, nor does it offer incentives for optimal development. The cost incurred by the institution is gradually overtaking its benefit. The ambiguous property rights are deemed to be a transitional institution during the development of land markets in urban China.

## 1. Introduction

China's economic reforms since the late 1970s have brought about tremendous changes in the country. The most significant change has occurred in the economy that has demonstrated a remarkable growth in

* Reprinted with the author's permission from *Urban Studies*, 42(8), pp. 1369–1390.

GDP at a rate of about 9 percent per annum on average since 1978. The quality of life of its citizens has improved markedly as a result. Market orientation and opening-up to the world are two key factors underpinning the economic miracle. Economic growth leads to physical change. It can be seen throughout China that infrastructure, urban amenities and housing have improved remarkably. China's cities have experienced a drastic transformation in the course of economic reforms. Urbanization has reached a new height after 30 years' stagnation (1949–1979) and, consequently, many more urban premises were built during the period 1980–2000 than in the period 1949–1979. Nevertheless, the fundamental achievement is the economic institutional change. The rules of the game have shifted from central planning to market orientation. An emerging urban land market is structured by newly evolved institutions which are responsible, to a large extent, for the phenomenon of rapid urban change. Formerly considered as a means of production, urban land is now regarded as an economic asset. The mode of China's urban land development and subsequently the built environment have thus been transformed significantly.

Based on a conceptual framework of institutions, this paper elaborates on how the socialist institution of people's land ownership has evolved into a new form to structure an emerging urban land market. After presenting the new institution of ambiguous property rights over urban land, the author argues that it is generated against the background of ongoing gradualist reforms and emerging new organizations. The ambiguous property rights serve the local growth coalition which is formed by two new organizations — the local developmental state and *danwei*-enterprises — a phenomenon in China's urban politics arising during the economic reforms. On the one hand, the ambiguous property rights contribute to a dynamic urban physical growth in many Chinese cities by creating a local property industry and opening up a land redevelopment market. On the other hand, the emerging land market structured by the ambiguous property rights is characterized by rent-seeking, hasty capitalization of land rents and inadequate order in land development. A distorted equilibrium of demand and supply, caused by the new institution, leads to building booms and oversupplies. It is argued that ambiguous property rights should be regarded as a transitional institution as they do not provide certainty — which institutions supposedly do — and they do not offer incentives for optimal land developments. An inadequate institution cannot survive for too long in an environment of market competition which pushes for further institutional change.

## 2. Transitional Institutions for the Land Market: A Conceptual Framework

Societies and markets are bound by institutions which are "the humanly devised constraints that structure political, economic, and social interactions" (North, 1991, p. 97). A society is deemed an organized community because individuals living together as group members share the same rules and customs which regulate their social behaviors. Institutions thus provide "regularities in behaviour which are agreed to by all members of a society and which specify behaviour in specific recurrent situations" (Schotter, 1981, p. 9). In the economic domain, institutions are deemed to be "sets of rights and obligations affecting people in their economic lives" (Matthews, 1986, p. 905). The functioning of an economic system depends on a whole set of institutional conditions. As institutions determine an incentive structure for the market, an efficient market should be shaped by institutions which minimize transaction costs and encourage competition through price and quality (North, 1998). Uncertainty in the interactions or transactions is effectively mitigated by institutions that limit the set of choices and increase the predictability of social behavior. On a pragmatic note, the World Bank (2002) defines institutions as rules, enforcement mechanisms and organizations. Organizations, whether they are political, economic or social, behave and perform as collective actors within a framework defined by institutions (Knight, 1992; Weimer, 1997).

Buildings or real estate are a special commodity in the market because of their heterogeneity, low liquidity, high transaction cost and location fixity. The real estate is thus geographically specific and differentiated in the market. Neoclassical economics holds such precepts that individuals behave rationally in maximizing utilities with preference, and relative prices drive the market towards a long-run equilibrium. Markets should therefore be structured as the players compete by price and quality rather than in other ways. Any real market is just a suboptimal deviation from the neoclassical ideal. However, since social interactions and market transactions are conditioned by institutions, in the same vein, the market of urban physical development is structured by institutions as well (Healey, 1992; Guy and Henneberry, 2002). Healey and Barrett (1990) suggest the structure-agency approach for the analysis of property development processes. Structure is "the framework within which individual agents make their choices" in the property market (Healey and Barrett, 1990, p. 90). Similarly, the notion of "structures of building provision" was coined by Ball (1998) to refer to "the contemporary network of relationships associated with the provision of particular types of building at specific points in time" (p. 1513). The structure within which agents make choices determines the development of the built environment. This structure, in the author's view, is the institution of property rights which are considered essential in the governance of the real estate market (Fischel, 1985; Webster and Lai, 2003). Clearly defined property rights are believed to be an imperative for economic efficiency. The Coase theorem specifies that free exchange with costless transactions tends to move resources to the highest-valued uses, independent of prior allocation of rights (Coase, 1960). However, in reality, transaction costs are always positive. The assignment of property rights thus matters for the achievement of efficiency.

Economic and social transformations suggest profound institutional change. Since 1978, significant changes with the single goal of national economic growth have occurred in China where a social transformation is being spearheaded by economic reforms. It has been determined that the reforms shall raise economic productivity — which had been in a dire situation under the central planning system — and install a market system to aggregate individual choices. Because of political constraints, gradualism prevails, which brings in an approach of trial and error in the implementation of new initiatives. Gradualism leads to dualism which means a co-existence of new and old institutions. It is understood that the old institutions, which formerly played a pivotal role in the outgoing planning system, have a vested interest in maintaining the status quo and are in a strong bargaining position to influence institutional change. Thus, not to become complete losers as a result of change, old organizations are given opportunities to adapt to the new game, to see if transformation can possibly proceed with the old actors managing the reforms.

Institutional change driven by gradual reforms thus produces institutions with the characteristic of transition (short-term) — the so-called transitional institutions which provide a link between the outgoing socialist planning system and an incoming system of market orientation. Not by design, but as a result of compromise and competition between the status quo interests and forward-looking forces, transitional institutions, tentative in nature, provide incentives for collaboration and coordinate economic activities among diverse actors. As the economic reforms progress to an advanced phase, transitional institutions will be phased out. In North's (1990) and Eggertsson's (1994) views, institutional change is always made marginal, incremental and path-dependent by an immense stock of social capital in the form of an institutional matrix. In this regard, institutional change is made by means of a series of transitional institutions.

Change of institutions is related to social choices and social choices are constrained by cultural norms. At this juncture, the role of informal institutions is brought to the scene. Institutions are composed of both formal rules like constitutions, regulations and laws, and informal constraints such as conventions, moral rules and social norms. Formal institutions are explicitly enforced by the state and organizations. When formal institutions are weak in maintaining order and managing transactions/interactions, informal institutions prevail. Transitional institutions are basically informal, as they are unwritten and implicit. Institutions are supposed to enhance certainty in the market by providing regularity and making market behaviors predictable (North, 1990). Although transitional institutions provide a framework for economic activities during the dynamic transformation, the informality of the institutional environment creates uncertainty. Uncertainty could prompt the orderly invention of a wide variety of schemes such as farming cooperatives, insurance and self-help groups to spread risks (Schotter, 1981). Uncertainty could also induce disorderly short-term behavior. In a close-knit homogeneous community, informal institutions as a product of collective action and unwritten codes of social conduct may serve to coordinate members' expectations and behaviors. Being culture-specific, informal institutions may not be sufficient to provide order in the absence of formal institutions when society becomes diverse and heterogeneous (World Bank, 2002). Conventions, moral rules and social norms are not necessarily shared and thus not necessarily observed among members of a diverse community (Mantzavinos, 2001; Elster, 1989). Although a move towards marketization, transitional institutions may not provide sufficient order and certainty to the emerging real estate market in urban China. Institutional change continues until order and certainty prevail.

## 3. The Advent of Ambiguous Property Rights

### 3.1. *Ambiguous property rights over urban land*

Since the founding of the socialist centrally controlled system in 1949, urban land in China has been nationalized and controlled by the state in the interests of the public. Local governments allocated land to users as a production means through directives, rather than by pricing mechanisms. Urban land was not considered a commodity according to the Marxist principles of socialist people's ownership and thus economic transactions of land were deemed illegal between owners and users.[1] After nationalization in the 1950s, China's urban economy became overwhelmingly state-owned. From 1954 to 1984, urban land was virtually a free good allocated through administrative channels (IFTE/CASS and IPA, 1992). State-owned enterprise (SOE) users' entitlement to land use rights became a unique institution incorporated in the formation of socialist cities. Free resources encourage users to over-consume without considering affordability. Land squandering was prevalent (Fung, 1981). As there were no incentives to relinquish occupied land — no compensation — land users held their land plots virtually in perpetuity. Land use rights, a distinctive socialist institution, extended SOE land users' *de facto* property rights over assigned state-owned land (Marcuse, 1996; Zhu, 2004a).

After a ten-year trial in the Shenzhen Special Economic Zone, commoditization and marketization of urban land have formally replaced the free allocation of land in all Chinese cities since 1988 when the National People's Congress approved an amendment to the 1982 Constitution that

---

[1] Clause 4, Article 10, of the 1982 Constitution stipulates: "Urban land belongs to the state. No organization or individual may appropriate, buy, sell or lease land, or unlawfully transfer it in other ways".

states: "the right of land use can be transferred in accordance with the law" (Zhu, 1999). Complementing an emerging market economy, public land leasing is legalized such that urban land can be leased to developers or users for a fixed period of time after a payment of rental in lump sum to the state. Land leasehold can be acquired through tender, auction or negotiation. After 30 years' practice of free allocation as a socialist production means, urban land has been restored as an economic asset.

Land leaseholds are supposedly acquired at market prices. Transfers of land rights through auction and tender are allocated through market mechanisms, reflecting the full market value of land, while purchasing leaseholds through negotiation is a practice where land prices are determined by negotiations between two parties: the local government as a seller and developers as buyers. Sales by auction and tender are transparent to the market, whereas sales through negotiation are non-transparent deals where land prices can vary very much. A dual land market has thus been invented (Zhu, 1994). Compared with the market of land acquisition through negotiation, the market of land acquisition by auction and tender is insignificant in terms of size. In the period 1988–1999, 36.4 sq kilometers of land were allocated through land leasing of which 97.7 percent was by negotiation, 2.0 percent by tender and 0.3 percent by auction in Shenzhen, a pioneer of the urban land reform (SZBS, 2000). During 1992–1999, 17 sq kilometers of land in Shantou were leased, 98.8 percent by negotiation and only 1.2 percent by tender and auction (STBS, 2000). Between 1992 and 2002 in Guangzhou, a total of 251 sq kilometers of land plots were transferred to applicants, of which 144 sq kilometers, accounting for 57 percent, were passed to SOEs with small payments (Li, 2002). Price disparities between the two modes of land supply are substantial. Price discounts implied in land leasing by negotiation are 80 percent on average and, in many cases, are as much as 100 percent (Liao, 1994). The old system of free allocation of land survives in the guise of land leasing by negotiation. This practice is derived from the ambiguous delineation of property rights over land between the principal and agents, i.e. between the central state, local governments and SOEs. The ambiguous property rights have arisen during the gradual reform of the economic system and with the emergence of two new organizations — the local developmental state and the *danwei*-enterprises.

### 3.2. *Changes in the economic system: Gradualism and dualism*

A planned economic system with central controls was adopted in 1949, and then top-down control mechanisms were installed, assisted by the nationalization of economic resources. The use and allocation of resources were determined by central plans. Prices, one of the most important mechanisms in the market system for resource allocation, bore little relationship to the equilibrium of demand and supply. Demand in the market was often ignored by the rigid planning system. After the disappointing performance of the planned economy for a period of 30 years, economic reform was launched in 1978 aiming towards the grand goal of building an efficient and strong economy. The rigid, centrally controlled planning system has been under restructuring in order to give room to bottom-up initiatives. Decentralization of economic management has set off an unprecedented transformation which is gradually replacing central directives with material incentives to the agents at local levels. Replacing the People's Commune, farm households become production units making decisions on what to grow and to sell at market prices after fulfilling the required planned output quotas. Urban SOEs are given autonomy in their production in the same manner. Commoditization and marketization, penetrating into the economic system at the margin initially, have been driving the change from a plan-controlled economy to a market-led one.

Nevertheless, institutional change brought about by the economic reform is intended in principle to improve productivity without fundamental changes to the system (Wang, 1994). The goal of establishing a socialist market economy has initiated changes in the economic organizations, but the political organizations, which used to be crucial components of the outgoing planned economy, are still more or less in place. A noticeable trait is that pragmatism has been substituted for socialist idealism. This pragmatism implanted in the reform process determines that transformation is incremental and gradual, as opposed to the drastic "shock therapy" adopted by the former Soviet Union and East European socialist countries. Gradualism is meant as an instrument to legitimize rather than undermine the existing political system. The reform has thus turned out to be a process of "muddling through" without a blueprint to guide the unprecedented changes. "Crossing the river by groping for stones" is a succinct adage revealing the underlying philosophy. It is exemplified by how the country is opened up to foreign capital and how non-state-owned sectors grow. Both foreign capital and the private sector were driven out after the Communist Party gained control over China in 1949. Foreign investment was sought out at first in four special economic zones set up in 1979, and then in 14 coastal open cities in 1984. Only in 1992 were cities in other regions granted autonomy to attract foreign investment with favorable policies (Qian, 2000). Initially, foreign partners were allowed as a minor party and later majority ownership was permitted. Foreign capital returning to China since 1978 has been in a dual process of gradual penetration: geographical expansion and ownership domination (Morris *et al.*, 2002). In the course of the reforms, non-state-owned enterprises have been growing and have become an indispensable component of the economy. State-owned and collective-owned enterprises accounted for 77.6 and 22.4 percent of the total industrial output in 1978, respectively. There were no private-owned industries then. In 1999, state-owned and collective-owned enterprises contributed 28.2 and 35.4 percent respectively and the remaining 36.4 percent was produced mainly by private-owned industrial firms (SBS, 2000).

In spite of these fundamental changes, gradualism remains the key spirit of the economic reform which has already been ongoing for a quarter of a century. Dualism, the co-existence of new and old institutions, thus emerges as a result of compromise and cooperation. It is meant to provide a mechanism that introduces market elements while retaining planning controls for the sake of social stability. It is expected to provide a path to transition by mitigating the effects of the redistribution of political powers and economic benefits entailed in the reform process. In short, it is "to implement a reform without creating losers" who are likely to hamper the reform (Lau *et al.*, 2000, p. 122). One of the dualist measures was dual-track pricing, implemented in the 1980s and early 1990s (Wu and Zhao, 1987). Lau *et al.* (2000, p. 121) explain its rationale in this way: a market track is introduced under which economic agents participate in the market at free-market prices, provided that they fulfill their obligations under the pre-existing plan.

It was applied to agricultural goods at first, and then extended to industrial goods and labor markets (Sicular, 1988; Byrd, 1991; Lin, 1992).

Markets are therefore expected to "grow out of the plan" (Naughton, 1995). Local governments as well as SOE agents take more responsibility for making decisions. Incentives for profit maximization mediated by the market have come into force on the one hand. On the other hand, socialist redistribution between profit-making and loss-making SOEs, coordinated by the remnants of planning control, remains effective to a certain extent (Xiao, 1991). Both coordination mechanisms of top-down directives and bottom-up initiatives are at work. Both material and coercive incentives, which link the principal's goals to the agents' performance, are in place to motivate agents (Zhu, 2000).

### 3.3. *Two new organizations hatched out during transition: The local developmental state and danwei enterprises*

The socialist state and SOEs are two essential actors in the outgoing centrally planned system. Acting as an omnipotent provider, the state, together with its agents — SOEs and local governments — dominated the economy and society. Without these two organizations, the centrally controlled economy would not have been sustained. The state is transforming itself from an economic producer and socialist welfare provider to an advocate of marketization. The socialist authoritarian state is changing from its preoccupation with political correctness to the pursuit of economic growth in order to legitimize itself by improving the lives of its citizens, with the progressive reforms that are gradually phasing out unsustainable socialist welfarism and letting the market take over its role of provision. In the same vein, SOEs as agents of the socialist state are shedding their obligatory social responsibilities to become independent modern enterprises.

As the leading paradigm for the development of East Asian capitalist economies, the developmental state places top priority on economic development, productivity and national competitiveness (Johnson, 1982). China's developmental state emerges from its origin as a socialist state in this context (White and Wade, 1988; Woo-Cumings, 1999). At the same time, devolution occurs in the central-local intergovernmental power structure and localities are given more latitude in making investment decisions and managing local growth. This process is led by the fiscal decentralization initiated in 1984 to change the fiscal system from profit remittance to taxation levy. Local fiscal revenue and expenditure were controlled by central planning to a great extent in the pre-reform era, as the control of revenue resources was one of the essential components of the centrally controlled planning system (Oksenberg and Tong, 1991; Huang, 1996). The kernel of revised fiscal contracts between the central and local governments is that the latter have become "residual claimants" of fiscal revenue — a strong incentive for local governments to pursue local economic development (Qian, 2000).

No longer being passive agents of the central government, China's provincial and municipal governments are made active actors pursuing local growth because of decentralization, which results in competition between the center and localities (Solinger, 1992; Wang, 1994; Nolan, 1995; Oi, 1995; Unger and Chan, 1995; Wong *et al.*, 1995; Huang, 1996). Localism has re-emerged in China's national politics as local governments compete with each other in pursuing development strategies to stimulate local growth and expand fiscal capacity (Wong, 1987, 1992). As a result, autonomous local governments are highly motivated to maximize local revenues and subsequent increases in the state budget deficit have compromised the central government's capacity (Breslin, 1996; Lin, 2000). China's local governments have become an economic interest group with their own policy agenda and preferences and thus have become the local developmental state — a term coined to capture its unique characteristics.

The developmental state plays an active and strategic role in guiding market forces to achieve the goal of economic growth. A capitalist developmental state is "a plan-rational economy with market-rational political institutions" (Johnson, 1995, p. 28). "Embedded autonomy", or insulation from political and social pressures, allows the developmental state to be relatively free from predation and rent-seeking (Evans, 1995). By this definition, China's local developmental state has close links (embedded) to society, but it is not independent from the political and business interests of society (insulation) (Zhu, 1999, 2002). In this regard, having the same rationale of pro-growth legitimization, China's local developmental state is different from the paradigm of Asian developmental states in three respects: its socialist origin, competition between localities and the tenure of its local leaders being dependent on the authorities at a higher level. Dependence is twofold. On the one hand, the common interests in local growth entice a reciprocal relationship between the local developmental state and business interest groups. Facing intense competition from other localities, the local developmental state endeavors to create a favorable business climate for businesses to prosper, which directly leads to local growth. On the other hand, political central control over local developmental states is still retained as a main instrument, for the Party-led central government to remain relevant. Despite the considerable experience gained by local officials in managing the locality, their political existence and advancement are still determined by the central state according to their performance. This performance has been largely measured by economic growth rates and urban physical changes. Short-term quantitative growth is thus pursued at the expense of long-term quality development.

The reform of SOEs is intended to substitute market mechanisms for mandatory planning coordination. Under the central planning system, the state and state-owned economic units or *danwei*[2] were closely related as one entity, rather than as two parties — the principal and independent agents. By separating management from the state ownership of enterprises, the SOE reform has taken several steps to change the business decision-making process and to improve production efficiency with instilled managerial responsibility and fnancial accountability (Aram and Wang, 1991; Fan, 1994; Perkins, 1995; Hope, 1996). After almost two decades of SOE reforms, SOEs have gained a certain degree of, but not complete, autonomy. It is believed that government officials are still making important decisions for many large-sized SOEs based on non-economic logic (Hu, 2000). Although there has been a remarkable achievement in the ownership change of enterprises (Xu and Wang, 1999; Zweig, 2001) and although non-state-owned firms contribute an ever-increasing share to the industrial output (Scalapino, 1999), SOEs remain the largest employers in the country. SOEs employed 78 percent of the urban workforce in 1978 and the figure was only reduced to 55 percent in

---

[2] State-owned units in socialist countries, or *danwei* in China, are a link in social redistribution chains. The *danwei*, literally meaning work unit in English, is a profound socialist institution which used to be essential and is, to a certain extent, still important to Chinese urban residents. The functions of *danwei* are more than just organizing required production. They are a mechanism through which the state distributes socialist welfare to workers (Li, 1993).

1999 (SBS, 2000). The SOEs' role of providing full employment, jobs for life and welfare to workers made SOEs a profound socialist institution in the pre-reform era (Putterman and Dong, 2000). Socialist comprehensive welfare has been phased out in the course of reforms, but a social security system is yet to be established.

Nevertheless, rising unemployment rates, increasingly a menace to social and political stability (Weller and Li, 2000), prevent the SOE reform from further deepening (Hu, 1996; Hassard *et al.*, 2002). SOEs still have to shoulder some of the social responsibilities on behalf of governments to avoid a massive outbreak of social problems. Having to retain redundant workers and shoulder the heavy burdens of welfare obligated to retired workers, SOEs can easily justify their continuous access to the soft-budget guarantees provided by the government, until the transfer of welfare provision (social safety net) from *danwei* to local governments finally takes place.[3] Thus, SOEs are concerned with profits and losses, but are not entirely responsible for them. The state has to help some loss-making SOEs survive for the overriding goal of political stability. Therefore, SOEs are transformed to take a dual role. Many SOEs are both an agent of the state (*danwei*) and an actor in the emerging market (enterprise). The term *danwei*-enterprise is coined to suggest this dual nature, between a quasi-state and an enterprise. *Danwei*-enterprises, being a hybrid of independent enterprises and apparatuses of the local developmental state, possess characteristics of both *danwei* and autonomous firms.

### 3.4. *Ambiguity to the advantage of localities*

The gradual reforms without a blueprint have led institutional change on an uncharted route. The distinctions between the governing rules of the two economic entities created by dualism are often blurred to the

---

[3] SOEs had heavy social burdens, providing an array of social services (housing, medical insurance, pensions). A quick look at the issue of retirees reveals the enormous social obligation borne by SOEs. Retirees accounted for 25 percent of the total number of urban workers in 1997; about 20 percent of SOEs' capital assets were buried in social projects; housing for employees cost SOEs an extra 35–40 percent of total wages; and the cost for medical care accounted for 12 percent of total wages (Liu, 1997).

advantage of parties with vested interests. The problematic formulation of central-local intergovernmental fiscal relations reflects the scope of central-local tensions regarding the extent of decentralization (Wong *et al.*, 1995). The local developmental state pushes local autonomy to the limit. Since 1978, the consistent growth of extra-budgetary funds, which are outside the central planning system, has testified to the extent of decentralization that localities have gained (Blecher, 1991; White, 1991; Wang, 1995). While decentralization is the spirit of the economic reforms, the central government does not wish to see its roles of central coordination and regional redistribution marginalized. The scope of decentralization is thus made negotiable, which induces competition between the center and localities. Competition without clear rules yields ambiguity.

Ambiguous property rights over state assets are pursued and administered by the local developmental state that aims to capture state assets as much as possible, for the advantage of localities. Economic growth, physical change and social stability are the fundamental objectives of the local developmental state, while *danwei*-enterprises struggle to survive and keenly pursue expansion. It is local growth that binds the two actors. Growth coalitions, similar to "urban regimes" (Mollenkopf, 1983; Logan and Molotch, 1987; Swanstrom, 1988; Stone, 1989; Zhu, 1999), are formed between the local developmental state and *danwei*-enterprises in China's urban politics. Ambiguous property rights are the key mechanism in the operation of growth coalitions. The local developmental state, because of its intimate involvement in the economic sphere, may still be engaged in redistribution between profit-making and loss-making SOEs in the management of local economies (Wei and Wang, 1997; Nanto and Sinha, 2002; Wang, 2002), instead of being a disinterested state for third-party enforcement of market rules and social redistribution. As agents of the local developmental state, *danwei*-enterprises are engaged in a dual role as production units for profit and as quasi-states because of their residual role in managing social stability. A reciprocal relationship is thus found between these two organizations. *Danwei*-enterprises receiving assistance in the form of asset appropriation need to shoulder some responsibilities on behalf of the local developmental state by retaining redundant workers (Wang, 2002) and undertaking unprofitable but socially significant projects (such as slum clearance and redevelopment of dilapidated high-density housing).[4]

However, with the separation of control from state ownership, *danwei*-enterprises begin to command the assets held and become agents in autonomous pursuit of their own interests. Principal-agent problems emerge as a consequence of there being no simultaneous privatization process. The line is often blurred between implicit taking of state subsidies and illegitimate poaching of state assets. The ambiguous property rights are to the advantage of local growth coalitions and at the expense of the central government's land revenue income. The local developmental state and *danwei*-enterprises are clear beneficiaries.

## 4. An Emerging Real Estate Market Structured by Ambiguous Property Rights

Economic change in China since 1978 is significantly reflected in the degree of marketization and openness. Increasingly autonomous SOEs, structural change in enterprise ownership and profits instead of commands as coordination mechanisms indicate how far the economy has progressed towards a market.[5] Decentralization and marketization create

---

[4] Shanghai's housing development and provision in the 1980s and 1990s are an example in illustration. Commoditization or privatisation leads to an increasing share of private housing in the market over the years and private housing has become the norm for housing supply since the late 1990s. There was no commodity housing in 1982. However, provision of commodity housing accounted for 95.2 percent of total housing space supplied in 2000 (SMBS, 2001a, 2001b). Commodity housing sold to households had to be subsidized by the state in the 1980s. While the percentage of households buying housing at market prices has been increasing since the late 1980s, *danwei*-enterprises have taken over the role of the state by assigning their employees subsidized housing which is purchased directly in the market. During 1982–1984, *danwei* acquired 31.0 percent of total housing units at market prices. In the period 1991–1993, *danwei* purchased 78.5 percent of total housing units in the market (SMBS, 1994b).

[5] Openness brings in competition and thus enhances consumer sovereignty. Only 3 percent of total retail sales in China were transacted at market prices in 1978 (Naughton, 1995, p. 14). By the late 1990s, 60–70 percent of goods and services had their prices determined in the market (Zhao, 1999). Imports and exports as percentages of GDP suggest how open an economy is to the world economy. Imports and exports only accounted for 5.2 and 4.6 percent of China's GDP in 1978 respectively. The percentages rose to 21.2 (imports) and 23.3 (exports) in 2002 (SBS, 2003) whereas the sum of exports and imports as a percentage of GDP is about 30 percent in America, Japan, India and Brazil (Woodall, 2004, p. 8).

an environment for competition and competition seemingly hatches out a market. Market orientation since the 1980s is deemed a key factor contributing to the extraordinary economic growth which has brought about rapid urbanization and urban land development. Between 1949 and 1978, urban population as a percentage of the total national population only increased from 10.6 to 17.9. By 2001, it had risen to 37.7 percent, with a net increment of 308.1 million urban residents between 1978 and 2001. As a result, the total urban built-up area increased from 9,386 sq kilometers (1985) to 24,027 sq kilometers (2001) and the total building floor space in cities increased from 2.32 billion sq meters (1985) to 11.01 billion sq meters (2001) (SBS, 2002). There were no commercially developed buildings before 1978. An increasing percentage of buildings has been produced by developers in the market since the 1980s; these are the so-called commodity buildings whose prices are determined by the equilibrium of demand and supply (see Table 9.1).

It appears that building supply responds to demand. Buildings as economic assets are seemingly sold and bought at prices determined by buyers and sellers. Albeit not perfectly and efficiently, property prices have been changing and adjusting according to situations in the market. During the period 1988–1994, Shenzhen's housing prices had fluctuations

Table 9.1.   Development of Commodity Buildings/Housing in China and Shanghai

|  | Commodity Building Floor Space as a Percentage of the Total Building Floor Space | Commodity Housing Floor Space as a Percentage of the Total Housing Floor Space |
|---|---|---|
| China |  |  |
| 1994 | 8.1 | NA |
| 1997 | 9.5 | NA |
| Shanghai |  |  |
| 1990 | 2.9 | 4.3 |
| 1994 | 13.5 | 23.7 |
| 1997 | 40.4 | 54.1 |

*Sources*: SBS (1995, 1998); SMBS (1991a, 1995a, 1998a).

of between +95 percent and −22 percent (ECSYRE, 1995). Entry into the development market does not seem restricted.

There were no developers at all in 1980. In 2001, there were 29,552 developers registered in China (SBS, 2002). However, China's emerging real estate market is not a neoclassical model where the "invisible hand" governs. It is structured by the transitional institution of ambiguous property rights.

If property rights are not clearly delineated, some valued assets will be left in the public domain, subject to open access (Barzel, 1989). Open access to land assets in the public domain brings in hasty capitalization of land assets before the option vanishes. Because of ambiguity, *danwei*-enterprises' land use rights take priority over the landowner's rights. In the context of gradual reforms that do not endorse any long-term measures, the ambiguous property rights are hardly protectable and stable. Although robust market demands for buildings and acute shortages of urban premises (resulting from suppressed building construction in the previous era of centrally controlled urbanization) press for supply, *danwei*-enterprises are also motivated to rush out hasty development projects in order to capitalize land assets held, rather than to maximize land value by waiting for the best timing and opportunity. Land plots could be taken back by the government (the landowner) if not developed promptly.

The ambiguous property rights further complicate the process of land development. Meant to provide certainty to ensure the maintenance of quality neighborhoods, land use planning control as a collective property right is made uncertain because of ambiguity. The land development right as a component of land rights should be defined by land use planning which regulates the land market according to how land should be developed. China's land use planning is adapting itself from being a constituent of the centrally controlled system to being a regulation authority for the emerging market economy. Rigid control is discarded and replaced by flexible and responsive rules. While the local developmental state is not a disinterested regulatory third party in the economic sphere, the land use planning system is used as a tool by the growth coalition which requires a great deal of discretion in the implementation of development projects. Land use planning is highly discretionary and decision-making in the planning process is not transparent at all (Zhu, 2004a). An underdeveloped legal system also contributes to an absence of effective development controls, as planning procedures and operations are often open to interpretation and manipulation by the authorities.[6] The land development right is highly unpredictable as it is ambiguously defined, which creates disorder in the land development market.

## 5. Ambiguous Property Rights: A Transitional Institution

### 5.1. *Performance*

Under the auspices of local growth coalitions, the institution of ambiguous property rights over urban land has helped to create a local property development industry and to open up a market for urban land redevelopment which was locked up by the old socialist institution. As a result, many of China's cities have seen tremendous urban physical growth since the late 1980s. Prior to 1980, the development of socialist cities was entirely a matter for the state, as the state owned all the means of production. All land and building developments were carried out either by governments on behalf of users or by occupants themselves. Marketization and rapid economic growth in the 1980s at first created a market of user demand for land and buildings from overseas investments and local businesses. A property development industry was needed to meet the market demand for premises. The substantial amount of capital required up-front, however, prevented SOEs from initiating developments. SOEs had not been moulded as real enterprises operating under market conditions and there was hardly any source from which to raise development finance. The first generation of local developers grew up by participating in joint ventures between foreign development capital and local land plots in the late 1980s. The local SOE partners were given access to land as initial capital to contribute to the venture. The ambiguous property rights allowed these SOEs to appropriate state land assets. A strong demand for buildings and initial state land assets brought back market-oriented local developers, after an absence of 40 years from China's cities (Zhu, 1999). In Guangzhou, for

---

[6] China's land use planning system is elaborated on thoroughly by Xu (2001), Ng and Xu (2000) and Xu and Ng (1998). An illustrious case about the workings of the planning system is provided by Xu (2001). During the period 1992–1996, the mayor of Guangzhou issued at least 2,000 memos to the city planning bureau to request planners to follow his suggestions in dealing with development applications.

example, there were 553 local developers in 1994. The number of developers went up to 925 in 2001 (GZBS, 2002).

Due to dynamic market demands, the widening gap between the potential capital value of "the highest and best land use" and the present capital value[7] of the existing land use constituted a powerful incentive for land redevelopment in many vibrant Chinese cities where many existing structures had been built before 1949. However, redevelopment of these brownfield sites remained hampered by the sitting land users, although land leasing has led to a development market for greenfield sites since 1988. There was hardly any leasing of brownfield sites for redevelopment before the early 1990s. Capitalization of the land capital value gap had a supply-side constraint, tenants' land use rights having become *de facto* ownership rights. SOE land tenants were then offered an option to develop land plots based on their land use rights, which was meant to eliminate the supply-side constraint, and land redevelopment could be carried out in response to market demand. This measure, based on the institution of ambiguous property rights, should be considered effective in freeing land redevelopment shackled by old institutions during the transition. A survey reveals that during 1992–2000 in a district of Shanghai, 77.6 percent of a total of 8.26 million sq meters of building floor space was developed on sites of that nature (Zhu, 2004a).

The era of economic reforms since 1978 can be divided into three periods with regard to the characteristics of land development: Period I (1978–1987) when land was still a free means of production; Period II (1988–1992) when greenfield land sites were developed extensively under the new regime of land commoditization; and Period III (1993 to present) when brownfield land sites are brought into the land market by *danwei* land users. According to a sample of five cities, land and building developments occurred in ever-increasing numbers (see Table 9.2). Nationally, on average, the floor areas of buildings under construction in 1995 were 80.3 percent more than those in 1990. An examination of seven provinces/municipalities (Shanghai, Zhejiang, Shandong, Guangdong, Hainan, Guizhou and Gansu) revealed that there were increments of between 14.6 percent (Gansu) and 127.6 percent (Zhejiang) during the same period (SBS, 1991, 1996).

---

[7] The present capital value of land is "net returns expected to be earned in future years" (Harvey, 1987, p. 97).

Table 9.2.  Development of Buildings (Floor Space on Average Every Year) (million sq meters)

|                              | Shanghai | Guangzhou | Wuhan | Xi'an | Chengdu |
|------------------------------|----------|-----------|-------|-------|---------|
| Period I, 1978–1987          | 8.35     | 3.92      | 2.88  | 1.88  | 6.19    |
| Period II, 1988–1992         | 9.58     | 6.29      | 5.36  | 2.11  | 10.49   |
| Period III, 1993–2000        | 21.97    | 12.62     | 10.13 | 4.23  | 17.95   |
| Increase rate, I–II (%)      | 14.7     | 60.5      | 86.1  | 12.2  | 69.5    |

Sources: SMBS (2002a); GZBS (2002); WHBS (2002); XABS (2002); CDBS (2002).

Shantou, a medium-sized city in Guangdong Province, saw its built-up area expand from 7.8 sq kilometers (1979) to 63.7 sq kilometers (1999) in a period of just 20 years (STBS, 2000). Dongguan, a county town in the same province, witnessed its urban area increasing from 16.2 sq kilometers (1988) to 41.1 sq kilometers (1993) (Yeh and Li, 1999). Between 1993 and 2000 in a district of Shanghai, 4.81 million sq meters of building floor area were constructed, while 2.49 million sq meters of old structures were demolished (SMBS, 1994b–2001b). The total building stock by 1990 was 9.08 million sq meters (SMBS, 1991b). These figures suggest that a quarter of the building stock was demolished and 53 percent was added during the period. Similarly, during the same period, building construction and demolition in the whole city of Shanghai were undertaken on an unprecedented scale: 131.2 million sq meters constructed and 30.5 million sq meters demolished (SMBS, 1994b–2001b). In all, 17.7 percent of the total building stock of 172.6 million sq meters in Shanghai Municipality in 1990 was demolished during 1993–2000.

## 5.2. Implications

The ambiguous property rights, however, induce rent-seeking. Price disparities between the two land markets (land leasing by auction/tender and land leasing through negotiation) generate rents.[8] It has been estimated that

---

[8] According to Krueger (1974) and Tullock (1993), rent-seeking normally arises in the context of artificial interference with markets by the state whose restrictions give rise to rent in a variety of forms. It is a societally costly pursuit of transfers, when individual efforts to maximize value generate social waste rather than social surplus (Buchanan, 1980, p. 4), the so-called welfare-reducing effects of political competition over redistribution (Olson, 1982).

during the period 1987–2000, 300,000 hectares of land were leased out nationwide, of which only 5 percent was through auction and tender.[9] Rent dissipation reportedly occurred at a rate of about 10 billion yuan every year at the cost of the state landowner's revenue income.[10] It is the two-tier incentive structure that has constructed the dynamics of building construction booms. On the one hand, the commoditization and marketization of buildings make property development a viable business driven by profit-pursuing. On the other hand, the capitalization of land rents generated between the two land markets is another driving force behind rapid land (re)development. Since property development projects on publicly leased land make up an insignificant fraction of the total supply of commodity space, the unprecedented urban physical change in the 1990s is mainly accounted for by the developments in another land market which was driven by property demand as well as by the capitalization of land rents.[11]

Oversupply of commodity buildings occurred as a result (Jackson, 1997; Zhao *et al.*, 1998). Shanghai was allegedly facing the biggest property glut in its history in the late 1990s (Lee, 1998; Haila, 1999). Between 1991 and 2000 in Guangzhou, 54.6 million sq meters of commodity buildings were on sale and only 30.5 million sq meters were sold. The unsold floor space accounted for 44 percent of the total. Similarly, during the same period, 30.4 million sq meters of commodity housing were on sale and only 22.5 million sq meters were sold (Li, 2002).

Hasty land developments are driven by landholders' rent-seeking behaviors, because rents generated from the dual land market cannot be safely stored for long during an uncertain transition period. Gradualism implies unpredictable changes and dualism will not be perpetual. The ambiguous property rights, based upon gradualism and dualism, are thus insecure. When uncertainty occurs, it prevents actors from making rational and the most appropriate decisions because they do not know the causality, which deprives actors of a long-term perspective. Land leasing

---

[9] See http://www.people.com.cn/GB/14857/15304/21521/2081658.html, accessed September 10, 2003.

[10] See http://www.peopledaily.com.cn/GB/14857/22238/28463/28464/2015058.html, accessed September10, 2003.

[11] Several in-depth case studies can be found in Wang and Hung (1997), Zhao *et al.* (1998), Wu and Zhang (2000) and Zhu (2002, pp. 50–51).

projects can wait for the best timing to be initiated because of secure property rights. Furthermore, risk is part and parcel of real estate businesses. Underpriced land causes a weak sense of risk-bearing, which makes developers less cautious in initiating projects than they would be if land were acquired at market prices. Uncertainty induces prompt capitalization of land rents. Capitalization of land rents can be materialized only through undertaking land (re)development. The opportunity of rent capitalization could be otherwise lost. Between 1997 and 2002, 1466 hectares, out of a total of 8,550 hectares of sites which were not promptly developed, were taken back from landholders by the Guangzhou municipal government (Li, 2002).

The ambiguous property rights compromise the third-party role of the state in the emerging land market. Having sampled the cases of development control dealt with by the Shanghai Municipal Planning Bureau in the 1980s, a survey disclosed that 46.8 percent of the cases were in discordance with the requirements of the land use master plans, after 3.3 times of negotiation (bargaining) on average for each case (Sun and Deng, 1997). The author's survey shows that the bargaining propensity did not change much in the 1990s. Numerous negotiations are observed from a sample of 23 cases which are selected from a census of 296 real estate projects conducted during the period 1992–2000.[12] The bargaining results in many discrepancies. After negotiations, revision rates in four development control parameters (land use, plot ratio, site coverage and building height) reach the extent of 71 percent. Bargaining even goes into the construction stage. Discrepancies in the same four planning parameters reach 34 percent between what is stipulated in land use planning and what is actually built. Almost all cases bargain for higher densities and more floor space. Externalities imposed by these alterations fail to internalize and certainty for the real estate market is seriously undermined. Furthermore, there are rents generated from changing land use and land use density. This planning system thus invites rent-seeking and creates disorder in the land development market.

---

[12] It is noticed that land acquired through open leasing is not subject to negotiation. Negotiations for changing land development parameters occur on land held by *danwei*-enterprises.

Table 9.3.   Comparison of the Quality of Office Property Developments

|  | Class A as a Percentage of the Total | Class B as a Percentage of the Total | Class C as a Percentage of the Total |
|---|---|---|---|
| Developments in the mode of land leasing | 74 | 26 | 0 |
| Developments in the mode of ambiguous property rights | 23 | 62 | 15 |

*Source*: Author's survey.
*Note*: Classification of office property is done by local real estate consultants based on building quality. Class A is the highest and Class C the lowest among the three classes, while Class B is in between. These statistics are based on a sample of 36 cases.

Suboptimal developments ensue. A comparison between two compatible groups (in similar locations) of redevelopments shows that land leasing projects are overall of higher quality than those projects with ambiguous property rights (see Table 9.3). Developers who have acquired land through land leasing at market prices are under cost pressure to distinguish their products from the competition of low-priced alternatives. As a result, a submarket emerges where tenants are willing to pay 30–40 percent more rent for office buildings developed in the land leasing mode. Office buildings developed in this mode saw an average vacancy rate of 7.1 percent (based on 19 samples) and those developed in the mode of ambiguous property rights suffered an average vacancy rate of 14.1 percent (based on 8 samples) by the end of 2002.

Rent-seeking inevitably implicates government officials in charge of land allocation. Between 1999 and 2002, there were 549,000 cases of corruption involved with land deals, and 3,800 officials were accused nationwide.[13] All the costs incurred by the institution of ambiguous property rights are increasingly becoming greater than its benefits.

---

[13] See http://www.people.com.cn/GB/2014899. html, accessed September 24, 2003.

## 5.3. *Pushing for Further Institutional Change*

Institutions are created to cope with pervasive uncertainty in the human world (Heiner, 1983) and institutions "reduce uncertainty by providing a structure to everyday life" (North, 1990, p. 3). Formation of rules thus aims to reduce complexity and uncertainty and to lower transaction costs (Williamson, 1985). Although providing incentives for land (re)development, the ambiguous property rights as unwritten and informal rules do not provide certainty for the emerging real estate market. Therefore, the ambiguous property rights are a transitional institution. Further institutional change is propelled by organizational change in the context of market competition. The local developmental state and *danwei*-enterprises, two prominent organizations during the gradual reforms, are given room and time by the ambiguous property rights to be transformed gradually while market mechanisms develop. The local developmental state adapts itself to fit into the market and *danwei*-enterprises evolve to become full market players.

The SOE reforms deepened in the mid-1990s when the term "socialist market economy" was officially coined, indicating the long-term direction of economic reforms. Privatization of small and medium-sized SOEs and the corporatization of large SOEs began. Many SOEs have since completed the transformation towards shareholding companies and have been listed on the Shanghai and Shenzhen Stock Exchanges (Broadman, 1995; Iskander, 1996). SOE's roles in urban physical development have been diminishing (see Table 9.4). In Guangzhou, SOE developers' share in the real estate development market in 1995 was 46.3 percent in terms of floor space. Their share in 2001 dropped to 13.3 percent (GZBS, 2002). Non-state-owned entities and private firms are taking over SOEs as main actors in the new economy. The *danwei* is fading out and *danwei*-enterprises are discarding their *danwei* responsibilities and becoming independent enterprises. The amount of housing purchased by *danwei* at market prices and then assigned to employees at subsidized prices has been decreasing. A total of 78.5 percent of all housing units in the market were sold to *danwei* in the period 1991–1993 (SMBS, 1994b). This dropped to 2.8 percent in 2002 (SMBS, 2003b).

Table 9.4. Investment in Fixed Assets by SOEs as a Percentage of the Total in Five Cities

| Year | Shanghai | Guangzhou | Wuhan | Xi'an | Chengdu |
|------|----------|-----------|-------|-------|---------|
| 1980 | 88.6 | 94.5 | 96.7 | 97.2 | 93.3 |
| 1985 | 80.9 | 86.4 | 78.5 | 88.2 | 71.8 |
| 1990 | 84.7 | 89.0 | 86.6 | 89.0 | 70.3 |
| 1995 | 59.8 | 61.9 | 59.0 | 59.8 | 50.2 |
| 2001 | 38.1 | 46.4 | 50.0 | 58.1 | 49.3 |

*Sources*: SMBS (2002a); GZBS (2002); WHBS (2002); XABS (2002); CDBS (2002).

Without insulation from the political and social interests of society, China's local developmental state is not a detached and disinterested state. A strong pro-growth position and weak leverage in guiding market forces make local governments and the state unable to play the role of the third party. The local developmental state is not so conducive to the construction of a market. The land use planning system is an illustrative case in this regard. Land use planning is intended to reduce or eliminate the impact of negative externalities and thus it is expected to lead to an efficient and equitable land use structure. Without appropriate land use planning controls, substandard overcrowded "urban villages" appear in many of Southern China's cities (Jin, 1999; Du, 1999; Zhu, 2004b). Suboptimal developments are mostly related to the land plots with ambiguous property rights. Market competition exposes the inferiority of these projects, resulting in high vacancy rates in these buildings. Slums in the midst of glittering modern buildings and a large amount of vacant buildings damage the credibility of local developmental states. Moreover, the local developmental state and *danwei*-enterprise coalition is gradually losing its relevance while *danwei*-enterprises are becoming autonomous enterprises. It is in the best interest of local governments to take the third-party role to provide order to the market where building development is increasingly commoditized (see Table 9.5).

Having seen rampant irregularities, rent dissipation and political threats caused by land-related corruption, the central government decided to clarify land rights, while the institution of ambiguous property rights has been found to be no longer serving its purposes in the advanced coastal

Table 9.5.   Commoditization of Building Development in Shanghai

| Year | Commodity Building Floor Area as a Percentage of Total Building Floor Area | Commodity Housing Floor Area as a Percentage of Total Housing Floor Area |
|------|------|------|
| 1998 | 46.7 | 63.3 |
| 2000 | 50.2 | 80.8 |
| 2001 | 64.0 | 90.8 |

*Sources*: SMBS (1999a, 2001a, 2003a).

cities. Since July 1, 2002, urban land leasing has been governed by Decree 11 — Regulations on Land Leasing through Auction and Bidding, issued by the Ministry of Land Resources on May 9, 2002. Since August 1, 2003, urban land leasing through negotiation has been strictly controlled by Decree 21 — Regulations on Land Leasing through Negotiation, issued by the same ministry on June 11, 2003. It appears that the state landowner's property rights over urban land have been strengthened. Since 2002, there have been 9 launches of land sales through transparent public bidding in Shanghai, which are publicized on the government website,[14] while during the period 1988–1995, only 9 out of a total of 1,303 land plots were allocated through tender (Zhao *et al.*, 1998).

Nevertheless, the ambiguous property rights may still be needed to advance local growth by strengthening local growth coalitions in less developed regions. Market-driven economic growth has not occurred evenly throughout the whole country (see Table 9.6). The degrees of marketization and commoditization are lower in the central and western regions where SOEs remain dominant in the economy. There are indications that the new decrees issued by the Ministry of Land Resources may not be strictly observed in less developed cities. As of 2003, there were 3,837 development zones nationwide with a total area of 36,000 sq kilometers, of which only 232 were approved by the central State Council and 1,019 by the provincial governments.[15] Most of the development zones without the blessing of

---

[14] See http://www.shanghai.gov.cn and http://www.shfdz.gov.cn/tdsyqcr/zbgg.asp, accessed October 20, 2003.

[15] See http://www.people.com.cn/GB/14857/22238/28463/28464/2015058.html, accessed September 10, 2002.

Table 9.6.   Regional Disparities in Economic Growth and Marketization (2000)

| Region | Population as a Percentage of Total | Urban Population as a Percentage of Total | GDP as a Percentage of Total | Development Commodity Building as a Percentage of Total | Percentage of Total Industrial Output Contributed by SOEs |
|---|---|---|---|---|---|
| Eastern region[a] | 42.4 | 52.2 | 59.4 | 62.4 | 38.0 |
| The rest[b] | 57.6 | 47.8 | 40.6 | 37.6 | 70.1 |

*Source*: SBS (2001).
*Notes*: [a] The eastern region comprises Beijing, Tianjin, Hebei, Liaoning, Shanghai, Jiangsu, Zhejiang, Fujian, Shandong, Guangdong, Guanxi and Hainan, with a land area of 1.3 million sq kilometers.
[b] The rest (central and western regions) consists of the remaining 19 provinces with an area of 8.3 million sq kilometers.

upper-level authorities are set up by localities in the central and western regions. Under the regime of ambiguous property rights, land in development zones has already been conveyed at very low prices to local-government-owned land developers, and thus is beyond the jurisdiction of the new decrees which only control land conveyance from local governments. It is perceived that the ambiguous property rights practised in the developed cities in the 1990s would still be practised in the developing cities in the 2000s, as the institution offers an incentive conducive to local growth in the initial stage of marketization.

## 6. Conclusion

China's emerging urban land markets are structured by the new institution of ambiguous property rights which has evolved from the socialist institution of people's ownership of land in the context of economic reforms characterized by gradualism and dualism. The new institution has helped the local growth coalition between the local developmental state and the *danwei*-enterprises in their endeavor to develop the local economy. It has also facilitated the release of land, formerly locked up by the old socialist institution, to the urban land redevelopment market. Although regarded as a positive change towards the establishment of land markets in a matrix of institutions related to central planning, the ambiguous property rights create land rents. Capitalization of land rents undermines the emerging land market: the distorted equilibrium between demand and supply leads to building booms and oversupplies, and the absence of the state as the third party gives rise to inadequate order in the land development market. The ambiguous property rights do not achieve what an institution should — providing certainty for the market and incentives for the optimal utilization of resources. The institution of ambiguous property rights is deemed transitional as the cost it incurs is increasingly becoming greater than the benefit it brings.

Building effective institutions for markets is a great challenge to many developing countries and transitional economies. In this endeavor, the state is a crucial actor and its capacity is a key factor. A critical test for the transitional economies, which are undergoing a makeover from a centrally controlled system to a market economy, is to build market mechanisms in their economies. Market failures are prevalent in many developing countries, evidenced by shortages of basic private/public goods such as housing and infrastructure. One of the characteristics of the Third World countries' urbanization is that informal developments dominate in their cities (Brennan, 1993). However, it has been argued that market failures are often caused by government failures (World Bank, 2002). A functional market would not exist without effective market institutions and building institutions for the market is a challenging task for the state as well as for the community. China's experience in establishing urban land markets has demonstrated that openness, competition and a capable and responsive government are the critical factors in the process of institutional change towards a market system. The state has a very constructive role to play in the building and managing of functional markets. Functional markets cannot be established instantly, as building market institutions is always a gradual process.

With broadening openness and intensifying competition, local economies of the advanced regions have progressed to a phase where it is quality development, instead of speedy but shoddy growth, that measures the performance of local governments. It is not so necessary for the local government to help SOEs at this stage as SOEs are increasingly being weaned from state subsidies to stand on their own feet and non-state-owned enterprises are taking a leading role in the economy. When the shortage of urban premises comes to an end, thanks to the economic reforms, inferior developments brought in by the transitional institution are exposed and discredit, rather than serve, the local developmental state. The continuous decentralization since the reforms has somehow been making the central government a regulatory state playing the role of the third party, while the local developmental state is an active actor in its local economy. Since 2002, the central government has reiterated that it should strengthen its governance of urban land leasing and has stressed its property rights over urban land.[16] Without an effective state serving as the third party, uncertainty could induce disorderly short-term behavior in the market. An orderly invention with measures to spread risks would be a viable option when there are governments maintaining order. Institutional change for the establishment of land markets in urban China is on the path towards a complete system of state land leasehold where the state principal's rights over land are fully in force.

## References

Aram, J.D. and Wang, X. (1991). "Lessons from Chinese State Economic Reform". *China Economic Review*, 2(1), pp. 29–46.

Ball, M. (1998). "Institutions in British Property Research: A Review". *Urban Studies*, 35(9), pp. 1501–1517.

Barzel, Y. (1989). *Economic Analysis of Property Rights*. Cambridge: Cambridge University Press.

Blecher, M. (1991). "Development State, Entrepreneurial State: The Political Economy of Socialist Economy in Xinju Municipality and Guanghan County". In G. Write (ed.), *The Chinese State in the Era of Economic Reform: The Road to Crisis*. Armonk, NY: M.E. Sharpe, pp. 265–291.

Brennan, E.M. (1993). "Urban Land and Housing Issues Facing the Third World". In J.D. Kasarda and A.M. Parnell (eds.), *Third World Cities: Problems, Policies and Prospects*. Newbury Park, CA: Sage Publications, pp. 74–91.

---

[16] Decree 11 [2002] regulates land leasing through auction and bidding. Decree 21 [2003] regulates land leasing through negotiation. Decree 71 [2004] requires that Decree 11 should be applied to all previous land leasing cases and those outstanding cases should be settled by August 31, 2004. In October 2004, Prime Minister Wen Jiabao spoke to local land bureau cadres on the central government's determination to manage national land assets effectively. The State Council released a document about strict controls over land leasing in December 2004.

Breslin, S.G. (1996). "China: Developmental State or Dysfunctional Development?" *Third World Quarterly*, 17(4), pp. 689–706.

Broadman, H.G. (1995). *Meeting the Challenge of Chinese Enterprise Reform*. Washington, DC: World Bank.

Buchanan, J.M. (1980). "Rent Seeking and Profit Seeking". In J.M. Buchanan, R.D. Tollison, and G. Tullock (eds.), *Toward a Theory of the Rent-Seeking Society*. College Station, TX: Texas A & M University Press, pp. 3–15.

Byrd, W.A. (1991). *The Market Mechanism and Economic Reforms in China*. Armond, NY: M.E. Sharpe.

CDBS (Chengdu Bureau of Statistics) (2002). *Chengdu Statistical Yearbook*. Beijing: China Statistics Publishing [in Chinese].

Coase, R.H. (1960). "The Problem of Social Cost". *The Journal of Law & Economics*, 3, pp. 1–44.

Du, J. (1999). "The Choices Faced by Urban Villages in the New Millennium". *City Planning Review*, 23(9), pp. 15–17 [in Chinese].

ECSYRE (Editorial Committee of Shenzhen Yearbook of Real Estate) (1995). *Shenzhen Yearbook of Real Estate, 1994*. Beijing: People China's Publishing.

Eggertsson, T. (1994). "The Economics of Institutions in Transition Economies". In S. Schiavo-Campo (ed.), *Institutional Change and the Public Sector in Transitional Economies*. Washington, DC: World Bank, pp. 19–50.

Elster, J. (1989). "Social Norms and Economic Theory". *Journal of Economic Perspectives*, 3(4), pp. 99–117.

Evans, P.B. (1995). *Embedded Autonomy: States and Industrial Transformation*. Princeton, NJ: Princeton University Press.

Fan, Q. (1994). "State-owned Enterprise Reform in China: Incentives and Environment". In Q. Fan and P. Nolan (eds.), *China's Economic Reforms — The Costs and Benefits of Incrementalism*. London: Macmillan, pp. 137–156.

Fischel, W.A. (1985). *The Economics of Zoning Laws: A Property Rights Approach to American Land Use Controls*. Baltimore, MD: The Johns Hopkins University Press.

Fung, K.I. (1981). "Urban Sprawl in China: Some Causative Factors". In L.J.C. Ma and E.W. Hanten (eds.), *Urban Development in Modern China*. Boulder, CO: Westview Press, pp. 194–221.

Goetz, E.G. and Clarke, S.E. (1993). *The New Localism: Comparative Urban Politics in a Global Era*. Newbury Park, CA: Sage.

Guy, S. and Henneberry, J. (eds.) (2002). *Development and Developers: Perspectives on Property*. Oxford: Blackwell Science.

GZBS (Guangzhou Bureau of Statistics) (2002). *Guangzhou Statistical Yearbook.* Beijing: China Statistics Publishing [in Chinese].

Haila, A. (1999). "Why is Shanghai Building a Giant Speculative Property Bubble?" *International Journal of Urban and Regional Research*, 23(3), pp. 583–588.

Harvey, J. (1987). *Urban Land Economics.* London: Macmillan.

Hassard, J., Morris, J., and Sheehan, J. (2002). "The Elusive Market: Privatization, Politics and State-enterprise Reform in China". *British Journal of Management*, 13(3), pp. 221–231.

Healey, P. (1992). "An Institutional Model of the Development Process". *Journal of Property Research*, 9, pp. 33–44.

Healey, P. and Barrett, S.M. (1990). "Structure and Agency in Land and Property Development Processes: Some Ideas for Research". *Urban Studies*, 27(1), pp. 89–104.

Heiner, R.A. (1983). "The Origin of Predictable Behavior". *American Economic Review*, 73(4), pp. 560–595.

Hope, N.C. (1996). "Opening Remarks". In H.G. Broadman (ed.), *Policy Options for Reform of Chinese State-Owned Enterprises.* Washington, D.C.: World Bank, pp. 13–16.

Hu, X. (1996). "Reducing State-Owned Enterprises' Social Burdens and Establishing a Social Insurance System". In H.G. Broadman (ed.), *Policy Options for Reform of Chinese State-Owned Enterprises.* Washington, DC: World Bank, pp. 125–148.

Hu, X. (2000). "The State, Enterprises, and Society in Post-Deng China: Impact of the New Round of SOE reform". *Asian Survey*, 40(4), pp. 641–657.

Huang, Y. (1996). *Inflation and Investment Controls in China.* Cambridge: Cambridge University Press.

IFTE (Institute of Finance and Trade Economics)/CASS (Chinese Academy of Social Sciences) and IPA (Institute of Public Administration) (1992). *Urban Land Use and Management in China.* Beijing: Jingji [in Chinese].

Iskander, M. (1996). "Improving State-owned Enterprise Performance: Recent International Experience". In H.G. Broadman (ed.), *Policy Options for Reform of Chinese State-Owned Enterprises.* Washington, DC: World Bank, pp. 17–86.

Jackson, D.G. (1997). *Asia Pacific Property Trends: Conditions and Forecasts.* New York: McGraw-Hill Books.

Jin, D. (1999). "A Survey on Urban Villages". *City Planning Review*, 23(9), pp. 8–14 [in Chinese].

Johnson, C. (1982). *MITI and the Japanese Miracle: The Growth of Industrial Policy: 1925–1975.* Stanford, CA: Stanford University Press.

Johnson, C. (1995). *Japan: Who Governs? The Rise of the Developmental State.* New York: Norton.

Knight, J. (1992). *Institutions and Social Conflict.* Cambridge: Cambridge University Press.

Krueger, A.O. (1974). "The Political Economy of the Rent-seeking Society". *American Economic Review*, 64, pp. 291–303.

Lau, L.J., Qian, Y.Y., and Roland, G. (2000). "Reform Without Losers: An Interpretation of China's Dual-track Approach to Transition". *Journal of Political Economy*, 108, pp. 120–143.

Lee, H.S. (1998). "DBS Land's Shanghai Bet". *Business Times* (Singapore), May 5.

Li, B. (1993). "Danwei Culture as Urban Culture in Modern China: The Case of Beijing from 1949 to 1979". In G. Guldin and A. Southall (eds.), *Urban Anthropology in China.* Leiden: E.J. Brill, pp. 345–352.

Li, H.W. (2002). *Urban Land Use and Management: A Case Study of Guangzhou.* Guangzhou: Guangdong People's Press [in Chinese].

Liao, K.Y. (1994). "China's Urban Land Market". In IFTE/CASS and IPA (eds.), *Urban Land Use and Management in China (Special Reports and Appendices).* Beijing: Economic Sciences Publishing [in Chinese].

Lin, J.Y.F. (1992). "Rural Reforms and Agricultural Growth in China". *American Economic Review*, 82, pp. 34–51.

Lin, S. (2000). "Too Many Fees and Too Many Charges: China Streamlines Its Fiscal System". Background Brief No. 66, East Asian Institute, National University of Singapore.

Liu, W. (1997). "On the Process of China's SOE Reforms". *Special Economic Zones' Economy*, 1, pp. 13–15 [in Chinese].

Logan, J.R. and Molotch, H.L. (1987). *Urban Fortunes: The Political Economy of Place.* Berkeley, CA: University of California Press.

Lu, Z.Y. (2001). "Achievement and Problems of SOE Reform, and Suggestions on Deepening Reform during the 10th Five-Year-Plan Period". *Financial and Trade Economics*, 1, pp. 12–14 [in Chinese].

Mantzavinos, C. (2001). *Individuals, Institutions, and Markets.* Cambridge: Cambridge University Press.

Marcuse, P. (1996). "Privatization and Its Discontents: Property Rights in Land and Housing in the Transition in Eastern Europe". In G. Andrusz, M. Harloe and I. Szelenyi (eds.), *Cities after Socialism: Urban and Regional Change and Conflict in Post-socialist Societies.* Oxford: Blackwell, pp. 119–191.

Matthews, R.C.O. (1986). "The Economics of Institutions and the Sources of Growth". *The Economic Journal.* 96, pp. 903–918.

Mollenkopf, J.H. (1983). *The Contested City*. Princeton, NJ: Princeton University Press.

Morris, J., Hassard, J. and Sheehan, J. (2002). "Privatization, Chinese-style: Economic Reform and the State-owned Enterprises". *Public Administration*, 80(2), pp. 359–373.

Nanto, D.K. and Sinha, R. (2002). "China's Banking Reform". *Post-Communist Economies*, 14(4), pp. 469–493.

Naughton, B. (1995). *Growing Out of the Plan: Chinese Economic Reform, 1978–1993*. Cambridge: Cambridge University Press.

Ng, M.K. and Xu, J. (2000). "Development Control in Post-reform China: The Case of Liuhua Lake Park". *Cities*, 17(6), pp. 409–418.

Nolan, P. (1995). "Politics, Planning, and the Transition from Stalinism: The Case of China". In H.J. Chang and R. Rowthorn (eds.), *The Role of the State in Economic Change*. Oxford: Clarendon, pp. 237–261.

North, D.C. (1990). *Institutions, Institutional Change and Economic Performance*. Cambridge: Cambridge University Press.

North, D.C. (1991). "Institutions". *Journal of Economic Perspectives*, 5(4), pp. 97–112.

North, D.C. (1998). "The Institutional Foundations of East Asian Development: A Summary Evaluation". In Y. Hayami and M. Aoki (eds.), *The Institutional Foundations of East Asian Economic Development: Proceedings of the IEA Conference held in Tokyo, Japan*. London: Macmillan, pp. 552–560.

Oi, J.C. (1995). "The Role of the Local State in China's Transitional Economy". *The China Quarterly*, 144, pp. 1132–1149.

Oksenberg, M. and Tong, J. (1991). "The Evolution of Central-Provincial Fiscal Relations in China, 1971–1984: The Formal System". *The China Quarterly*, 125, pp. 1–32.

Olson, M. (1982). *The Rise and Decline of Nations*. New Haven, CT: Yale University Press.

Perkins, F. (1995). "Productivity Performance and Priorities for the Reform of China's State-owned Enterprises". Economics Division Working Papers 95/1, Research School of Pacific and Asian Studies, Canberra.

Putterman, L. and Dong, X.Y. (2000). "China's State-owned Enterprises: Their Role, Job Creation, and Efficiency in Long-term Perspective". *Modern China*, 26(4), pp. 403–447.

Qian, Y.Y. (2000). "The Process of China's Market Transition (1978–1998): The Evolutionary, Historical, and Comparative Perspectives". *Journal of Institutional and Theoretical Economics*, 156(1), pp. 151–171.

Reich, R.B. (1991). *The Work of Nations: Preparing Ourselves for 21st-century Capitalism*. New York: Alfred A. Knopf.

SBS (State Bureau of Statistics) (1991, 1995, 1996, 1998, 2000, 2001, 2002, 2003). *China Statistical Yearbook*. Beijing: China Statistics Press [in Chinese].

Scalapino, R.A. (1999). "The People's Republic of China at Fifty". *National Bureau of Asian Research Analysis*, 10(4), pp. 1–30.

Schotter, A. (1981). *The Economic Theory of Social Institutions*. Cambridge: Cambridge University Press.

Sicular, T. (1988). "Plan and Market in China's Agricultural Commerce". *Journal of Political Economy*, 96, pp. 283–307.

SMBS (Shanghai Municipal Bureau of Statistics) (1990a–2003a). *Shanghai Statistical Yearbook*. Beijing: China Statistics Publishing [in Chinese].

SMBS (1989b–2001b). *Shanghai Real Estate Market*. Beijing: China Statistical Publishing [in Chinese].

Solinger, D.J. (1992). "Urban Entrepreneurs and the State: The Merger of State and Society". In A.L. Rosenbaum (ed.), *State & Society in China: The Consequences of Reform*. Boulder, CO: Westview, pp. 121–142.

STBS (Shantou Bureau of Statistics) (2000). *Shantou Statistical Yearbook*. Beijing: China Statistics Publishing [in Chinese].

Stone, C. (1989). *Regional Politics: Governing Atlanta 1946–1988*. Lawrence, KS: University of Kansas Press.

Sun, S.W. and Deng, Y.C. (1997). "A Study of the Role of Urban Planning in Shanghai". *Urban Planning Forum*, 2, pp. 31–39 [in Chinese].

Swanstrom, T. (1988). "Semisovereign Cities: The Politics of Urban Development". *Polity*, 21(1), pp. 83–110.

SZBS (Shenzhen Bureau of Statistics) (2000). *Shenzhen Yearbook of Statistics*. Beijing: China Statistical Publishing [in Chinese].

Tullock, G. (1993). *Rent Seeking*. Cheltenham: Edward Elgar.

Unger, J. and Chan, A. (1995). "China, Corporatism, and the East Asian Model". *The Australian Journal of Chinese Affairs*, 33, pp. 29–53.

Wang, H. (1994). *The Gradual Revolution*. New Brunswick, NJ: Transaction.

Wang, H.K. and Hung, C.T. (1997). "Shanghai's Industrial Relocation under Land Marketization: A Case Study on Shanghai Electrical Instrument Works". Paper presented at International Symposium on Marketisation of Land and Housing in Socialist China, Hong Kong Baptist University, October/November [in Chinese].

Wang, S. (1995). "The Rise of the Regions: Fiscal Reform and the Decline of Central State Capacity in China". In A.G. Walder (ed.), *The Waning of the Communist State—Economic Origins of Political Decline in China and Hungary*. Berkeley, CA: University of California Press, pp. 87–113.

Wang, X. (2002). "State-owned Enterprise Reform in China: Has It Been Effective". In R. Garnaut and L. Song (eds.), *China 2002: WTO Entry and World Recession*. Canberra: Asia Pacific Press at the Australian National University, pp. 29–44.

Webster, C. and Lai, L.W.C. (2003). *Property Rights, Planning and Markets: Managing Spontaneous Cities*. Cheltenham: Edward Elgar.

Wei, S.J. and Wang, T. (1997). "The Siamese Twins: Do State-owned Banks Favor State-owned Enterprises in China?" *China Economic Review*, 8(1), pp. 19–29.

Weimer, D.L. (1997). "The Political Economy of Property Rights". In D.L. Weimer (ed.), *The Political Economy of Property Rights: Institutional Change and Credibility in the Reform of Centrally Planned Economies*. Cambridge: Cambridge University Press, pp. 1–20.

Weller, R.P. and Li, J. (2000). "From State-owned Enterprise to Joint Venture: A Case Study of the Crisis in Urban Social Services". *The China Journal*, 43, pp. 83–99.

WHBS (Wuhan Bureau of Statistics) (2002). *Wuhan Statistical Yearbook*. Beijing: China Statistics Publishing [in Chinese].

White, G. (1991). "Basic-level Government and Economic Reform in Urban China". In G. White (ed.), *The Chinese State in the Era of Economic Reform: The Road to Crisis*. Armonk, NY: M.E. Sharpe, pp. 215–242.

White, G. and Wade, R. (eds.) (1988). *Developmental State in East Asia*. New York: St Martin's.

Williamson, O.E. (1985). *The Economic Institutions of Capitalism: Firms, Markets, Relational Contracting*. New York: The Free Press.

Wong, C.P.W. (1987). "Between Plan and Market: The Role of the Local Sector in Post-Mao China". *Journal of Comparative Economics*, 11, pp. 385–398.

Wong, C.P.W. (1992). "Fiscal Reform and Local Industrialization: The Problematic Sequencing of Reform in Post-Mao China". *Modern China*, 18(2), pp. 197–227.

Wong, C.P.W., Heady, C., and Woo, W.T. (1995). *Fiscal Management and Economic Reform in the People's Republic of China*. Hong Kong: Oxford University Press.

Woo-Cumings, M. (ed.) (1999). *The Developmental State*. Ithaca, NY: Cornell University Press.

Woodall, P. (2004). "The Dragon and the Eagle: A Survey of the World Economy". *The Economist*, October 2–8, pp. 1–24.

World Bank (2002). *Building Institutions for Markets: World Development Report 2002*. New York: Oxford University Press.

Wu, J. and Zhang, G.H. (2000). "Large Scale Urban Redevelopment in the 1990s — Empirical Survey of Jing'an District". *Urban Planning Forum*, 4, pp. 47–54 [in Chinese].

Wu, J.L. and Zhao, R.W. (1987). The Dual Pricing System in China's Industry". *Journal of Comparative Economics*, 11, pp. 309–328.

XABS (Xi'an Bureau of Statistics) (2002). *Xi'an Statistical Yearbook*. Beijing: China Statistics Publishing [in Chinese].

Xiao, G. (1991). "State Enterprises in China: Dealing with Loss-makers". *Transition (World Bank)*, 2(11), pp. 1–3.

Xu, J. (2001). "The Changing Role of Land-use Planning in the Land-development Process in Chinese Cities: The Case of Guangzhou". *Third World Planning Review*, 23(3), pp. 229–248.

Xu, J. and Ng, M.K. (1998). "Socialist Urban Planning in Transition: The Case of Guangzhou, China". *Third World Planning Review*, 20(1), pp. 35–51.

Xu, X. and Wang, Y. (1999). "Ownership Structure and Corporate Governance in Chinese Stock Companies". *China Economic Review*, 10(1), pp. 75–98.

Yeh, A.G.O. and Li, X. (1999). "Economic Development and Agricultural Land Loss in the Pearl River Delta, China". *Habitat International*, 23(3), pp. 373–390.

Zhao, M., Bao, G.L., and Hou, L. (1998). *Reforms of Land Use System and Development of Cities and the Country*. Shanghai: Tongji University Press [in Chinese].

Zhao, R. (1999). "Review of Economic Reform in China: Features, Experiences and Challenges". In R. Garnaut and L. Song (eds.), *China: Twenty Years of Economic Reform*. Canberra: Asia Pacific Press, pp. 185–199.

Zhu, J.M. (1994). "The Changing Land Policy and Its Impact on Local Growth: The Experience of the Shenzhen Special Economic Zone, China, in the 1980s". *Urban Studies*, 31(10), pp. 1611–1623.

Zhu, J.M. (1999). *The Transition of China's Urban Development: From Plan-controlled to Market-led*. Westport, CT: Praeger.

Zhu, J.M. (2000). "Urban Physical Development in Transition to Market". *Urban Affairs Review*, 36(2), pp. 178–196.

Zhu, J.M. (2002). "Urban Development under Ambiguous Property Rights". *International Journal of Urban and Regional Research*, 26(1), pp. 41–57.

Zhu, J.M. (2004a). "From Land Use Right to Land Development Right: Institutional Change in China's Urban Development". *Urban Studies*, 41(7), pp. 1249–1267.

Zhu, J.M. (2004b). "Local Developmental State and Order in China's Urban Development during Transition". *International Journal of Urban and Regional Research*, 28(2), pp. 424–447.

Zweig, D. (2001). "China's Stalled 'Fifth Wave': Zhu Rongji's Reform Package of 1998–2000". *Asian Survey*, 41(2), pp. 231–247.

## CHAPTER 10

# Urban Land Expansion and Economic Growth*

*Ding Lu*

China's hyper economic growth in recent years has occurred with the rapid expansion of urban land use. Whether such urban land expansion is efficient remains questionable. Using China's data for 31 provincial economies during 1996–2007, this study applies the neoclassical growth accounting model to assess the distinctive contribution of urbanized land to economic growth. The finding shows rather low contribution rates of urban land expansion to economic growth. This empirical evidence suggests low efficiency in urban land uses, which is rooted in a series of institutional weaknesses of the land market.

## 1. Introduction

It is well known that China, which accounts for about one fifth of the global population, has achieved rapid economic growth of over 9 percent per annum over the past three decades. A less well known but indispensable dimension of this hyper-growth story is the massive scale of urbanization and rapid expansion of urban land use. From 1980 to 2008, while per capita income shot up eleven times, the urbanization rate, measured by the share of population living in urban areas, rose from about 19 percent to 46 percent (Fig. 10.1). Since the mid-1980s, city built-up

* The paper was presented at American Economic Association ASSA Meetings 2009, January 3–5, San Francisco, USA. The author thanks the discussants and audience for valuable comments.

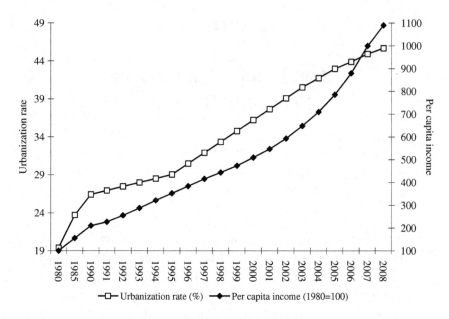

Figure 10.1.    Urbanization rate and per capita income index (1980–2008).

*Source*: NBSC (1996–2009).

*Note*: Urbanization rate is percentage of population resident in urban areas.

areas have been expanding by 6.2 percent per annum while the number of urban residents has risen by 10–22 million per annum. Since China's per capita arable land is less than half of the world's average, such a rapid expansion of land use for industrial and commercial development naturally raises concerns over its efficiency.[1]

Like China, many developing countries have experienced dynamic urban expansion with more land resources developed for urban use. To measure the contribution of urbanized land to economic growth is not only academically interesting but also useful for policy-making regarding land regulation and urbanization management. In the growth accounting literature, however, land assets are generally treated as part of the

---

[1] According to World Bank data, in 2005, China's per capita arable land was 0.10 hectares as compared to the world average of 0.22 hectares.

physical capital stock and the distinctive contribution of land resources to economic growth has generally been ignored.

Only in recent years has there been a revival of interest in the role of land in economic growth based on new evidence in empirical studies. For instance, Jorgenson and Nomura (2007) include the capital cost of land in their study on the productivity gaps between the US and Japanese industries. Diewert and Lawrence (2000) find that neglecting land and inventories in growth accounting could result in underestimation of average total factor productivity (TFP) growth rates by one fifth to one sixth for the Canadian economy during 1963–1996.

In this paper, we will first review the status of land in the growth accounting literature and explain why it is useful to identify and assess the distinctive contribution of urbanized land to economic growth. We will then highlight the phenomenal urban land expansion as part of China's growth experience. A growth accounting model is applied to estimate the role of urban land use in the rapid economic growth.

## 2. Land in Growth Accounting Literature

In classical economics, land is one of the basic production factors, like labor and capital. Since the early 20th century, however, land has "lost" its importance in modern mainstream economic literature. Land property has been treated as a form of fixed asset and generally regarded as part of the capital stock. The remarkable change of status of land in the literature can be attributed to a series of theoretical and practical reasons. Gaffney (1994) gives an in-depth political-economic account of some of these reasons. Ryan (2002) offers a comprehensive literature review of how the concept and importance of land as a production factor have evolved in economic science. In this section, we will focus on the approach to the role of land in the growth accounting literature.

In principle, the neoclassical growth accounting model is readily available for measuring the contribution of all production factors, including land. Following the seminal work of Solow (1957), with a general production function

$$Y = A(t) f(x_1, x_2, \ldots) \tag{1}$$

where $Y$ is output, $x_i$'s are production factors, and $A(t)$ represents shifts of the production function, the contribution of all production factors can be accounted for in the following manner:

$$\frac{\dot{Y}}{Y} = \frac{\dot{A}}{A} + \sum_i \omega_i \frac{\dot{x_i}}{x_i} \qquad (2)$$

where $\dot{Y}/Y$ and $\dot{x_i}/x_i$ are the growth rates of output and inputs respectively, $\omega_i = A\, \partial f/\partial x_i \cdot x_i/Y$, is $x_i$'s share of total income. With a competitive factor market, a factor's marginal product, $A\, \partial f/\partial x_i$ equals its price, $v_i$, so $\omega_i = v_i\, x_i/Y$, by Euler's theorem (Solow, 1957). The practice of growth account-ing, however, has generally avoided measuring explicitly the role of land in economic growth by treating land cost as part of the capital expense. A major reason for including land input as part of capital input (or simply ignoring it) is that doing so simplifies the modeling. In particular, when constant returns to scale are assumed, a two-factor (capital and labor) version of model (1) can be easily employed for analysis of per capita (or per worker) output growth, as done by Solow (1957):

$$y = Y/E = A\,(K/E)^\beta = A\,k^\beta \qquad (3)$$

where $y$ is per worker output, $E$ is employed labor input, $k$ is per worker capital stock, and $\beta$ is the capital share of income.

The second reason is that most growth accounting studies deal with aggregate economies and assume the total land resources to be unchanged over time. A good example is Denison's study on sources of long-term growth of the US economy. He treated the total land input in the period 1929–1969 as unchanged, since "the total acreage of private land (within which residential land is a tiny proportion of the total area) has changed very little during the period covered" (Denison, 1974, p. 57). Therefore, in his results, the contribution of land to total output growth is zero.

Third, for industry-level growth and productivity studies, data on land input are not easy to get. For instance, according to a study on the sources of the growth of 33 US industries in 1980–2000 by Jorgenson, Ho and Stiroh (2007), the US Federal Reserve Board published detailed data on land values and quantities in its Balance Sheets for the US Economy through 1995, but no longer does so since the underlying data has become unreliable. Jorgenson, Ho and Stiroh (2007) use the limited land data available in the Flow of Funds Accounts of the United States and historical data described in one of the authors' earlier studies to estimate a price and a quantity of private land. The result is a quantity series that "varies very little, so its major impact is to slow the growth of capital stock and capital input" (Jorgenson, Ho and Stiroh, 2007, p. 16).

Thanks to the above reasons, land as a distinctive input has largely been absent in most growth accounting studies, particularly those regarding aggregate economies and regional economies. There is, however, some pressing need to measure the contribution of land input to economic growth more seriously.

Land developed for industrial and commercial uses is indispensable to modern economic growth. Parallel to industrialization that transfers the mainstay of the labor force from the agricultural sector to the industrial and other modern sectors, urbanization expands urban areas and concentrates more and more economic activities and a greater share of population on the urban land. For historical and geographical reasons, patterns of land use intensity vary from country to country and region to region. Patterns of land use intensity also determine the features of urbanization and economic development. Their variations must have significant implications on productivity and growth efficiency. For instance, Nomura (2005) points out that a remarkable contrast between the US and Japan is that the share of land in nominal capital stock in the year 2000 was 23.6 percent in the US as compared to 43.5 percent in Japan, even after a decade-long asset price deflation in the latter. Since land price in Japan is much higher than that in the US, neglecting land in measuring capital input could severely underestimate Japan's TFP and exaggerate the productivity gap between Japan and the US.

Evaluating the role of urbanized land as a separate production factor could improve our understanding of inter-regional and international growth disparities. For many developing economies, property ownership, especially with regard to land, may be poorly defined and the real estate market is often rudimentary and underdeveloped. Where pecuniary values of land are hard to evaluate, land-related assets cannot be easily counted as part of the capital expense, as is the case in the Jorgenson capital account approach.[2] The early history of capitalism is littered with notorious cases of land expropriation by powerful interest groups such as the enclosure of land in pre-industrialization Britain. In many of today's Third World countries, abuse of compulsory purchase or eminent domain by state powers is not a rare phenomenon. In rapidly growing China, the compulsory acquisition of farmers' land for urban development or expropriation of (urban) private estate for redevelopment has been a main source of social unrest in recent years (Chen *et al.*, 2008).

Finally, including land in growth accounting should provide a more accurate assessment of the contribution of other factors to economic growth. For example, without considering the role of land distinctively, the capital share of income may be exaggerated. The estimation of the contribution of capital to output growth and, consequently, the estimation of total factor productivity growth may both be distorted.

## 3. Urban Land Expansion in China's Rapid Economic Growth

China's recent experience of hyper economic growth and massive urbanization highlights the importance of assessing the role of urbanized land in growth. As shown in Tables 10.1 and 10.2, since the mid-1980s, 10–22 million people have become urban residents every year, causing the urban population to rise by 2.4 times. Meanwhile, the total size of city built-up areas has expanded by the rate of 1,267 sq kilometers per year, increasing the total size of city built-up areas by about 3.9 times. This momentum of rapid urbanization is likely to continue in the coming years.

The fact that city built-up areas have been expanding by 5.3 pecent per annum since the mid-1980s gives rise to an intriguing issue: How has this rapid urban expansion contributed to the country's hyper economic growth of over 9 percent per annum in those years? Exploring this issue is not only academically interesting but also important with public policy implications.

---

[2] Jorgenson (1990) pioneered the approach in the literature to improve the measurement of capital cost and sources of income by providing estimates of capital stocks and rental prices, classified by four asset classes — producers' durable equipment, non-residential construction, inventories, and land — and three legal forms of organization — corporate and non-corporate business and non-profit enterprises.

Table 10.1.  City Built-up Areas and Urban Population (1985–2008)

| | City Built-up Area (sq km) | Urban Population (million) | Land Requisition (sq km) | City Population Density (Official*) (person per sq km) | Urban Population Density (Estimated*) (person per sq km) |
|---|---|---|---|---|---|
| 1985 | 9,386 | 250.94 | | | 26,736 |
| 1990 | 12,856 | 301.95 | | | 23,487 |
| 1995 | 19,264 | 351.74 | | | 18,259 |
| 1996 | 20,214 | 373.04 | 1,018 | 367 | 18,454 |
| 1997 | 20,791 | 394.49 | 519 | 440 | 18,974 |
| 1998 | 21,380 | 416.08 | 516 | 459 | 19,462 |
| 1999 | 21,525 | 437.48 | 340 | 462 | 20,325 |
| 2000 | 22,439 | 459.06 | 447 | 441 | 20,458 |
| 2001 | 24,027 | 480.64 | 1,812 | 588 | 20,004 |
| 2002 | 25,973 | 502.12 | 2,880 | 754 | 19,333 |
| 2003 | 28,308 | 523.76 | 1,606 | 847 | 18,502 |
| 2004 | 30,406 | 542.83 | 1,613 | 865 | 17,853 |
| 2005 | 32,521 | 562.12 | 1,264 | 870 | 17,285 |
| 2006 | 33,660 | 577.06 | 1,396 | 2,238 | 17,144 |
| 2007 | 35,470 | 593.79 | 1,216 | 2,104 | 16,741 |
| 2008 | 36,295 | 606.67 | 1,345 | 2,080 | 16,715 |

*Source*: NBSC (1996–2009).
*Notes*: *Numbers under "City Population Density" are official figures, which appear to be inconsistent over years and across regions. Numbers under "Urban Population Density" are estimated by dividing urban population by built-up area. It is noteworthy that "Urban Population" includes both city and township residents while "City Built-up Area" may not include built-up areas in townships. The density statistics are therefore sensitive to the administrative definitions of townships and cities.

For academic interest, exploring the issue will help us understand better the role of urban land use in the economy. The strong association between urbanization and development has inspired plenty of explanations in the literature of urban economics and development economics, such as the theories featuring economies of agglomeration, economies of localization, and economies of urbanization or clustering. Generally speaking, those theories highlight the benefits to producers and consumers from both the economies of scale and economies of scope brought about by the geographic concentration of urban economic activities. Little research, however, has been done to explicitly measure the contribution of urban land use to overall economic growth.

Table 10.2.   Built-up Area and Urban Population: Growth & Increment (1985–2007)

|  | Annual Growth Rate | | Annual Increment | |
| --- | --- | --- | --- | --- |
|  | Built-up Area (%) | Urban Population (%) | Built-up Area (sq km) | Urban Population (million) |
| 1985–1990 | 6.5 | 3.8 | 694 | 10.2 |
| 1990–1995 | 8.4 | 3.1 | 1,282 | 10.0 |
| 1995–1996 | 4.9 | 6.1 | 950 | 21.3 |
| 1996–1997 | 2.9 | 5.8 | 577 | 21.5 |
| 1997–1998 | 2.8 | 5.5 | 588 | 21.6 |
| 1998–1999 | 0.7 | 5.1 | 145 | 21.4 |
| 1999–2000 | 4.2 | 4.9 | 915 | 21.6 |
| 2000–2001 | 7.1 | 4.7 | 1,587 | 21.6 |
| 2001–2002 | 8.1 | 4.5 | 1,946 | 21.5 |
| 2002–2003 | 9.0 | 4.3 | 2,335 | 21.6 |
| 2003–2004 | 7.4 | 3.6 | 2,098 | 19.1 |
| 2004–2005 | 7.0 | 3.6 | 2,115 | 19.3 |
| 2005–2006 | 3.5 | 2.7 | 1,139 | 14.9 |
| 2006–2007 | 5.4 | 2.9 | 1,810 | 16.7 |
| 2007–2008 | 2.3 | 2.2 | 825 | 12.9 |
| 1985–2008 | 5.3 | 4.2 | 1,267 | 18.3 |

*Source*: Based on Table 10.1.

For public policy-making, the land issue is extremely important in today's Chinese economy. As pointed out by Ding (2007), China's unprecedented urban development in recent decades can be attributed to two institutional settings, i.e. the land use rights system and land acquisition. In China's Constitution, all land is state-owned. In the mid-1980s, however, local governments were authorized to acquire land from rural collectives for conversion into state-owned land. Meanwhile, the introduction of tradable land use rights allowed the local governments to lease the land to users/developers and allowed the latter to resell or sublease the land use rights. These reforms led to the emergence of a real estate market and a boom in urban land development. Ding (2003) observes that the tradable land use rights and land acquisition authority have become an important source of revenues for local governments to finance large-scale urban redevelopment, infrastructure building, and other local-budget-funded projects. The land acquisition laws and regulations give the local governments substantial discretion in determining the exact compensation values. The local governments also enjoy monopoly power in setting leasing terms and prices to the developers.

Compared to the pre-reform centrally planned system, these settings are no doubt important institutional progress that has promoted the efficiency of land use and urban development. They have, however, also been flawed institutions that serve as hotbeds for bureaucratic corruption and instruments for public expropriation of land from disadvantaged land users such as farmers and urban residents. In recent years, land expropriation has become the number one cause of social protests and riots, beating other causes such as environmental pollution, corruption and judicial unfairness (McBride, 2008; Chen *et al.*, 2008). Given the importance of urban land use, quantitative measurement of its contribution to economic growth will offer a useful reference for public policy making regarding land uses.

## 4. Growth Accounting with Land Input

We now attempt to apply (2) to the measurement of the contribution of urban land ($L$) expansion to China's economic growth:

$$\frac{\dot{Y}}{Y} = \frac{\dot{A}}{A} + \lambda \frac{\dot{E}}{E} + \beta \frac{\dot{K}}{K} + \theta \frac{\dot{L}}{L} \tag{4}$$

where $\lambda$, $\beta$, and $\theta$ are the income shares of labor, capital, and land respectively.

We collected a dataset for 31 provincial economies over the period 1996–2007 from NBSC (1996–2008). All pecuniary statistics of gross regional product and capital are deflated by their relevant accumulative price indices with the base year 1995 as 1.[3] Following the standard

---

[3] China revised its GDP figures based on a nationwide economic census in 2004. The indices of gross regional product data back to 2001 published in NBSC (2006, 2007) have been used to account for the adjusted GDP statistics.

perpetual inventory approach used in Zhang and Zhang (2003), we estimated the gross capital stocks as

$$K_t = \frac{FC_t - \Phi_t}{P_t} + K_{t-i} \tag{5}$$

where $K_t$ is the gross capital stock in year $t$, $FC_t$ is fixed capital formation
in year $t$, $P_t$ is an accumulative price index with year 1995 as 1, derived
from the annual price indices for fixed assets, and $\Phi_t$ is capital depreciation. The initial values for the capital stock are also estimated in the same
way as in [Zhang and Zhang (2003).][4]

Since fixed capital formation includes investment in real estate, we
need to exclude that from our accounting for capital stock so that the net
contribution of (non-land) capital assets can be measured. We use the
ratios between investment in real estate and fixed capital formation as a
proxy to the proportion of capital stock invested in real estate. While the
national data for these ratios are available for the whole period under
study (Fig. 10.2), the provincial data are available only for the latest few

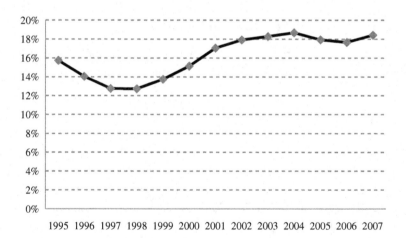

Figure 10.2.    Real estate investment's share of total fixed capital investment.
*Source*: NBSC (1996–2008).

---

[4] $K_0 = I_0/(\gamma + \delta)$, where $\delta$ is the depreciation rate assumed to be 5 percent and $\gamma$ is the growth rate of
real investment.

Table 10.3.　National GDP, Total Employment, Net Capital Stock, and Built-up Area

| | GDP (100 million yuan, at 1995 prices) | Total Employment ($E$, 10,000 persons) | Net Capital Stock ($K_N$, 100 million yuan, at 1995 prices) | City Built-up Area ($L$, sq km) | Index (1996 = 100) | | | |
|---|---|---|---|---|---|---|---|---|
| | | | | | GDP | $E$ | $K_N$ | $L$ |
| 1996 | 545 | 62,838 | 101,021 | 20,214 | 100 | 100 | 100 | 100 |
| 1997 | 597 | 63,667 | 114,391 | 20,791 | 110 | 101 | 113 | 103 |
| 1998 | 641 | 62,360 | 128,690 | 21,380 | 118 | 99 | 127 | 106 |
| 1999 | 691 | 62,494 | 142,572 | 21,525 | 127 | 99 | 141 | 106 |
| 2000 | 751 | 62,979 | 156,697 | 22,439 | 138 | 100 | 155 | 111 |
| 2001 | 811 | 63,053 | 170,417 | 24,027 | 149 | 100 | 169 | 119 |
| 2002 | 889 | 63,780 | 188,654 | 25,973 | 163 | 101 | 187 | 128 |
| 2003 | 983 | 64,863 | 212,404 | 28,308 | 181 | 103 | 210 | 140 |
| 2004 | 1,085 | 66,309 | 242,699 | 30,406 | 199 | 106 | 240 | 150 |
| 2005 | 1,207 | 68,027 | 283,672 | 32,521 | 222 | 108 | 281 | 161 |
| 2006 | 1,348 | 69,750 | 331,473 | 33,660 | 248 | 111 | 328 | 167 |
| 2007 | 1,513 | 71,351 | 384,853 | 35,470 | 278 | 114 | 381 | 175 |
| Growth rate per annum (%) | | | | | 9.73 | 1.16 | 12.93 | 5.24 |

*Source*: NBSC (1997–2008).

years (2004–2007). For years 1995–2003, we use the time trends of the national ratios to derive the provincial ratios from their 2004–2007 values.

The statistics for employed labor ($E$) is the number of total employed persons and that of urban land use ($L$) is developed area (or built-up area). Table 10.3 and Fig. 10.3 summarize the sizes and growth trends of GDP, employment, (net) capital stock, and urban built-up area from 1996–2007. It is worth noting that during these years while real GDP grew by 278 percent, capital stock increased by 381 percent, and urban land use rose by 178 percent. Employment growth has been the slowest: it even declined in 1997–1998 and attained only a 114 percent rise for the whole period.

The labor share of income, $\lambda$, is the ratio of compensation of employees to gross regional product, calculated from provincial GRP statistics. To get the land share of income, we first estimated average urban land prices in provincial economies from the value and space of annual land purchases by real estate developers, which are available from 2002. The

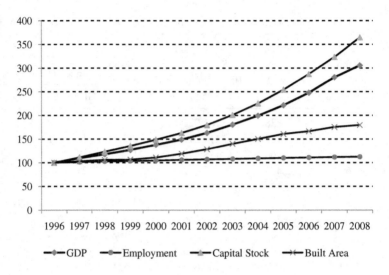

Figure 10.3.    Growth trends of GDP and main input factors (1996–2008).

*Source*: NBSC (1996–2009).

*Note*: 1996 = 100.

national data of these statistics are available back to 1997 and have been used as time trends to derive provincial land prices for years before 2002 from recent-year numbers (see Fig. 10.4 for the national average land purchase price from 1997 to 2007). Assuming that the land use right is purchased for 50 years and the long-term interest rate is 5 percent, we derive the annual value of land ($\alpha$) from its purchase price.[5] With the definition $\theta = \alpha L/Y$, we calculated the land share of income for each provincial economy. Under constant returns to scale, the capital share of income is $\beta = 1 - \lambda - \theta$.

Figure 10.5 summarizes the changing shares of labor, capital, and land in total income. It is notable that labor's share of income has been declining since 1996 while land's share of income has risen significantly after 2002.

---

[5] According to the State Council (1990), the maximum number of years for land use rights that can be purchased from the local governments are as follows: 70 years for residential use, 40 years for commercial, tourism, or entertainment uses, 50 years for all other uses (including industrial use).

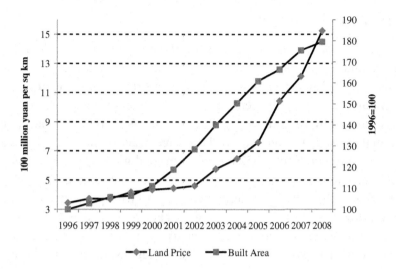

Figure 10.4. National average land purchase price and city built-up area index (1997–2008).

*Source*: Estimated by the author from NBSC (1996–2009).

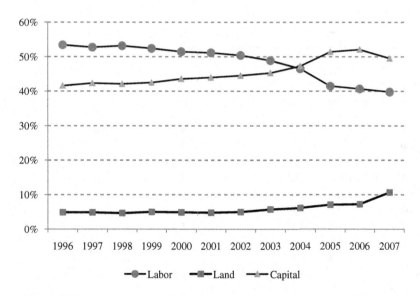

Figure 10.5. Shares of labor, capital, and land in national income (1996–2007).

*Source*: Estimated by the author from NBSC (1996–2008).

*Note*: The percentage values are the average factor share of income weighted by provincial GRP.

## 5. Findings

Applying the data to (4), we obtained the contributions of growth of labor, capital, and (urban) land to GRP growth from 1997 to 2007, as presented in Table 10.4. These results show that China's rapid economic growth (at an average rate of 11.5 percent per annum measured by weighted average of provincial GRPs) from 1997 to 2007 was mainly driven by rapid capital accumulation (at an annual rate of 12.9 percent, accounting for 6.1 percent per annum or contributing 52.6 percent of total growth) and the residual term (accounting for 4.6 percent per annum or contributing 40.1 percent of total growth), which is interpreted as total factor productivity growth from technological progress or efficiency gains. The increase of labor and land inputs has, however, played a relatively insignificant role: employment growth has contributed only 0.5 percentage points to annual growth while urban land expansion has contributed to only 0.3 percentage points to annual growth.

The low contribution of employment growth to total economic growth is understandable given that it was the slowest growing factor during the period

Table 10.4.    Contribution to GRP Growth by Factor

| Year | Sources of Growth Rate (%) | | | | | % Contribution | | | |
|------|------|-------|---------|------|--------|-------|---------|------|--------|
|      | GRP  | Labor | Capital | Land | Others | Labor | Capital | Land | Others |
| 1997 | 11.0 | 0.7 | 5.8 | 0.1 | 4.4 | 6.6 | 52.2 | 1.1 | 40.1 |
| 1998 | 9.7 | −1.1 | 5.4 | 0.1 | 5.3 | −11.5 | 55.3 | 1.4 | 54.8 |
| 1999 | 8.8 | 0.1 | 4.6 | 0.0 | 4.0 | 1.6 | 52.6 | 0.5 | 45.3 |
| 2000 | 9.6 | 0.5 | 4.3 | 0.2 | 4.6 | 4.7 | 45.1 | 2.2 | 47.9 |
| 2001 | 9.6 | 0.0 | 3.8 | 0.4 | 5.4 | −0.1 | 39.8 | 4.2 | 56.1 |
| 2002 | 10.9 | 0.5 | 4.8 | 0.4 | 5.1 | 5.0 | 44.1 | 4.1 | 46.9 |
| 2003 | 12.2 | 0.8 | 5.7 | 0.6 | 5.2 | 6.5 | 46.8 | 4.5 | 42.2 |
| 2004 | 13.6 | 1.1 | 6.7 | 0.5 | 5.4 | 7.8 | 49.3 | 3.5 | 39.4 |
| 2005 | 13.1 | 1.1 | 8.6 | 0.4 | 3.0 | 8.3 | 65.6 | 3.4 | 22.7 |
| 2006 | 13.7 | 1.1 | 8.8 | 0.2 | 3.6 | 7.7 | 64.2 | 1.8 | 26.3 |
| 2007 | 14.4 | 0.9 | 8.1 | 0.5 | 4.8 | 6.5 | 56.3 | 3.5 | 33.7 |
| Annual mean | 11.5 | 0.5 | 6.1 | 0.3 | 4.6 | 4.5 | 52.6 | 2.8 | 40.1 |

*Note*: GRP growth rates are the weighted average of 31 provincial economies by their GRP level. Factor contribution rates are the weighted average of provincial economies by their factor size.

1997–2007 (at a rate of less than 1.2 percent per annum as in Table 10.3). The negative growth in 1997–1998 and near-zero growth in 1999–2001 correspond to the low or negative contribution rates of employment to total economic growth in those years. When employment growth picked up after 2001, the contribution rates of labor to overall economic growth also rose.

Remarkably, the contribution of land to economic growth has been even lower (0.3 percentage points on average). This has been the case even though urban land use expanded at a rate of 5.24 percent per annum during the period (ref. Table 10.3). This puzzling performance could be a sign of inefficient use of land for urban development.

For comparison, we also did a two-factor growth accounting analysis in a traditional way: measuring only the contributions from labor (employment) and gross capital stock without deducting real estate investment from the total fixed capital investment expense. Table 10.5 compares the results from the two-factor model with that from the three-factor model. Without identifying and assessing the contribution of land, the two-factor

Table 10.5. Contribution to GRP Growth by Factor: Two-Factor Model vs. Three-Factor Model

| Year | | Two-Factor Model | | | Three-Factor Model | | | |
|---|---|---|---|---|---|---|---|---|
| | GRP | Labor | Capital | Others | Labor | Capital | Land | Others |
| 1997 | 11.0 | 0.7 | 6.0 | 4.3 | 0.7 | 5.8 | 0.1 | 4.4 |
| 1998 | 9.7 | −1.1 | 6.0 | 4.8 | −1.1 | 5.4 | 0.1 | 5.3 |
| 1999 | 8.8 | 0.1 | 5.7 | 2.9 | 0.1 | 4.6 | 0.0 | 4.0 |
| 2000 | 9.6 | 0.5 | 5.6 | 3.5 | 0.5 | 4.3 | 0.2 | 4.6 |
| 2001 | 9.6 | 0.0 | 5.7 | 4.0 | 0.0 | 3.8 | 0.4 | 5.4 |
| 2002 | 10.9 | 0.5 | 6.1 | 4.2 | 0.5 | 4.8 | 0.4 | 5.1 |
| 2003 | 12.2 | 0.8 | 7.2 | 4.3 | 0.8 | 5.7 | 0.6 | 5.2 |
| 2004 | 13.6 | 1.1 | 8.0 | 4.6 | 1.1 | 6.7 | 0.5 | 5.4 |
| 2005 | 13.1 | 1.1 | 9.6 | 2.4 | 1.1 | 8.6 | 0.4 | 3.0 |
| 2006 | 13.7 | 1.1 | 10.2 | 2.5 | 1.1 | 8.8 | 0.2 | 3.6 |
| 2007 | 14.4 | 0.9 | 10.8 | 2.7 | 0.9 | 8.1 | 0.5 | 4.8 |
| Annual mean | 11.5 | 0.5 | 7.3 | 3.7 | 0.5 | 6.1 | 0.3 | 4.6 |

*Note*: GRP growth rates are the weighted average of 31 provincial economies by their GRP level. Factor contribution rates are the weighted average of provincial economies by their factor size.

model overestimates the contribution of capital while underestimating the contribution of "others" (i.e. total factor productivity growth). Specifically, the two-factor model overestimates capital's contribution to growth on average by 1.2 percentage points out of 6.1 percentage points while it underestimates the residual contribution on average by 0.9 percentage points out of 4.6 percentage points. For both sources, the over/underestimates amount to 21 percent of the results of the three-factor model.

## 5. Concluding Remarks

In this paper, we consider the need for measuring the distinctive role of land in economic growth. We then conduct an exercise of growth accounting to measure the contribution of urbanized land input to GDP growth using data for China's provincial economies.

There are two major findings of this growth accounting study. One is that urbanized land has contributed rather little (0.3 percentage points) to China's recent economic growth although the city built-up areas have expanded as fast as 5.24 percent per annum since 1996. Figure 10.6 shows

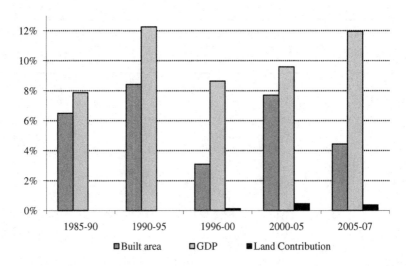

Figure 10.6.    Annual growth rates of built-up area and GDP vs. GDP growth contributed by urban land expansion.

*Source*: Tables 10.3 and 10.4.

that annual growth rates of city built-up areas since the mid-1980s have been fast for most years. However, the contribution of urban land use to GDP growth has been rather minimal.

The second finding is that ignoring land as a distinctive input factor leads to significant overestimation of capital's contribution to growth and underestimation of productivity gains. This result is consistent with the finding by Diewert and Lawrence (2000) not just in direction but also in magnitude: using data for Canada, the duo found that neglecting land and inventories in growth accounting could result in underestimation of average total factor productivity growth rates by one fifth to one sixth. Our results suggest that a two-factor model has underestimated average total factor productivity by 21 percent as compared to the results of a three-factor model. On top of that, the contribution of capital is overestimated by roughly the same magnitude.

Our first finding has important policy implications. China's Constitution defines all land to be state-owned. Before the mid-1980s, all land use rights were administered by the centrally planned system. The authorization of local governments to acquire farm land for urban development and lease (state-owned) land use rights to users/developers began in the mid-1980s. The promulgation of a Regulation on Use Right Grant and Transfer for Urban State-owned Land in 1990 established the basic procedural framework for land use right lease and transaction (State Council, 1990). In 1992–1993, the ruling Communist leadership reached a major consensus[6] to engage in a wholesale transition towards a market-based economy and open up the economy further to foreign investment. Beijing's call for speeding up reform and openness emboldened the local governments to act more aggressively in land acquisition for local industrial/urban development. Meanwhile, a series of reforms, including the privatization of urban housing estates, led to the emergence of a real estate market and a boom in urban land development in the first half of the 1990s. The 1999 amendment of the land acquisition law (ref. Ding [2003, 2007] for details) and

---

[6] This collective consensus in the top leadership was reached after the paramount leader Deng Xiaoping called for fundamental reforms to the economic system in his famous South China tour. See Wong and Zheng (2001) for details of the historical significance of Deng's South China tour (or *Nanxun*).

China's accession to the WTO at the turn of the century injected a new dose of stimulus into urban expansion. The increase of the contribution of urban land to economic growth in 2000–2005 and the sharp rise of land prices after 2002 may reflect the impact of these reforms.

Institutional weaknesses of China's real estate market, however, abound. In the process of reform, government bureaucracy, particularly at the local government level, has amassed tremendous monopoly power in determining the terms and conditions of land requisition and use right lease and sales. Grabbing land for urban development and expansion has become a money spinner for local officials either for the local government budget or for private gain. Power abuse in land requisition has thus become a hotbed for bureaucratic corruption and an instrument for public expropriation of land from disadvantaged land users such as farmers and urban residents. It is no wonder that land expropriation has become a major cause of legal disputes, mass protests, and social unrest in recent years. Based on anecdotal observations, many believe that those institutional weaknesses have led to inefficient and wasteful uses of land resource for urban expansion. Our finding of rather low contribution rates of urban land expansion to economic growth provides the first empirical evidence of low efficiency in urban land uses.

Our second finding reveals the estimation problems due to the neglect of the distinctive role of land in the growth accounting literature. Further studies need to be carried out by using different data and by adopting more sophisticated model designs (for instance, to take into account human capital input). The benefits of assessing the distinctive contribution of land to economic growth can only be verified and confirmed by comparing the results of growth accounting models with and without land as a major input factor.

## References

Chen, Gang, Lye, L.F., Yang, D. and Wang, Z. (2008). "China's Politics in 2007: Power Consolidation, Personnel Change and Policy Reorientation". Briefing Series 33, The China Policy Institute, Nottingham University.

Denison, Edward F. (1974). *Accounting for United States Economic Growth, 1929–1969*. Washington, DC: Brookings Institution.

Denison, Edward F. (1985). *Trends in American Economic Growth, 1929–1982.* Washington, DC: Brookings Institution.

Diewert, Erwin W. and Lawrence, Denis A. (2000). "Progress in Measuring the Price and Quantity of Capital". In Lawrence J. Lau (ed.), *Econometrics and the Cost of Capital: Essays in Honor of Dale W. Jorgenson.* Cambridge: The MIT Press, Chapter 11, pp. 273–326.

Ding, Chengri. (2003). "Land Use Policy Reform in China: Assessment and Prospects". *Land Use Policy,* 20(2), pp. 109–120.

Ding, Chengri. (2007). "Policy and Praxis of Land Acquisition in China". *Land Use Policy,* 24(3), pp. 1–13.

Gaffney, Mason. (1994). "Land as a Distinctive Factor of Production". In Nicolaus Tideman (ed.), *Land and Taxation.* London: Shepheard-Walwyn, pp. 39–102.

Jorgenson, Dale W. (1990). "Productivity and Economic Growth". In E. Berndt and J. Triplett, (eds.), *Fifty Years of Economic Measurement.* Chicago: University of Chicago Press, pp. 19–118.

Jorgenson, Dale W., Ho, Mun S., and Stiroh, Kevin J. (2007). "The Sources of Growth of U.S. Industries". In D. Jorgenson, M. Kuroda and K. Motohashi (eds.), *Productivity in Asia: Economic Growth and Competitiveness.* Cheltenham: Edward Elgar.

Jorgenson, Dale W. and Nomura, Koji. (2007). "The Industry Origins of the U.S.-Japan Productivity Gap". *Economic Systems Research,* 19(3), pp. 315–341.

McBride, Edward. (2008). "China's Quest for Resources". *The Economist* (UK), March 13.

National Bureau of Statistics of China (NBSC) (1996–2007). *China Statistical Yearbook.* Beijing: China Statistics Press.

National Bureau of Statistics of China (NBSC) (1999). *Comprehensive Statistical Data and Materials on 50 Years of New China.* Beijing: China Statistics Press.

National Bureau of Statistics of China (NBSC) (2005). *China Compendium of Statistics: 1949–2004.* Beijing: China Statistics Press.

National Bureau of Statistics of China (NBSC) (2008). Communique on National Economic and Social Development 2007, http://www.stats.gov.cn.

Nomura, Koji. (2004). *Measurement of Capital and Productivity.* Tokyo: Keio University Press [in Japanese].

Nomura, Koji. (2005). "Toward Reframing Capital Measurement in Japanese National Accounts". KEO Discussion Paper No. 97.

Ryan, Christopher K. (2002). "Land as a Factor of Production". *American Journal of Economics and Sociology,* 61(5), pp. 7–25.

Solow, Robert. (1957). "Technical Change and the Aggregate Production Function". *Review of Economics and Statistics*, 39(3), pp. 312–320.

State Council (1990). Regulation on Use Right Grant and Transfer for Urban State-owned Land. State Council Executive Order No. 55.

US Bureau of Labor Statistics (2007). *Preliminary Multifactor Productivity Trends (24 May 2007)*. Washington DC: US Department of Labor.

US Bureau of Labor Statistics (2007b). *Technical Information about the BLS Multifactor Productivity Measures (September 26, 2007)*. Washington DC: US Department of Labor.

Wong, John and Zheng Yongnian (eds.) (2001). *The Nanxun Legacy and China's Development in the Post-Deng Era*. Singapore, New Jersey and London: Singapore University Press and World Scientific.

Zhang, Xiaobo and Kevin H. Zhang. (2003). "How Does Globalisation Affect Regional Inequality within a Developing Country? Evidence from China", *The Journal of Development Studies*, 39(4), pp. 47–67.

CHAPTER 11

# Rural-Urban Migration and Urbanization in China*

*Kevin Honglin Zhang and Shunfeng Song*

Since 1978 China has experienced a rapid and unprecedented process of urbanization, created by the largest flow of rural-urban migration in history in the world. This paper attempts (a) to assess the role of city-ward migration in China's urbanization in 1978–1999 and (b) to empirically investigate the factors behind the migration boom with time-series and cross-section data. We find that (a) rural-urban migration made dominant contributions to the Chinese urban population growth; (b) while moving together with the Chinese economy, the causal link runs from economic growth to migration, not vice versa; (c) inter-province migrants were encouraged by the rural-urban income gap and discouraged by the geographic distance to destinations; and (d) the number of intra-province migrants is positively related to the rural-urban income gap and urban population in that province.

## 1. Introduction

As a result of the rapid economic growth in the two decades since the initiation of economic reforms in 1978, China has been experiencing rapid urbanization created by the largest flow of rural-urban migration in history in the world. According to the Chinese government, the urban population share in China rose significantly from 18 percent in 1978 to

---

* Reprinted with the authors' permission from *China Economic Review*, 14, pp. 386–400.

31 percent in 1999, and urban population rose by 222 million (SSB, 2000), compared with the entire US population of 280 million. The actual levels of urbanization and migrants could be higher, however, if the huge number of floating people is considered. What is striking in the Chinese experience is not only the size of the increase in its urbanization levels in such a short period of time, but also the magnitude of urban population growth. What can explain the timing and the extent of China's urbanization? What role does the rural-urban migration play in the process of urbanization?

Many studies have examined China's rural-urban migration and urbanization, including Chang (2002), Chang and Brada (2002), Hare (1999), Knight and Song (1999), Seeborg, Jin, and Zhu (2000), Song (2001), Song and Zhang (2002), Wu (1994), and Zhao (1999). However, empirical analyses of the determinants of the rural-urban migration and its role in China's urbanization have been limited. In particular, we are still uncertain about the magnitude of migrants and the factors behind the rising migration. This paper attempts to close the gap by (a) computing the number of annual rural-urban migrants through decomposing urban growth into natural growth and net migration and (b) investigating empirically the determinants of migration at national and regional levels with time-series and cross-section data. Policy implications may be derived on how the Chinese government should balance the inevitably large rural-urban migration and the growing urban unemployment.

This study is interesting in several aspects. First, like many developing countries, the problems of unemployment and poverty have begun to emerge in China as a result of rapid urbanization in the last two decades, along with other problems such as a progressive overloading of housing and social services, increased crime, pollution, and congestion. Given the serious problems, it is desirable for us to know the factors contributing to the urbanization and city-ward migration so that corresponding policies may be derived. Second, China's experience since 1978 contrasted sharply with its slow and even stagnated urban growth in the 1960s and the 1970s. While many studies have examined the pre-reform patterns of migration and urbanization, few studies have been devoted to assessing the post-reform patterns. Third, as the most populous country, China is an interesting case for migration studies. China can also offer fascinating comparisons with other developing countries, since China differs to a certain extent from other developing countries in its migration and urbanization due to the uniqueness of its country size and development experience. Studies of such comparisons and differences may help derivè policy implications under various circumstances.

The main findings may be summarized as follows: First, the Chinese rural-to-urban migration was a dominant source (75 percent) of the growth of its urbanization in 1978–1999. Second, while the Chinese migration is accompanied by its economic growth, the direction of their causal link runs from the latter to the former, not vice versa. The downward time trend of the overall migration in 1978–1999 may imply rising costs of urbanization that limit the increase of migrants. Third, the rural-urban income gap seems to be a strong driving force behind city-ward migration both within and across provinces. Finally, geographic distance discourages inter-province migrants, and intra-province migration is positively associated with the size of the provincial urban population.

The rest of the paper is organized as follows: Section 2 describes the characteristics of China's migration and urbanization. An analytical framework is introduced in Section 3. Section 4 shows our empirical investigation. Finally we make concluding remarks in Section 5.

## 2. Patterns of Migration and Urbanization in China: 1978–1999

The level of urbanization is usually measured by the share of urban population in total population. A rise in a country's urbanization level could be caused either by migration from rural to urban areas, or faster population growth in urban areas than in rural areas. Like for other countries in the early stage of industrialization, rural-urban migration is the main source of urbanization growth in the current China.

To see how much the migration contributes to the Chinese urbanization, we decompose the annual urban growth into two parts: the natural growth of the urban population and net urban migration. The amount of natural urban growth in a year is obtained by multiplying the urban population in that year by the natural growth rate of the urban population, which is equal to the difference between the birth rate and death rate.[1] The magnitude of city-ward migrants in that year thus is the remaining part of the increase in total urban population after taking off the natural urban growth. The resulting figures showing the natural urban growth and net migration for the period 1978–1999 are presented in Table 11.1.

Although the exact number of individual migrants is still difficult to ascertain due to the absence of an authoritative national survey, the prominent presence of migrants in Chinese cities is hardly disputable.[2] A recent publication by the Chinese State Statistical Bureau and Ministry of Labor and Social Security (SSB-MLSS, 1999), *China Labor Statistical Yearbook 1999*, reports the rural labor force flow and employment by provinces at the end of 1998 and the increase in the single year of 1998. Based on the information provided in the *Yearbook*, we computed the regional shares of total migrants, inter-province migrants, and intra-province migrants by province and by coastal inland area. The results are presented in Table 11.2.

The overall patterns of Chinese urbanization and rural urban migration may be discerned from Table 11.1, which also includes total and urban population and the average growth of each indicator for two ten-year subperiods and the entire period of 1978–1999.[3] Table 11.2 displays the regional patterns of city-ward migration. Several points are worth mentioning.

---

[1] The natural growth rate of the urban population is measured by the natural city growth rate (SSB, 2000). While the two rates may not be identical, the differences should be small. Even for the city rate, no data are available for years 1979, and 1981 through 1988. The missing data are restored by projection based on both the natural city growth rates in the remaining years and the correlations between the natural growth rate of the total population and the natural city growth rate.

[2] In China's largest cities, at least one out of every five persons is a migrant, and rural migrants account for over three quarters of all migrants in large Chinese cities (Wang and Zuo, 1999). The migrants in Shanghai, China's largest city, rose tenfold from 0.26 million in 1981 to 2.81 million in 1993, and correspondingly the migrant share in total residents rose from less than 5 percent to 21.7 percent (Sun, 1997).

[3] Data on China's urbanization had been a somewhat tricky question in the sense that data from different sources or the same sources at different times may not be consistent due to the problem of the frequently changing definitions of urban and rural population. However, recent efforts made by the Chinese government have led to its urban statistics to be closer to reality. For instance, the adjusted data on the Chinese urban population and levels of urbanization in *China Statistical Yearbook 2000* (SSB, 2000) based on a population census seem to have no significant differences from what was suggested by several studies (Wu, 1994; Zhang and Zhao, 1998).

Table 11.1.  Urbanization and Rural-Urban Migration in China: 1978–1999

| Year | Total Population (10,000) | Urban Population (10,000) | Urbanization | | | Natural Growth | | Net Migration | |
|---|---|---|---|---|---|---|---|---|---|
| | | | Level (%) | Growth Rate (%) | Growth in Persons (10,000) | Growth in Persons (10,000) | Share (%) | Growth in Persons (10,000) | Share (%) |
| 1978 | 96,259 | 17,250 | 17.92 | 2.11 | 582 | 144 | 24.76 | 438 | 75.24 |
| 1979 | 97,542 | 18,494 | 18.96 | 5.80 | 1,244 | 144 | 11.59 | 1,100 | 88.41 |
| 1980 | 98,705 | 19,139 | 19.39 | 2.27 | 645 | 158 | 24.51 | 487 | 75.49 |
| 1981 | 100,072 | 20,175 | 20.16 | 3.97 | 1,036 | 200 | 19.36 | 835 | 80.64 |
| 1982 | 101,654 | 21,479 | 21.13 | 4.81 | 1,305 | 228 | 17.45 | 1,077 | 82.55 |
| 1983 | 103,008 | 22,270 | 21.62 | 2.32 | 791 | 206 | 25.99 | 585 | 74.01 |
| 1984 | 104,357 | 24,017 | 23.01 | 6.45 | 1,746 | 210 | 12.01 | 1,537 | 87.99 |
| 1985 | 105,851 | 25,094 | 23.71 | 3.01 | 1,077 | 247 | 22.89 | 831 | 77.11 |
| 1986 | 107,507 | 26,366 | 24.53 | 3.45 | 1,272 | 281 | 22.12 | 991 | 77.88 |
| 1987 | 109,300 | 27,674 | 25.32 | 3.24 | 1,308 | 315 | 24.11 | 992 | 75.89 |
| 1988 | 111,026 | 28,656 | 25.81 | 1.94 | 982 | 313 | 31.91 | 669 | 68.09 |
| 1989 | 112,704 | 29,540 | 26.21 | 1.55 | 884 | 310 | 35.11 | 574 | 64.89 |
| 1990 | 114,333 | 30,191 | 26.41 | 0.75 | 651 | 306 | 47.01 | 345 | 52.99 |
| 1991 | 115,823 | 30,543 | 26.37 | -0.14 | 352 | 282 | 80.21 | 70 | 19.79 |

(*Continued*)

Table 11.1. (Continued)

| Year | Total Population (10,000) | Urban Population (10,000) | Urbanization | | | Natural Growth | | Net Migration | |
|---|---|---|---|---|---|---|---|---|---|
| | | | Level (%) | Growth Rate (%) | Growth in Persons (10,000) | Growth in Persons (10,000) | Share (%) | Growth in Persons (10,000) | Share (%) |
| 1992 | 117,171 | 32,372 | 27.63 | 4.77 | 1,829 | 255 | 13.94 | 1,574 | 86.06 |
| 1993 | 118,517 | 33,351 | 28.14 | 1.85 | 979 | 267 | 27.27 | 712 | 72.73 |
| 1994 | 119,850 | 34,301 | 28.62 | 1.71 | 950 | 269 | 28.32 | 681 | 71.68 |
| 1995 | 121,121 | 35,174 | 29.04 | 1.47 | 872 | 261 | 29.86 | 612 | 70.14 |
| 1996 | 122,389 | 35,949 | 29.37 | 1.15 | 776 | 264 | 34.02 | 512 | 65.98 |
| 1997 | 123,626 | 36,989 | 29.92 | 1.86 | 1,040 | 322 | 30.96 | 718 | 69.04 |
| 1998 | 124,810 | 37,942 | 30.40 | 1.60 | 953 | 310 | 32.54 | 643 | 67.46 |
| 1999 | 125,909 | 38,893 | 30.89 | 1.61 | 951 | 289 | 30.44 | 662 | 69.56 |
| Annual Average Growth and Shares | | | | | | | | | |
| 1978–1988 | 1.44 | 4.79 | 0.79 | 3.72 | 1,199 | 245 | 20.41 | 945 | 79.59 |
| 1989–1999 | 1.11 | 2.79 | 0.47 | 1.66 | 1,024 | 314 | 30.63 | 710 | 69.37 |
| 1978–1999 | 1.29 | 3.79 | 0.65 | 2.63 | 1,058 | 266 | 25.12 | 793 | 74.88 |

*Sources*: Computed from *China Statistical Yearbook 2000* (SSB, 2000) and *Comprehensive Statistical Data and Materials on 50 Years of New China* (SSB, 1999a).

*Notes*: The share of natural urban growth is defined as the percentage of natural growth of urban population in total urban growth in persons. The remaining part of total urban growth is the share of net migration.

Table 11.2.  Rural-Urban Migrants at the End of 1998 by Province: Shares in Nation

| | Migrants from the Reporting Province | | | | | Migrants in the Reporting Province | | | |
| | Total | Inter-Province | Intra-Province | | | Total | Inter-Province | Intra-Province | |
| Regions | (%) | (%) | (%) | Share in Total | Region | (%) | (%) | (%) | Share in Total |
|---|---|---|---|---|---|---|---|---|---|
| *Coastal areas* | *18.80* | *11.12* | *33.79* | *61.15* | *Coastal areas* | *68.93* | *75.54* | *60.22* | *37.71* |
| Jiangsu | 3.61 | 2.71 | 5.39 | 50.77 | Guangdong | 30.9 | 36.57 | 23.43 | 32.73 |
| Shandong | 3.56 | 2.36 | 5.91 | 56.50 | Zhejiang | 9.54 | 11.92 | 6.40 | 28.97 |
| Hebei | 3.52 | 2.66 | 5.23 | 50.53 | Fujian | 6.08 | 6.31 | 5.77 | 40.98 |
| Guangdong | 3.12 | 0.45 | 8.31 | 90.63 | Jiangsu | 4.58 | 3.06 | 6.59 | 62.07 |
| Others | 4.99 | 2.94 | 8.95 | 61.04 | Others | 17.82 | 17.67 | 18.02 | 43.63 |
| *Inland areas* | *81.20* | *88.88* | *66.21* | *27.75* | *Inland areas* | *31.07* | *24.46* | *39.78* | *55.25* |
| Sichuan | 18.97 | 19.68 | 17.83 | 31.98 | Sichuan | 4.94 | 1.02 | 10.11 | 88.26 |
| Henan | 14.17 | 14.94 | 12.87 | 30.91 | Henan | 4.23 | 2.75 | 6.17 | 63.01 |
| Anhui | 10.83 | 13.90 | 3.80 | 11.93 | Shaanxi | 2.89 | 2.25 | 3.72 | 55.63 |
| Hunan | 7.90 | 10.11 | 3.76 | 16.21 | Hubei | 2.41 | 1.44 | 3.70 | 66.09 |
| Jiangxi | 6.12 | 8.10 | 2.40 | 13.33 | Xinjiang | 2.30 | 3.52 | 0.69 | 13.03 |
| Others | 23.21 | 22.15 | 25.55 | 37.46 | Others | 14.30 | 13.47 | 15.38 | 46.44 |
| *Nation* | *100.00* | *100.00* | *100.00* | *100.00* | *Nation* | *100.00* | *100.00* | *100.00* | *100.00* |

*Source:* State Statistical Bureau and Ministry of Labor and Social Security of China (1999a), *China Labor Statistical Yearbook 1999*, Beijing: China Statistics Press.

*Note:* All numbers are percentage in nation, except shares in total for intra-province, which are percentage in the reporting province. For instance, 50.77 percent for Jiangsu Province indicates the share of intra-province migrants in total city-ward migrants of Jiangsu. The 31 administrative units in China consist of 23 provinces (Hebei, Liaoning, Shandong, Jiangsu, Zhejiang, Fujian, Guangdong, Hainan, Guangxi, Jilin, Heilongjiang, Shanxi, Anhui, Jiangxi, Henan, Hubei, Hunan, Sichuan, Guizhou, Yunnan, Shaanxi, Gansu, and Qinghai), 4 autonomous regions (Inner Mongolia, Guangxi, Ningxi, and Xinjiang), and 4 municipalities (Beijing, Tianjin, Shanghai, and Chongqing). Both autonomous regions and municipalities enjoy the same status as province. The newly established municipal city of Chongqing was dropped from the sample of empirical analyses due to unavailability of the data before 1996. To be consistent, the city of Chongqing was still treated as part of Sichuan Province. The coastal areas include 3 municipalities and 8 provinces as follows: Beijing, Tianjin, Shanghai, Hebei, Liaoning, Shandong, Jiangsu, Zhejiang, Fujian, Guangdong, and Hainan. The remaining provinces are considered as inland areas.

First, the urban population grew much faster than the total population, especially in the first ten years. While the total population rose on average at a rate of 1.29 percent per annum, the rate for the urban population was 3.79 percent, almost threefold. The difference was even larger in 1978–1988, with 1.44 percent versus 4.79 percent. As a result of the faster growth of the urban population, the level of urbanization increased from about 18 percent in 1978 to 31 percent in 1999, a rise of 13 percentage points, with 8 percentage points in 1978–1988 and 5 percentage points in 1989–1999. In terms of urban growth in persons, the increase of the urban population in the two decades reached as much as 222 million. In other words, more than 10 million people joined the body of urban population per year in the period of 1978–1999.

Second, the rural-urban migration was the dominant source of the Chinese urban growth in 1978–1999. In the two decades since 1978, about 174 million people (more than the total population of many large countries in 1998, such as Brazil [166 million] and Russia [147 million]) moved from rural areas to cities, creating the largest flow of migration in history in the world. This unprecedented scale of migration constituted 75 percent of the total increase in urban population in that period. The contribution of the migration to urban growth in 1978–1988 (80 percent) was larger than that in 1989–1999 (69 percent). The number of migrants in most years of the first decade was about 10 million. Two single years, 1984 and 1992, witnessed the migration of as many as 15 million.

Third, most of the migration took place across provinces, from inland rural areas to coastal urban areas. As figures in the first half of Table 11.2 show, 81 percent of the total migrants and 89 percent of inter-province migrants came from inland areas. Moreover, most of the inland migrants (72 percent) were inter-province migrants. In contrast, migrants from coastal areas constituted a small part of the nation, and most of them (61 percent) limited their movements within the home provinces. Regarding the question of where the inter-province migrants go, figures in the second half of Table 11.2 offer an answer. More than two thirds (69 percent) of total migrants, and three quarters of inter-province migrants (76 percent), went to coastal areas. In summary, the main direction of the Chinese city-ward migration was from the western inland areas to the eastern coastal areas.

Fourth, distance mattered in the migration. The provinces that had the most emigrants were Sichuan (19 percent of the nation), Henan (14 percent), Anhui (11 percent), Hunan (8 percent), and Jiangxi (6 percent). They were also the top five provinces in terms of inter-province emigrants. The provinces that had the most immigrants were Guangdong (31 percent of the nation), Zhejiang (10 percent), and Fujian (6 percent). They were also the top three provinces in terms of hosting inter-province migrants. By looking at a provincial map of China, one can easily realize that the provinces with the most emigrants in general are geographically closer to the provinces with the most immigrants. The rural people of many provinces in the northeast, northwest, and southwest seemed to be discouraged by the distance in their decision to move to the eastern coastal areas.

Many factors have been identified in the literature to explain China's migration and urbanization, such as economic reforms, relaxation of the migration-control policy, and the rural-urban income gap. To systematically investigate the determinants of the migration boom, we first establish an analytical framework on the basis of well-known theories of migration and urbanization. Then we specify and estimate empirical models, through which evidence may be derived from time-series and cross-section data.

## 3. Driving Forces of Migration and Urbanization: A Theoretical Framework

The first theory of migration and urbanization in developing countries is the labor surplus model.[4] The model assumes that two sectors exist in a developing economy: a traditional rural sector with zero marginal labor productivity and a modern urban industrial sector with high productivity. Central to the theory is that rural-urban migration is a natural and output-gain process in which surplus labor is withdrawn from the rural sector to provide the needed manpower for urban industrial growth. Urbanization thus augments national income through short-run efficiency gains due to

---

[4] The classical version of this theory, the dual economy model, was developed by Lewis (1955), Fei and Ranis (1964) and Jorgenson (1961). Extensions of the theory were made by Kelley, Williamson and Cheetham (1972).

shifts of labor from low to high marginal productivity employment and long-run growth effects due to higher accumulation rates in urban sectors. Therefore, output growth, trend acceleration, and rising migration and urbanization are likely outcomes of the labor surplus model.

The most influential model of rural-urban migration was suggested by Todaro (1969), which was extended by Harris and Todaro (1970), Zarembka (1972), Stiglitz (1974), and Corden and Findlay (1975). The model starts from the assumption that migration proceeds in response to urban-rural differences in expected income rather than actual earnings. The source of the rural-urban income differential is "a politically determined minimum urban wage at levels substantially higher than agricultural earnings" (Harris and Todaro, 1970, p. 126). Migrants consider the various labor market opportunities available to them in the rural and urban sectors and choose one that maximizes their expected gains from migration. The model predicts that migration rates in excess of urban job opportunity growth rates are not only possible but also rational and even likely in the face of wide urban-rural expected income differentials.

The literature also suggests some other factors that may influence rural-urban migration and urbanization, (see the survey by Williamson, 1988). For the purpose of this study, we focus on those relevant to China's experience in the last two decades. For example, agricultural land scarcity may push rural labor to the cities. Arable land shortage may account for heavy rural-urban migration due to the low level of per capita arable land in China. This shortage may generate a powerful rural push when the price of agricultural products remains unchanged institutionally. Institutional factors may matter as well in city-ward migration. Government policies that may lead to such migration include urban-bias measures, such as urban-oriented price distortions, government manipulation of capital markets, and public investment distributions.

## 4. Empirical Analyses of Determinants of Rural-Urban Migration

### 4.1. *Analyses with time-series data*

As suggested in the theories in the preceding section, the Chinese rural-urban migration should be a natural and inevitable consequence of economic development, because economic development entails a massive shift of labor and other inputs from rural sectors to urban sectors. This suggests a positive impact of economic development (measured by the growth rate of real income) on the magnitude of city-ward migration. The size of migration is also affected positively by the rural-urban income gap and the shortage of arable land in rural areas.[5] The resulting regression model of the national migration with time-series data in 1978–1999 thus is

$$M_t = \alpha_0 + \alpha_1 G_t + \alpha_2 Y_t + \alpha_3 L_t + \alpha_4 A_t + \alpha_5 Ts + \varepsilon_t \qquad (1)$$

where $M_t$ is the number of net city-ward migrants in year $t$, $G$ represents the income gap between rural and urban areas, $Y$ is the growth rate of real GDP, and $L$ indicates per capita arable land.

We include two more explanatory variables in the regression model: the share of agricultural employment ($A$) and the time trend ($T$), following the standard treatment in the literature (e.g. Mills and Becker, 1986). Since the output of industrial and services production is mostly sold outside the urban areas, both the industry and services influence (but are not influenced by) the urban population and migration. There is thus a case for including the share of industry and services among the explanatory variables. Alternatively it would be equivalent for us to use the share of agricultural employment. The time trend variable ($T$), which takes values 1 through 22 from 1978 to 1999, may capture effects of an upward or downward trend in the magnitude of migration that cannot be explained by the explanatory variables in the model.

Some variables that influence migration are not included in Eq. (1) due to considerations of data availability or model specifications. For instance, urban unemployment, which affects expected urban income, should enter the model with a negative sign as high unemployment can halt migration flows. Unfortunately, no reliable data on China's urban unemployment are available. The official data indicate a very low urban

---

[5] China has been characterized by its sharp and wide rural-urban divide. This divide arose from the socialist industrialization process, which created a hastened heavy-industry base at the expense of its rural population. The vast rural population not only endured much lower standards of living than urban dwellers, they were also prevented from migrating to cities (Knight and Song, 1999).

unemployment rate, being 2.8 percent in 1994, 2.9 percent in 1995, 3.0 percent in 1996, 3.1 percent in both 1997 and 1998 (SSB, 1998). Another example is changes in administrative units and population policies that definitely influence urban population and migration. Since the policy changes were not one-time increases or decreases but gradual, it seems inappropriate to introduce a policy variable in the regression model with time-series data.

Annual data on the rural-urban migration is constructed based on the concept that the total growth of the urban population is the sum of the natural growth of the urban population and net rural-urban migration, as discussed in Section 2 and shown in Table 11.1.[6] All data on explanatory variables are obtained from *China Statistical Yearbook 2000* (SSB, 2000) and *Comprehensive Statistical Data and Materials on 50 Years of New China* (SSB, 1999a). The rural-urban income gap ($G$) is measured by the ratio of urban per capita disposable income to rural per capita net income. Per capita arable land ($L$) is defined as the ratio of cultivated areas (in hectares) to total agricultural population.[7]

The regression results of Eq. (1) with the time-series data in 1978–1999, which are presented in Table 11.3, suggest significant and positive effects of economic development on the Chinese rural-urban migration. This finding is consistent with the theoretical predictions. The significant negative coefficient of $T$ seems to indicate that factors other than those included in the model contribute to a downward time trend in the level of migration. The downward trend of annual migrants might result from rising costs of urbanization or implicit administrative controls on migration. The insignificant coefficients of the rural-urban income gap and per capita arable land seem to be surprising at the first glance. But the

---

[6] The floating population is not included in the city-ward migrants, because most floating people in urban areas are temporary residents in nature under explicit and implicit administrative controls on rural-urban migration. Therefore they are not included in the official statistics of urban population. The official data on inter- and intra-province migration does not include the floating population either.

[7] No data on cultivated areas for years 1996, 1997 and 1998 in all Chinese government publications of statistics, because a new agricultural census, which was completed in October 1996, suggested a larger amount of cultivated area in 1999 than what was expected. For the purpose of consistent time-series data on per capita arable land, we use the pre-census data for 1978–1995, and constructed the data for the last four years by projection.

Table 11.3. Determinants of Rural-Urban Migration in China: 1978–1999

| Dependent Variable: Log (Number of Migrants) | | |
|---|---|---|
| Independent Variables | Coefficients | *t*-Statistic |
| Constant (*C*) | 15.18** | 2.67 |
| Change in urban-rural income gap (*G*) | 0.57 | 0.70 |
| Growth rate of real GDP (*γ*) | 0.13* | 2.01 |
| Change in per capita arable land (*L*) | −2.19 | −0.95 |
| Agricultural employment share (*A*) | −0.12 | −1.54 |
| Time trend (*T*) | −1.32* | −1.89 |
| $R^2$ | 0.32 | |
| *F*-statistic | 13.92*** | |

*Note*: The sample size is 22. The asterisks ***, **, and * indicate levels of significance at 1 percent, 5 percent, and 10 percent, respectively.

puzzle can be solved easily by considering the following fact: While China indeed has a large income gap between rural and urban areas (the range of the ratio of urban to rural per capita income is 2.04–2.86) and suffers from a shortage of arable lands (the range of per capita arable land is 0.27–0.35 hectares) relative to most developing countries, the changes in the two variables over the period 1978–1999 are quite small. In fact, potential city-ward migrants have been encouraged substantially by the rural-urban income gap and the limited arable land, but they may not respond significantly to a small change in the two indices.

A specification test is necessary to examine whether or not the migration model is subject to simultaneity bias, since the labor surplus model implies a possible feedback from migration to economic development. The standard Granger causality test is conducted with two lags, and the results are reported in Table 11.4. The null hypothesis that the Chinese economic development (measured by the logarithm of per capita income) does not Granger-cause migration is rejected at the 5 percent level of significance, while the hypothesis of the exogeneity of migration cannot be rejected. This finding thus not only complements our results from the structural model of Eq. (1), but also suggests that China's rural-urban migration in the last two decades is basically a consequence of its rapid economic growth. The interpretation of the causality tests is as follows. While theoretical predictions may suggest positive effects of rural-urban

Table 11.4.   Granger Causality Tests of the Link between Migration and Income Growth

| Null Hypotheses and Estimating Equations | $F$-Statistic |
|---|---|
| Growth of real income ($Y$) does not Granger-cause migration ($M$) | |

$$\ln M_t = a_0 + \sum_{i=1}^{2} a_i \ln M_{t-i} + \sum_{j=1}^{2} b_j \ln Y_{t-j} + u_t \qquad 4.25^{**}$$

Migration ($M$) does not Granger-cause growth of real income ($Y$)

$$\ln Y_t = c_0 + \sum_{i=1}^{2} c_i \ln Y_{t-i} + \sum_{j=1}^{2} d_j \ln M_{t-j} + v_t \qquad 1.85$$

*Note*: The asterisks ** indicate the level of significance at 5 percent.

migration on economic growth through efficiency-enhancing structural changes, it does not seem to be true for the case of China due to its huge population body and rural surplus labor. China has been struggling for a long time with the potential increase in urban unemployment in the process of industrialization, and the resulting migration policy is to strictly control labor mobility through the household registration system (World Bank, 1997). Even though the controls have been relaxed gradually since 1978, many implicit restrictions on rural-urban migration still remain to avoid explosive urban unemployment (Wang and Zuo, 1999). Thus migration in general follows job creation in urban industrial and service sectors (Song, 2001).

### 4.2. *Analyses with cross-section data*

While the estimations of Eq. (1) are useful for us to better understand the Chinese migration, the specification with time-series data is limited in revealing the patterns of the migration at regional levels and the roles played by the rural-urban income gap and the shortage of arable land. To take advantage of the information on the regional migration shown in Table 11.2, we specify a simple regression model that emphasizes the role of the rural-urban income gap, arable land, and geographic distance in determining the cross-province migration in China. The resulting specification is given as

$$MS_i = \beta_0 + \beta_1 LAND_i + \beta_2 YGAP_i + \beta_3 DISTANCE_i + \mu_t \qquad (2)$$

where $MS_i$ indicates the share of emigrants in total agricultural population in province $i$ at the end of 1998, $LAND_i$ is per capita arable land for province $i$, and $YGAP_i$ is per capita income gap between urban areas in the top four migration-host provinces and rural areas in province $i$, as indicated in Table 11.2, and $DISTANCE_i$ measures the physical distances between province $i$ and the top four migration-host provinces. The variable of urban unemployment is not included in the model due to problems of data. According to the Chinese government, the urban unemployment rate for major cities was lower than 2 percent in 1998 (SSB, 1999). The regressions that include the urban unemployment rate indicate no improvements over those without the variable, and the coefficient of the unemployment variable is insignificant at conventional levels as well. We do not include in the equation the variable of institutional factors that no doubt influenced the migration substantially, because the variation in the policy variable within China (or across provinces) was negligible.

Equation (2) constitutes the basis for our cross-section estimations of the determinants of Chinese city-ward migration. In particular, this specification will be estimated directly for the total number of emigrants of a province and for the inter-province emigrants by 1998. For the intra-province emigrants (measured by the share of intra-province migrants in total agricultural population in province $i$ at the end of 1998, denoted by $MSIN_i$), Eq. (2) can be modified slightly to reflect the actual motivations for migration. We replace $YGAP$ with $YGAPIN$, which represents the income gap, measured by the ratio of per capita income in urban areas to rural areas within a province. The variable of $DISTANCE$ is dropped because no information is available on the sources and destinations of intra-province migrants. We introduce urban population ($UP$) as an explanatory variable to reflect the hypothesis that a province with a greater urban population and urban concentration tends to attract larger numbers of immigrants in a cumulative manner due to agglomeration economies.[8] The regression model for intra-province migration thus is

$$MSIN_i = \gamma_0 + \gamma_1 LAND_i + \gamma_2 YGAPIN_i + \gamma_3 UP_i + v_t. \qquad (3)$$

---

[8] Thanks go to an anonymous referee for the suggestion of including urban population in the model.

The data on migrants are taken from *China Labor Statistical Yearbook 1999* (SSB, 1999b), and data on all independent variables are from *China Statistical Yearbook 2000* (SSB, 2000) and *Comprehensive Statistical Data and Materials on 50 Years of New China* (SSB, 1999a). $LAND_i$ is measured as the average ratio of arable areas (in hectares) to total agricultural population in province $i$ in the five-year mid-period (i.e. 1986–1991). $YGAP_i$ is constructed as the ratio of average per capita income of urban areas in the top four migration-host provinces (Guangdong, Zhejiang, Fujian and Jiangsu) to per capita income of rural areas in province $i$. To avoid fluctuations in a single year, we use the five-year average ratio in the mid-period (i.e. 1986–1991) for $YGAP_i$. The similar procedure of the five-year average in the mid-period is used for constructing $YGAPIN_i$ and $UP_i$.

In addition to regressions for migrants by the end of 1998, Eqs. (2) and (3) are to be estimated for migrants in 1998 as well. All of the explanatory variables are measured in the same way as estimations for migrants by 1998 but take the value in 1997, instead of the five-year average in the mid-period. These regressions may enable us to see if any changes took place in 1998 relative to the entire period.

The estimates of the cross-section data for the migrants by the end of 1998 and in 1998 are obtained by the ordinary least squares technique. In both cases, the number of observations is 28 rather than 31 provinces and municipalities due to unavailability of data.[9] Tables 11.5 and 11.6 report parameter estimates of various models, from which the following main points emerge.

(a)  The overall performance of estimates in the regressions for total migrants and inter-province migrants in Table 11.5 is satisfactory, and better than the regressions for intra-province migrants. Values of $R^2$ in all cases are around 50 percent, suggesting reasonable explanatory power of the models. The fit of the regressions is good as well. The

---

[9] The data on migrants for Shanghai and Tibet and the data on all explanatory variables for Chongqing before 1997 are not available. Although it became a newly established municipality, Chongqing in this study is treated as part of Sichuan Province as it was before 1996. For detailed information about the 31 provinces and municipalities in China, see the notes in Table 11.2.

Table 11.5.   Cross-section Estimates of Migration Models: Total Migrants by 1998

| Independent Variables | Total Migrants | | Inter-Province Migrants | | Intra-Province Migrants | |
|---|---|---|---|---|---|---|
| | Coefficient | *t*-Statistic | Coefficient | *t*-Statistic | Coefficient | *t*-Statistic |
| C | 373.88*** | 3.16 | 255.66*** | 2.92 | −102.23* | −1.75 |
| LAND | −24.01 | −0.40 | −14.47 | −0.31 | −19.69 | −1.21 |
| YGAP | 83.25*** | 2.80 | 65.06*** | 2.96 | | |
| DISTANCE | −307.29*** | −4.18 | −232.71*** | −4.27 | | |
| YGAPIN | | | | | 51.11** | 2.35 |
| UP | | | | | 0.07*** | 4.32 |
| $R^2$ | 0.51 | | 0.52 | | 0.49 | |
| F-statistic | 8.40*** | | 8.72*** | | 7.75*** | |

*Note*: The number of observations is 28 for all estimations. The asterisks ***, **, and * indicate levels of significance at 1 percent, 5 percent, and 10 percent, respectively. The dependent variable is the share of emigrants in total agricultural population in a province.

Table 11.6.   Cross-section Estimates of Migration Models: Migrants in 1998

| Independent Variables | Total Migrants | | Inter-Province Migrants | | Intra-Province Migrants | |
|---|---|---|---|---|---|---|
| | Coefficient | *t*-Statistic | Coefficient | *t*-Statistic | Coefficient | *t*-Statistic |
| C | 112.24*** | 3.31 | 70.07** | 2.72 | −15.62 | −0.84 |
| LAND | 1.88 | 0.10 | 0.84 | 0.06 | −6.20 | −1.19 |
| YGAP | 20.80** | 2.44 | 17.51** | 2.71 | | |
| DISTANCE | −91.25*** | −4.33 | −65.73*** | −4.10 | | |
| YGAPIN | | | | | 8.70* | 1.75 |
| UP | | | | | 0.02*** | 3.49 |
| $R^2$ | 0.50 | | 0.48 | | 0.39 | |
| F-statistic | 7.94*** | | 7.41*** | | 5.20*** | |

*Note*: The number of observations is 28 for all estimations. The asterisks ***, **, and * indicate levels of significance at 1 percent, 5 percent, and 10 percent, respectively. The dependent variable is the share of emigrants in total agricultural population in a province.

regression *F*-statistics are significant at the conventional levels of almost 100 percent in all cases except those for intra-province migrants.

(b)   For the models of total migrants and inter-province migrants in Table 11.5, the estimated coefficients of *YGAP* and *DISTANCE* are significant at 1 percent and have the correct signs. The results support the widely held view that the large flows of city-ward migration might have been encouraged substantially by the rural-urban income gap between home and host provinces, and that migrants respond negatively to the distance between home and host provinces. The findings are quite consistent with the theoretical predictions and empirical results from existing studies (e.g. Mills and Becker, 1986; Wang and Zuo, 1999).

(c)  The insignificance of the coefficient for *LAND* is not quite expected. According to the World Bank (2000, pp. 118–120), Chinese per capita arable land was 0.10 hectares in both periods of 1979–1981 and 1995–1997, much lower than most countries in the world.[10] The shortage of arable land and the large labor surplus in rural China no doubt generated a powerful push for city-ward migration, which should be reflected in a cross-country estimation.[11] However, in our study with the cross-province data, variations in per capita arable land among provinces within China are so small that no significant response is observed from migrants.

(d)  Intra-province migration is positively affected by urban-rural income gap within a province (*YGAPIN*) and provincial urban population (*UP*), as suggested by the significant coefficients of the two variables. It seems safe to say that the income gap between rural and urban areas indeed is a powerful driving force of both inter- and intra-province migration. City-ward intra-province migrants are also encouraged by agglomeration economies.

(e)  The pattern of parametric estimates for migrants in 1998 in Table 11.6 is in general the same as that for migrants by 1998 in Table 11.5, suggesting virtually no changes in the migration determination between the year 1998 and the period before that year.

---

[10] For low-income countries excluding China and India, per capita arable land was 0.23 hectares in 1979–1981 and 0.18 hectares in 1995–1997. The corresponding figures for mid-income countries are 0.24 and 0.35, and those for high-income countries are 0.46 and 0.41 (World Bank, 2000).

[11] China has been a labor surplus country for a long time. Even by the 1950s, most arable land was already cultivated and further increases in the labor force contributed little to increase agricultural output.

Overall, our findings are consistent with the widespread belief and most theoretical predictions mentioned above. In the long-term time-series context, the city-ward migration was a consequence of China's rapid economic growth in the period of 1978–1999. It was the increase in per capita income, which brought China to a higher level of economic development, that caused large flows of rural-to-urban migrants. At the regional level, both inter and intra-province migrants responded positively to the rural-urban income gap. While inter-province migrants were negatively affected by the geographic distance between source and destination provinces, intra-province migrants in a province were positively influenced by the urban population size of the province.

## 5. Concluding Remarks

There has been widespread concern among Chinese policy makers about the pace of the rural-urban migration and urbanization in the recent years. The large floating population and number of city-ward migrants have been singled out as a few of the major economic and social problems in China. This paper addresses the factors behind China's rapid migration and urbanization on the basis of both time-series and cross-section estimations. The findings of the article can be summarized as follows. Once again, the main source of China's urban growth in the last two decades was rural-urban migration, which in turn resulted from China's rapid economic growth. Both inter- and intra-province rural-to-urban migrants were encouraged by the income gap between the rural home and urban destinations. While geographic distance discouraged inter-province migration, the urban population size of a province had positive effects on the intra-province migration of that province.

Some policy implications regarding migration and urban unemployment may be drawn from this study. First, the pace and scale of the city-ward migration and urbanization should be determined by and be consistent with economic growth as well as development levels. Although a theoretical feedback of migration to economic growth is suggested, no evidence is found in the Chinese case. Our time-series analyses show that the nationwide migration boom in the last two decades was a consequence of China's rapid economic growth, not vice versa. The slowdown in migration in the 1990s, even under the same growth rate of GDP as in the 1980s, seems to imply the rising costs of migration and urbanization. Excessive rural-urban migration and urbanization relative to economic growth may create serious problems of unemployment and poverty due to the limited absorption capacity of both the industry and urban social services. Therefore, certain administrative controls on rural-urban migration may be still necessary in the short run for restraining explosive unemployment.

Second, the Chinese government should be prepared to deal with increasing city-ward migrants in the near future due to the potential growing rural-urban income gap. Since China joined the World Trade Organization at the end of 2001, the rural-urban inequalities are expected to increase further, because rural incomes will be further depressed by increased agricultural imports, and urban incomes may rise through expanding labor-intensive manufacturing exports. With the widening gap, more country-dwellers may be driven into the cities, putting even greater pressure on urban unemployment. The Chinese authorities may have two policy options: one is to create jobs in urban industries and services, which is beyond the scope of this study, and the other is to control migration, which is related to the findings of this study. Reducing the rural-urban income gap may be a powerful policy instrument to control the pace of migration and urbanization. Because migrants respond significantly to differentials between the rural and urban incomes, it is important that imbalances between economic opportunities in rural and urban areas are minimized. For example, since inter-province migrants mainly move from inland rural areas to coastal urban areas, any measures to reduce the inland-coastal income disparities may not only decrease the number of such migrants but also improve development opportunities for the vast inland areas.

### References

Chang, Hsin Gene. (2002). "Urbanization and Unemployment in China". In A. Chen, G. Liu, and K. Zhang (eds.), *Urbanization and Social Welfare in China*. Aldershot: Ashgate.

Chang, Hsin Gene and Brada, Josef C. (2002). "China's Urbanization Lag during the Period of Reform: A Paradox". University of Toledo and Arizona State University Working Paper.

Corden, W. and Findlay, R. (1975). "Urban Unemployment, Intersectoral Capital Mobility and Development Policy". *Economica*, 42, pp. 59–78.

Fei, J.C.H. and Ranis, G. (1964). "A Theory of Economic Development". *American Economic Review*, 51, pp. 533–565.

Hare, Denise. (1999). "'Push' versus 'Pull' Factors in Migration Outflows and Returns: Determinants of Migration Status and Spell Duration among China's Rural Population". *Journal of Development Studies*, 35(3), pp. 45–72.

Harris, John R. and Todaro, Michael P. (1970). "Migration, Unemployment, and Development: A Two-sector Analysis". *American Economic Review*, 60, pp. 126–142.

Jorgenson, D.W. (1961). "The Development of a Dual Economy". *Economic Journal*, 71, pp. 309–334.

Kelley, A.C., Williamson, J.G., and Cheetham, R.J. (1972). *Dualistic Economic Development: Theory and History*. Chicago: University of Chicago Press.

Knight, John and Song, Lina (1999). *The Rural-Urban Divide: Economic Disparities and Interactions in China*. Oxford: Oxford University press.

Lewis, Arthur W. (1955). *The Theory of Economic Growth*. Homewood, IL: Irwin.

Mills, Edwin S. and Becker, Charles M. (1986). *Studies in Indian Urban Development*. New York: Oxford University Press.

Seeborg, Michael C., Jin, Zhenhu and Zhu, Yiping. (2000). "The New Rural-Urban Labor Mobility in China: Causes and Implications". *Journal of Social Economics*, 29, pp. 39–56.

Song, Shunfeng. (2001). "City Size and Urban Unemployment: Evidence from China". *World Economy & China*, 9(1), pp. 46–53.

Song, Shunfeng and Zhang, Kevin Honglin. (2002). "Urbanization and city-size distribution in China, *Urban Studies*, 39, pp. 2317–2327.

State Statistical Bureau (SSB) of China (1999). *Comprehensive Statistical Data and Materials on 50 Years of New China*. Beijing: China Statistical Press.

State Statistical Bureau (SSB) of China (1998, 1999b and 2000). *China Statistical Yearbook 1998, 1999* and *2000*. Beijing: China Statistical Press.

State Statistical Bureau and Ministry of Labor and Social Security (SSB-MLSS) of China (1999). *China Labor Statistical Yearbook 1999*. Beijing: China Statistical Press.

Stiglitz, J. (1974). "Wage Determination and Unemployment in LDCs". *Quarterly Journal of Economics*, 88, pp. 194–227.

Sun, Changming. (1997). "Floating Population in Shanghai: A Perspective on Social Transformation in China. In T. Scharping (ed.), *Floating Population and Migration in China: The Impact of Economic Reforms.* Hamburg, Germany: Institute of Asian Studies, pp. 201–215.

Todaro, Michael P. (1969). A Model of Labor Migration and Urban Unemployment in Less Developed Countries". *American Economic Review*, 59, pp. 138–148.

Wang, Feng, and Zuo, Xuejin. (1999). "Inside China's Cities: Institutional Barriers and Opportunities for Urban Migrants". *American Economic Review: Papers and Proceedings*, 89(2), pp. 276–280.

Williamson, Jeffery G. (1988). Migration and Urbanization". In H. Chenery and T.N. Srinivasan (eds.), *Handbook of Development Economics*, Vol. I. Amsterdam: Elsevier-North Holland, pp. 425–465.

World Bank. (2000). *World Development Indicators.* Washington DC: World Bank.

Wu, Harry Xiaoying. (1994). "Rural to Urban Migration in the People's Republic of China". *China Quarterly*, 139, pp. 669–698.

Zarembka, P. (1972). *Toward A Theory of Economic Development.* San Francisco: Holden-Day.

Zhang, L. and Zhao, Simon X.B. (1998). "Re-examining China's 'Urban' Concept and the Level of Urbanization". *China Quarterly*, 154, pp. 330–381.

Zhao, Yaohui. (1999). "Leaving the Countryside: Rural-Urban Migration Decisions in China". *American Economic Review: Papers and Proceedings*, 89(2), pp. 276–280.

CHAPTER 12

# Demography, Migration, and Regional Income Disparity*

*Ding Lu*

More than one tenth of China's total population has become the so-called floating population, consisting of mostly rural migrants who are away from their place of household registration for more than six months. Migration improves the efficiency of interregional resource allocation and enhances the welfare of residents in both the poor and rich regions. However, massive migration from low-income regions to high-income regions redistributes the so-called demographic dividends across regions by restructuring regional demographics. The poor regions with net outward migration thus face a major challenge regarding how to maximize the benefits of labor mobility and control its negative impact on their economies.

## 1. Introduction

For three decades, China has sustained hyper economic growth of above 9 percent per annum. With this rate of growth, the economy doubles its size every eight years. Hundreds of millions of people have been lifted out of poverty. A disturbing feature of China's hyper economic growth has been its uneven occurrence across the country's vast regions. The income disparity between the rich coastal regions and the poor inland regions as well as between the urban areas and rural areas has been widened.

* Reprinted and revised from EAI Background Briefs, No. 399 (2008).

Meanwhile, China's interregional labor mobility has increased substantially since the late 1980s. A major part of this increasing labor mobility comes from the flow of rural migrant workers (*nongmin gong*), who go to work in urban areas without becoming permanent urban residents due to various institutional restrictions. When an official census started to collect data about domestic migrations in 1987, there were only 15.2 million migrants who were away from their place of household registration for more than six months. That accounted for only about 1.5 percent of China's population. The such defined floating population increased to 30 million by 1990, 56 million by 1995, 80 million by 2000, and 140 million by 2004, more than one tenth of the total population (National Population and Family Planning Commission, 2005). It further rose to 221 million in 2010, accounting for 16.5 percent of the total population. (National Bureau of Statistics of China, 2011) The increase in interregional labor mobility poses new challenges to the regional governments, especially those with net outward migration. Good public policies are needed to maximize the benefits and minimize the costs of labor migration across regions.

The rapid increase of labor migration has occurred not only between rural and urban areas but also across different provincial economies. According to China's Population Census, between 1985 and 1990, the accumulated cross-province migration was over 11.06 million. By 2000, the number of people not living in the provinces of their own household registration reached 42.42 million. By 2005, the number rose to 47.79 million.

According to our estimation,[1] in 2000–2005, all the nine richest provincial economies experienced net inward migration (indicated by positive net migration ratios). Meanwhile, most of the net outward migrating provincial economies had below-median-level per capita incomes (Fig. 12.1). This pattern of migration from low-income regions to high-income regions has continued the earlier trends of migration.[2]

---

[1] We estimate the provincial economies' net migration volume, $m_t$, in the following way: $m_t = \Delta N_t - g_{nt} N_{t-1}$, where $\Delta N_t = N_t - N_{t-1}$, which is the change of total population of residents in year $t$, and $g_{nt}$ is the annual natural growth rate of the resident population. We then define net migration ratio in the period from year 0 to $t$ as $Z_t = \sum_{i=0}^{t} \{ m_t / [(N_0 + N_t)/2] \}$.

[2] Earlier studies show strong and significant correlations between per capita incomes and net population inflows in the period 1985–1990 (Yao, 2003).

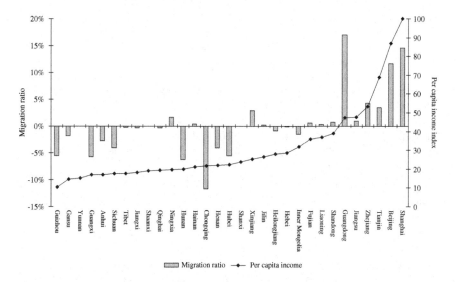

Figure 12.1. Provincial per capita income (2005) and migration ratio (2000–2005).
*Source*: National Bureau of Statistics of China (2001–2006), *China Statistical Yearbook*, Beijing: China Statistics Press.

As shown in Table 12.1, of the ten provincial economies with the highest net outward migration, only Inner Mongolia has a per capita income above the national average level. None of these economies have attained a per capita household consumption above the national average. It is also notable that the poor, out-migrating provincial economies have generally higher juvenile dependency ratios (i.e. younger populations).

Such massive migration from low-income regions to high-income regions has a profound impact on the interregional allocation of labor resources. In particular, it redistributes the so-called demographic dividends[3] across regions by substantially restructuring the regional demographics.

---

[3] Demographic dividends arise from a particular period of demographic transition. In most parts of the world, population growth has roughly been through a three-phase transition in recent history. In the initial stage, both the fertility rate and death rate are high and life expectancy is short so the population growth is relatively slow with a high dependency ratio (i.e. dependents-to-working-age-adults ratio) with a large number of children to take care of. When economic modernization arrives with improved public health care, better diets, and rising income, the death rate (especially the infant mortality rate) starts to plummet and people live longer. The growing divergence between the high

Table 12.1.   Provincial Economies with Largest Net Migration Ratios (2005)

| | Per Capita GDP Index | Dependency Ratio | | | Per Capita Household Consumption | Net Migration Ratio (2000–2005) |
|---|---|---|---|---|---|---|
| | | Gross | Juvenile | Elderly | | |
| Guizhou | 10.31 | 57.58 | 44.65 | 12.93 | 17.55 | −5.5% |
| Gansu | 14.48 | 44.15 | 33.74 | 10.41 | 18.89 | −1.8% |
| Guangxi | 16.99 | 49.92 | 35.60 | 14.32 | 21.39 | −5.8% |
| Anhui | 17.06 | 49.66 | 34.56 | 15.10 | 19.86 | −2.7% |
| Sichuan | 17.47 | 48.74 | 32.50 | 16.24 | 21.35 | −4.1% |
| Hunan | 19.99 | 40.53 | 26.30 | 14.23 | 25.67 | −6.2% |
| Chongqing | 21.86 | 46.27 | 30.23 | 16.04 | 25.93 | −11.6% |
| Henan | 21.92 | 41.58 | 29.92 | 11.66 | 22.96 | −4.1% |
| Hubei | 22.18 | 39.00 | 26.25 | 12.75 | 25.69 | −5.6% |
| Inner Mongolia | 31.71 | 33.32 | 22.74 | 10.57 | 28.90 | −1.4% |
| **National** | 27.33 | 40.10 | 27.39 | 12.71 | 29.82 | |
| Shandong | 38.89 | 34.90 | 21.48 | 13.42 | 34.61 | 0.7% |
| Guangdong | 47.25 | 40.45 | 30.05 | 10.39 | 50.47 | 17.0% |
| Jiangsu | 47.56 | 35.88 | 21.11 | 14.77 | 40.57 | 0.9% |
| Zhejiang | 53.29 | 36.01 | 21.63 | 14.39 | 52.35 | 4.3% |
| Tianjin | 68.86 | 28.79 | 16.31 | 12.48 | 58.13 | 3.4% |
| Beijing | 86.96 | 26.74 | 13.03 | 13.70 | 92.60 | 11.7% |
| Shanghai | 100.00 | 26.53 | 11.39 | 15.14 | 100.00 | 14.6% |

*Source*: Compiled from National Bureau of Statistics of China (2006), *China Statistical Yearbook*, Beijing: China Statistics Press.

birth rate and the falling death rate accelerates population growth and leads to an unprecedented expansion of the population size which is a feature of the second stage of demographic transition. Sooner or later, with further development and rise in the standard of living, the fertility rate starts to decline and population growth slows. At this third stage of demographic transition, the falling birth rate converges with the lower death rate over time and eventually leaves little population growth. In the post-transition era, as the falling fertility rate nears or drops below the replacement level, population growth eventually comes to a halt and even starts to decline. With low birth rates and lengthening life expectancy, an aging society emerges. When demographic transition enters the third phase, as the birth rate starts to fall, the baby boomers from earlier years enter working age while the dependency ratio declines since there are fewer kids to be fed. Both the slowing population growth and the rising saving rate (thanks to a bulging working-age portion of the whole population) are favorable to capital accumulation and the rise of per capita income. Since the labor force grows at a faster rate than the total population, per capita income must rise as long as the growing labor force is sufficiently employed. These benefits thus bring in demographic dividends or a window of development opportunity. Human capital accumulation is also accelerated thanks to smaller family sizes and rising incomes that favor higher-quality child rearing.

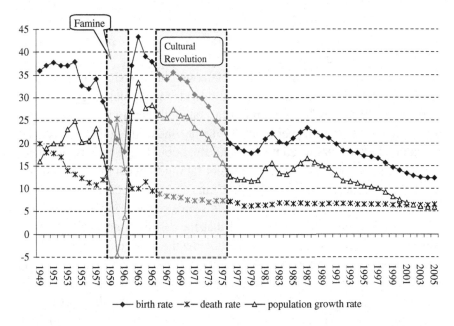

**—♦— birth rate —×— death rate —△— population growth rate**

Figure 12.2.   Birth rate, death rate, and natural growth rate of population (1949–2005) (per 1,000 persons).

*Source*: National Bureau of Statistics of China (1999), *Comprehensive Statistical Data and Materials on 50 Years of New China*; Beijing: China Statistics Press; National Bureau of Statistics of China (2005), *China Compendium of Statistics: 1949–2004*, Beijing: China Statistics Press; Institute of Population and Labor Economics, Chinese Academy of Social Sciences (1985–2006), *Almanac of China's Population*, ACP press.

## 2. Demographic Consequences of Mass Migration

At the national level, China's economic takeoff has benefited tremendously from demographic dividends over the past three decades. From 1949 to 1970, China was in the second phase of demographic transition.

As shown in Fig. 12.2, except for the 1959–1961 famine, the annual death rate declined continuously from 1.7–2.0 percent in 1949–1952 to 0.76 percent in 1970. Meanwhile, the annual birth rate hovered between 2.9 percent and 4.3 percent for all years except for 1959–1961, bringing two waves of baby booms — the first in 1949–1954 when the birth rate stayed above 3.6 percent for six years and the second in 1962–1965 when the birth rate shot up above 3.7 percent for four years. The enlarged gap between the birth rate and the death rate resulted in an unprecedented growth of population at an annual rate of over 1.6 percent through 1949–1970 except during the 1959–1961 famine.

China entered the third phase of demographic transition in the early 1970s, when the government started nationwide family planning programs. Between 1970 and 1979, the total fertility rate fell sharply from 5.81 births per woman to 2.75 births per woman. The decline of the total fertility rate accelerated after 1980 when the one-child-per-couple policy was launched and promoted. The total fertility rate kept falling to reach the replacement level of 2.1 per woman around 1990.[4] China's fertility decline within a relatively short time period is drastic, rarely seen elsewhere in the world. The United Nations Secretariat estimated that the fertility rate in 2000–2005 was around 1.7 births per woman, well below the replacement level of 2.1 births per woman (United Nations Secretariat, 2006).

China's population structure in the 1970s and 1980s was largely a bottom-heavy one, characteristic of a young population with a fast-growing labor force. From 1975 to 2005, the combined effects of the second-wave baby boomers entering working age and the continuous fall of the fertility rate have moved the overall dependency ratio downwards, while most of the first-wave baby boomers had not yet grown out of their productive age.

As seen in Fig. 12.3, the juvenile dependency ratio (between the population aged 0–14 and the population aged 15–64) fell all the way from over 70 percent in 1970 to below 30 percent after 2000, while the elderly dependency ratio (between the population aged 65+ and the population aged 15–64) remained relatively stable below 10 percent. The overall dependency ratio (between the population aged 0–14 and 65+ and the population aged 15–64) thus fell from nearly 80 percent to below 40 percent. Such a very favorable demographic change coincided with the crucial years of China's market-oriented reform and economic

---

[4] Despite the declining fertility rate, the crude birth rate rebounded in the 1980s, when 9 out of 10 years saw birth rates above 2.0 percent. The bulging birth rates were largely caused by the coincidental arrival of the marriage-childbirth tides with the two waves of the earlier baby boomers due to the fact that many first-wave baby boomers had to delay planning their families through the chaotic Cultural Revolution (1966–1976). The birth rate soon resumed its falling trend by the end of the 1980s and dropped all the way down to below 0.15 percent per annum by the turn of the century.

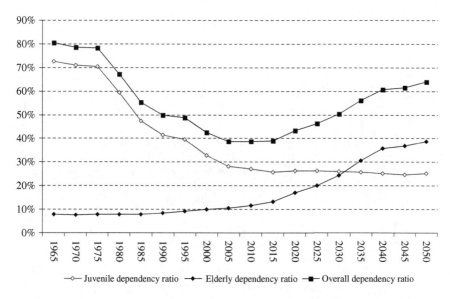

Figure 12.3.    China's juvenile, elderly and overall dependency ratios (1970–2050).

*Source*: United Nations Secretariat (2006), *World Population Prospects: The 2006 Revision and World Urbanization Prospects: The 2005 Revision*, http://esa.un.org/unpp; National Bureau of Statistics of China (1999), *Comprehensive Statistical Data and Materials on 50 Years of New China*, Beijing: China Statistics Press; National Bureau of Statistics of China (2005), *China Compendium of Statistics: 1949–2004*, Beijing: China Statistics Press.

*Notes*: Juvenile dependency ratio = population aged 0–14 to population aged 15–64; elderly dependency ratio = population aged 65 and above to population aged 15–64; overall dependency ratio = (population aged 0–14 and population aged 65+) to population aged 15–64.

takeoff. During 1982–2000, roughly 15 percent of China's growth was attributable to demographic dividends (Mason and Wang, 2005).

In most places in the world, the demographic dividend period lasted for at least five decades. In China, however, the demographic transition has occurred as if in fast-forward, resulting in a much shorter and transitory dividend period. All indicators of demographic trends suggest that China has already entered a post-transition era of a fast aging population. By 2000, China's population age structure was that of a mature population, where the largest shares were found in the working-age cohorts. China's population age structure is projected to become a very old one by 2030. From 2005 to 2025, China's population aged over 65 will double in size to about 200 million people. From 2015 onwards,

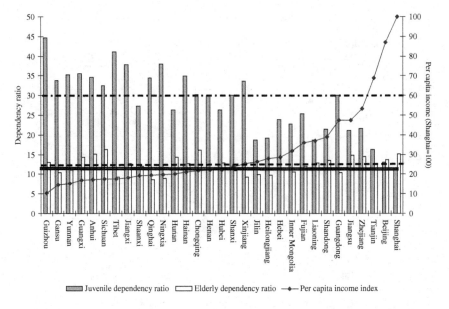

Figure 12.4.    Regional disparity of per capita income and dependency ratio (2005).

*Source*: Compiled from National Bureau of Statistics of China (2006), *China Statistical Yearbook*, Beijing: China Statistics Press.

*Note*: "==" refers to median per capita income, "- - -" refers to median elderly dependency ratio, and "–·–" is median juvenile dependency ratio.

the overall dependency ratio will rise sharply, boosted by the rapid aging of the population (Fig. 12.3).

Across China, demographic patterns are highly heterogeneous. As shown in Fig. 12.4, there is a rough correspondence between aging and per capita income. The five richest provincial economies have the oldest population structures. Most lower-income provinces have relatively younger populations. Generally the rich provinces are in the later phase of demographic transition while the poor ones are more likely at the earlier phase of transition. The poor inland regions appear to have some more years to enjoy the demographic dividends or the window of development compared to the rich coastal regions.

Unfortunately, greater labor mobility across regions has somehow diluted the demographic dividends for the poor regions, most of which have net outward migration. The outward migration of the working-age population from the poor regions to the rich coastal regions has helped the latter cope with the problems of an aging population by injecting young workers into the labor force. It nevertheless shrinks the size of the labor force in the poor regions and raises their dependency ratios.

Table 12.2 compares the changes in demographic structures in ten poor regions with net outward migration and seven rich regions with net inward migration between 2000 and 2006. During the period 2000–2006, in the seven rich provincial economies, the ratios of working-age population declined on average by 5.6 percentage points while in the ten poor regions the ratios declined by 11.3 percentage points. Meanwhile, the

Table 12.2.   Changes in Demographic Structure (2000–2006)

|  | 2000 | | | 2006 | | |
|---|---|---|---|---|---|---|
|  | Aged 0–14 | Aged 15–64 | Aged 65+ | Aged 0–14 | Aged 15–64 | Aged 65+ |
| *Poor 10 average* | 24.6 | 68.7 | 6.7 | 29.3 | 57.4 | 13.4 |
| Guizhou | 30.3 | 63.9 | 5.8 | 42.2 | 45.3 | 12.5 |
| Gansu | 27.0 | 68.0 | 5.0 | 30.8 | 58.8 | 10.4 |
| Guangxi | 26.2 | 66.6 | 7.1 | 32.3 | 54.6 | 13.1 |
| Anhui | 25.5 | 67.0 | 7.5 | 31.2 | 53.9 | 14.9 |
| Sichuan | 22.7 | 69.9 | 7.4 | 28.9 | 54.7 | 16.4 |
| Hunan | 22.2 | 70.5 | 7.3 | 25.2 | 60.0 | 14.8 |
| Chongqing | 21.9 | 70.2 | 7.9 | 28.2 | 55.3 | 16.6 |
| Henan | 25.9 | 67.1 | 7.0 | 29.4 | 59.2 | 11.4 |
| Hubei | 22.9 | 70.8 | 6.3 | 23.2 | 63.4 | 13.4 |
| Inner Mongolia | 21.3 | 73.4 | 5.3 | 21.4 | 68.4 | 10.3 |
| *Rich 7 average* | 17.9 | 73.5 | 8.6 | 18.2 | 67.9 | 13.9 |
| Shandong | 20.8 | 71.1 | 8.0 | 20.3 | 67.0 | 12.7 |
| Guangdong | 24.2 | 69.8 | 6.1 | 27.8 | 62.4 | 9.8 |
| Jiangsu | 19.7 | 71.6 | 8.8 | 20.2 | 64.8 | 15.0 |
| Zhejiang | 18.1 | 73.1 | 8.8 | 20.0 | 66.6 | 13.4 |
| Tianjin | 16.8 | 74.9 | 8.3 | 15.6 | 70.8 | 13.6 |
| Beijing | 13.6 | 78.0 | 8.4 | 12.7 | 73.1 | 14.3 |
| Shanghai | 12.2 | 76.3 | 11.5 | 10.5 | 71.0 | 18.6 |
| *National average* | 22.9 | 70.1 | 7.0 | 25.5 | 61.8 | 12.7 |

*Source*: Compiled from National Bureau of Statistics of China (2001, 2007), *China Statistical Yearbook*, Beijing: China Statistics Press.

average ratios of elderly population climbed by 5.3 percentage points in the seven rich regions while sharply doubling by 6.7 percentage points in the ten poor regions. The poor regions are quickly losing their demographic dividends to the rich ones.

Figure 12.5 compares the changes in average demographic structures during 2000–2006 in the rich regions and the poor regions. Compared to the rich regions, the poor regions experienced a sharper drop in working-age population ratios and a more drastic rise in elderly population ratios.

Going back to Fig. 12.4, it is alarming that some of the below-median-income provinces have already displayed above-median elderly dependency ratios, such as Guizhou, Guangxi, Anhui, Sichuan, Hunan, and Chongqing. The situation in some provinces like Shaanxi, Hunan, and Hubei are more worrying since they have below-median juvenile dependency ratios but near- or above-median elderly dependency ratios, indicating fast aging in the near future. Since the per capita incomes in

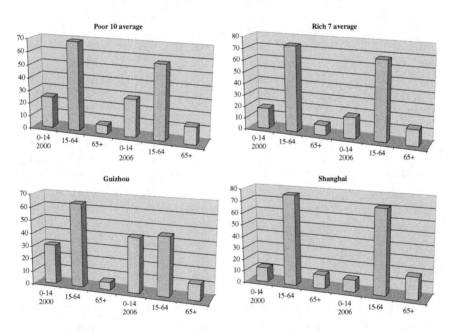

Figure 12.5.    Changes in demographic structures (2000–2006).

*Source*: Same as Table 12.2.

these provinces are below the median, they are likely to be trapped in a state of "getting old before getting rich". Another problematic group consists of the three northeast provinces, Liaoning, Heilongjiang, and Jilin, which are located in the heavy-industry "rustbelt", with high ratios of loss-making state-owned enterprises. All three have juvenile dependency ratios only two thirds of the median level and near-median elderly dependency ratios, which again foretell fast aging ahead.

## 3. Labor Migration and Migrants' Welfare

Despite its detrimental impact on the poor regions' demographic structures, labor migration enhances the efficiency of labor resource allocation across regions. It improves the welfare of the residents in the poor regions as well as in the rich regions. In regions where labor is relatively scarce, its rate of return (i.e. wage rate) is relatively higher than that of other factors. Such differences in rates of return for production factors are the basis of differing comparative advantages of regional industries and products as well as what motivates the movement of production factors. Migrant workers from the poor regions surely gain from migrating to take better-paid jobs in the rich regions. The existence of rural surplus labor only bolsters the efficiency gains of migration to sectors and regions of booming demand for workers.

This process of factor price equalization benefits not only the workers from the poor regions but also the employers in the rich regions since they can hire workers at lower labor costs. The resulting lower production costs will eventually be passed to the general public (especially the consumers) in all regions through the lower prices of goods and services.[5]

Poor regions may also benefit from labor mobility through its impact on human capital accumulation (Razin and Yuen, 1997). Migration of

---

[5] Factor price equalization through factor mobility thus helps to close the income gap between the poor and rich regions. It is, however, only a necessary condition for interregional income convergence and not a sufficient one. Per capita income is $y = (wL + rK)/L = w + r K/L = w + r k$, where $w$ is wage rate, $r$ is rate of return to capital, and $L$ and $K$ refer to labor and capital respectively. Even if $w$ and $r$ are equalized across regions, the occurrence of convergence in $y$ will depend on whether per worker capital stock, $k$, converges. According to the neoclassical steady-state growth model, $k$ may vary due to different saving rates and/or population growth rates across regions.

workers from low-wage (human-capital-poor) regions to high-wage (human-capital-rich) regions can create an indirect channel of productivity transmission across regions if some of those workers continue to accumulate human capital in their homeland regions (by, for instance, investing in their children's education there). In the process of wage equalization through migration, the prospect of getting better-paid jobs provides incentives for those left behind to raise the rate of human capital accumulation, thus leading to equalization of the levels of human capital and hence the levels of per capita income across regions.

Another way the poor regions can benefit from the outward migration of labor is through migrant workers' remittances back home. As shown in Fig. 12.6, for almost all provincial economies whose per capita household

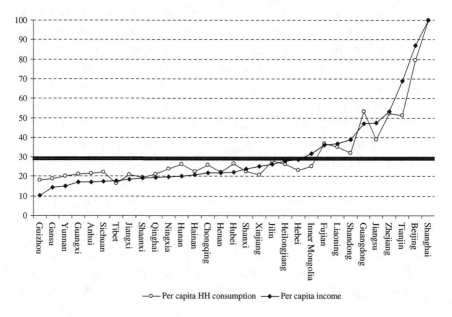

Figure 12.6.   Provincial per capita income and per capita household consumption (2005).

*Source*: National Bureau of Statistics of China (2006), *China Statistical Yearbook*, Beijing: China Statistics Press.

*Notes*:

1. Provincial per capita income and household consumption are indices with those of Shanghai set to be equal to 100.

2. "==" refers to national per capita household consumption level.

consumption levels fall below the national level, their per capita house-hold consumption indices are above their per capita GDP indices. That happens largely thanks to the migrant workers' remittances. The migrant workers' remittances not only lift the consumption of their family members who stay behind, but also increase the saving and investment rates in the homeland. Higher savings and faster accumulation of capital stock are the preconditions for faster growth of per capita income.

Finally, labor mobility is generally more effective than capital mobility in equalizing incomes across regions due to the fact that capital owners usually do not migrate with their capital. Capital flows will change the per worker capital stock and thus the per capita gross domestic product (GDP, the value of final products produced in a region) across regions but it will not change the per capita gross national product (GNP, the value of income earned by the residents of a region) across regions if capital owners stay where they are. In contrast, labor mobility leads to migration and thus changes the per capita GDP as well as the per capita GNP, leading to more effective convergence in per capita income levels.

## 4. Challenges to the Regions with Net Outward Migration

Despite the above benefits, the regions face a major challenge regarding how to maximize the benefits of labor mobility and control the negative impact of losing the demographic dividends. Unfortunately, the current institutional environment in China is far from conducive for the poor regions to gain sufficient benefits from outward migration of their labor.

One of my recent empirical findings shows that, since the mid-1990s, the constraining effect of the dependency ratio on per capita income in the rich coastal regions has only been *half* of the average level in all regions. In other words, the rich coastal regions have been significantly less constrained by the rising dependency ratio (Lu, 2008). It is evident that the increased labor mobility has brought in biased benefits to regions with net inward migration. If this pattern of welfare effects continues, greater interregional labor mobility will only aggravate the interregional disparity in development as the poor regions lose their most productive workers to emigration.

In particular, the household registration system and other institutional barriers continue to keep the migrant labor force "floating" or "temporary" without being assimilated by the urbanization process in high-income areas. The fact that a great proportion of the migrant workers' dependents are left behind in their homeland means that the demographic structures in the poor regions have deteriorated. The remarkably higher dependency ratios in most poor regions and higher elderly dependency ratios in some poorest areas (ref. Figs. 12.4 and 12.5, Table 12.2) substantiate this observation. As time passes, a great proportion of the poor regions' population spend the most productive years of their lives outside the local economy only to return to their homeland after becoming aged dependents themselves. Therefore gaps in per capita income across regions are more likely to be persistent and even enlarged. Migrant workers' remittances can moderate the gaps but that is not enough to close them as shown in Fig. 12.6.

Even migration's spillover benefits of faster human capital accumulation in the homeland may be discounted since the fruits of human capital accumulation will eventually be drained away by the outward migration of the more productive workers. Sociologists in China have well-observed that, with their parents being separated or away for jobs from the homeland, children of migrant workers suffer severe disadvantages in the quality of their school education. The issue has raised serious concerns among the public. By 2007, there were about 150 million rural migrants working in urban areas. About six million of these migrants' children had moved with their parents to live in urban areas but many of them could not receive equal opportunity for school education like the children of permanent urban residents. Another 22 million of the migrant workers' children had been left behind in the rural homeland, accounting for 17 percent of the total schooling-age cohort. Without direct care by their parents, these "left-behind children" (*liushou ertong*) face various psychological and social problems.[6]

---

[6] "Standing Committee of National People's Congress Concerns over the Education Problems Faced by Children of Rural Migrant Workers", Xinhua News Agency, June 28, 2007 (www.gov.cn).

## 5. Policy Options for the Poor Regions

The long-term effects of labor mobility on interregional income disparity depend on the migration patterns. If the migrant workers from inland and rural areas are allowed to establish permanent residence with their dependents in the coastal and urban areas, the migration will improve the age structure in the rich provinces as well as the welfare of those migrant workers and their dependents. By moving their dependents with them, the detrimental impact of labor emigration on the homeland demographic structure is kept at a minimum. Meanwhile, they will not only be contributors to the rich regions' GDP but also become the income earners of these regions' GNP. The wage rate in their hometown regions will also be raised as labor becomes relatively scarce there thanks to emigration. In the longer run, most emigrants who established residence in the rich regions will not return to add to the burden of elderly dependency on their homeland population after their retirement. Many of them, as investors, can be expected to be more prone to find invest-ment opportunities in their original homeland, as evident in the mainstay role played by overseas Chinese investors in the early years of China's opening-up. In contrast, if the household registration system and other institutional barriers continue to keep the migrant labor force "floating" around the coun-try, the interregional income disparity is likely to persist and get worse.

For the governments in the regions with net outward migration, it is important to understand that outward migration of labor is driven by mar-ket forces and should not be resisted. To maximize the benefits from labor migration and minimize its negative impact, we recommend the following policy options.

Removing the institutional barriers to permanent migration of rural workers and their dependents to urban areas should be a long-term goal at the national level. The poor-region governments should persistently lobby and push for an overhaul of the nationwide household registration system to achieve that goal.

At the local level, the provincial governments should move ahead to lower and disassemble the barriers to rural-to-urban migration in their administrative territories. Rural migrant workers who can find jobs in local cities or towns and are willing to move there with their dependents should be welcome and supported by the government authorities. This will make local cities and towns more attractive to them to settle in. Meanwhile, improving the physical and socioeconomic infrastructure of local urban areas to absorb more rural migrants should be a priority of local government budget plans.

Governments of poor regions may negotiate with governments of rich regions to agree on policies and regulations that will facilitate the assimilation of migrant workers in the urbanization process in rich regions. Such coordination among the regional governments will make it easier for workers from poor regions and their families to establish permanent residence in rich regions.

Much can be done to improve the local business environment through investment in infrastructure, institutional reforms, and policy changes to attract more inward capital flows, especially inward direct investment from other regions or abroad. Continuous inward investment will raise the capital-labor ratio in the local economy, create more jobs, enhance labor productivity, and therefore raise the local wage rate.

## References

Lu, Ding. (2008). "Regions with Net Outward Migration: Issues and Challenges". Paper presented at International Conference on China's Regional Economic Development: Cooperation, Challenges & Opportunities for Singapore, May 9–10, Singapore.

Mason, Andrew and Wang, Feng. (2005). "Demographic Dividends and China's Post-reform Economy". Paper presented to the International Union for the Scientific Study of Population, XXV International Population Conference, Tours, France, July 18–23.

National Population and Family Planning Commission (2005). *China's Population.* www.chinapop.gov.cn, accessed September 20, 2005.

National Bureau of Statistics of China (NBSC) (2011). *Main Results of the Sixth National Population Census of 2010.* http://www.stats.gov.cn

Razin, Assaf and Yuen, Chi-Wa. (1997). "Factor Mobility and Income Growth: Two Convergence Hypotheses". *Review of Development Economics*, 1(2), pp. 171–190.

United Nations Secretariat (2006). *World Population Prospects: The 2006 Revision* and *World Urbanization Prospects: The 2005 Revision.* http://esa.un.org/unpp.

Yao, Zhongzhi. (2003). "Labour Movement and Regional Disparity". 世界经济 (*The World Economy*), 4, pp. 35–44.

# CHAPTER 13

# Epilogue

*Ding Lu*

A review of the past 30 years of China's urbanization experience reveals the challenges the country faces in the next stage of development. The most serious challenges include the environmental challenge, the urban governance challenge, and the migration challenge. How China answers these challenges will define the pace and features of the great urbanization in the coming years.

## 1. The Unique Experience of China's Urbanization

The massive urbanization of China in the past three decades is characterized by two aspects: One is the rapid growth of the urban population, which has expanded by over four percent or 15 million per annum since 1985. In other words, Chinese cities and towns have taken in more than 400 million people from the rural area since the early 1980s. The other phenomenon is the fast expansion of urban built-up areas, which have been growing by over five percent or 1,200 sq kilometers per annum in the same period. The total number of cities rose from 193 in 1978 to 655 in 2008 (Chapter 1 and Chapter 10).

As discussed in this book, several developments have been driving the fast pace and massive scale of this great urbanization. The most powerful driving force is of course China's successful economic takeoff launched by its market-oriented reform 30 years ago. Since then, economic growth has been sustained at hyper rates and generated tremendous wealth for the Chinese people. Capital accumulation and technological progress have

raised productivity and industrialized the economy, allowing a large number of rural laborers to be freed from farmlands and be hired by other
industries. Large-scale urbanization is indispensable to this process.

What is unique for China is the drastic change in state policy towards
urbanization and a series of fundamental reforms in key institutions that
determine the pace and direction of urbanization. Right from the start of the
market-oriented reform 30 years ago, the Chinese Communist leaders discarded the Marxist "anti-urban" ideology and Maoist self-sufficiency
doctrine for regional economies. The state-compelled urban-to-rural mass
migration was quickly reversed. The war-preparing endeavor to build inland
military industrial bases was abandoned and replaced by systematic efforts
to revive and open up the coastal cities to foreign investment (Chapter 3).

Interface with foreign companies soon made it necessary to reintro-
duce the market for urban land and properties. That eventually and
inevitably led to the literal rewriting of China's socialist Constitution in
1988 to allow the use rights of the supposedly state-owned urban land to
be transferred and traded (Chapters 7 and 8). With more and more state-
owned enterprises being restructured and privatized and more and more
people working with the prospering private sector, the dominance of the
all-state-owned public housing regime had to go. Mass privatization
of public housing and sale of land use and development rights to commercial developers gave birth to a booming housing market in the 1990s
(Chapter 3). The re-emergence of a real estate market has reinvigorated
urban redevelopment. With delegated authority to oversee urban land use
right sales and development, local governments have played an active role
in guiding and planning for urban expansion and redevelopment. The rent
accrued to the newly developed or redeveloped urban land has generated
lucrative business opportunities as well as juicy revenues for the local
governments and their officials (Chapter 9).

All this has created tremendous incentives for government officials,
*danwei*-enterprises, real estate business players, and various investors to
drive the expansion and redevelopment of Chinese cities. In the domain
of local governments, urban planning became very pro-business and pro-
growth, and was easily bent to adapt to various business interests of real
estate development (Chapters 3 and 4). Local-government-sanctioned
urban development has accelerated the conversion of farmland for

non-agriculture use and caused tensions with the legal protection of arable land and farmers' rights (Chapter 5). The spectacular expansion of urban areas has been inevitably accompanied by various efficiency problems (as examined in Chapters 6 and 10).

The rapid industrialization and booming urban economy became powerful magnetic fields for rural surplus labor, resulting in a huge out-flow of migrant rural workers into the urban area (Chapter 11). Until the recent decade, the central government had attempted to encourage *in situ* transformation of rural surplus labor into local towns and small (county-level) cities but not large and megacities. Although the policy opened the door for rural migrants to live and work permanently in small (county-level) cities and towns, it maintained the *hukou* (household registration) system that has kept a large number of *nongmin gong* (rural migrant work-ers) from gaining full resident status in large cities. The practice has not only left its marks on city-size distribution (Chapter 2) but also has had profound effects on interregional development in the context of demo-graphic changes (Chapter 12).

The expansion of city clusters and the rising role of megacities in eco-nomic growth have eventually prompted the policy makers to change their mind. Over the years the small-town consensus in urban planning was phased out and gave way to a more balanced urbanization strategy. A new guideline was adopted in 2007 to "promote balanced development of large, medium-sized and small cities and towns on the principle of bal-ancing urban and rural development, ensuring rational distribution, saving land, providing a full range of functions and getting larger cities to help smaller ones" (Chapter 3).

As shown in Chapter 1, China has huge potential for rapid urbaniza-tion in the coming years. While China's per capita income has reached the average middle-income countries' level (Fig. 1.1), its urbanization rate is still about five percentage points lower than the latter's (Fig. 1.4). Since the early 1990s China has entered a period of rapid urbanization. Now it is still in the middle of the second phase of the S-curve of a steep upward slope.

To successfully maintain this momentum and ensure a smooth urban-ization, China needs to answer several big challenges. How China answers these challenges will define the pace and direction of urbaniza-tion in the coming decades.

## 2. Environmental Challenge

After 30 years of hyper economic growth and rapid urbanization, China has largely exhausted its extensive mode of growth that depends much on cheap labor and exploitative use of natural resources. Given the sheer size of China's economy and population, it is simply not sustainable for China to keep growing by consuming its own and the global natural resources at the current pace. Although the size of its economy measured by purchasing power parity (PPP) is only two thirds of that of the US economy, China has already overtaken the US as the world's largest emitter of greenhouse gas and energy-consuming economy (Fig. 13.1). China's environmental problems include water pollution, water shortage, air pollution, hazardous waste, soil erosion, loss of forests and grasslands, and loss of species and habitat (Ma and Ortolano, 2000).

Environmental degradation has reached a choking level. "Chinese cities often seem wrapped in a toxic gray shroud. Only one percent of the country's 560 million city dwellers breathe air considered safe by the European Union".[1] By the turn of the century, China had 16 of the 20 most

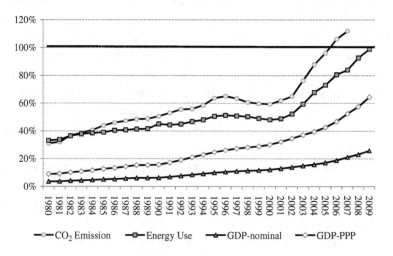

Figure 13.1.  China's GDP & $CO_2$ emission.

*Source*: World Bank online databank, http://databank.worldbank.org.

---

[1] Joseph Kahn and Jim Yardley (2007), "As China Roars, Pollution Reaches Deadly Extremes", *New York Times*, August 26.

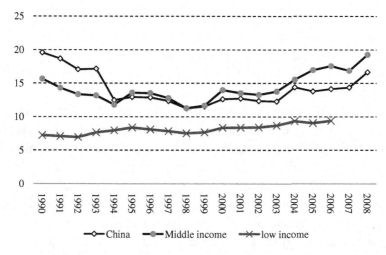

Figure 13.2.   Gap between gross and net adjusted savings.

*Source*: World Bank online databank, http://databank.worldbank.org.

polluted cities in the world (World Bank, 2001, p. 26). Over the past 20 years, the gap between China's gross national savings and its adjusted net savings has been about 14 percent of GDP (Fig. 13.2).[2] This gap has displayed a rising trend in recent years. Most of this gap can be explained by the depletion of a variety of natural resources and damages from carbon dioxide and particulate emissions.

Woo (2007), an eminent China observer, warns that water shortage will be the most likely factor to make China's high growth unsustainable in the coming years. E. Economy, another expert on China, observes that two thirds of China's approximately 660 cities have less water than they need and 110 of them suffer from severe shortages. The depletion of underground water has caused the sinking of the country's wealthiest cities: Shanghai and Tianjin had sunk by more than six feet during the 15 years to 2004. Moreover, the aquifers in 90 percent of Chinese cities are polluted, more than 75 percent of the river water flowing through China's urban areas is considered unsuitable for drinking or fishing, and about

---

[2] Adjusted net savings = gross national savings – consumption of fixed capital + current public expenditure on education – estimates of the depletion of a variety of natural resources – damages from carbon dioxide and particulate emissions.

30 percent of the river water throughout the country is unfit for use in agriculture or industry. "As a result, nearly 700 million people drink water contaminated with animal and human waste" (Economy, 2007, p. 38). According to a special report by *The Economist*, water pollution and scarcity knock 2.3 percent off China's GDP annually.[3]

How will China answer this challenge while continuing to expand its urban population by tens of millions every year? Urban living has the potential to be greener than other ways of life thanks to the economies of scale and agglomeration effects. By staying close to where you work and shop, sharing with more people public transportation and public utilities such as provision of power, heat, water, and drainage and waste disposal systems, residents living in a densely populated urban area may enjoy lower per capita energy consumption and pollution emissions than people living elsewhere. However, to maximize the benefits of scale economies and agglomeration, careful urban planning and smart zoning are a must since urban dwelling and building have strong externalities, positive or negative. For instance, ill-planned public transport and bad zoning may reinforce car use and cause more pollution. Inappropriate building codes and hasty construction may lead to short-lived and energy-inefficient estates. All these problems are common in China's hasty expansion of urban boundaries, where the construction of buildings accounts for 30 percent of the country's carbon emissions.[4]

To make urban development greener and more ecologically sustainable, the key is to make it incentive-compatible for local governments and property developers to practise good urban planning, effective plan enforcement, and green code compliance. Unfortunately, the current governance structure provides strong incentives for local governments to rapidly develop and redevelop urban areas with little regard for environmental consequences.

## 3. Urban Governance Challenge

As seen in Fig. 13.3, since the tax-sharing reform of 1994, the local governments' revenues have fallen short of their fiscal expenditures by nearly

---

[3] John Grimond (2010), "For Want of a Drink: A Special Report on Water", *The Economist*, May 20.
[4] Banyan (2010), "Asia's Alarming Cities", *The Economist*, July 1.

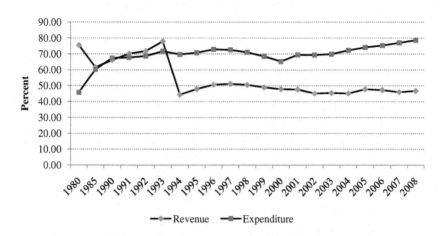

Figure 13.3.   Local governments' fiscal share.
*Source: China Statistical Yearbook 2009.*

30 percent. Since land sale income has become a chief source of extra-tax revenue to shore up local government budgets, the local officials have the incentive to create more land development deals and maximize land sale revenues.

Meanwhile, in the Chinese political regime, local economic growth is one of the primary criteria for bureaucratic evaluation and promotion. This has motivated local officials to create more urban development projects to drive local GDP growth. Entering the 2000s, local governments have become more active in selling land development rights and happier to push for higher land transfer prices to get the much-wanted funds for developing urban infrastructure and other GDP-maximizing investment projects. In 2009 alone, local governments had received an additional income of 1.5 trillion yuan from land transfer, or more than one third of their total revenue.[5] The increase in land transfer receipts is most noticeable in megacities that have witnessed the most rapidly rising real estate prices over the past decade.

Given the strong growth of China's economy, huge economic rent is accruing quickly to limited urban land resources (Fig. 13.4). Real estate

---

[5] Ministry of Finance (2010), "Statistics on Nationwide Land Transfer Revenues and Expenses", April 13.

Figure 13.4.    China's real estate market (1999–2009).

*Source*: National Bureau of Statistics.

development has become the most lucrative business. Ever since Rupert Hoogewerf launched the *Hurun Report* China Rich List in 1999, the real estate (property) tycoons have been the largest business category in this list every year. The 2010 *Hurun Report* observes:

> Property is still the biggest wealth creator for the Hurun Rich List, with 20.1 percent listing property as one of their key industries. The percentage has been steadily decreasing, from over half in the first year of 1999 to 23.1 percent last year. ... Of all the industries, China's property tycoons are far and away richer than tycoons from any other industry. The average wealth of the Top Ten Richest Property Developers is more than double the average wealth of the next richest industries of retail and IT.[6]

The local governments' overreliance on income from land sales for fiscal funds, dubbed "*tudi caizheng*" in Chinese, and the local officials' zealous pursuit of local GDP growth have made local officials deeply involved in the business interests in the property market. This has led to several consequences. First, it fuels hasty urban expansion and redevelopment that contributes to environmental degradation. As discussed in

---

[6] "Zong Qinghou of Wahaha Tops Hurun Rich List 2010", http://hurun.net, accessed on Dec 1, 2010.

Chapter 4, local urban planning has become so pro-business and pro-growth such that blue plans and zoning programs are often bent and revised to meet business interests.

Second, it creates a hotbed for rent creation and rent-seeking. Cai (2008) observes a symbiotic relationship between the property developers and government officials in charge of urban development. According to the 2010 *Hurun Report,* "China's property tycoons have the strongest political endorsement of any industry bar the steel sector. Twelve of the Property Top Fifty are delegates to the CPPCC, NPC or CPC".[7] The power of local officials to bend the land requisition rules and construction codes to favor those who have won their sponsorship is widely perceived as a chief cause of many corruption scandals.

Third, focused on land sale revenues from high-end "commodity housing", the local governments have little interest in providing low-cost "subsistence housing" for low-income households.[8] The rising prices of commodity housing and the shortage of low-cost housing have frustrated middle- and low-income households and caused social resentment. A survey by the Chinese Academy of Social Science (CASS) suggests that at the end of 2009, about 85 percent of urban respondents claimed that they were unable to afford a new flat even with mortgages.[9] Another survey by the People's Bank of China shows that about 72.5 percent of residents consider the current level of housing prices "too high to be acceptable".[10] In main metropolitan centers, the housing price per sq meter almost invariably amounts to 50–100 percent of average annual income. Based on these ratios, to secure an average flat of 90 sq meters, an average working family in Beijing and Shanghai will have to work for more than 50 years before they can pay for their loan in full as compared to 5–10 years in the developed world (Lu and Huang, 2010).

---

[7] *Ibid.* CPPCC refers to Chinese People's Political Consultative Conference, NPC refers to National People's Congress, and CPC refers to Communist Party of China.

[8] "Commodity housing" (*shangpin fang*) refers to housing developed by profit-oriented developers and sold at market prices. Since 2007, the central government has pledged to provide low-cost "subsistence housing" (*baozhangxing zhufang*) to be rented or sold to lower-than-middle-income households.

[9] Chinese Academy of Social Sciences (2009), *2010 China Economic Bluebook*, Beijing: Social Science Literature Press.

[10] Wenwei Po (Hong Kong) (2010) June 18.

Finally, hasty urban expansion driven by the alliance between local officials and property developers often leads to land being grabbed from farmers or urban residents of the redeveloped areas without proper compensation. Land requisition sometimes ends up in violent confrontation between the land-clearing agents and the farmers or residents. Although the Chinese media is not allowed to report such incidents, an anecdotal check shows the severity of the problem. In "China Election and Governance", a non-profit online forum, there are over 800 posted discussions on *zhengdi chaiqian* (land requisition and property demolition) Many of these are about the "demolition (of property) with violence".[11]

Although there are calls for political reform to help "break the unholy alliance" between government officials and business people (Yu, 2010), the entrenched political-economy interests will not make it easy to remold the system. The reform of urban governance is likely to be gradual like most other sensitive reforms in China. The introduction of property tax at the local level is likely to be the first step to phase out the local governments' overreliance on land sale revenues. A related key issue in urban governance is how to deal with the influx of rural migrant workers.

## 4. Migrant Challenge

China's *hukou* (household registration) system distinguishes between the residential rights of the urban and the rural residents and fortified a dual labor market structure that discriminates against the rural migrant workers. As presented in Chapter 3, past reforms have made it much easier for rural migrants to move permanently to small (county-level) cities and towns but permanent migration to large cities is still a dream beyond reach for most *nongmin gong* (rural migrant workers). City governments welcome rural migrant workers to meet the needs of local development but usually take various measures to protect the privileges of the incumbent urban residents by keeping the in-migrants "temporary" and limiting their access to local public services. In Fig. 13.5, one can see that, across China's 31 provincial economies, the more urbanized places are associated with a larger proportion of population without a local *hukou*.

---

[11] China Election and Governance website, http://www.chinaelections.org, accessed on Dec 15, 2010.

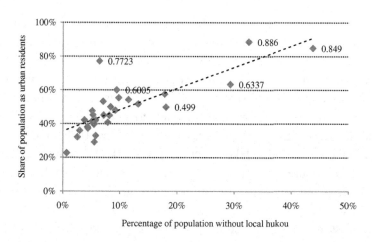

Figure 13.5.   Urbanization rate vs. no-*Hukou* rate (2008).

*Source*: *China Statistical Yearbook 2009.*

Fan (2010) highlights another factor that has kept rural migrant workers from staying permanently in the cities. He observes "a striking difference between China and some other developing countries", that is, "Chinese cities, large and small, lack any sign of significant urban poverty or slums". However, he does not think, like many do, that the *hukou* system might have contributed to this phenomenon. Although without an urban *hukou* rural migrant workers are not entitled to many urban public services, nothing really prevents them from staying and working in the urban areas for long. Instead, he believes that China's rural land tenure system is the anchor that ties the migrant workers to their homeland. Under this system, each rural household is entitled to hold a lease for a piece of the collectively owned village farmland for 30 years and may sublease it to other farmers but never has the full property right to it. Unable to sell or mortgage the land, rural residents have to remain rooted in their homeland to keep one's entitlement to the land. To a migrant worker, the leasehold in the home village serves as a social safety net of last resort. Fear of losing this entitlement and a lack of formal social insurance elsewhere are therefore the main reasons that most migrant workers will eventually return to their rural homeland.

China's current social security system was initiated in the late 1990s following the "three-pillar model" of old-age security recommended by the World Bank (1994), i.e. a publicly managed system with mandatory participation and the limited goal of reducing poverty among the old; a privately managed mandatory savings system; and voluntary savings. The system has been gradually assembled and built up for people with urban *hukou* since then. A main weakness of the system is its fragmented administration across regions. As a major step to unify the system, China's Social Insurance Law (passed on October 28, 2010, by the National People's Congress and to take effect on July 1, 2011) sets the goal that the basic social insurance endowment funds will gradually realize national coordination and other social insurances will gradually realize provincial coordination. It also set the goal to have a nationally uniform social security numbering system based on personal ID numbers which will allow individuals to transfer their basic endowment and medical insurances freely across regions of different coordinating administrations.[12] Compared to the problem of administrative segmentation, financial sustainability is an even more serious challenge (Lu, 2010). With a quickly aging population in many cities, the overall ratio between the contributing employees and the retirees has declined quickly from 4.4 in 1993 to below 3 in recent years.[13]

For the rural *hukou* holders, the social insurance system was merely at the stage of experimental practice at the local (usually the county or even village) level until 2009. It was only in September 2009 that the State Council issued a guideline for developing a nationwide rural old-age insurance system,[14] of which the benefits are much more modest as compared to those in cities. Adopting such a segregated two-track social insurance system reflects the fact that Beijing's policy makers do not want rural migrants to compete with the limited social safety net benefits reserved for the urban *hukou* holders.

Given the status quo of China's social security system and its direction of reform, rural-urban segregation by the *hukou* system is still a

---

[12] Social Insurance Law of the People's Republic of China, National People's Congress website, www.npc.gov.cn, accessed October 29, 2010.

[13] China Economic Research Center of Peking University (2007), *Transitional Notional Defined Contribution*.

[14] State Council (2009), "Guidelines for Establishing the New Rural Old-Age Insurance", *State Council Gazette*, No. 32.

necessity in the foreseeable future. If the rural land tenure system is not reformed and social insurance continues to be segregated, many rural migrant workers will not take the leap to abandon their entitlement to rural land leasehold. On the other hand, for urban *hukou* holders in the cities, a dual urban labor market where rural laborers are available for hire at discounted wage rates serves many of their daily needs, especially in the service sector. Such a labor market is also a source of cheap labor for urban industries. Meanwhile, to maintain and improve the level of public services received by the incumbent urban *hukou* holders, the policy makers have to be cautious about giving too many new migrants full entitlement to such services in the cities. Therefore, the easing of restrictions of the *hukou* system in large cities will likely be gradual and incremental, subject to a subtle balance of the political-economy interests of all sides.

## References

Cai, Jinming. (2008). "Rent Seeking by Power Becomes Rampant and Property Sector Becomes Corruption Hotbed Due to Officials Business Collusion". http://www.people.com.cn, Dec 11, 2008.

Economy, Elizabeth C. (2007). "The Great Leap Backward? The Costs of China's Environmental Crisis". *Foreign Affairs*, 86(5), pp. 38–59.

Fan, Gang. (2010). "Urbanizing China". www.project-syndicate.org, accessed on Dec 30, 2010.

Lu, Ding. (2010). "China's Rapid Demographic Transition and Its Challenges to Social Security System". Paper presented at International Conference on China's Social Policy Reform: Challenges and Direction, July 30–31, Singapore.

Lu, Ding and Huang, Y. (2010). "China's 'New Deal' Measures to Cope with Its Bubbling Housing Market", EAI Background Briefs, No. 544.

Ma, Xiaoying and Ortolano Leonard. (2000). *Environmental Regulation in China: Institutions, Enforcement, and Compliance*. Oxford: Rowman & Littlefield Publishers.

Woo, Wing T. (2007). "What are the High-Probability Challenges to Continued High Growth in China?" Paper prepared for the conference "Assessing the Power of China: Political, Economic, and Social Dimensions" co-sponsored by the Institute for China Studies at Seoul National University, and the POSCO Research Institute (POSRI) in Seoul, South Korea, May 30–31.

World Bank (1994). *Averting the Old Age Crisis: Policies to Protect the Old and Promote Growth*. Oxford: Oxford University Press.

World Bank (2001). *China Development Report*. Washington DC: World Bank.

Yu, Yongding. (2010). "China Has Reached a Critical Moment and Economic Growth May Stop". http://www.caogen.com/blog/index.aspx?ID=182, accessed Dec 26, 2010.

# Major Events of China's Urban Development (1949–2010)

*Ding Lu*

| Date | Event |
|------|-------|
| 1949 | • National Land Bureau was set up under Ministry of Internal Affairs to unify the management of national land resources |
| 1953 | • The 1st Five-Year Plan was started, with a guideline for urban development of "Focused construction, steady progress" |
| | • State monopoly purchase and rationing of staple goods such as food, edible oil and cotton imposed nationwide |
| | • Central government issued Instructions on Persuading Peasants from Moving Into Cities Blindly |
| 1954 | • National People's Congress promulgated the first Constitution of the PRC, which |
| | ○ pledged to protect citizens' ownership of means of production and peasants' ownership of land |
| | ○ declared the goal of transforming urban private/capitalist businesses into socialist ones |
| | ○ announced that the state, for the public interest, could acquire urban and rural land and means of production by purchase, expropriation, or confiscation |

| | |
|---|---|
| | • Campaign to transform the urban capitalist industries was launched and all capitalist firms (hiring more than eight employees) were restructured to socialist units in the name of "public-private joint ventures" in a few years |
| 1954–1956 | • Management of urban land and rural land was separated with the setting up of the Ministry of Agriculture |
| 1955–1959 | • Campaign to collectivize agriculture eliminated private land ownership in rural areas and led to the emergence of the People's Communes as the main administrative regime in rural areas |
| 1950–1957 | • With Soviet aid, 694 major industrial projects were built during the 1st Five-Year Plan period |
| | • Six new cities were built, 20 cities were substantially expanded, 74 cities were moderately expanded |
| | • Urbanization rate rose from 10.6 percent to 15.4 percent, with annual increase of urban population by 4.45 million |
| 1957 | • Central government issued Instructions on Forbidding Rural Residents from Flowing Out Blindly |
| 1958.01 | • National People's Congress passed the Regulations on Household Registration |
| 1958–1959 | • The Great Leap Forward campaign caused a temporary surge of industrial output and employment, causing the urban population to rise from 13 percent to 16 percent of total population. |
| | • National People's Congress passed the PRC Regulations on Household Registration — the household registration system was introduced |
| 1959–1961 | • Three-year famine caused the loss of dozens of millions of lives |

|  |  |
|---|---|
| | • Food rationing reinforced the household registration system |
| | • Central government decided (1961) to reduce urban population by 20 million in three years |
| 1961–1963 | • 25.46 million employees were laid off, of which 16.41 million were *xia fang* (sent down) by the government to migrate with their families from urban to rural areas, resulting in a reduction of 26 million of urban population |
| | • Government called on urban youth to migrate to rural areas |
| 1964–1980 | • Beijing launched the plan to build the Third Front industries and relocate factories from coastal cities to inland provinces. In 16 years, a total of 205 billion yuan was invested and over 4 million technicians and workers were sent to build 1,100 industrial projects in inland provinces |
| 1966.05 | • Tianjin upgraded to a provincial municipality (after Beijing and Shanghai) |
| 1968–1977 | • During the *Shangshan Xiaxiang* (Down to the countryside) campaign, the government sent 17 million urban high-school graduates to live and work in rural areas as "rusticated youth" |
| 1978–1984 | • Rural economic reform gradually dissolved collective farming, leading to fast productivity rise in agriculture; rural non-agriculture employment rose from 252 million to 567 million as total agricultural output increased by one third |
| | • More than 20 million rusticated urban youth and *xiafang* technicians and workers were allowed to return to their former hometown urban residence |
| | • Urbanization rate recovered upward trend, rising from 17.92 percent to 23.01 percent |
| 1980 | • National urban planning meeting in Beijing reached the small-town consensus; "Strictly |

|          |                                                                                                                |
|----------|----------------------------------------------------------------------------------------------------------------|
|          | control the size of large cities, rationally develop medium-sized cities, and vigorously promote the development of small cities and towns" became the national guideline for urban development |
|          | • The first four special economic zones, Shenzhen, Zhuhai, Shantou, and Xiamen, were launched |
|          | • State Council promulgated Interim Provisions for Construction Land Use by China-Foreign Joint Ventures, which authorized fee levies on land use |
|          | • State Council allowed individuals to build, own, and buy housing estates |
| 1981     | • State Urban Construction Commission was authorized to oversee land use and development in urban areas |
| 1982     | • Shenzhen Special Economic Zone promulgated Interim Provisions on Land Use Administration and started collecting urban land use fees; Guangdong City followed and started collecting urban land use fees |
|          | • State Council promulgated Rules for Compulsory Deportation of the Homeless and Beggars in Urban Areas |
|          | • Land Administration Bureau under Ministry of Agriculture was set up to oversee rural land use |
| 1982.12  | • The 4th Edition of the People's Republic of China Constitution was promulgated. Clause 10 of the Constitution specifies that "Urban land is state-owned" and "rural land and suburban land are collectively owned"; "No organizations or individuals may appropriate, buy, sell, or lease land, or unlawfully transfer it in any way" |
| 1982–1985 | • State-subsidized sale of housing estates was tried in 160 cities and 300 towns |
| 1984.01  | • Central government allowed peasants that engage in non-agricultural activities to migrate to towns |

|          | and obtain household registration status there, beginning a policy to encourage *in situ* urbanization in rural areas |
| 1984.05 | • Central government gave the status of coastal open cities (COCs) to 14 coastal cities (Shanghai, Guangzhou, Tianjin, Dalian, Qinhuangdao, Yantai, Qingdao, Lianyungang, Nantong, Ningbo, Wenzhou, Fuzhou, Zhanjiang, and Beihai), delegating to their municipal governments the right to approve foreign investment projects |
| 1984 | • State Council approved first batch of 15 national economic and technological development zones |
| 1984–1986 | • People's Communes were officially dissolved and replaced by township governments as the rural administrative authority |
|          | • In 1984 the criteria for the designation of official town status were lowered and the rural administrative system was reformed by "converting townships to towns" (撤乡建镇) and "making towns administrative villages" (镇管村), leading to the designation of 2,583 towns in the next two years, and a total of 14,539 towns by 1992 |
|          | • In 1986 the criteria for the designation of city status were lowered and the local government administrative structure was further reformed by "converting prefectures to cities" (撤地建市) and "making cities administrative counties" (市管县), leading to a rapid increase in the number in cities (from 193 in 1978 to 434 in 1988, and 479 in 1991) |
|          | • Township & village enterprises (TVEs) boomed |
| 1985.01 | • State mandatory purchase of agricultural products was replaced by state-farmer contract purchase. Farmers were allowed to sell their products in the free market after fulfilling their state contracts |

| | |
|---|---|
| 1985.09 | • Central government promulgated guidelines for state-owned enterprise reform, allowing SOEs to produce for markets after fulfilling state plans |
| 1984–1987 | • Emergence of millions of "floating people", consisting mainly of rural-urban migrant workers |
| 1986 | • State Council set up an ad hoc commission on housing reform |
| | • State Council set up State Land Management Bureau to oversee land use in urban and rural areas |
| 1987.09 | • The first leasing deal of land use right was sealed in Shenzhen |
| 1987.11–12 | • Shanghai and Shenzhen promulgated rules for land use right transaction |
| 1988.01 | • State Council held First National Housing Reform Conference and adopted a national housing reform schedule |
| 1988.04 | • National People's Congress made amendments to the Constitution: |
| |     o Clause 10 now states: "the right of land use can be transferred in accordance with the law" |
| |     o Clause 11 now allows private economy to exist and develop in legally defined scope |
| | • Hainan Island became the 5th special economic zone |
| 1988.09 | • State Council promulgated Interim Provisions for Urban Land Use Tax to authorize local governments to collect land use tax for all urban land |
| 1988–1989 | • Government cracked down on "floating population" and forced 13 million migrants back to rural residence |
| 1989.12 | • The government promulgated the Law of Urban Planning, which upheld the guideline of "Strictly control the size of large cities, rationally develop medium-sized cities, and vigorously promote the development of small cities and towns" |

| | |
|---|---|
| 1990.04 | • Central government launched Pudong New Area in Shanghai |
| 1990.05 | • State Council promulgated Interim Provisions for Granting and Assigning Leaseholds in State-owned Urban Land |
| 1991.10 | • State Council held Second National Housing Reform Conference, pushing housing reform by gradually raising public housing rent |
| 1992 | • Chinese Communist Party's 14th National Congress reached the consensus to build a "socialist market economy" after its paramount leader Deng Xiaoping called for comprehensive reform of the economic system |
| | • Central government decided to extend the practice of 14 coastal open cities (designated in 1984) to five inland cities along the Yangtze River, 13 border cities, 11 inland provincial capitals |
| 1993 | • Agricultural goods markets were liberalized and food rationing was abandoned |
| | • State Council held Third National Housing Reform Conference, switching focus of reform to selling public housing |
| 1993.11 | • State Council promulgated Interim Provisions for Value-added Tax on Land |
| 1994.07 | • State Council issued Decision on Deepening Urban Housing Reform |
| | • National People's Congress passed the Law on Real Estate Administration |
| 1992–1994 | • National and provincial governments launched hundreds of various development zones |
| 1995.01 | • Ministry of Finance promulgated Detailed Measures to Implement Interim Provisions for Value-added Tax on Land |
| 1995.03 | • State Land Administration Bureau issued Notice on Clearing Up Idled Construction Land for Non-agriculture Uses |

| | |
|---|---|
| Through the 1990s | • Strong demand for industrial labor attracted dozens of millions of rural-urban migrant workers to urban areas |
| 1997.03 | • Chongqing City upgraded to a provincial municipality |
| 1997.06 | • Central government approved reform of household registration system for small cities and towns, allowing rural residents who have jobs and homes in small cities and towns to obtain urban *hukou* |
| 1997.07 | • China resumed its sovereignty over Hong Kong, which became a special administration region of China. |
| 1998.04 | • Ministry of Land and Resources was set up to enforce central government's power of land management, especially to protect the cultivated land resources |
| 1998.07 | • State Council issued Notice on Further Deepening Urban Housing Reform and Promoting Housing Construction, ending the in-kind housing rationing system |
| 1998.10 | • Chinese Communist Party's Central Committee highlighted development of small cities and towns as a "big strategy" for rural economic and social development |
| 1999.12 | • China resumed its sovereignty over Macau, which became the second special administration region of China |
| 2000.01 | • Central government set up an ad hoc leading group on West China Development |
| 2000.10 | • The 10th Five-Year Plan pledged to "break up the system that separates rural from urban populations, reform urban household registration system, remove unreasonable restrictions on rural labor to be employed in cities and towns, and guide rural surplus labor to orderly flow between regions as well rural and urban areas" |

|            | |
|------------|--|
|            | • The 10th Five-Year Plan proposed an urban development guideline: "Develop small cities and towns with emphasis, actively develop medium-sized and small cities, optimize functions of regional hub cities, and develop large cities' leading role, and guide the orderly development of city clusters" |
|            | • The 10th Five-Year Plan launched the West China Development Strategy |
| 2001.04   | • State Council issued Notice on Consolidating Administration of State-owned Land Assets, requiring all land use right sales with two or more interested parties to go through a legal tender or auction procedure |
| 2001.05   | • State Council clarified that rural residents that have jobs or homes in county-level cities and other designated towns are allowed to register as permanent urban households in these places |
| 2001.10   | • Ministry of Finance and State Development Commission canceled seven statutory fees levied on migrant workers |
| 2001.12   | • China became the 143rd member of the World Trade Organization |
|            | • Guangdong became the first province to abandon the registration divide between rural and urban households |
| 2002.05   | • Ministry of Land Resources promulgated Regulation on Tender, Bidding, and Auction for Granting and Assigning State-owned Construction Land Use Right |
| 2002.12   | • Chinese Communist Party's 16th National Congress acknowledged the "inevitable trend of industrialization and modernization for surplus rural labor to move to non-agricultural industries and to cities and towns". It defined "the path to urbanization with Chinese characteristics" as "to raise the level of urbanization gradually and |

|  |  |
|---|---|
| | persist in the coordinated development of large, medium and small cities and small towns". |
| 2003 | • State Council issued notices about management of rural migrant workers' employment in cities and their children's schooling needs |
| | • Central government promulgated Plan to Train Rural Migrant Workers 2003–2010 |
| | • State Council issued Notice about Promoting Continuous and Healthy Development of Real Estate Market, leading to a new round of housing market boom |
| 2003.06 | • State Council promulgated Rules for Aid and Administration of the Homeless and Beggars in Urban Areas to replace Rules for Compulsory Deportation of the Homeless and Beggars in Urban Areas |
| 2004.03 | • Premier Wen Jiabao announced a five-year plan to phase out taxes on all agricultural products |
| 2003.07–2004.08 | • Central government |
| |    o temporarily suspended approval for new development zones and expansion of existing development zones |
| |    o cracked down on activities that violated legal procedures of granting and assigning leasehold land use rights |
| |    o issued Rules of Economic Housing Administration, pledging to provide low-priced economic housing for middle- and low-income households |
| 2004–2005 | • The "vertical leadership" reform was launched at the provincial level which put local land management departments under direct administration of corresponding departments at the next higher level |

| | |
|---|---|
| 2005–2006 | • Central government implemented a series of measures to curb the rise of real estate prices |
| 2005.06 | • State Council authorized Shanghai Pudong New Area to be a comprehensive reform pilot area |
| 2006.05 | • State Council authorized Tianjin's Binhai New Area to be a comprehensive reform pilot area for urban development<br>• Central government implemented some new measures to curb the fast rise of real estate prices |
| 2006.12 | • State Council amended Interim Provisions for Urban Land Use Tax to raise urban land use tax substantially |
| 2007.03 | • National People's Congress passed and promulgated the Real Right Law, which provides legal protection of ownership of realities and chattels |
| 2007.06 | • State Council granted Chengdu and Chongqing the status of comprehensive reform pilot area for urban-rural integrated development |
| 2007.09 | • Ministry of Land Resources made amendments to Regulation on Tender, Bidding, and Auction for Granting and Assigning State-owned Construction Land Use Right |
| 2007.10 | • Chinese Communist Party's 17th National Congress proclaimed the following "path of urbanization with Chinese characteristics": "we will promote balanced development of large, medium-sized and small cities and towns on the principle of balancing urban and rural development, ensuring rational distribution, saving land, providing a full range of functions and getting larger cities to help smaller ones. Focusing on increasing the overall carrying capacity of cities, we will form city clusters with mega cities as the core so that they can boost development in other areas and become new poles of economic growth". |

| 2007.12 | • State Council authorized Wuhan City Circle and Changsha-Zhuzhou-Xiangtan city cluster to be comprehensive reform pilot areas for resource-economizing and environmentally friendly development<br>• State Council promulgated Interim Provisions on Farm Land Occupation Tax |
|---------|---|
| 2008.01 | • The Urban and Rural Planning Law came into effect |
| 2009.05 | • State Council authorized Shenzhen to be a comprehensive reform pilot area |
| 2010.04 | • State Council authorized Shenyang Economic Zone and Shanxi Province to be comprehensive reform pilot areas |
| 2010.10 | • Central Committee of the Chinese Communist Party proposed the 12th Five-Year Plan Guideline, including a "primary function area" strategy |
| 2010 | • Central government implemented a series of measures to curb the fast rise of urban housing prices |

Compiled by Ding Lu.

## References

*Baidu Baike* (Encyclopedia). baike.baidu.com.

Chen, Donglin. (2006). "The Third-Front Constructions: An Industrial Heritage". *Zhongguo Guojia Dili* (*China National Geography*), 6, qkzz.com accessed August 14, 2010.

National Bureau of Statistics of China (NBSC) (2009). "Achievements of Urban Social Economic Development". PRC 60th Anniversary Series Report No. 10. www.stats.gov.cn, accessed on July 15, 2010.

National Bureau of Statistics of China (NBSC) (2011). *Main Results of the Sixth National Population Census of 2010.* http://www.stats.gov.cn

Niu, Fengrui, Pan, Jiahua and Liu, Zhiyan (eds). (2009). *Zhongguo Chengshi Fazhan 30 Nian (Urban Development in China: 30 Years 1978–2008)*. Beijing: Social Sciences Academic Press [in Chinese].

Wu, Fulong, Xu, Jiang and Yeh, Anthony Gar-On. (2007). *Urban Development in Post-reform China: State, Market and Space*. London and New York: Routledge.

Xia, Yongxiang and She, Qigang. (2002). "The General Law of Worldwide Urbanization and China's Practice. In Yongjun, Chen and Aimin, Chen (eds.), *Zhongguo Chengshihua (An Analysis of Urbanization in China)*. Xiamen: Xiamen University Press, pp. 3–13 [in Chinese].

# Index

"abolishing townships and
establishing towns" (*che xiang
jian zhen*)   45
administrative villages
(*xingzhengcun*)   78
agglomeration   128
agricultural land   7, 8, 83, 101, 104,
105, 109–111, 120, 197, 200, 288
Anhui   30, 35, 47, 55, 285, 287,
304, 309, 310
anti-urbanization/anti-urbanism   26,
33, 34, 44
arable land   31, 99–103, 105,
109–111, 115–117, 119, 120, 260,
288–293, 296, 319
Asian Olympic Games   170
auction and tender   227, 241

Beijing   7, 17, 29, 32, 35, 44, 47,
48, 55, 56, 58, 64, 70, 83, 120,
134, 137, 140, 142–148, 150, 151,
155, 161, 162, 164, 169, 170–172,
185, 187, 196, 247, 275, 285,
303–305, 307–309, 312, 325, 328
Birmingham   64, 68
Brasilia   66
brownfield sites   192, 197, 198, 239
Building Permit   86, 207, 214

built-up area (or built area)   3, 59,
74, 77, 79, 126, 131, 134, 149,
150, 154, 166, 172, 196, 197, 200,
236, 240, 264–266, 269, 271, 274,
275, 317

Canberra   66
capitalization   8, 149, 188, 192,
199, 222, 237, 239, 241, 242, 248
central business district (CBD)   7,
51, 79, 81, 82, 125, 127–129, 132,
140–148, 150, 172, 199
city-size distribution   6, 11–14,
19–21, 319
City Beautiful and Neighborhood
Unit   66
Chaoyang district (in Beijing)   142,
173, 183
Chengdu   56, 74, 240, 245
Chinese Academy of Social Science
305, 325
Chongqing   17, 30, 48, 56, 137,
141, 144, 146, 285, 294, 304, 309,
310
city classifications   42
Coase theorem   193, 224
county-level cities   17, 57,
132, 326

prefecture-level cities   17,
      126, 127
central municipalities   17
"producer cities" vs. "consumer
      cities"   34, 52, 53
coastal open cities (COCs)   47, 48,
      50, 229
collectively-owned enterprises   75,
      76, 229
collective land ownership   78
commoditization and marketization
      (of urban land or housing estates)
      77, 192, 194, 197, 226, 228, 241
Communist Party of China (CPC)
      33, 59, 325
comparative advantage   36, 120, 311
congestion pricing   152
conglomeration   36
Constitution (PRC)   7, 50, 77, 78,
      163–165, 168, 195, 197, 225, 226,
      266, 275, 318
"converting prefectures to cities (*che
      di jian shi*)"   46
county towns (*xian zhen*)/county
      seats (*xian cheng*)   17, 18, 41
corruption   163, 168, 217, 243, 245,
      267, 276, 325
Cultural Revolution (1966–1977)
      15

*danwei*   7, 8, 50, 51, 131, 149, 150,
      152, 155, 165, 200–206, 210–212,
      214, 217, 221, 222, 227, 230,
      232–235, 237, 239, 242, 244, 245,
      247, 318
Daqing oilfield   36

demographic dividends   301,
      303–305, 307, 308, 310, 313
demographic structure   309–311,
      314, 315
demographic transition   9, 303–308,
      329
Deng (Xiaoping)   41, 47, 50, 198,
      275
dependency ratio   303, 304,
      306–311, 313, 314
developmental planning   63–65,
      70–72, 78, 81, 90–92
Dewai (in Beijing)   170
Dongguan   84, 85, 240
dual economy   107, 113, 114, 287
dual land development mode   202
dual land market   227, 241

economic growth   1, 5, 8, 9, 39, 53,
      56, 59, 63, 64, 66, 68, 70, 72, 78,
      83, 90, 92, 100, 127, 129, 152,
      156, 161, 162, 166, 193, 222, 224,
      230–232, 234, 236, 238, 246, 247,
      259–265, 267, 272–276
economic structure   23, 53
environmental degradation   320,
      324

family planning programs   306
famine   33, 37, 105, 106, 305,
      306
fertility rate   303, 304, 306
fiscal decentralization   49, 230
floating population   9, 24, 48, 50,
      134, 290, 297, 301, 302
foreign concessions   33

foreign direct investment (FDI)/foreign investment   24, 25, 27, 33, 47, 48, 50, 52, 53, 69, 109, 132, 133, 167, 198, 229, 275, 318

foreign-invested enterprises (FIEs)   24, 25

food rationing   45

Fujian   11, 17, 30, 35, 38, 46, 47, 52, 55, 247, 285, 287, 294

Fuzhou   17

Gansu   30, 35, 55, 239, 285, 304, 309

Garden City   66

GDP (Gross Domestic Product)   2, 23, 30, 40, 41, 47, 58, 73, 75, 76, 80, 85, 101–103, 105, 107, 110, 116–118, 121, 127, 132–134, 161, 222, 235, 247, 267, 269, 270, 274, 275, 289, 291, 298, 304, 313, 315, 320, 321–324

Gross National Product (GNP)   313, 315

Gross Regional Product (GRP)   267, 269, 271–273

Geographic Information System (GIS) database   171

gradualism   72, 161, 194, 199, 224, 228, 229, 241, 247

"grain self-sufficiency" policies   111, 119, 120

Granger causality   291, 292

Great Famine   105, 106

Great Leap Forward   37, 39, 105

greenfield sites   191, 192, 197, 239

Guangdong   30, 33, 35, 46, 55, 138, 239, 240, 247, 285, 287, 294, 304, 309

Guangzhou   49, 70, 80, 83–86, 137–140, 162, 207, 227, 238, 240–242, 244, 245

Guangxi   30, 35, 55, 117, 285, 304, 309, 310

Guiyang   25

Guizhou   30

Haidian district (in Beijing)   173

Hainan   30, 35, 55, 120, 137, 239, 247, 285

Hangzhou   32, 74, 137, 139

Hebei   30, 35, 55, 247, 285

Heilongjiang   30, 35, 55, 285, 311

Henan   30, 35, 55, 56, 285, 287, 304, 309

heavy industries   15, 25, 33

HOV (high occupied vehicle) lanes   152

Hongqiao (in Shanghai)   88, 89, 133, 197

Huaihai Road (in Shanghai)   88–90

Huangpu District (in Shanghai)   199, 206

*Huang Cheng* (emperor's residence)   169

Hubei   30, 35, 45, 55, 285, 304, 309, 310

*hukou* (household registration) system   9, 37, 319, 326

human capital   276, 304, 311, 312, 314

Hunan   30, 35, 55, 285, 287, 304,
     309, 310
*Hurun Report*   324, 325

income disparity   301, 315
Industrial Development Certificates
     (IDCs)   67
"industrialization without
     urbanization"   74
*nei qu* (inner district)   169
inland   8, 15, 25, 35, 38, 47, 48, 54,
     107, 117, 282, 285, 286, 298, 301,
     308, 315, 318
Inner Mongolia   30, 35, 55, 285,
     303, 304, 309
*in situ* urbanization   46, 57, 58, 78

Japan   52, 75, 235, 263
Jiangmen   84, 85
Jiangsu   26, 30, 35, 47, 55, 107,
     108, 247, 285, 294, 304, 309
Jiangxi   30, 35, 47, 55, 285, 287
Jing'an (in Shanghai)   81, 83, 84,
     88, 89
Jilin   30, 35, 55, 285, 311

labour mobility   136, 292, 301, 302,
     308, 311, 313, 315
land acquisition/land requisition   8,
     134, 165, 166, 203, 210, 211, 214,
     216, 227, 266, 267, 275, 276, 325,
     326
Land Administration Law   162, 168
land development right (LDR)   8,
     72, 191–193, 199, 202–217, 237,
     238, 303, 312, 314, 323

Land Development Permit   86, 207
(land) leasing system   7, 161
land market   6–8, 50, 63, 65, 71–73,
     80, 87, 91, 92, 127, 150, 161–168,
     171, 172, 175, 183, 185, 187, 188,
     191–195, 206, 209, 213, 216, 217,
     221–223, 227, 237, 239–242,
     247–249, 259
land price   110, 128, 129, 164,
     168, 169, 171–175, 178,
     181–185, 187, 213, 227, 263,
     269, 270, 276
Land Reforms (1949–1955)   105
land rent   8, 78, 80, 83, 169, 178,
     183, 184, 186, 192, 209, 211, 222,
     241, 242, 248
land sale revenue   323, 325, 326
land use intensity   7, 99–101,
     108–115, 117–119, 127, 128, 142,
     148, 164, 263
land use plan/Land Use Master Plan
     6, 64–66, 70, 71, 78–80, 86, 87,
     90, 91, 191, 192, 206–208,
     212–214, 216, 237, 238, 242, 245
Land Use Planning Note   86, 207,
     208, 212, 214
land use rights   7, 8, 50, 51, 72,
     77, 161–163, 165, 167–169,
     171–173, 191, 195, 199–202,
     210, 226, 237, 239, 266, 270, 275
"leave the land (farming) but not
     the rural areas" (*li tu bu li xiang*)
     44
Las Vegas   82
"left-behind children" (*liushou
     ertong*)   314

Liaoning   30, 35, 55, 247, 285, 311
local developmental state   8, 63, 64,
    70, 71, 78, 79, 86–88, 92, 216,
    221, 222, 227, 230–235, 237, 244,
    245, 247, 249
local governments   6, 7, 50, 51,
    53, 56, 68–70, 72, 101, 107, 153,
    154, 162, 163, 168, 197, 201,
    211, 226, 227, 230, 231, 233,
    245, 247, 248, 266, 267, 270,
    275, 318, 322–326
London   67, 82, 142
Lujiazui (in Shanghai)   8, 35, 77,
    81, 83, 88, 89, 133, 191, 192,
    196–200, 202–204, 209, 240, 246,
    282, 285
Luoyang   25

marketization   51, 69, 75–77, 192,
    194, 197, 226, 228, 230, 235, 238,
    241, 246, 247
Marxist ideology/Marxism   33, 77,
    195
Mao (Zedong)   15, 35–37, 41, 43,
    53, 100, 318
mayor   57, 70, 72, 83, 207, 238
migration
        inter-province migration   9,
        297
        rural-urban migration/ urban-
        to-urban migration   4, 6, 8,
        9, 23–25, 27, 279, 280, 281,
        283, 286–289, 291, 292,
        297, 298
        state-compelled   37–40, 53,
        318

migration control policy
    287
migration ratio   302–304
military-industrial complexes   35
Ministry of Foreign Economic
    Relations and Trade (MOFERT)
    121
Ministry of Labor and Social
    Security   282, 285
Ministry of Land Resources   217,
    246
Moscow   82
multiple-cropping index   99, 100,
    104, 107, 108, 112–116, 118
multiple transport modes   152
Munich   82

Nanchang   81, 82
Nanjing   32, 53, 74, 137
National People's Congress   57,
    197, 226, 314, 325, 328
nationalization   195, 226, 228
natural villages (*zirancun*)   78
neoclassical growth (accounting)
    model   8, 259, 261
Ningxia   30, 35, 55, 120, 303, 308,
    312
neoclassical economics   193, 223
New Lanark   64, 66
newly industrialized Asian (NIA)
    countries   100
number of cities   3, 11–13, 17, 18,
    35, 41, 42, 54, 317

Office Development Permit   67
one-child-per-couple policy   306

one-note-and-two-permits system
86, 207
open-door policy 17, 24, 27, 43,
161
Opium War 32

Pareto law, the 6, 12–15, 19–23,
26
Pearl River Delta 58, 84, 85
People's Bank of China 325
People's Communes 36, 37, 43
People's Republic of China (PRC)
12, 15, 19, 29, 30, 33, 46, 57, 92,
105, 328
per capita income 1, 3–5, 30, 54,
126, 259, 260, 291, 293, 294, 297,
302–304, 308, 310–314, 319
Port Sunlight 64
population density 30, 52, 59,
128–130, 141, 151, 152, 164, 167,
265
"production first, living conditions
second" 34, 36
principle of regional economic self-
sufficiency 35
production responsibility system
43
property right 6, 65, 71, 72, 80, 92,
191, 193–196, 202, 204, 217, 221,
222, 224, 226, 227, 234, 235,
237–249, 327
Provisional Act of Land Use Taxation
on State Owned Urban Land 163
Provisional Act of Land Value
Increment Tax on State Owned
Land 163

Provisional Regulation of Land Use
Rights Granting and Transferring
of State Owned Land in Cities and
Towns 163, 168
public transit 130, 131, 152
Pudong (Development Zone) 47,
48, 51, 79, 163, 167, 197, 246,
247
purchasing power parity 320

Qianmen district (in Beijing) 143,
146–148, 151, 161, 162, 164,
169–172, 185, 187, 325
Qinghai 30, 32, 35, 54, 55, 285
Qinghai-Tibet Plateau 32

rank-size rule 13, 15, 19, 20
Radiant City 66
real estate 5, 7, 29, 48, 50, 51, 72,
74, 88, 109, 126, 163, 167, 168,
191, 193, 196, 206, 208, 212, 215,
216, 223, 224, 226, 235, 237,
242–244, 263, 266, 268, 269, 273,
275, 276, 318, 323, 324
Regulations on Land Leasing through
Auction and Bidding 246
Regulation on Use Right Grant and
Transfer for Urban State-owned
Land 275
rent-seeking 51, 213, 216, 217, 231,
240–243, 325
rent dissipation 8, 221, 241, 245
rural migrant workers (*nongmin
gong*) 9, 302
rural-urban income gap 279, 281,
287, 289–292, 296–298

scale economies 136, 156, 322
self-sufficiency 35–37, 99, 100,
105, 106, 109, 111, 119, 120, 318
Shanghai 8, 29, 33, 35, 36, 47–49,
51, 52, 55, 70, 74, 76, 77, 80, 81,
83, 84, 86–89, 120, 133, 134, 137,
140, 150, 191, 192, 196–204, 206,
209, 211, 212, 216, 235, 236,
239–242, 244–246, 247, 282, 285,
294, 304, 309, 312, 321, 325
Shanghai Municipal Ordinances on
Urban Land Management 200,
202
(Shanghai) Management of Housing
Demolition and Tenant Relocation
ordinance 200
Shanghai Municipal Planning Bureau
242
Shandong 30, 35, 55, 239, 247,
285, 303, 304, 308, 309
Shantou 227, 240
Shanxi 30, 56, 106, 285
Shaanxi 30, 35, 55, 285, 310
*shehui zhuyi quanmin suoyouzi*
(socialist people's ownership)
195
*shengdi* (raw land without urban
infrastructure and land levelling)
169
Shenyang 74, 86
Shenzhen 3, 25, 49, 50, 70, 83–85,
108, 133, 137, 139, 140, 145, 197,
226, 227, 236, 244
*shudi* (improved land) 167, 169
Sichuan 30, 35, 55, 107, 108, 285,
287, 294, 304, 309, 310

Silk Route 32
Singapore 66, 141, 206
small-town consensus 29, 44, 46,
49, 56, 319
*Social Insurance Law* 328
social security system 233, 327,
328
socialist collectivization 37
"socialist market economy" 17, 50,
244
sown area 99–109, 115, 119, 120
Soviet (Union) 33, 228
Special Economic Zones
(SEZs)/Special Economic
Development Zones (SEDZs) 7,
46, 50, 108, 109, 125, 127, 128,
132, 229, 163, 167
State Council 45, 46, 49, 51, 54,
57, 132, 168, 246, 249, 270, 275,
328
state-owned enterprises (SOEs) 15,
77, 192, 194, 195, 200, 201,
227–230, 232–235, 238, 244–248,
311
strategic concept plan 63, 65, 79,
86, 91
"strictly control the development of
large cities" 37

Tiananmen Square 172, 173, 185,
198
Tianjin 29, 33, 35, 47, 48, 55, 58,
74, 120, 134, 247, 285, 304, 309,
321
Tibet 30, 32, 35, 54, 55, 120,
294

Third Front/"three-front" project 25, 35

topographic features (China) 31

total factor productivity (TFP) 261, 263, 264, 272, 274, 275

"town administrating villages" (*zhen guan cun*) 45

Town and Country Planning Act 67

township (*xiang/zhen*) 78

township and village enterprises (TVEs) 44, 46, 107

treaty ports 33

"*tudi caizheng*" 324

United Nations Secretariat 306, 307

United States (of America) 14, 31, 263

university towns 7, 125, 127, 128, 132, 137, 139, 140, 155

Urban Housing and Real Estate Management Act 163

urban infrastructure 5, 12, 26, 37, 40, 43, 45, 48, 51, 53, 80, 153, 162, 166–169, 323

urban land market (see land market) 6, 7, 72, 80, 161, 167, 187, 192, 213, 222, 247, 248

Urban Planning Law 46, 56

urban population 1–4, 8, 9, 11, 15–18, 26, 27, 31, 35, 37–42, 53, 55, 58, 73, 75, 104, 106, 110, 116, 118, 121, 134, 161, 162, 166, 167, 236, 264–266, 279, 280–282, 284, 286, 289, 290, 293, 296, 297, 317, 322

urban policy/urbanization policy 25, 26, 34, 41, 56, 58

urban planning 6, 46, 52, 56, 58, 63–68, 70–72, 78, 86, 90–92, 150, 163, 185, 206, 318, 319, 322, 325

Urban Planning Act 78, 86, 206

"urban villages" 245

urbanization level 73, 75, 280, 281

urban-rural segregation 40

urban spatial expansion 149, 156, 161

"using industry to subsidize agriculture" (*yi gong bu nong*) 44

VMT (vehicle miles traveled) 131, 152, 154

*wai qu* (outer district) 169, 183

Washington, D. C. 64, 142, 151

working-age population 9, 309

World Bank 2, 4, 156, 194, 196, 199, 223, 225, 248, 260, 292, 296, 320, 321, 328

World Trade Organization (WTO) 276, 298

Wuhan 240, 245

Xiamen 11, 17, 137

*xia fang* ("sending down") campaigns 38

Xi'an 240, 245

Xinjiang 30, 35, 55, 285

Xintiandi (project) 89

Yangtze River 32, 47, 48, 58
Yellow River 32
*"Yi Liang Wei Gang, Gang Ju Mu Zhang"* (Food must be taken as a core; once it is grasped, everything falls into place) 106
Yunnan 30, 35, 55, 285

Zhaoqin 84, 85

Zhejiang 30, 35, 55, 139, 239, 247, 285, 287, 294, 304, 309
*"zhengdi chaiqian"* (land requisition by property demolition) 326
Zhongguancun (in Beijing) 170
Zhuhai 85, 86
zoning 65, 68, 80, 153, 213, 322, 325

Printed in the United States
By Bookmasters